PATHS TO
What People Do and Think About Going to law

ONE WEEK LOAN

0 6 APR 2005

101\108

3 0 'N '008

2

Paths to Justice:
What People Do and Think About Going to Law

PROFESSOR HAZEL GENN

Faculty of Laws
University College London

With
Sarah Beinart
Steven Finch
Christos Korovessis
Patten Smith
Members or former members of
The National Centre for Social research

Funded by the Nuffield Foundation

·HART·
PUBLISHING

OXFORD – PORTLAND OREGON
1999

Hart Publishing
Oxford and Portland, Oregon

Published in North America (US and Canada) by
Hart Publishing c/o
International Specialized Book Services
5804 NE Hassalo Street
Portland, Oregon
97213-3644
USA

Distributed in the Netherlands, Belgium and Luxembourg by
Intersentia, Churchillaan 108
B2900 Schoten
Antwerpen
Belgium

Distributed in Australia and New Zealand by
Federation Press
John St
Leichhardt
NSW 2000

Hart Publishing Ltd is a specialist legal publisher based in
Oxford, England.
To order further copies of this book or to request a list of other
publications please write to:

Hart Publishing Ltd, Salter's Boatyard, Oxford OX1 4LB
Telephone: +44 (0)1865 245533 or Fax: +44 (0)1865 794882
e-mail: mail@hartpub.co.uk

British Library Cataloguing in Publication Data
Data Available
ISBN 1 84113–039–7 (paperback)

Typeset by Hope Services (Abingdon) Ltd.
Printed in Great Britain on acid-free paper
by Page Bros (Norwich) Ltd

Foreword

Lawyers, and especially those who spend their time in and around the courts, tend to think that their world is at the centre of the universe. The way to resolve disputes about legal matters is in court, the way to court is through the lawyers, and the lawyers will go a good distance along that way before settling the dispute by agreement, thus avoiding the risks and uncertainties of asking the judge to do it for them.

But to do them credit, many lawyers recognise that to expect every dispute to follow this path would be quite unrealistic. It would be far too costly, of legal resources, of court time, and of much more besides. In recent years, therefore, there has been much discussion, and many attempts, not only to find ways of making the court process more accessible and affordable to ordinary people, but also to divert disputes away from the courts, into various recognised forms of "alternative dispute resolution".

The judiciary are by and large enthusiastic supporters of the thinking behind the new Civil Procedure Rules, which resulted from Lord Woolf's Report on Access to Justice. The legal profession are making the best of it. But what do the general public think? How do the reforms fit in with the experience and expectations of the general public about the resolution of their legal problems?

Way back in 1994, the Nuffield Foundation, with its longstanding interest in access to justice issues, began to wonder how much was known about the public's own experience of the law and legal processes. We began by wondering how much they knew about the law and the legal system, and considered commissioning work on the "public understanding of law", much as we had earlier commissioned work on the public understanding of science. But a series of meetings with interested professionals and researchers soon convinced us that this would simply reveal what we already knew: that most people have very little knowledge about the law itself and what they have is often inaccurate.

Far more interesting and relevant to the current debate about access to justice, however, were two questions: how often do people experience problems which might have a legal solution—conceptualised in this study as "justiciable events"—and how do they set about solving them?

We therefore commissioned Professor Hazel Genn of University College London, together with the National Centre for Social Research (then Social and Community Planning Research), to carry out this ambitious study. With the help of a steering group, they turned the concept "justiciable event" into a concrete series of examples of problems which individuals might encounter in their everyday lives and which might have a legal solution: including problems with goods and services, debts, housing, employment, divorce and separation, children and much else. They then devised a questionnaire which was used to screen a random sample of over 4,000 people in England and Wales to find out how common these problems were. The answer was that some of them were very common and that problems, like buses, tend to come in convoy rather than on their own.

Those who had recent experience of problems which they themselves did not think trivial were asked to take part in a longer interview about what they had done, the outcomes achieved, and their views about it all. Over 1,000 people did so.

Mostly they did take some action but only a very few of these problems ended up in courts of law or in tribunals, and only a tiny proportion in what is now called "alternative dispute resolution". Whether or not they did depended more upon the sort of problem it was than upon the sort of people they were. The great strength of this study, apart from its methodological rigour and independence, is its focus upon the types of problems experienced and people's reactions to them, rather than upon the types of people who experience problems. It has much to tell us about the different reactions to different problems, as well as the public's experience of the more formal legal system.

It has come at a particularly opportune time, with the new Civil Procedure Rules resulting from the Woolf Report implemented in April 1999 and the restructuring of publicly funded legal services under the Access to Justice Act 1999 almost upon us.

There is already more to come, in the shape of a parallel survey in Scotland to be published next year, and two follow up studies of people in this sample who had particular types of experience: Jane Lewis and Mavis Maclean are following up the 200 people who experienced divorce or separation, and Professor Genn and colleagues at the National Centre are following up those who actually experienced court, tribunal and formal alternative dispute resolution processes in more detail. We also hope that others will wish to examine the data from this study in more depth: it will be put (suitably anonymised) on public deposit for secondary analysis.

The Foundation is most grateful to Professor Genn and the National Centre for all that they have done. We are also grateful to the members of the advisory group who worked extremely hard to refine the concepts and questionnaires. Above all we are grateful to the many members of the public who shared their views and experiences with the researchers. We hope and expect that this exciting survey will inform debate and public policy making for a long time to come.

The Hon Dame Brenda Hale
Trustee of the Nuffield Foundation

Contents

Foreword by The Hon. Dame Brenda Hale
   Trustee of the Nuffield Foundation   v
Acknowledgements   xi
List of Figures   xiii
List of Tables   xvi

Chapter 1.   Introduction   1
Chapter 2.   The Landscape of Justiciable Problems   21
Chapter 3.   Strategies for Resolving Justiciable Problems   67
Chapter 4.   The Response to Problems of Different Types   105
Chapter 5.   Outcomes   145
Chapter 6.   Fulfilling Objectives?   179
Chapter 7.   Experiences and Perceptions of the Legal System   215
Chapter 8.   Paths to Justice: Which Way Now?   249

Appendix A   Technical Report   265
Appendix B   Logistical Regression Analysis Results   275
Appendix C   Questionnaires   289

Acknowledgements

Work began on this ambitious project at the end of 1996 and on an equivalent survey of Scotland during 1997. Although the developmental stages of the research enjoyed the luxury of a relatively steady pace offered by the Nuffield Foundation, the rapid introduction of civil justice reforms in England and Wales, most particularly the development of the Community Legal Service, created considerable pressure to complete the analysis of the survey and release the findings into the public domain while policy was still being developed and debated. The results of the survey in Scotland will be published as a companion volume next year and, in addition to providing a comparable map of paths to justice in Scotland, it will offer a chance to analyse some of the themes emerging from this study in greater depth.

This research could not have been accomplished without the contribution of a large number of people. First, the project benefited greatly from the wisdom of a distinguished Advisory Panel who generously gave their time to attend meetings at the Nuffield Foundation and to offer guidance on the design and analysis of the research. The Panel has been chaired by Dame Brenda Hale and the members of the Panel are: Patrick Allen (Hodge, Jones and Allen); Professor John Baldwin (Institute of Judicial Administration, Birmingham University); District Judge Carlos Dabezies; David Gladwell (Head of Civil Justice Division, Lord Chancellor's Department); Professor Roger Jowell (National Centre for Social Research); District Judge Nic Madge; Sarah Tyerman (previously Research Manager Lord Chancellor's Department and now Secretary of the Neill Committee on Standards in Public Life); Sue Warner (Central Research Unit, Scottish Office); Carole Willis (Controller, Research and Policy Planning Unit, The Law Society); and Marlene Winfield (National Consumer Council).

Sharon Witherspoon (Assistant Director of the Nuffield Foundation) has provided unwavering and enthusiastic support throughout the life of the project and her insights and incisive critiques have been of immense value. On a personal level, I have very much enjoyed the opportunity of working closely with her and am deeply grateful for all that she has contributed to the research.

The fieldwork for the project was expertly carried out by the National Centre's team of interviewers. The quality of the data available for analysis was a direct result of the care with which interviews were undertaken and the interest in the research shown by interviewers. I would also like to record my gratitude to Kit Ward and Hilary Legard who conducted lengthy and challenging qualitative interviews to supplement the screening and main survey interviews. The insights gained as a result of their skilful interviewing techniques have greatly enriched the study.

I would also like to thank Theresa O'Neill, assistant to Sharon Witherspoon, for her help in maintaining liaison between the researchers, the Foundation, and the Advisory Panel. As always, I am grateful to my assistant Helen Ghosh at University College London, for her invaluable hard work and calm competence.

Special thanks are due to Richard Hart and the team at Hart Publishing for producing this volume under extreme time pressure and for their good-natured tolerance of last minute amendments.

Finally, I am grateful to Daniel Appleby for his continuing willingness to read drafts and check numbers in the middle of the night, and to Bea and Matt for giving me a sense of proportion.

Hazel Genn
University College London

List of Figures

Figure 2.1   Incidence of problems of different types reported in screening survey.   24

Figure 2.2   No action taken to resolve justiciable problem by problem type.   38

Figure 2.3   Action taken to try and resolve problems with receiving faulty goods or services.   39

Figure 2.4   Reasons for not taking action to resolve problems with faulty goods and services.   40

Figure 2.5   Types of problems to do with money.   41

Figure 2.6   Action taken to resolve problems to do with money.   42

Figure 2.7   Breakdown of problems to do with employment.   43

Figure 2.8   Reasons for taking no action to resolve employment problems.   44

Figure 2.9   Problems to do with owning residential property.   45

Figure 2.10   Reasons for not taking action to resolve problems with owning residential property.   45

Figure 2.11   Problems to do with living in rented accommodation.   46

Figure 2.12   Reasons for not taking action to resolve problems with living in rented accommodation.   47

Figure 2.13   Problems with relationships and family matters.   48

Figure 2.14   Actions taken about problems with relationships and family matters.   48

Figure 2.15   Reasons for not taking action to resolve relationship and family problems.   49

Figure 2.16   Problems to do with children under 18.   50

Figure 2.17   Actions taken about problems with children under 18.   50

Figure 2.18   Actions taken about injuries or work-related ill health.   52

Figure 2.19   Reasons for not taking action to do with injury or work-related ill health.   52

Figure 2.20 Actions taken about discrimination, unfair treatment
             by police, immigration, medical negligence.   53

Figure 2.21 Reasons for taking no action about discrimination,
             unfair treatment by police, immigration, medical
             negligence.   54

Figure 3.1   Broad strategy for dealing with justiciable problems. 68

Figure 3.2   First source of advice.   83

Figure 3.3   Second source of advice.   84

Figure 3.4   First advice in relation to respondents' income.   86

Figure 3.5   Advice obtained from a solicitor at any point while
             resolving problem in relation to respondents' income. 87

Figure 3.6   Percentage obtaining advice by problem type.   88

Figure 3.7   First adviser by problem type.   89

Figure 3.8   Advice from solicitors and other advisers by type of
             problem.   89

Figure 5.1   Paths and outcomes following non-trivial justiciable
             problems.   147

Figure 5.2   Involvement in formal legal proceedings by problem
             type.   150

Figure 5.3   Respondents' reports of type of court/tribunal dealing
             with problem.   152

Figure 5.4   Outcome of justiciable problems—plaintiffs and
             defendants compared.   153

Figure 5.5   Outcome in relation to advice.   154

Figure 5.6   Final outcome of different problem types.   155

Figure 5.7   Outcome of consumer problems.   157

Figure 5.8   Outcome of employment problems.   158

Figure 5.9   Outcome of divorce and separation problems.   159

Figure 5.10 Outcome of neighbour problems in relation to
             advice.   160

Figure 5.11 Outcome of money problems in relation to advice.   161

Figure 5.12 Outcome of accidental injury and work-related ill
             health.   162

Figure 5.13 Outcome of problems with landlords.   163

Figure 5.14 Financing of legal action by problem type.   169

Figure 5.15 Cost of resolving disputes excluding legal costs.   169

Figure 6.1   Main objectives in taking action.   183

Figure 6.2   Amount of claim where respondent seeking
             lump sum.   187

Figure 6.3   "Was this more, less or about the same amount
             of money as you had hoped for?"   188

Figure 6.4   "Was this more, less or about the same amount of
             money as you had expected to pay?"   189

Figure 6.5   Impact of sorting out problem in relation to
             outcome.   195

Figure 6.6   "Did solving this problem take a shorter time than
             expected, about as long as expected, or a longer time
             than expected?"   195

Figure 6.7   Achievement of main objectives by problem type.   197

Figure 6.8   Perceptions of fairness of adjudication among
             those who won and lost.   202

Figure 7.1   "Courts are an important way for ordinary people
             to enforce their rights."   227

Figure 7.2   "If I went to court with a problem, I am confident
             that I would get a fair hearing."   230

Figure 7.3   "The legal system works better for rich people than
             for poor people."   234

Figure 7.4   "Lawyers' charges are reasonable for the work
             they do."   236

Figure 7.5   "Most judges are out of touch with ordinary people's
             lives."   240

List of Tables

Table 2.1 Incidence of problems of different types by age.   29

Table 2.2 Mean number of problems experienced by those with problems of a given sort.   30

Table 2.3 Estimates of rates per thousand, numbers of adults in England and Wales affected by problems and total numbers of problems of different types during previous five years.   32

Table 2.4 Percentage overlap between the incidence of eligible problems.   33

Table 2.5 Incidence of problems of different types; impact of applying the triviality criterion.   37

Table 2.6 Breakdown of main survey sample by problem type.   55

Table 2.7 Comparison of characteristics of main survey sample of respondents experiencing justiciable problems with general population.   57

Table 2.8 Comparison between main sample profile and the general population.   58

Table 4.1 Factors determining need for advice.   143

Table 6.1 Negative and positive effects of sorting out problem.   192

1

Introduction

"I'd like more access to justice and less access to the courts."
(Survey respondent)

It is perhaps remarkable that, in a period of unprecedented upheaval in the procedures for resolving civil disputes through the legal system, and historical alterations in the public funding of legal advice and representation[1], both the protagonists and opponents of change lack a solid empirical foundation for their respective positions. The rather unusually intense spotlight currently trained on the civil courts has been said to reveal a system in crisis: procedures that are too complicated; courts that are too slow; lawyers who are too aggressive; litigants who are bewildered and traumatised by their experiences; and an unquantified body of citizens whose access to the courts to vindicate rights is barred by these features. But where is the evidence for these assertions?

Discussion about access to justice and lack of access to justice proceeds largely in the absence of reliable quantitative data about the needs, interests and experiences of the community that the system is there to serve. There is as little information available about who litigates and why they litigate as there is about who chooses not to litigate and who feels that they are being denied access to the courts. We have surprisingly scant knowledge of the kinds of cases that actually reach the civil courts or the dispute resolution activity that takes place in the shadow of the courts. We have little information about what the civil justice system delivers and the extent to which the courts are regarded as valuable or irrelevant to those for whom they ostensibly exist. The result is that we lack a context for evaluating proposals for change, and we lack the basic accounting data that might help us to know whether new policies implemented have changed things for the better, for worse, or not at all.

---

[1] See the reports by the Rt Hon the Lord Woolf, MR *Access to Justice: Interim Report*, Lord Chancellor's Department 1995; *Access to Justice: Final Report*, Lord Chancellor's Department 1996; *Modernising Justice*, A Consultation Paper, Lord Chancellor's Department, November 1998, HMSO; *Access to Justice Act* 1999.

The absence of comprehensive information about the operation of the civil justice system is a weakness at a time when far-reaching changes to procedure and the funding of civil actions are simultaneously being introduced. Lord Woolf's fundamental review of the civil justice system, which began in 1994, and which reported in 1995 and 1996, recommended changes that he argued would alter the landscape of civil litigation in the future. His vision for the new culture and approach to civil litigation involves a single, simplified, plain English set of rules for the High Court and county courts which are to be operated by the judiciary in the light of an "overriding objective"—the exhortation to deal with cases "justly". This is to be achieved by ensuring that parties are on an equal footing; by saving expense; by dealing with cases in a proportionate manner with regard to the amount of money at stake, the importance and complexity of the issues in dispute, and the financial position of the parties. The overriding objective also requires that cases are dealt with expeditiously and fairly, and that court resources are allocated in an appropriate manner. In the post-Woolf world of civil litigation it is now the judiciary who are to control the pace of litigation. They have acquired wide case-management powers, including the initial allocation of civil actions to one of a number of "tracks[2]", responsibility for ensuring that civil actions are dealt with proportionately, and the power to penalise parties and their solicitors for failure to deal expeditiously with cases.

The emphasis on proportionality, speed, limited procedures and pressure toward early case-settlement is designed to drive down the cost of litigation to parties, to make court procedure more comprehensible and thus improve access to justice. The centrality of out of court settlement in the new landscape has led to a growing interest in diverting cases away from the courts and toward private dispute resolution processes such as mediation, conciliation and arbitration (ADR). In order to ensure that parties and their legal representatives actively explore the possibility of achieving settlement by private ADR, the new rules of court give judges the power to direct parties to try to settle their differences by means of ADR and to stay court proceedings for this

---

[2] The "small claims track" for cases with a value of up to £5,000 (excluding personal injury actions and housing disrepair cases with a value over £1,000); the "fast track" for cases with a value of between £5,000 and £15,000 (involving fixed trial dates, simplified procedures, limited trial length and capping of costs payable to counsel for appearing at a fast track trial); and the "multi-track" for cases over £15,000 or of particular complexity, where judges are required actively to manage the progress of the action.

purpose[3]. The emphasis in the Woolf report on the value of ADR and the high-profile given to it in "preparation for Woolf" judicial training has led to considerable interest among the judiciary for what is seen as a relatively novel approach to the resolution of civil disputes. The development of court-based local ADR initiatives[4] and judicial enthusiasm for ADR suggest that the diversion of civil cases from public to private dispute resolution is likely to increase.

At the same time as litigants and lawyers are grappling with these procedural modifications to the civil justice system, an historic transformation is taking place in the public funding of legal services. In the culmination of attempts to control exponential increases in expenditure on legal aid during the past two decades, the government has embarked on a reform programme involving the capping of government expenditure on legal advice and representation, delivery of publicly-funded legal services by means of contracting with suppliers, the removal of many categories of civil action from the ambit of public funding, and the expansion of conditional fee arrangements[5].

The Access to Justice Act 1999, which provides the statutory footing for these and other changes to the legal system, announces the establishment of a "Legal Services Commission" which will have responsibility for the public funding of legal services and for a "Community Legal Service". Under the new funding regime the Legal Services Commission will maintain a "Community Legal Service Fund" which will pay for advice and representation services provided through the Community Legal Service. The Commission has a broad responsibility to set priorities for the funding of services in light of assessments of the need for services of different types, in relation to different areas or communities in England and Wales, and in relation to different categories of case.

[3] Where the court of its own initiative considers that a stay of proceedings while the parties try to settle their case by alternative dispute resolution would be appropriate, the court will direct that the proceedings be stayed for one month. Civil Procedure Rule 26.4(2)(b). This can be extended for such a period as the court considers appropriate, 26.4(3).

[4] A permanent mediation scheme has been established at the Central London County Court and other regions are planning to introduce similar schemes. For an evaluation of the mediation scheme based at the Central London County Court and a discussion of the issues arising from the mediation of civil disputes see Hazel Genn, *Central London County Court Pilot Mediation Scheme: Evaluation Report*, London, Lord Chancellor's Department, Research Series 4/98, 1998.

[5] Often referred to as "no win no fee" arrangements under which a solicitor receives no fee if the case is unsuccessful, but may charge an "uplift" or success fee if the case succeeds.

The new criteria for the funding of legal advice and representation will be incorporated into a "Funding Code" devised by the Commission. The Code is required to reflect a number of factors such as: the likely benefit of funding services in relation to their cost; the availability of funds and likely future demands on the capped budget of the Community Legal Service Fund; the importance of the matter facing an individual and the availability of alternatives to public funding (for example obtaining legal advice and representation on a conditional fee basis); the prospect of success in the dispute; the conduct of the individual in relation to the request for public funding; and the public interest. Moreover, the growing emphasis on ADR is reflected in S8(3) of the Act, which requires that the new Funding Code should reflect "the principle that in many family disputes mediation will be more appropriate than court proceedings".

The Act also amends previous legislation[6] so that conditional fee arrangements are permitted in all types of civil cases except family proceedings. The combined effect of the wide availability of conditional fee arrangements and the Funding Code criteria means that certain categories of civil dispute, such as personal injury litigation, which are currently funded by Legal Aid will no longer be eligible for publicly funded legal advice and representation. It has been argued that the effects of cash-limiting the funds available for the Community Legal Service Fund, more stringent eligibility criteria, and the use of contracts to provide legal services will reduce rather than increase access to justice for members of the public on low incomes[7].

The Legal Services Commission has the responsibility of establishing and developing the new "Community Legal Service" in order to provide general information about the law and legal system and the availability of legal services; to provide advice and to provide help in preventing or settling or otherwise resolving disputes about legal rights and duties; it also has a responsibility to help in the enforcement of judgments; and to provide help in relation to legal proceedings that do not concern a dispute. Those who provide advice and assistance through the Community Legal Service are expected to improve the range, quality, and accessibility of services offered to those members of the public in need of such ser-

---

[6] S27 of the Access to Justice Act 1999 amends S58 of the Courts and Legal Services Act 1990 which allowed for the use of conditional fees for only three classes of action: personal injury actions, insolvency proceedings, and actions concerning human rights.
[7] See for example M. Zander (1998), "The Government's Plans on Legal Aid and Conditional Fees", 61 *Modern Law Review*, 798–822; Law Society, *Justice For All*, 1999.

vices. The growing emphasis on keeping cases out of court is reflected in the responsibility of Community Legal Service providers to "take seriously the need to achieve the swift and fair resolution of disputes without unnecessary or unduly protracted proceedings in court"[8].

These are therefore busy times for civil justice policy. The legal profession, the judiciary and potential customers of the courts are grappling with the changes introduced by the Woolf reforms. The architecture of the Community Legal Service is still at the design stage, as is the difficult task of determining priorities and the nature of the need for legal advice and representation that is to be met by the Service. These developments are taking place without the benefit of broad contextual information about the incidence of civil disputes and problems concerning legal rights and obligations, or the behaviour, expectations and needs of the public in seeking to achieve satisfactory resolutions to those disputes and problems.

This book is an attempt to fill some of the existing information void and to provide a factual basis that will inform debate and policy choices. It presents the results of a national survey of households in England and Wales. The broad primary objective of the study was to establish the frequency with which members of the public are faced with problems for which a legal remedy exists ("justiciable problems"), to map the response of the public to those problems, whether and where they go for help, and the results. Although the study represents the most comprehensive attempt to estimate the volume of such problems from the "bottom-up", it builds on a well-established tradition, in many different legal cultures, of measuring what have been defined as the "legal needs" of the public and the use of legal services.

THE "LEGAL NEEDS" TRADITION

The unquestionable difficulty of arriving at any sensible definition of what might constitute a "legal need" has not prevented a substantial research industry from engaging, periodically, in the practice of measuring legal need. Some of the earliest studies of legal need were carried out in North America in the 1960s and the tradition spread to Europe and England[9]. The approach of the studies was to devise a list of

---

[8] Access to Justice Act 1999, Part I, S4 (4)(a)–(c).
[9] Carlin and Howard, 1965 "Legal Representation and Class Justice", 12 *UCLA Law Review*, 381–437; Abel Smith, Zander and Brooke, *Legal Problems and the Citizen*,

problems for which it might be useful to use a lawyer, or for which researchers thought a lawyer ought to be used, and to ask respondents whether they had experienced such problems and if so whether they had, indeed, used a lawyer to solve the problem. These research studies provided some useful insights into differential use of legal services. Their weakness, however, was in the narrowness of the approach. Much of the work inevitably focused on the kind problems taken to private legal practitioners and the central question of who used lawyers and why. The answer was frequently that use of lawyers was strongly related to social class[10]. The Royal Commission on Legal Services in England in 1977 followed a similar pattern of questioning and concluded that a large number of people who needed legal services were not getting them, and recommended a number of measures regarded as necessary to improve access to justice[11].

Other studies of the use of legal services in England over the last twenty years indicate that the range of civil issues on which solicitors and CABx are consulted is relatively narrow, limited to buying and selling houses, making wills, claiming compensation for an accident or dealing with a family dispute[12]. It has been suggested that few people seek help with social welfare problems, consumer problems, debt, or housing matters, and little is known about what attempts are made to deal with these problems outside of the formal legal system. It is unrealistic to assume that those who do not seek formal resolution do nothing at all.

ESTIMATING "PROBLEMS"

The error emerging from many of the early studies of legal needs was the tendency to focus on the kinds of *people* who use legal services, rather than on the kinds of problems which are taken to lawyers. Conceptualising potential legal problems as though they were in some way homogeneous was a serious flaw.

Heinemann, 1973; Johnsen "Problems in Planning Legal Services" in Blankenburg (ed), *Innovations in the Legal Services*, Gunn and Hain, 1980.

[10] J. Griffiths, "The Distribution of Legal Services in the Netherlands", 1977, 14 *British Journal of Law and Society*, 260.

[11] Royal Commission on Legal Services (1979), *Final Report*, HMSO Cmnd 7648.

[12] J. Jenkins et al, *Survey of Use of Legal Services*, London, Law Society, 1989; MVA Consultancy, *Consumer Study of Knowledge and Use of Legal Services*, London, 1994.

Towards the end of the 1970s dissatisfaction with the narrow definition of legal needs used in existing studies led to a change in approach.
In 1971 the American Bar Association and the American Bar
Foundation, in partnership, undertook a comprehensive study of how
the public used lawyers. Rather than attempting to measure legal need,
the objective of the study was to determine the circumstances under
which members of the public seek the advice or help of lawyers, and to
identify factors that appeared to influence decisions to consult or not to
consult lawyers[13]. Respondents were asked whether they had experienced a wide range of problems and what they had done about them.
One of the key findings was that use of lawyers to resolve problems was
largely influenced by the nature of the problem being faced, and that
members of the public made their decisions about whether or not to use
lawyers as a result of a careful weighing of the likely costs against
potential benefits.

In 1994 the American Bar Association carried out a further
"Comprehensive Legal Needs Study" which aimed to explore both
quantitatively and qualitatively situations with "a legal dimension"
encountered by low and moderate income American households. The
objectives were to estimate the nature and number of situations faced
by households that raised legal issues and to see what steps were taken
in dealing with those situations. The research was based on interviews
with 3,000 respondents and the principal findings of the study were that
about half of the households surveyed faced one or more situations in
the previous twelve months that could have been addressed by the system of civil justice; that nearly three quarters of those situations faced
by low-income households did not find their way into the justice system; and that two-thirds of the situations faced by moderate-income
households did not find their way into the justice system[14].

The most common problems experienced concerned housing and
real property, personal finance and consumer issues. Other important
findings of the study were that the most common course of action in
dealing with a legal need for members of both low and moderate
income households was to try and handle the situation on their own.
While moderate-income households turned to the legal system as the
second most frequent response, the second most common response

---

[13] Barbara A Curran, *The Legal Needs of the Public*, American Bar Foundation,
Chicago, 1977.
[14] *Legal Needs and Civil Justice*, Major Findings of the Comprehensive Legal Needs
Study, American Bar Association, Chicago, 1994.

among low-income households was to take no action at all. The most common problems taken to the civil justice system were family and domestic issues.

In the United Kingdom there have been two recent, linked surveys of the use of legal and other services to resolve civil disputes. The first, was conducted in England and Wales by the National Consumer Council in 1995[15] and the second, using comparable questions was carried out in Scotland in 1997[16]. The NCC survey was based on an omnibus survey of 8,358 members of the public over the age of 16 in which respondents were asked if they had been involved in any one of 13 types of civil dispute in the past three years. The questioning was introduced by a statement referring to Lord Woolf's Inquiry into access to justice and they key question for estimating the prevalence of "legal needs" was as follows: "In the last three years, have you been involved in a serious dispute about any of these matters?" The matters referred to were: damage to a vehicle; divorce; medical/injury; unpaid debt; faulty goods; neighbour; problem at work; local authority/government/agency; faulty services; custody/access to children; landlord/tenant rights; will/estate; repossession of home.

The study estimated that 13% of the population had suffered a "serious dispute" relating to one of the 13 listed types of disputes in the previous three years, a very high proportion of whom (about 4/5) sought outside help about resolving the dispute, most often from a solicitor or CAB. The most common disputes reported related to damage to vehicles (18%), divorce (10%), personal injury (including medical negligence) (10%), unpaid debts (9%), and faulty goods (8%). The survey found that three-quarters of those reporting having experienced a serious dispute were potential plaintiffs and one quarter were potential defendants. Among potential *plaintiffs*, the most frequent type of dispute mentioned concerned faulty goods and services or accidental injury. The most common type of disputes reported during the survey in which the respondent was a potential *defendant* concerned home repossession, debts, and access to children or neighbour disputes.

Interesting though the findings are, there are important limitations to the NCC study. The relatively low incidence of "disputes" reported reflects the nature of the question asked rather than the frequency with which respondents were likely to have experienced, say purchasing a faulty appliance, a problem at work, or a problem with a neighbour.

[15]   *Seeking Civil Justice*, National Consumer Council, 1995.
[16]   *Civil Disputes in Scotland*, Scottish Consumer Council, 1997.

What the survey measured was not the prevalence of events raising issues about legal rights or obligations that citizens must deal with in their day-to-day lives, but events that respondents defined as a "serious dispute" in the context of questioning about the civil justice system and Lord Woolf's Inquiry into access to justice. As a result no information was obtained about how problems that had not become defined as "serious disputes" had been handled by the public. Moreover, because the study was based on an omnibus survey only a limited number of questions could be asked in order to explore public responses to such disputes (26 questions were asked in all).

UNDERSTANDING THE PROPENSITY TO SUE

Despite some of the conceptual shortcomings of studies of use of legal services and traditional attempts to measure "unmet legal need", empirical studies of differential use of legal services have provided solid evidence that many citizens involved in predicaments for which legal remedies are available, do not seek legal advice or attempt in any other way to pursue any formal legal remedy for the problem[17].

The observation of this prevalent failure to seek legal remedies where they are theoretically available has led some scholars to focus their energies on the early stages of disputes in order to theorise disputing behaviour, although this has been hampered by a lack of empirical data. One of the most influential theories on disputing behaviour[18] visualises access to justice as a path with barriers, which some travellers will surmount, while others fall by the wayside. The logical steps along the path involve the recognition of particular kinds of events as "injurious" (naming); the identification of the event as a grievance for which another is responsible (blaming); the confrontation of the wrongdoer with the complaint (claiming); and finally, if the response of the wrongdoer is unsatisfactory, the decision to pursue a remedy through the courts. According to this model, the litigants who find their way into the formal dispute resolution system are those who, following the occurrence of a potentially injurious event, attribute blame to another person or body, have the consciousness of a legal remedy, and

---

[17] See for example Harris, D et al *Compensation and Support*, Clarendon Press, 1984, on use of legal services by personal injury victims.

[18] Felstiner, W et al (1981) "The Emergence and Transformation of Disputes: Naming, Blaming, Claiming . . .", 15 *Law and Society Review* 631.

are prepared to seek such a remedy rather than simply ignoring the event (lumping it) or attributing the event to bad lack or an act of God. Although this model is a helpful starting point in identifying the psychological processes and structural barriers that affect choice, it is important not to underestimate the complex interaction of factors that influence decisions about how to deal with problems raising legal issues and the fact that the model may be more appropriate for certain types of legal problem than for others. Indeed, one of the difficulties of theorising about disputing behaviour in the access to justice context has been the failure to recognise the *dissimilarity* of problems for which legal remedies exist and the responses to those problems. Not everyone involved in circumstances for which a legal remedy is available necessarily feels a sense of grievance. Not everyone blames another. Those who claim may not blame and those who blame may not claim. Not everyone is interested in the remedy that is provided by the law. Those who neither blame nor claim may not necessarily "lump it", but may seek a self-help remedy that is likely to secure a desired outcome.

A later study of plaintiffs in personal injury actions[19] which challenges and develops some of the ideas in the "naming, blaming, claiming model" revealed a complicated relationship between attribution of blame and the requirements of the law, and concluded that the idea that blame logically precedes consideration of legal action is faulty. Lloyd-Bostock (1984) argues that knowledge of the legal remedy or information about the availability of a legal remedy is very important to reasoning processes and claiming behaviour. Indeed, in many cases "the way in which accident victims attribute fault for their accidents and responsibility for compensating them is a reflection of, rather than reflected in, the law . . . fault, including moral fault, does not necessarily imply liability and . . . where it does, it is probably a justification rather than a reason for claiming damages[20]."

OBJECTIVES IN LITIGATING

It is clear that many factors may influence the decision to take action or to commence legal proceedings and an important issue will be what the litigant hopes or believes he will achieve by undertaking formal legal

---

[19] Lloyd Bostock, "Fault and Liability for Accidents", Chapter 4 in Harris et al, 1984 op. cit.

[20] pp 159–160.

action. Research that focuses in detail on motivation for claiming is in short supply and the meagre evidence available can be difficult to interpret. The NCC survey attempted to explore motivation for taking action to resolve serious disputes. This was done by including a question which asked, "What did you most want the law to help you to achieve?" and then asking respondents to choose, from a list of eight outcomes, the one that was most important to them. The results of the NCC study show that only one-third of respondents said that financial compensation was the most important thing that they wanted to achieve, despite the fact that the principal remedy offered by the legal system for the winning party in a civil claim is financial compensation. Prevention of similar occurrences in the future and apologies, which respondents to the NCC survey frequently mentioned as primary objectives in taking action, are goals for which the legal system is not well suited.

A questionnaire to plaintiffs in medical negligence claims also included a question concerning the most important factors in the decision to litigate. Respondents were asked to say for each of a number of suggested objectives which were "very important, important or not important"[21]. The objectives most frequently rated as "very important" were to prevent a similar thing happening to someone else, to make the doctor/hospital admit that something had gone wrong, discovering more about what happened and obtaining the right treatment. Less than half of the respondents said that obtaining compensation was a "very important" factor in the decision to sue, despite the fact that that is the only remedy that the legal system can deliver as a result of a negligence action.

These findings are difficult to understand within the context of cases that are expensive to pursue, take many years to conclude and are often extremely stressful for all involved. Both studies sought to identify objectives for claiming from a list of pre-coded alternatives, but the subtlety of objectives in claiming and the way that objectives might change during the course of seeking resolution of a problem, as well as the reasons for not making a legal claim, are matters which require further exploration.

---

[21] Hazel Genn "Access to Just Settlements: The Case of Medical Negligence" in A Zuckerman & R Cranston (Eds) *Reform of Civil Procedure: Essays on "Access to Justice"*, Oxford, Clarendon Press, 1995. (pp 393–412).

THE PATHS TO JUSTICE SURVEY

The decision to conduct a national study of the response of the public to justiciable problems was taken in 1996, in the context of debate about lack of access to justice and impending policy changes to the civil justice system. Since that time the absence of available information about the public need for advice and assistance in relation to the resolution of justiciable problems has become more evident with the recent proposals for the establishment of a Community Legal Service.[22] Moreover, the growing emphasis on the desirability of diverting civil cases away from the public courts and towards private dispute resolution processes (ADR) begs some important questions.

In order to make any sensible decisions about how the civil justice system might better serve the needs of the public, it is necessary to gain an understanding of how justiciable problems are managed *now*; what the public's preferences are in seeking a resolution of their problems; what drives decisions to begin or avoid litigation; and to try and identify those who genuinely feel that their desired access to court-based solutions is barred. The Paths to Justice Survey was designed to address these questions.

The focus of the study was on the behaviour of the public in dealing with non-trivial justiciable civil problems and disputes, as potential plaintiffs or potential defendants. The approach represented an attempt to map strategies from the bottom-up and was distinctive in that it was not limited to use of legal services to achieve court-based solutions for disputes and grievances. The study was designed to include the widest range of events (experienced by individuals as private persons) for which legal remedies are available under the civil justice system, subject only to a "triviality" threshold. Whether or not individuals were included or excluded from the study depended crucially on several key definitions used in the study as follows:

"Justiciable event": For the purposes of the study a justiciable event was defined as a matter experienced by a respondent which raised legal issues, whether or not it was recognised by the respondent as being "legal" and whether or not any action taken by the respondent to deal with the event involved the use of any part of the civil justice system.

---

[22] See Lord Chancellor's Department, *Consultation Paper on the Community Legal Service*, HMSO, May 1999.

Fourteen broad categories and over sixty sub-categories of justiciable event were identified for inclusion in the study ranging across employment, divorce, family, money, health, injury, immigration, property, discrimination issues etc (see Chapter 2 for full list). The justiciable events included in the study related only to *civil* matters, so where a respondent had been the victim of a crime this was not normally included. However, there were situations where violence raised the possibility of civil actions and these cases were included.

"Non-trivial": In order to avoid the study being swamped with trivial matters it was necessary to impose a triviality threshold. Using imposed or self-selected severity thresholds involved difficulties. For example, imposed thresholds ignore respondents' perceptions of the importance of an event. If a respondent felt that the threshold was too low they might be irritated by having to answer further questions about a matter to which they attached little importance. If the threshold was set too high, a respondent might feel frustrated about not being permitted to talk about a matter that was important to them. On the other hand, self-selected severity inevitably involves differential interpretation of terms such as "serious" and "major", resulting in the loss of information about strategies adopted to deal with some relatively serious events and the possibility of being swamped by relatively trivial events. In the end a mixture of imposed and self-selected triviality criteria was adopted. This involved a two stage approach: first respondents were asked to report all justiciable events that they had experienced as defined by the study irrespective of the seriousness of the event; second, events that had been reported were excluded from further questioning if respondents said that they had taken no action whatsoever to deal with the problem because the problem had not been regarded as important enough to warrant any action. Thus exclusion from further investigation was based on respondents' subjective perceptions of triviality. Some events, however, were automatically deemed to be relevant for further investigation. These were, divorce, being threatened with or the subject of legal proceedings, or having considered or commenced legal proceedings against another person or organisation[23]. Finally, events were not included in the main survey if respondents said that they had

[23] The American Bar Association Comprehensive Legal Needs Study (1994) adopted a slightly different approach. Some matters were included automatically such as homelessness, discrimination, dismissal from work. For all other types of events the questions were framed in such a way that words such as "serious problem/dispute" or "major difficulties" were incorporated into the question.

taken no action to deal with the problem because they did not regard themselves as being in dispute since they believed that the other side was right, or that no one was to blame.

"Private individuals": The study was concerned with the response of *individuals* to justiciable events. Thus businesses, institutions, associations, etc were excluded from the study. This raised some difficulties when an individual was in business on his own account and it was decided that such individuals would be included if they reported a justiciable event occurring in their private capacity, but that any justiciable event occurring in relation to their work activities would be excluded. A self-employed plumber suing an electrician who carried out work on the plumber's house would therefore be included. If, however, the same plumber had been sued by a householder as a result of his own faulty workmanship, that event *would not* be included in the study.

Objectives

The survey was designed to provide information and offer analyses of the following:

- The *incidence* of justiciable problems within the population.
- The *responses* of the public to justiciable problems, including use of legal and other advice sources, alternative dispute resolution methods, self-help strategies (and what these entail—for example involving the police in civil disputes), and simply doing nothing.
- Perceived *barriers* to access to justice, including the types of issues that are being denied access to the courts, when access is desired; the factors perceived as representing the main barriers to access—such as cost, lack of information, lack of confidence.
- The *motivation* for taking action to resolve problems and for using courts or alternative forms of dispute resolution, or for avoiding legal processes.
- The *outcome* of different strategies for resolving justiciable disputes and the cost.
- The public's *experiences and perceptions* of legal proceedings, the courts, and the judiciary.

Central to the survey's objectives and subsequent analysis was a desire to convey the *dissimilarity* of the range of justiciable problems that might face members of the public at different times, and the way in which strategies for the resolution of justiciable problems are as much influenced by the characteristics of the problem as by the characteristics of the person experiencing the problem.

Method[24]

The research comprised four distinct stages:

(i) Qualitative developmental work involving group discussions to assist in the design of the screening questionnaire.

(ii) A face-to-face screening survey of the general population of adults (over 18) conducted in their homes, designed to estimate the incidence of events for which legal remedies exist ("justiciable problems") in the five years since January 1992. This involved a random sample of 4,125 individuals ("the screening survey").

(iii) Follow-up face-to-face interviews with 1,134 adults in their homes who had been identified as having experienced a non-trivial justiciable problem during the previous five years ("the main survey").

(iv) In-depth face-to-face qualitative interviews with 40 respondents who had experienced a justiciable problem ("the qualitative interviews").

Qualitative Developmental Work

The screening survey was preceded by a lengthy developmental stage in order to ensure that the questions included on the screening questionnaire covered the widest possible range of potentially justiciable problems, not merely the more obvious events that many people would recognise as being potentially "legal" problems. Moreover, it was important that the wording of the questions was appropriate, containing comprehensive memory prompts in order to maximise recall and reporting. The developmental work included a series of group discussions with members of the public, solicitors, and advice agency workers. The discussions took place during evenings and lasted for about two hours. All group discussions were tape-recorded and verbatim transcripts produced.

---

[24] A full technical report is provided in Appendix A.

Topics explored during group discussions with members of the public included: experiences of justiciable events and the terminology used by the public when referring to "justiciable problems"; the various strategies adopted to try and resolve justiciable problems; the range of advice sources used by the public in dealing with justiciable problems; experience of the accessibility of advice and assistance; motivations for taking action to try and resolve problems; experience of and attitudes to the legal profession, the courts, and the judiciary.

Group discussions with solicitors and advice agency workers included exploration of the range of justiciable events dealt with by them; the types of advice and assistance provided for different categories of justiciable problem; routes to advisers and perceived barriers to advice; and perceptions of clients' attitudes to taking legal or other action to resolve justiciable problems.

In addition to group discussions, several pilot surveys of the screening questionnaire and the main questionnaire were carried out in order to obtain a rough estimate of the likely strike rate for the main survey, and to modify and refine questions in the light of experience.

The Screening Survey

A random sample of 4,125 individuals aged 18 or over was screened in order to determine whether or not they had experienced problems of various sorts during the previous five years ("the survey period")[25]. Interviewers presented respondents with a series of show cards each of which showed a list of problems of a particular type and respondents were asked whether or not they had experienced one or more of the problems on each card since January 1992. There were fourteen broad categories of problems and over sixty problem sub-categories included on the screening survey. The full range of questions asked, together with the material on the show cards is reproduced in Appendix C. The results of the screening survey are discussed in Chapter 2.

---

[25] Although it would have been extremely enlightening to be able to compare experiences of respondents from different ethnic backgrounds, this was not feasible on the basis of a simple random sample of the population. Such analysis would require a special sample design, which was not achievable within the available budget.

Main Survey

Respondents who said that they had experienced problems of a particular type were then asked for each problem mentioned (up to a maximum of three) whether they had taken any of a list of actions which were also shown on a card. Those saying that they had not taken any of these actions were then asked to say why not, again choosing their reasons from a card. Respondents were deemed eligible for a main interview if they had experienced one or more problems from the problem show cards and had *either* taken one of the specified actions about it *or* indicated that the reason they had not taken any such action was not to do with the triviality of the problem. In addition, respondents were automatically deemed eligible for a main interview if they had been involved in divorce proceedings, had legal action taken against them, had been threatened with legal action over a disagreement, or had started, or considered starting, court proceedings. If respondents mentioned having experienced more than one problem during the survey period, they were asked about the second most recent problem in the main interview. The second most recent problem was chosen in order to increase the likelihood that sufficient time would have elapsed for a resolution to have been achieved.

The main survey questionnaire covered the experiences of those who sought to deal with their problems or disputes through the legal system, those who used alternative methods of dispute resolution, those who adopted self-help strategies, and those who did nothing at all to seek a resolution of their problem or dispute. The interview covered details of the justiciable problem and what was at stake; the strategy adopted by the respondent, if any, in trying to achieve a resolution of the problem; details of any advice and assistance obtained; use and experience of legal processes; objectives in taking action; outcomes achieved. The survey also dealt with experiences and perceptions of those who did not use legal processes. All respondents were also questioned about attitudes to the courts, judiciary, and lawyers[26]. The main survey interviews lasted on average around forty-five minutes.

---

[26] A copy of the main questionnaire is reproduced at Appendix C.

Qualitative Study

Although the screening survey and main survey provided reliable estimates of the incidence of justiciable events and responses to those events, qualitative interviews were conducted to provide in-depth information about behaviour, decision-making and motivation, permitting a more detailed tracing of the *processes* through which disputes were handled. In particular, qualitative interviews were able to explore in detail: influences on decisions about how to deal with disputes and problems; motivations and objectives underlying choices about particular courses of action; experiences of using legal and other advisers; perceived barriers to advice; experience of being involved in legal proceedings. The qualitative interviews also provided important information to supplement attitudinal questions posed on the main survey about attitudes to the courts and legal services[27].

Respondents included in the qualitative follow-up stage of the research were recruited from those who had been interviewed in the main survey and were selected on the basis of a mix of problem types and responses to those problems. Qualitative interviews were therefore conducted with respondents who had taken no action to resolve their justiciable problem; those who had taken action to resolve their problem and who had done so without seeking any advice or assistance; respondents who had sought advice from an advice agency or non-legal adviser and then handled the problem themselves; respondents who had sought legal advice and resolved the problem without becoming involved in court proceedings; and respondents who had sought legal advice and resolved their problem following a court or tribunal hearing.

All interviews were tape-recorded and verbatim transcripts produced. The interviews lasted for about one hour on average.

STRUCTURE OF THE BOOK

Chapter Two uses the results of the screening survey to estimate the incidence of different kinds of justiciable problems as reported by respondents to the screening survey, together with brief information about whether respondents took any action to deal with the problem.

[27]   The topic guide used in the qualitative interviews is reproduced at Appendix A.

The Chapter identifies the most common problems experienced by members of the public, demographic variations in the reporting of justiciable problems, and the frequency with which individuals experienced problems of a particular kind during the survey period. For each of the fourteen broad problem areas covered in the screening survey, estimates are provided of the number of problems occurring per 1,000 population and the total number of problems occurring within the population of England and Wales. There is also information provided about the types of problems that tend to cluster together. The second section of Chapter Two provides a breakdown of the main survey sample, based on the selection of respondents experiencing a "non-trivial" justiciable problem during the previous five years, and the demographic characteristics of respondents experiencing problems of different types are described.

Chapter Three begins with an overview of the public response to justiciable problems, analysing the characteristics of "lumpers", "self-helpers", and those who obtained assistance in the process of resolving their problem. In order to gain a better understanding of the public need for advice in dealing with justiciable problems the Chapter describes barriers and pathways to advice, the choice of advisers, expectations of advisers, the nature of advice received and satisfaction with that advice.

Chapter Four lays bare the various strategies adopted by respondents in dealing with justiciable problems of different types and looks in more detail at some of the issues discussed in Chapter Three in relation to particular problem types. In the final section of Chapter Four, the results of multivariate analysis are presented in order to gain a better understanding of the factors associated with the likelihood that advice would be obtained during the process of resolving disputes.

In Chapter Five the outcome of attempts to resolve problems are analysed. The Chapter reports the proportion of all those experiencing a justiciable problem who succeeded in achieving a resolution of their problem, the proportion who abandoned their attempts to seek a resolution and the proportion who became involved in legal proceedings. Differences in outcome are analysed in relation to whether or not advice was obtained and the kind of advice obtained, as well as in relation to the type of problem experienced. In the second section of the chapter the cost of taking action to resolve problems is described, together with information about those respondents whose legal costs were covered by Legal Aid or other sources. The final section of the

Chapter uses the results of multivariate analysis to explain the factors most strongly associated with different problem outcomes, for example whether any resolution was achieved by agreement, or whether there was a court hearing or whether no resolution was achieved at all.

Respondents' motivations for taking action and the fulfilment of objectives are the subject of Chapter Six. The Chapter summarises the reported motivation of respondents for taking action to resolve justiciable problems and describes differences in motivation depending on the type of problem being experienced. There is also a summary of the amount of money being pursed or defended and the types of non-money remedy desired by respondents. Differences between problem types in the extent to which respondents' objectives were achieved are described, as are perceptions of the fairness of the outcomes obtained. The final section of the Chapter discusses the results of multivariate analysis identifying factors associated with the achievement of objectives and perceptions of fairness of outcome.

In Chapter Seven the experiences of those involved in ADR and court processes are described, followed by a detailed analysis of responses to attitude questions about the legal system. These data are supplemented by analysis of qualitative interviews in which respondents were given the opportunity to expand on their views of the legal system. The material in the chapter provides useful contextual information that can contribute to understanding of the influences on the public when they make decisions about how to deal with justiciable problems.

The concluding Chapter highlights some of the main findings of the study and draws together the various threads running through the discussion in previous chapters. It considers the significance of the courts in the resolution of civil disputes and the policy strategies that might rationally flow from the understanding of the needs and preferences of the public gained from the study.

A technical report providing details of sampling, response rates, data collection methods and weighting procedures is provided at Appendix A. Appendix B describes in more detail the approach of the multivariate analyses reported in Chapters 4, 5, and 6, and presents the full results of the analyses. The screening questionnaire, main survey questionnaire, and advance letter are reproduced at Appendix C.

2

The Landscape of
Justiciable Problems

The purpose of this chapter is to estimate the incidence of justiciable problems as defined in the survey and to look very broadly at public responses to these problems. The estimates are based on the replies of a random sample of 4,125 adults who were asked during a screening survey to recall whether they had experienced any of a wide range of problems during the previous five years and if so when, and on how many occasions. The analysis in this chapter is the first comprehensive attempt to assess the frequency with which the population of England and Wales faces a wide range of justiciable problems.

The range of problems included in the survey and the wording used to describe those problems were developed on the basis of focus group meetings with advice agencies, members of the public, and solicitors, followed by piloting of questionnaires. After testing the wording of the screening survey and making some modifications, the survey was conducted during autumn 1997 and spring 1998. In the final form of the questionnaire, interviewers presented respondents with a series of cards, each of which showed a list of problems of a particular type, and respondents were asked whether or not they had experienced one or more of the problems on each card since January 1992. The types of problems covered in the screening survey were:

- Employment problems
- Problems relating to owning residential property
- Problems with renting out rooms or property
- Problems to do with living in rented accommodation
- Problems with faulty goods or services
- Problems to do with money
- Problems to do with relationships and other family matters
- Problems connected with having children aged less than 18

- Injuries and health problems arising from accidents or poor working conditions requiring medical treatment
- Problems with discrimination in relation to sex/race/disability
- Problems with unfair treatment by the police
- Problems with immigration or nationality issues
- Problems with receiving negligent/wrong medical or dental treatment

Because it was important to encourage memory recall, on each of the show cards dealing with a particular category of problem, there was a series of memory prompts indicating the kinds of problems that might arise in the general category. So, for example, the show card dealing with employment problems offered the following prompts:

- Losing a job (*e.g. unfair dismissal, dispute about redundancy package*)
- Getting pay or a pension
- Other rights at work (*e.g. maternity leave, sickness pay, holiday entitlement, working hours*)
- Changes to terms and conditions of employment
- Unsatisfactory or dangerous working conditions
- Harassment at work
- Unfair disciplinary procedures

In addition to this range of justiciable "problems", respondents were also asked whether, apart from anything already reported, they had been involved in divorce proceedings, had had legal action taken against them, had been threatened with legal action over a disagreement, or had started or considered starting court proceedings for any reason.

Respondents who said that they had experienced any of these problems were then asked for each problem mentioned (up to a maximum of three) whether they had taken any of a list of actions which were also shown on a card as follows:

- Talked/wrote to other side about problem
- Sought advice about trying to solve problem
- Threatened other side with legal action
- Went to court/tribunal/arbitration or started case
- Went to mediation or conciliation
- Took problem to an ombudsman
- Took other action to try to solve the problem
- Did nothing

Those saying that they had not taken any of the actions on the card were then asked to say why not, again choosing their reasons from a card as follows:

• Other side was already taking action
• Thought it would cost too much
• Thought it would take too much time
• Did not think anything could be done
• Did not think it was very important
• No dispute/Thought the other person/side was right
• Was scared to do anything
• Thought it would damage relationship with other side
• Other reason

Respondents were deemed eligible for a "main" interview if they had experienced one or more problems and had either taken one of the specified actions to deal with the problem, or had failed to take action for a reason other than the triviality of the problem or that there was no dispute. Respondents were also included in the main survey if they had been involved in divorce proceedings, had had legal action taken against them, had been threatened with legal action over a disagreement about something, or had started or considered starting legal proceedings.

THE MOST COMMON PROBLEMS AND THEIR INCIDENCE

In total, about 40% of all respondents who answered the screening survey reported having experienced one or more justiciable problem during the previous five years. The type of problems most frequently experienced were those relating to faulty goods and services (experienced by eleven percent of the total sample); money problems (experienced by nine percent of the total sample); injuries/health problems resulting from accidents or poor working conditions (eight percent of the sample); owning residential property (eight percent); living in rented accommodation (seven percent), employment problems (six percent), relationships and family matters (six percent) (Figure 2.1). The problems least frequently experienced by the sample were those relating to: negligent medical or dental treatment (two percent of the sample); discrimination as a result of race, sex or disability (one percent of the sample); unfair treatment by the police (one percent of the

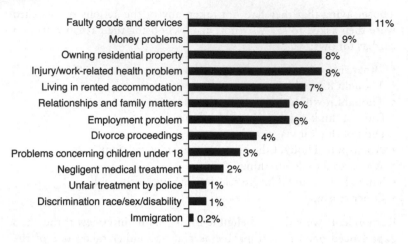

Figure 2.1. Incidence of problems of different types reported in screening survey. (Base = 4125)

sample); immigration or nationality issues (less than one percent of the sample).

Having been asked about experiences of specific problem types, respondents were then asked some additional questions in order to ensure that all those who had been involved in, or considered starting, any kind of legal proceedings were included in the main survey. Respondents were asked whether "apart from anything you have already told me about in this interview—since January 1992, has any legal action been taken against you, for example have you been sent a solicitor's letter or had court proceedings started against you?" and some additional questions about taking legal action and being threatened with legal action (see questionnaire in Appendix C for full text of questions). These "catch-all" questions produced some additional positive cases. About three percent of the sample reported that they had been the subject of legal action, about two percent of the sample reported having been *threatened* with legal action where they disputed the demand being made, and about two percent of the sample reported that they had started or *considered* starting some kind of legal proceeding through court, mediation or ombudsman.

The results of the screening survey can be compared with results of three recent roughly comparable surveys: the ABA study of the legal needs of low and moderate-income households in the United States published in 1994 ("ABA study")[1], the National Consumer Council Study of experiences of civil disputes in England and Wales published in 1995 ("NCC study")[2], and a national survey of legal service needs carried out for the New Zealand Legal Services Board ("New Zealand study") published in 1999[3].

The ABA study found that 40 percent of low income households and 46 percent of moderate income households had experienced one or more "legal needs" during the calendar year 1992, a legal need being defined as having experienced one or more of 17 categories of problem or situation[4]. The high incidence rate during a one year period is at least in part due to two important features of the study that are different from the present study. First, the ABA study was based on households and counted problems that had affected any person who was a member of the household at the time of the interview. Second, the ABA study included a number of matters not included in the present study, for example the need for advice about setting up a business, concerns about the community or regional environment, and concerns about inadequate or inferior municipal services, such as rubbish collection, holes in the pavement, inadequate public transport.

The most common needs reported in the ABA study concerned housing conditions or real property transactions (13% of low and 10% of moderate income households), personal finance and consumer needs (13% of both income categories), family and domestic legal needs (8% of low and 6% of moderate income households), employment (7% of low and 10% of moderate income households), personal or economic injury stemming primarily from accidents (6% of low and 9% of moderate income households). The range of the most common problems

---

[1] *Legal Needs and Civil Justice*, Major Findings of the Comprehensive Legal Needs Study, American Bar Association, Chicago, 1994.

[2] *Seeking Civil Justice*, National Consumer Council, 1995.

[3] G M Maxwell, C Smith, P Shepherd, A Morris, *Meeting Legal Service Needs*, prepared for the New Zealand Legal Services Board, Institute of Criminology, Victoria University of Wellington, 1999.

[4] For example, having experienced "unsafe or unhealthful conditions in rental housing, like the landlord frequently failing to provide heat, hot water, electricity, or working plumbing; a serious problems with cockroaches, mice or rats; or unsafe conditions, like electrical problems, that the landlord didn't correct." Unlike the current study, the ABA study included reports of needs that affected households in relation to business matters. A specific area of need was "legal needs of small businesses and farms".

and their incidence in the ABA study is similar to that reported in the screening survey.

The New Zealand study involved a national survey of 5,431 households in 1997. Respondents were asked how often they had experienced each of 27 different disagreements or problems in the previous three years and were given the option of reporting on any other disagreement or problem. The problems were those capable of a legal solution through the courts or through the assistance of lawyers. The survey found that 51% of the sample reported having experienced problems in the previous three years and over half of those reported having experienced more than one problem. The most common problems were disputes over consumer issues (experienced by 15% of the sample); traffic accident involving injury or damage (experienced by 11%); disagreements with an employer or employee (9%); problems about money being owed to the respondent (7%); disagreements with neighbours (7%). About 4% of the sample reported problems to do with divorce and separation. These figures appear to be roughly consistent with those of the present study, although the higher total incidence rate is probably accounted for by differences in methodology, for example the fact that disputes in the course of business were included, as was being suspected or charged with a crime (experienced by 3% of the sample).

The NCC study found that 13% of the general population of England and Wales had recent experience of at least one serious civil dispute relating to the thirteen problem areas asked about, corresponding to five million people among the population in England and Wales. This figure is much lower than the 40% of respondents in the present study who had experienced a justiciable problem in the previous five years. It is also lower than the ABA study. However, the NCC study adopted a less comprehensive approach than either the present study or the ABA study. The NCC study counted only those members of the public who reported having experienced one of 13 types of "serious civil disputes" in the previous three years[5]. Thus the range of matters about which respondents were asked was much narrower than in the present study, which used 14 broad problem categories and about 65 different sub-categories of problem to prompt memory and to indicate the kinds of problems and events to be reported. The use of the criterion of "serious dispute" in the NCC study meant that those respondents who had experienced a problem, but had avoided the mat-

---

[5] See discussion in Chapter 1 for text of the question and categories used.

ter from becoming a "serious dispute" by satisfactorily taking direct action, would probably not have been included in the NCC study although they would have been included in the present study. The differences between the overall incidence rate achieved in the two studies can also be partly accounted for by the longer reference period used in the present study (five years rather than the three-year reference period used in the NCC study).

There were also some differences between the two studies in the estimated incidence of specific problem types, although this is largely a result of different definitions of problem categories in the two studies. The most common problems reported in the NCC study were damage to a vehicle (18%), divorce (10%), injury (10%), unpaid debt (9%), faulty goods (8%), problems with neighbours (8%), problems at work (8%), dispute with local authority/agency (8%). Those problem categories that are directly comparable with the present study, such as, injury and problems at work show that the NCC estimates are very similar. Other categories are more difficult to compare. For example, in the present study faulty goods and services were categorised together and had an incidence rate of 11%. In the NCC study faulty goods had an incidence rate of 8% and faulty services an incidence rate of 7%. The incidence rate for divorce in the NCC study is significantly higher than that in the present study (10% in the NCC study as compared with 4%). However, the figure for the incidence of divorce proceedings derived from the screening survey in the present study represents simply those respondents who had been involved in divorce proceedings during the previous five years, whereas the NCC study refers to people "involved in a serious dispute about divorce". It is therefore likely that the NCC figure includes matters that would have been categorised in the present study under "relationships and family matters" which included division of money, pensions or property in connection with divorce or separation; and getting or paying maintenance of child support payments.

DEMOGRAPHIC VARIATIONS

The only demographic information collected on the screening questionnaire was the age and sex of respondents[6]. Analysis of prevalence

---

[6] Full demographic information was collected during the main survey and is used throughout the analysis of main survey findings discussed in the following chapters.

of justiciable disputes in relation to these factors indicated that there were no meaningful differences between men and women in the extent to which they reported having experienced justiciable problems during the study period. This finding is consistent with the NCC study, which found few gender differences in the reporting of involvement in civil disputes. Some 38% of men and 40% of women reported having experienced one or more justiciable problem during the previous five years. Moreover, within each problem type the proportion of men and women reporting having experienced the event was virtually identical.

There were, however, some differences in experience depending on age (Table 2.1). Younger people were more likely to have experienced problems than their older counterparts: over half of those aged between 18 and 34 had experienced one or more problems, whereas less than a quarter of those aged 65 or over had done so, and the incidence of most problem types declined with increasing age. Some of these differences can be plausibly linked with age-related changes in life-style, notably those relating to problems with employment, living in rented accommodation, and having children under 18. However, the explanations for other age-related trends, such as those relating to faulty goods and services and money, is less obvious. The NCC study also found some age differences in the reporting of experience of civil disputes that are roughly consistent with the findings of the present study, although the differences in problem categorisation made direct comparisons rather difficult.

Although the demographic and social classification data collected about screening respondents was rather limited, further analysis of the demographic characteristics of those reporting having experienced justiciable disputes in comparison with the general population is presented in the final section of this chapter.

FREQUENCY OF JUSTICIABLE PROBLEMS

Many members of the public interviewed in the screening survey reported having experienced problems of a particular type on more than one occasion during the survey reference period. For most broad categories of problems the average number of problems experienced by individuals during the survey reference period was somewhere between 1.2 and 1.5 (Table 2.2). However, the average number of times people experienced a particular category of problem was notably higher for

Table 2.1. Incidence of problems of different types by age[7]

Type of problem		Age					
	Total %	18–24 %	25–34 %	35–44 %	45–54 %	55–64 %	65+ %
Faulty goods or services	11	11	15	16	11	8	6
Money	9	15	12	11	8	8	6
Injury/work-related health problem needing treatment	8	9	9	8	8	7	6
Owning residential property	8	8	11	11	9	5	6
Living in rented accommodation	7	11	10	8	4	7	3
Employment	6	8	8	8	7	5	2
Relationships and family matters	6	9	7	7	6	5	4
Divorce proceedings	4	7	5	5	4	3	3
Children under 18	3	3	3	6	4	1	1
Subject to legal action	3	5	4	5	3	4	2
Negligent medical/dental treatment	2	3	2	1	2	2	1
Threatened with legal action	2	3	2	3	2	*	1
Started/considered legal action	2	3	3	3	2	2	1
Discrimination race/sex/ disability	1	*	1	2	1	*	1
Unfair treatment by the police	1	2	2	1	1	1	–
Renting out rooms or property	1	1	2	2	1	1	*
Immigration problem	*	*	1	1	–	–	–
Any problem	39	52	51	45	32	34	23
Unweighted base[8]:	4125	359	747	766	691	559	820
Weighted base:	4125	376	767	752	692	545	804

---

[7] Note that in all tables the symbol "*" denotes a non-zero quantity of less than half a per cent and the symbol "–" denotes zero.

[8] The number of unclear answers is not shown in these tables because it varied by type of problem.

Table 2.2. Mean number of problems experienced by those with problems of a given sort

Type of problem	Mean no. of problems	Weighted Base
Injury/work-related ill health	1.97	308
Living in rented accommodation	1.78	287
Renting out rooms or property	1.46	43
Money	1.46	384
Threatened with legal action	1.45	64
Subject to legal action	1.44	135
Owning residential property	1.43	335
Started/considered legal action	1.43	92
Children under 18	1.42	122
Faulty goods or services	1.38	448
Relationships and family matters	1.38	216
Discrimination, unfair treatment by the police, immigration, medical negligence	1.31	127
Employment	1.21	249

certain problem types. For example, the average number of problems experienced in the previous five years relating to renting property was 1.78, and for accidental injury and work-related health problems the average number of problems experienced was nearly two for those experiencing such problems (1.97). In effect this means that individuals were more likely to experience problems of these types in clusters i.e. if they experienced the problem *at all* they were likely to experience it on more than one occasion.

INCIDENCE OF JUSTICIABLE PROBLEMS: NATIONAL ESTIMATES

Having calculated the proportion of the sample that experienced certain types of justiciable problems, and the average number of times that each type of problem was experienced by individuals in the sample, it is possible to combine the information in order to show the proportion of all justiciable problems falling into any particular problem category, and to estimate rates per thousand population for each problem category. This information appears in Table 2.3. The estimates suggest that in a statistically representative sample of 1,000 adults there would be 392 people who had experienced 1,031 problems over the survey reference period (2.6 problems each). The most numerous problems experienced by the sample were those relating to:

• faulty goods and services (153 problems per 1,000 adults)
• money (138 problems per 1,000 adults)
• living in rented accommodation (124 problems per 1,000 adults)
• owning residential accommodation (119 problems per 1,000 adults).

It is also possible to estimate the total number of adults in England and Wales affected by each type of problem over the survey reference period and the total number of problems of each type experienced over this period[9]. Overall it was estimated that about 41,496,000 problems were experienced by 15,785,800 adults aged 18 and over (of a population of 40,237,000 people belonging to this age group) (Table 2.3).

PROBLEM CLUSTERS

In addition to looking at the incidence of problem types and the frequency with which individuals experienced problems of a certain type, an analysis was carried out in order to describe the *different* kinds of problems that survey respondents had experienced during the previous five years. Table 2.4 presents a cross-tabulation of the overlap between the incidence of different types of problems occurring during the survey reference period that had been defined as non-trivial[10]. From this table it can be seen that, for example, respondents reporting employment problems during the previous five years were also quite likely to have experienced money problems (30%), consumer problems (24%), or problems to do with owning property (22%). Respondents who were involved in divorce proceedings during the previous five years were very likely also to report family problems (59%), problems to do with children (19%), or money problems (19%). Victims of accidental injury or work-related ill-health were quite likely to mention that they

[9] These estimates are affected by the way in which a "problem" is operationally defined. In making them, problems have been calculated as something linked to the individual. Thus two people involved in the same problem (whether on the same side or on different) sides would be counted twice.

[10] For technical reasons, justiciable problems that were regarded by respondents as too trivial to warrant taking any action were excluded from this analysis.

Table 2.3. Estimates of rates per thousand, numbers of adults in England and Wales affected by problems of different types, and of total number of problems of different types during previous five years

	Number of problems per 1,000 population over 18	Estimate of number of adults with problem of this type	Total number of problems that are of this type
Faulty goods or services	153	4,474,354	6,153,132
Money	138	3,778,254	5,534,387
Living in rented accommodation	124	2,812,566	5,000,462
Owning residential property	119	3,351,742	4,798,019
Accident or work-related health problem	90	3,025,822	3,620,699
Relationships and family matters	83	2,406,173	3,324,849
Employment	73	2,442,386	2,945,029
Divorce proceedings	47	1,722,144	1,722,144
Subject to legal action	47	1,323,797	1,904,812
Discrimination, unfair treatment by the police, immigration, medical negligence	46	1,408,295	1,843,317
Problem with children under 18	43	1,227,229	1,740,455
Started/considered taking legal action	33	929,475	1,329,056
Threatened with legal action	24	659,484	953,219
Renting out rooms or property	16	430,536	626,559

had experienced money problems during the previous five years (21%) or employment problems (16%).

Respondents who reported having experienced money problems during the previous five years were likely also to have experienced consumer problems (26%), problems with rented accommodation (20%) and employment problems (20%).

These findings show clearly that respondents reporting having experienced a justiciable problem in the previous five years often experienced a problem more than once *and* more than one type of problem. While 20% of the population reported having experienced only one non-trivial justiciable problem during the previous five years, a further

Table 2.4. Percentage overlap between the incidence of eligible problems

	Total	Q2 Employment problem	Q3 Owning resid. property	Q4 Renting out property	Q5 Living in rented accomm.	Q6 Faulty goods/ services
Unweighted base	4125	232	314	41	243	424
Weighted base	4125	234	304	41	264	424
	%	%	%	%	%	%
Q2 Employment	6	–	17	31	14	13
Q3 Owning residential property	7	22	–	22	9	20
Q4 Renting out property	1	5	3	–	4	4
Q5 Living in rented accomm.	6	15	8	27	–	11
Q6 Faulty goods or services	10	24	28	44	18	–
Q7 Money	9	30	22	41	27	22
Q8 Divorce	4	8	8	9	10	8
Q9 Family matters	5	12	11	15	12	11
Q10 Children	3	7	7	19	8	5
Q11 Accident or injury	5	15	11	10	11	11
Q12 Police etc.	3	10	4	23	11	7

	Q7 Money	Q8 Divorce	Q9 Family matters	Q10 Children	Q11 Accident or injury	Q12 Police etc.
Unweighted base	351	179	205	116	218	100
Weighted base	359	176	198	114	223	106
	%	%	%	%	%	%
Q2 Employment	20	10	14	15	16	23
Q3 Owning residential property	18	13	17	20	15	13
Q4 Renting out property	5	2	3	7	2	9
Q5 Living in rented accomm.	20	15	16	19	13	27
Q6 Faulty goods or services	26	18	24	18	22	29
Q7 Money	–	19	21	23	21	30
Q8 Divorce	9	–	52	29	6	12
Q9 Family matters	11	59	–	38	9	15
Q10 Children	7	19	22	–	8	10
Q11 Accident or injury	13	7	10	15	–	12
Q12 Police etc.	9	7	8	9	6	–

14% reported having experienced two or more problems during the five year period. Looking more closely at those who had experienced more than one problem in the previous five years, eight percent of the population reported having experienced two problems; 4% reported having experienced three problems; two percent reported having experienced four problems; 0.5% of the population reported having experienced five problems; 0.3% had experienced six problems; 0.1% had experienced seven problems; and 0.02% reported having experienced as many as eight different problems during the five year period covered by the survey.

Table 2.4 shows the ways in which problems of different types tend to cluster and an additional analysis was undertaken to identify the most common pairs of problems occurring together during the five years of the survey reference period.

The analysis of the relationship between pairs of problem types shows that those problem types most commonly experienced together were:

- Divorce and family matters (0.53)[11]
- Family matters and children (0.26)
- Divorce and children (0.20)
- Employment problems and money problems (0.19)
- Problems with owning residential property and consumer problems (0.17)
- Problems with rented accommodation and money problems (0.17)
- Employment problems and owning residential property (0.14)

The results of the screening survey, suggest therefore, that problems and misfortune have a tendency to come in clusters. This finding is consistent with other studies of legal problems and misfortune, and with studies of the experience of crime victims[12]. For example, aside from the obvious clustering of divorce with problems concerning the care of children, empirical studies of the consequences of divorce have demonstrated the disruption to families caused by the forced sale of the fam-

---

[11] Correlation matrix. Figures in brackets represent the strength of the correlation.

[12] Surveys of criminal victimisation consistently reveal the clustering of incidents of victimisation. Certain individuals will be a victim of crime on more than one occasion during a survey reference period and such people may experience repeated instances of the same crime or instances of different crimes being committed against them. For a discussion of this phenomenon see Hazel Genn, "Multiple Victimisation", in M Maguire and J Pointing (eds) *Victims of Crime: A New Deal?* Open University Press, Milton Keynes, 1988.

ily home, and the frequent poverty and dependence on benefits that affects the lone parent shouldering childcare responsibilities after divorce. "[T]he burden of child-rearing after divorce falls mainly on [women's] shoulders and with lower wages for women combined with the opportunity costs of child-rearing, we have a growing population of economically vulnerable female-headed households.[13]"

Similarly, empirical studies of the financial consequences of accidental injury and work-related ill health have shown that many victims suffer financial hardship and have problems with benefits in the immediate aftermath of an injury as a result of being unable to work[14]. In addition there may be longer-term employment consequences and financial hardship if the victim suffers a substantial degree of residual disability, even if compensation for the injury was obtained via the legal system. A study of the long term financial effects of personal injury conducted by the Law Commission showed that as well as losing earnings from work, accident victims often incur other costs (for example for medical treatment, rehabilitation etc) or suffer other losses, and other household members may have to give up work altogether as a result of the victim's accident, thereby causing a *further loss* in household income. The Law Commission study found that nine in ten victims of serious injury had received state benefits since the date of their accident. The report concluded that having to pay extra costs while living on a reduced income resulted in many accident victims experiencing financial problems, and many borrowed money or accumulated debts as a result of their accident.[15]

Certain types of situations can have a cascade effect. For example, threatened repossession of the family home can lead to marital strain and breakdown, mental health problems, leading to difficulties at work and problems in caring for children. The operation of problem clustering was vividly illustrated by one unfortunate member of the sample in the present study, who lost his wife, health, job, home and children in the space of a few years:

> "I got divorced a few years ago. After the divorce I had to take out an extra mortgage to pay off my wife. I was a manager for a big company and had

[13] L J Weitzman and M Maclean (eds), *Economic Consequences of Divorce*, Oxford, Clarendon Press, 1992, p 9.
[14] D Harris et al, *Compensation and Support for Illness and Injury*, Oxford, Clarendon Press, 1984.
[15] *Personal Injury Compensation: How Much is Enough?*, London, Law Commission, Report No 225, 1994.

been there for 20 years. I had a heart attack in the middle of the night through the stress of working so hard and then had a bypass operation. I was off work for about a year. When I went back to work they offered me redundancy and I took it because I naively believed I would be able to get another job. But it left me unemployed for a year. The redundancy money all disappeared because I was paying the mortgage out of the redundancy money. It soon disappears if you are expecting to get a job and you don't get one. I was forced in the end to get rid of the house which I lived in with my two boys. I actually sold it about two weeks before I got repossessed. I got this job as a resident warden in a homeless hostel because it was somewhere to live as well. It was desperation. You can imagine the stress of it with the divorce, a bypass, a redundancy, and repossession all one year after the other. It was a great strain."

The financial vulnerability, emotional impact, and other consequences that can flow from many kinds of justiciable problem have implications for the type of advice and assistance that is needed when members of the public seek help to deal with problems. As will be seen from some of the case studies in Chapters 3 and 4, those who seek advice ostensibly about a single issue may have a bundle of underlying problems or difficulties that require unpacking before any viable resolution can be achieved.

TRIVIALITY THRESHOLD

In order to exclude from further analysis justiciable problems regarded by survey respondents as too trivial to bother about, all those who reported having experienced a problem during the survey reference period were asked whether they had taken any action to deal with the problem and if not, why they had failed to take action. Those respondents who reported lack of action in the screening survey because the problem was not regarded as important enough to warrant action were not included in the follow-up main survey[16].

However, the impact of applying the triviality criterion was relatively small for most problem types. As the discussion in the following section will show, rather few problems were reported in the survey that respondents had regarded as being too trivial to do anything about,

---

[16] In addition, those respondents who said that they had not taken action because they were not in dispute or believed that the other side was right were not included in the main survey.

although they may have failed to take action for other reasons. So, for example, in the screening survey some six percent of the sample reported having been involved in a problem relating to their employment. After removing those cases in which respondents said that the employment problem was not important enough to take action, the estimate for non-trivial employment problems remains at six percent of the total sample (Table 2.5). This suggests that in most cases respondents had either forgotten or chose not to report events regarded as trivial, leaving the population estimates for "non-trivial" justiciable events almost identical to those for all justiciable events reported.

An exception to this general pattern, however, was found in relation to injury and work-related illness victims where a high proportion of respondents took no action to resolve problems, generally because they thought that no one was to blame for the accident or that the event was

Table 2.5. Incidence of problems of different types since 1992: impact of applying the triviality criterion

	Estimate of incidence in adult population before applying triviality criterion	Estimate of incidence in adult population after applying triviality criterion
	%	%
Employment	6	6
Owning residential property	8	7
Renting out rooms or property	1	1
Living in rented accommodation	7	6
Faulty goods or services	11	10
Money	9	9
Relationships and family matters	6	5
Children under 18	3	3
Injury/work related ill health involving doctor/dentist/ hospital visit	8	5
Discrimination/ unfair treatment by police/immigration/medical negligence	4	3
Unweighted base:	4125	4125
Weighted base:	4125	4125

not important enough to warrant taking action, despite the fact that it had involved a visit to a hospital, doctor or dentist.

THE INCIDENCE OF DIFFERENT PROBLEMS AND WHETHER ANY ACTION TAKEN

The following sections describe in more detail the nature of the problems reported by respondents during the screening survey. Relatively brief information is also given about whether or not respondents reported during the screening survey having taken any action, no matter how limited, to try and resolve the problems that they had reported, since this information was used as the basis for inclusion in the main survey. Figure 2.2 below shows that although action was to taken to try and resolve most problems, there was some variation between different types of problem. For example, when problems concerned children, action was almost always taken to seek some kind of resolution. On the other hand, no action was taken to seek a resolution for around one in three problems relating to unfair treatment by the police, discrimination, accidents, and work-related ill health. Full information about respondents' strategies for resolving disputes and their use of advisers, based on comprehensive information obtained in the main survey, is presented and discussed in Chapters 3 and 4.

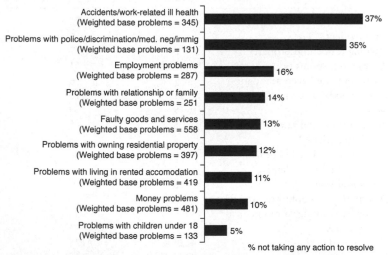

Figure 2.2. No action taken to resolve justiciable problem by problem type.

Problems with receiving faulty goods or services

The most common type of justiciable problem experienced by the general population sample involved faulty goods or services. Eleven per cent of the total sample had experienced one or more of these types of problems during the survey reference period, and the problems seemed to be especially pronounced among respondents aged between 35 and 44. The average number of problems experienced by those reporting consumer problems was 1.38 per person.

Brief information obtained on the screening survey about action taken to deal with consumer problems revealed that the vast majority of respondents took action to try and remedy consumer problems. Some steps had been taken to resolve the problem for about 87% of the consumer problems that had been experienced and reported in the survey. The most common action taken was to speak or write to the other side, but only in a minority of cases was advice sought about how to resolve the problem (30% of consumer problems). In some cases legal action was threatened, and a tiny minority of respondents said that their consumer problem had led to court proceedings or was dealt with by an ombudsman (Figure 2.3). In no cases did respondents mention taking the problem to mediation.

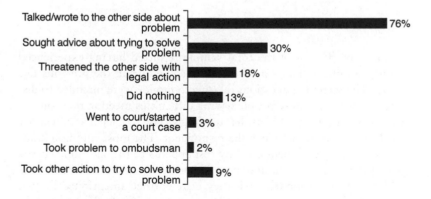

Figure 2.3. Action taken to try and resolve problems with receiving faulty goods or services. (Weighted base = 558)

In about thirteen per cent of cases respondents had taken no action whatsoever to try and resolve the problem. The most common reason given for failing to take any action at all was that the respondent did not think that anything could be done about the problem (22% of those failing to take action and 3% of all consumer problems) or that it was unimportant (3% of all consumer problems) (Figure 2.4). A detailed discussion of the most common approaches to dealing with consumer and other disputes, based on information obtained during the main survey, appears in Chapter 4.

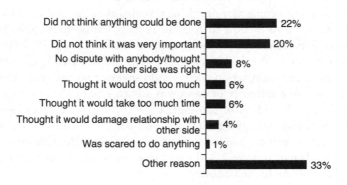

Figure 2.4. Reasons for not taking action to resolve problems with faulty goods and services. (Unweighted base = 78)

Problems to do with money

About nine percent of the total sample reported having experienced money problems that were difficult to solve during the previous five years. The screening questions relating to money were intended to distinguish between those people having difficulties meeting their outgoings, from specific problems that might give rise to a legal action either by the respondent or against the respondent. The most common kinds of money problems mentioned by respondents to the screening survey were problems over refusal of benefits, pensions, grants or loans by the DSS to which respondents felt they were entitled (mentioned by two per cent of all respondents and about one-quarter of all money problems); getting someone to pay money that was owed to the respondent (2% of the whole sample); problems relating to disputed or incorrect bills (2% of the total sample sample and about one-fifth of all money problems); disputed or incorrect tax demands (2% of the whole sample). Less common problems reported were: insurance companies unfairly rejecting claims; receiving incorrect information or advice about financial products; unfair refusal of credit (Figure 2.5). Among those respondents who mentioned having experienced a money problem during the survey reference period, the average number of money problems experienced was 1.46.

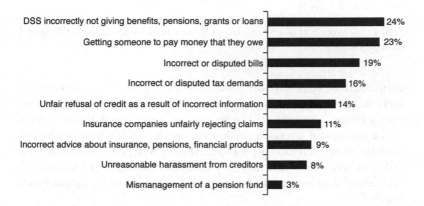

Figure 2.5. Types of problems or disputes that were difficult to solve to do with money since January 1992—percentages of all money problems reported. (Weighted base problems = 481)

Respondents were very likely to have taken action to deal with money problems. In about nine out of ten money problems reported in the screening survey, respondents said that they had taken some action to try to resolve the problem. Most often this involved writing or talking to the other side. Advice was sought for only about one in three money problems experienced by the sample and for only a very small proportion of money problems did the respondent go to court either to pursue or defend a claim (Figure 2.6).

In the very small proportion of cases (one in ten) in which respondents had failed to take any action to resolve a money problem, the most common reasons given for the failure were because the respondent thought that the problem was unimportant (26%) or that nothing

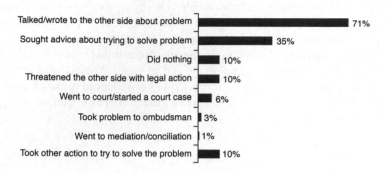

Figure 2.6. Action taken to resolve problems to do with money. (Weighted base problems = 481)

could be done to resolve the problem (15%). There were, however, a large number of "miscellaneous" reasons that were not easily classified into a group. These miscellaneous reasons represented almost a third of the reasons for not taking action among the small minority who did nothing about their money problem. About seven percent of those who failed to take action said that they thought it would cost too much to take action and about four per cent said that it would take too much time.

Employment problems

About six percent of the total sample had experienced one or more problems relating to their employment. The most common types of employment problem suffered were: losing a job (41% of employment problems experienced and 3% of the sample as a whole) and experiencing changed terms or conditions of employment (26% of employment problems and 2% of the whole sample). Other types of employment problems experienced with rather less frequency were harassment at work; unsatisfactory or dangerous working conditions; getting pay or a pension; other rights at work; unfair disciplinary procedures (Figure 2.7).

Among those reporting having experienced employment problems, the average number of these problems experienced during the previous five years was 1.21.

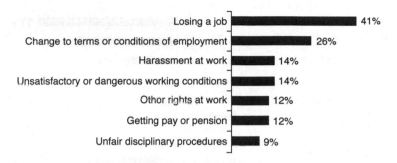

Figure 2.7. Breakdown of problems or disputes that were difficult to solve to do with employment since January 1992—percentages of all employment problems reported (Weighted base problems = 287)

An analysis of employment problems by age revealed that for each type of employment problem, the proportion of respondents experiencing it tended to *decrease* with increasing age, and this was most notable after retirement age. There was no significant difference between men and women in the incidence of employment problems.

Respondents took some action to deal with about three-quarters of their employment problems. By far the most common actions taken were seeking advice about the problem (56%) and talking or writing to the other side (52%). In a relatively substantial minority of cases (14%) the respondent had threatened legal action. The approach to dealing with employment problems is explored more fully in Chapter 4.

In about sixteen percent of employment problems, respondents said that they had done nothing about the problem. This is a relatively *high* figure in comparison with other problem types. The main reasons given by respondents for doing nothing about their employment problem were that they did not think that anything could be done (mentioned for about a third of problems where no action taken), or that they thought that the other side was right (mentioned for a little over a quarter of employment problems where no action taken). In about two percent of cases respondents took no action because they thought that it would cost too much, in about four percent of cases respondents thought that it would take too much time, and in about five percent of cases respondents were too scared to take action about employment problems. In a further two percent of cases no action was taken because

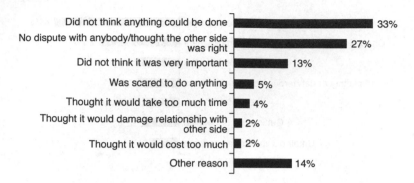

Figure 2.8. Reasons for taking no action to try and resolve employment problems. (Unweighted base = 55)

the respondent thought that taking action would damage their relationship with the other side (Figure 2.8).

Problems with owning residential property

About eight percent of the sample had experienced one or more problems to do with owning residential property and the average number of problems experienced during the previous five years was 1.43 per person. The most frequently experienced problems in this category were to do with neighbours (five percent of the whole sample and 57% of all problems with residential property), problems relating to buying and selling property (two percent of the sample and 17% of problems with property), alterations to property or planning permission, communal repairs or maintenance or repossession of the home (Figure 2.9).

Respondents had taken one or more actions in respect of 88% of problems experienced. The main actions taken by respondents were to talk or write to the other side about the problem (66% of problems) and to seek advice about solving it (56% of problems). In about 14% of problems the action taken was to threaten the other side with legal action. About four percent actually became involved in legal proceedings, about one percent went to mediation/conciliation, and a similar proportion took their case to an ombudsman.

Respondents had taken no action to try and resolve their problems to do with owning property in about 12% of cases, which is a relatively

Figure 2.9. Problems or disputes that were difficult to solve to do with owning residential property since January 1992—percentages of all residential property problems reported. (Weighted base problems = 397)

low rate of inaction in comparison with some other problem types. The main reasons mentioned for doing nothing were: thinking that nothing could be done; feeling that actions would damage the respondent's relationship with the other side involved in the problem; feeling that the problem was not very important; and feeling that there was no dispute/that the other side was right (Figure 2.10). In a small minority of cases no action was taken because it was feared that it would cost too much (7% of cases where no action taken).

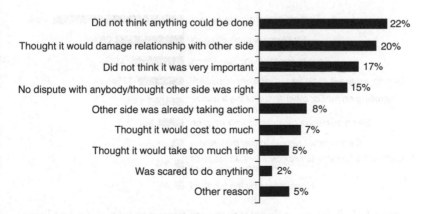

Figure 2.10. Reasons for not taking action to resolve problems with owning residential property. (Unweighted base = 60)

Problems to do with living in rented accommodation

About seven percent of the total sample had experienced problems relating to living in rented accommodation and the average number of problems experienced was 1.78. The main problems with living in rented accommodation were with getting the landlord to do repairs (mentioned by three per cent of all respondents and nearly half of all those with a problem in this category) and problems with neighbours (two per cent of the sample and about one quarter of those with a problem in this category). Other problems mentioned with some frequency were poor or unsafe living conditions (about one percent of the total sample and about a fifth of problems in this category), getting a deposit back from the landlord (just under one fifth of problems). In around one in ten cases the problem related to being evicted or being threatened with eviction (Figure 2.11).

Generally the proportion of people experiencing these problems declined with respondent age; this was especially marked for problems with getting the landlord to do repairs.

Respondents had taken some action to try to resolve problems in about 89% of cases. Respondents had spoken or written to the other side in about two thirds of cases (69%) and had sought advice for slightly over a third (37%) of problems about renting property. In no cases had there been a mediation or had the case been taken to an ombudsman. In about five percent of cases legal proceedings had been

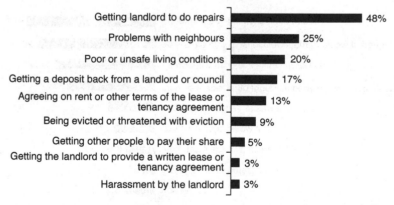

Figure 2.11. Problems or disputes that were difficult to solve to do with living in rented accommodation since January 1992—percentages of problems reported. (Weighted base problems = 419)

threatened and in about two percent of cases there had been court or tribunal proceedings.

In about one in ten of all problems to do with renting property (11%) respondents had done nothing about their problems. This figure is relatively low compared with some of the other problem categories. The main reasons given for failure to take action was a belief that nothing could be done (about three percent of all those with a problem to do with renting and about one-quarter of those not taking action), or that the problem was not important enough to take action (about 4% of all those with a rental problem and 38% of those not taking action) (Figure 2.12).

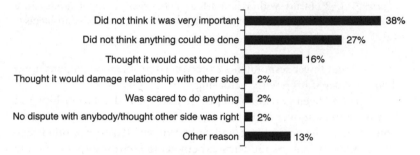

Figure 2.12. Reasons for not taking action to resolve problems to do with living in rented accommodation. (Unweighted Base = 45)

Problems to do with relationships and other family matters

About six percent of the sample had experienced problems to do with relationships and other family matters during the survey reference period. Respondents who reported these kinds of problems had experienced an average of 1.38 since January 1992. Three per cent of all respondents had experienced problems with getting or paying child maintenance during the survey reference period, and two per cent had experienced problems with the division of money or property in connection with a divorce or separation and problems after the death of a family member (Figure 2.13). About one percent of the sample as a whole (representing about one in five of those mentioning family problems) reported that they had experienced violent or abusive relationships with a partner, ex-partner or other family member. There was

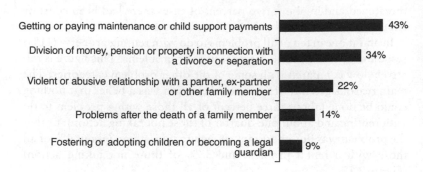

Figure 2.13. Problems with relationships and other family matters since January 1992—percentages of problems reported. (Weighted base problems = 251)

evidence that fewer respondents experienced problems attendant upon divorce or separation with increasing age.

Advice had been sought about problems to do with relationships and family matters in over half of all cases (57%) and in a similar proportion of cases the respondent had talked or written to the other side (49%). One in four respondents experiencing relationship and family matters said that they had started a court or tribunal case, which is a relatively high proportion by comparison with other problem types (Figure 2.14).

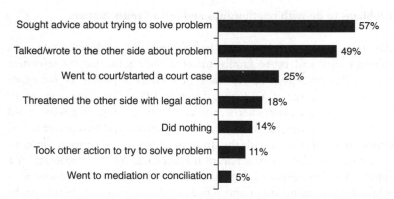

Figure 2.14. Actions taken about problems with relationships and family matters; all such problems since January 1992. (Weighted base all problems = 251)

About 14% of respondents experiencing family or relationship problems did not take any action to deal with the problem and this figure is relatively low when compared with other problem types, although not the lowest. The most common reasons for not taking action in order to try and resolve a problem relating to relationships and family matters were either that the respondent did not think that anything could be done about the problem, or that the respondent was worried that taking action might damage their relationship with the other party involved in the problem. This indicates the extent to which failure to take action is based on a sense of helplessness or anxiety about the repercussions of taking action when respondents are faced with these kinds of problems. In no case did respondents say that their failure to take action to resolve the problem was because they thought it would take too much time or would cost too much (Figure 2.15).

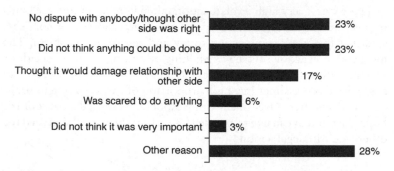

Figure 2.15. Reasons for not taking action to try and resolve relationship and family problems. (Unweighted base = 35)

Problems to do with children

The most frequently mentioned problems experienced in connection with children, involved getting children to a desired school or obtaining the kind of education that they needed (2% of the total sample and 4% of all those respondents with children), and residence and contact problems (1% of the total sample and 3% of those with children). Less common problems involved exclusion from schools and children being taken into care by the Local Authority (Figure 2.16).

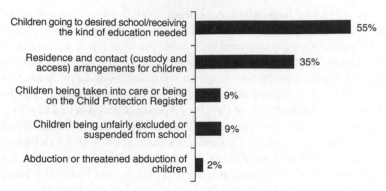

Figure 2.16. Problems or disputes that were difficult to solve to do with children under 18 since January 1992—percentages of problems reported. (Weighted base problems = 133)

There was a very high level of action taken in relation to these kinds of problems. In more than 90% of the problems reported, respondents said that they took some action to try and resolve the problem. The most common actions taken were talking or writing to the other side or seeking advice about the problem (Figure 2.17). Respondents also began legal proceedings in a high proportion of cases relating to problems with children. Over one in four respondents started a court or tribunal case and one in five respondents said that they had threatened the other side with legal action.

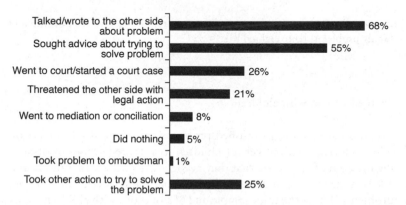

Figure 2.17. Actions taken about problems with children; all such problems since January 1992. (Weighted base = 133)

In only five percent of cases did respondents say that they had done nothing to try and resolve the problem concerning children under 18. This is a very low figure by comparison with other problem types and indicates the importance attached to resolving problems of this nature when they occurred. In the few cases in which respondents said that they had taken no action to try and resolve the problem, the main reason given was either that nothing could be done about the problem or that the problem was not sufficiently important to warrant taking action. In cases relating to children, therefore, it appears that problems were never regarded as being too much trouble or too costly to pursue.

Injuries and health problems

Nine per cent of respondents had suffered an injury or health problem resulting from an accident or from poor working conditions in the survey reference period. Seven per cent had experienced a problem of this sort that required a visit to a doctor, hospital, or dentist. This was used as a severity threshold and only those with injuries requiring a visit to the doctor, were administered the follow-up questions on actions and (if relevant) reasons for doing nothing.

Respondents took action to obtain a remedy for fewer problems of this type than they did for any other problem type. In over *one third* of cases of accidental injury or work-related ill health, respondents did nothing. In the sixty three per cent of problems where respondents took action, the main approach was to seek advice (39%) and talk or write to the other side (28%) (Figure 2.18).

The failure of over one in three respondents experiencing an accidental injury or work related illness requiring medical treatment is explored in more detail in Chapter 4. At the screening stage the reason most often given by injury victims for failure to take action was because respondents felt that they were not in dispute or that the other side was right—in other words that they did not believe that anyone else was to blame for the injury or ill-health. Other common reasons for not taking action were that respondents thought that the problem was not important enough to justify taking action, that nothing could be done, or that it would take too much time. Very few respondents said that their failure to take action was because of concern about cost (Figure 2.19).

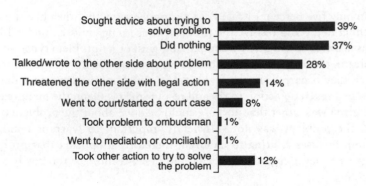

Figure 2.18. Actions taken about injuries or work-related ill health; all such problems since January 1992. (Weighted base problems = 345)

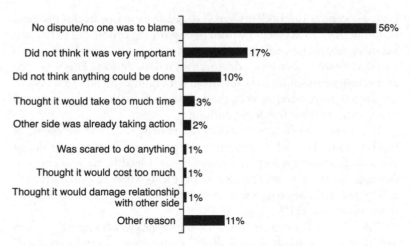

Figure 2.19. Reasons for not taking action to deal with injury/work-related ill health. (Weighted base = 137)

Problems with discrimination, unfair treatment by the police, immigration, nationality or medical negligence

These heterogeneous problems were presented to respondents together on the same show card and were treated as a single group of problems for the purposes of asking the follow-up questions about actions undertaken and reasons for doing nothing. For this reason they are discussed together here.

A relatively small proportion of the sample had experienced any problems of these sorts. Two per cent of the sample as a whole had suffered some form of medical negligence during the survey reference period. One per cent or fewer respondents had any experience of discrimination, unfair treatment by the police or of immigration or nationality issues.

There was a relatively low level of action taken to resolve this group of problems. Respondents said that they had taken some action to resolve the problem in about two thirds (65%) of cases. The most common action taken was talking or writing to the other side (42% of problems), or seeking advice (27%) (Figure 2.20).

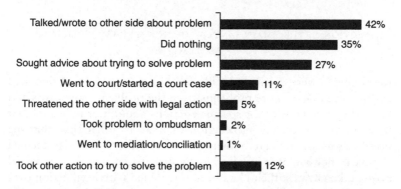

Figure 2.20. Actions taken about discrimination, unfair treatment by the police, immigration/nationality or medical negligence. (Weighted base = 131)

Respondents did nothing about one third of the problems in this category, which is a very high proportion. The chief reasons given for failure to take action were that it was believed that nothing could be done about the problem or because the problem was not considered to be important (Figure 2.21).

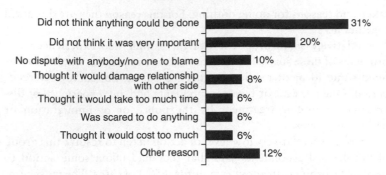

Figure 2.21. Reasons for taking no action to resolve disputes about discrimination, unfair treatment by the police, immigration/nationality or medical negligence. (Unweighted base = 49)

SECTION 2. THE "MAIN SAMPLE" OF NON-TRIVIAL JUSTICIABLE
PROBLEMS

Respondents were deemed eligible for a main interview if they had experienced one or more problems from the problem show cards and had either taken one of the specified actions about it or indicated that they had not taken any such action for reasons other than that the problem was too trivial to bother with. Respondents were also deemed eligible if they had been involved in divorce proceedings, had had legal action taken against them, had been threatened with legal action over a disagreement about something, or had started or considered starting court proceedings. Overall 1,419 of the 4,125 individuals screened (34%) were eligible for the main survey. A breakdown of the main survey respondents according to the type of non-trivial problem for which they were selected is presented in Table 2.6. The comparison shows that the pattern of problem types about which respondents were successfully interviewed in the main survey reflects almost exactly the pattern reported in the screening survey.

REDEFINING PROBLEM TYPES

The analysis of data obtained during the screening survey has been presented in a way that is consistent with the structure of the screening

Table 2.6. Breakdown of main survey sample by problem type

Problem category reported in screening questionnaire	% of problems reported in screening survey	% of problems in main survey	Unweighted number of cases in main survey
Employment	7	9	107
Owning residential property	12	11	128
Renting out property	2	2	18
Living in rented accommodation	12	11	121
Faulty goods and services	15	17	197
Money	13	15	168
Divorce proceedings	4	4	49
Family matters	8	5	62
Children under 18	4	3	36
Accidental injury/ work-related ill health	9	11	121
Discrimination/police ill treatment/immigration/ clinical negligence	4	3	40
Subject to legal action	5	3	39
Threatened with legal action	2	2	18
Started or considered legal proceedings	3	3	30
Unweighted base	4125	1134	1134

questionnaire. However, as will be evident, many of the problems experienced by respondents that were collected together under broad categories of problem type in the screening questionnaire do not logically fit well together for analytical purposes. In order to reveal differences in approach and outcome for respondents experiencing different types of justiciable problem, the subcategories of problems were regrouped into nine categories that were more meaningful and which would offer sufficient cases in each subgroup for comparisons to be undertaken.

These nine problem types are as follows:

Problems with neighbours [including those owning and those renting property].

Divorce and separation [including divorce proceedings, problems with ex-partners, problems about residence and contact, problems about payment of maintenance, violent or abusive relationships with a partner, or ex-partner].

Employment problems

Consumer problems [including goods and services]

Accidental injury and [excluding medical negligence]
work-related ill health

Problems over money [including money owed, insurance companies rejecting claims, incorrect bills, unfair tax demands, incorrect advice about insurance, pensions, etc., mismanagement of pension fund, unfair refusal of credit, harassment from creditors].

Freehold problems [alterations to property, planning permission, buying or selling property, communal repairs or maintenance, repossession of the home, squatters].

Problems with landlords [poor/unsafe living conditions, getting deposit back, getting landlord to do repairs, agreeing terms of lease, harassment by landlord, eviction or threats of eviction].

Tribunal matters [DSS benefits and education problems].

Since the number of cases reported in the screening survey relating to renting out property, the police, immigration, discrimination and medical negligence was very small, these cases have tended to be excluded from full analyses which specifically compare problem types.

COMPARISON OF MAIN SURVEY SAMPLE WITH GENERAL POPULATION

Aside from age and gender differences in the reporting of justiciable problems discussed earlier, it was not possible to collect comprehensive demographic data about respondents at the screening stage. This information was collected, however, for all respondents selected for the main survey and it is therefore possible to make some broad comparisons between the characteristics of the sample of respondents reporting non-trivial justiciable problems during the previous five years with the characteristics of the general population. This information is presented as a rough guide to the ways in which the sample is similar to, and differs from, the population at large.

Table 2.7 suggests that the sample of respondents reporting justiciable disputes and interviewed in the main survey was slightly younger than the general population and that women were slightly over-represented by comparison with the general population. As far as economic activity is concerned the sample of respondents experiencing justiciable disputes was more likely to be economically inactive than the general population. Although the proportion of respondents who were unemployed was similar to that in the general population, the main survey sample had a relatively high proportion of people who were long-term sick or disabled (6%) or looking after the home (14%).

The social class and educational profile of the main survey sample was compared with external sources such as the Census of the population in 1991, and recent major government surveys such as the General Household Survey (GHS) and the Health Survey for England (HSE). Overall, the social class profile of the main sample seems to be very

Table 2.7. Comparison of characteristics of main survey sample of respondents experiencing justiciable disputes with general population

	% Main survey sample	% General Population 1997
Age		
18–24	11	11
25–34	29	16
35–44	26	14
45–54	16	13
55–64	7	10
65 or older	8	15
Sex		
Male	44	49
Female	56	51
Economic Activity		
In employment	61	73
Unemployed	4	5
Economically inactive	34	22

similar to the general population when compared with these sources. There are, however, some differences in the educational qualification profile of the main sample, although definitions may not be directly comparable across sources. It seems that the main sample of respondents experiencing justiciable problems has a higher proportion of respondents with a university degree than the other sources have found. The results are summarised in Table 2.8 below.

Table 2.8. Comparison between main sample profile and the general population

	Main Sample	Census 1991[17]	GHS[18]	HSE[19]
Social class[20]	%	%	%	%
I (Professional)	5	5	4	4
II (Intermediate)	30	27	27	26
III (Skilled Non-Manual)	25	24	26	25
III (Skilled Manual)	18	21	19	20
IV (Semi-skilled)	15	17	18	18
V (Unskilled)	7	7	6	7
Educational qualifications[21]				
No qualifications	20	N/A	31	37
Degree etc. *(Degree/Higher degree (or degree level qualification) Teach)*	29	11[22]	11[23]	11[24]
A levels etc. *"A" levels/ "AS" levels/SCE Higher ONC/OND BEC/ TEC/BT*	20	N/A	23[25]	24[26]
Other *(O-levels/GCSEs/ungraded/ other)*	32	N/A	35	28

[17] Based on the 1% household Sample of Anonymised Records (SAR).
[18] Social class estimates are for England only, while educational qualifications are for Great Britain.
[19] England only.
[20] Social class is based on respondent's own job (or last job if not in employment). Excluding those in the Armed Forces and any that have never worked.
[21] This definition applies to the main survey sample only.
[22] Defined as: "higher degree, degree, diploma, etc".

The broad similarity of the main survey sample of respondents who experienced justiciable problems with the general population indicates the extent to which problems of this nature are experienced across all social, educational and demographic boundaries.

CHARACTERISTICS OF RESPONDENTS EXPERIENCING PROBLEMS OF DIFFERENT TYPES[27]

Consumer problems

Those respondents reporting consumer problems who were interviewed in the main survey were predominantly in the 25 to 54 age groups with a roughly even gender split. Most were in full or part time work (62%) although there were substantial minorities who were retired (16%) or looking after the home (14%). Virtually none of those interviewed about consumer problems was unemployed (1%) (although about 3% of the sample as a whole were unemployed). The income distribution of those complaining of consumer problems was rather different from the sample as a whole. Whereas about one third of the sample as a whole had incomes of below £10,000, fewer than one in five of those reporting consumer problems had incomes of that level (18%). At the other end of the spectrum, about 30% of those reporting consumer problems had incomes in excess of £32,000 as compared with about 21% in the sample as a whole.

Those reporting consumer problems were more likely than the sample as a whole to have obtained higher educational qualifications and somewhat less likely to have no qualifications, although one in five of those reporting consumer problems had no qualifications. Respondents with consumer problems were also more likely than the

---

23 Defined as: "Degree or equivalent".

24 Defined as: "degree/degree level qualification (including higher degree)".

25 Defined as: "higher education below degree level", "GCE A-level or equivalent".

26 Defined as: "teaching qualification", "nursing qualifications SRN, SCM, SEN, RGN, RM, RHV, midwife", "HNC/HND, BEC/TEC Higher, BTEC Higher/SCOTECH Higher", "ONC/OND/BEC/TEC/BTEC not higher", "City and Guilds Full Technological Certificate", "City and Guilds Advanced/Final Level", "City and Guilds Craft/Ordinary Level", "A-levels/Higher School Certificate".

27 This analysis has been carried out for those categories of problems for which the largest number of unweighted cases was available in the main sample. Those categories not included were disputes over freehold property, disputes concerning benefits, education, unfair treatment by the police, immigration, and medical negligence.

sample as a whole to be owner occupiers (80% as compared with 63% in the sample as a whole).

Over half of the complaints were against shops, mail order companies, travel agents and holiday companies (58%); about one in five complaints were against tradesmen such as plumbers and electricians (22%); and a small minority were complaints about professional services (5%). The remainder was spread across a wide range of persons and organisations.

Employment Problems

The age distribution of respondents interviewed about employment problems in the main survey was, unsurprisingly, slightly younger than that in the sample as a whole. Rather more men than women were interviewed about employment problems although in the sample as a whole there were more women than men. Again, unsurprisingly, among those reporting employment problems a higher proportion were in full or part-time work than in the sample as a whole, but the proportion who were unemployed at the time of the interview was the same as in the sample as a whole (3%). A much lower proportion of those with employment problems had retired or were looking after the home at the time of the interview than in the sample as a whole.

The income distribution of those complaining of employment problems was somewhat different from the sample as a whole. Although about half had incomes of below £20,000, which is similar to the whole sample, far fewer had incomes of below £10,000 than in the sample as a whole (17% as compared with 31%).

The educational profile of those interviewed about employment problems, as might be expected, showed somewhat higher levels of education than in the whole sample. There were also higher levels of home ownership and much lower levels of renting among those reporting employment problems.

The overwhelming majority of employment problems were with the respondent's employer although around one in ten cases concerned a work colleague.

Divorce proceedings and separation problems

This category includes cases relating to divorce proceedings and also other problems in relationships between partners, for example spousal violence and disputes over contact with children. Among those included in this category some 42% were included because they had been involved in divorce proceedings during the previous five years; 40% had reported a dispute with their ex-partner in relation to family matters such as child maintenance, division of property or violence; and 16% were in dispute with their ex-partner in relation to children under the age of 18. Some two percent were in dispute with the Child Support Agency.

Those respondents reporting divorce and separation problems who were interviewed in the main survey were predominantly in the 25 to 54 age-range. More women than men in the sample had reported a divorce and separation problem (57% of those reporting these problems were women and 43% were men). Over half of those interviewed about divorce and separation problems were in full-time work (56%) and another 10% were in part-time work. About 17% were looking after the home and or family, which is only a little higher than the average for the sample as a whole (14%). A small proportion of those interviewed about divorce or separation were unemployed (6%), but this figure is slightly higher than the figure for the sample as a whole.

The household income distribution of respondents interviewed about divorce and separation problems was somewhat different from that of the sample as a whole, having a higher proportion of respondents on *low* incomes. About 41% of those interviewed about divorce and separation problems had household incomes of less than £10,000 as compared with 33% in the sample as a whole.

As far as education is concerned, respondents interviewed about divorce and separation problems were slightly less likely than the sample as a whole to have a degree level qualification, but more likely to have A levels or equivalent. The proportion with no qualifications was the same as for the whole sample.

Respondents experiencing divorce or separation were slightly more likely than the sample as a whole to be living in rented accommodation (41% as compared with 34% in the sample as a whole); and more likely to be renting from the council (60% of those in rented accommodation renting from the Council as compared with 46% of the whole sample renting from the Council).

Problems with neighbours

Neighbour disputes represented the most common problem experienced by those reporting problems to do with owning property and was also the second most common problem experienced by those reporting problems relating to living in rented accommodation (second only to the difficulty of getting landlords to carry out repairs to the premises). In the main survey about three-quarters (74%) of those interviewed about problems with neighbours were living in property that they owned and the other quarter were living in rented accommodation.

The age distribution of those experiencing problems with neighbours was rather different from the sample as a whole, with a significantly higher proportion of those with neighbour problems being in the 65+ age bracket (17% of those with neighbour problems were in this age group as compared with only seven percent of the sample as a whole). There were also fewer respondents in the 25–44 age bracket complaining of neighbour problems as compared with the sample as a whole. Connected with the age distribution is the fact that women were over-represented among those complaining of neighbour problems (72% of those with neighbour problems compared with 55% in the sample as a whole). A difficulty with neighbours is clearly something that disproportionately afflicts older women.

Respondents experiencing neighbour problems were less likely than the sample as a whole to be economically active, with some 18% retired from work as compared with 9% of the sample as a whole. However, over half of those interviewed about neighbour problems were in full or part time employment.

Those experiencing problems with neighbours were also more likely to have lower household incomes than the sample as a whole, although the pattern is not entirely consistent. The proportion with household incomes of less than £10,000 is little different from the sample average, although those with neighbour problems were more likely to have incomes of between £10,000 and £20,000 than the sample as a whole (42% as compared with 29%) and correspondingly less likely to have incomes in the £20,000 to £40,000 bracket (17% compared with 27% in the sample as a whole).

The educational profile of those interviewed about neighbour problems is similar to that of the sample as a whole, with about a third of respondents having degree level qualifications or higher. There was, however, a slightly higher proportion with no qualifications (32% compared with 22% in the sample), which is again probably related to the relatively high number of older women reporting neighbour problems.

Those complaining of problems with neighbours were much more likely than the sample as a whole to own the property in which they lived and less likely to be renting their home.

Money problems

Among those interviewed in the main survey about money problems excluding disputes relating to DSS benefits, the most common problems related to a dispute with a bank, building society or mortgage company (23%), a utility (22%), some other company (16%), an insurance company (14%), or the local authority (9%).

The age distribution of respondents interviewed about money problems reflected closely the age distribution of the sample as a whole and there were equal proportions of men and women reporting such problems. The economic activity of those reporting money problems was also not significantly different from the sample as a whole, with about two-thirds of those with money problems in work.

The income distribution of those complaining of problems to do with money did differ somewhat from that of the sample as a whole. All brackets were roughly similar except that there were fewer with incomes in excess of £32,000 (5% as compared with 12% in the sample as a whole).

As far as education was concerned, those reporting problems to do with money were slightly less likely than the sample as a whole to have degree level qualifications and more likely to have qualifications no higher than O levels.

Although over half of those reporting money problems owned their home or were buying it with a mortgage, a higher proportion of this group than the sample as a whole were living in rented accommodation, although more likely than the sample average to be renting it privately (52% as compared with 36% in the sample).

Accidental injury and work-related ill health

Those respondents interviewed about injury and work-related ill health requiring medical treatment had most often suffered an accident or illness at work (35%) or a road accident (33%). About five percent had suffered accidents in a shop, about three percent in a restaurant or café, and about nine percent were in dispute with the council as a result of falls in the street or other public places.

Among those interviewed about accidents and ill-health there was a slightly higher proportion of respondents over 65 than in the sample as a whole (14% as compared with 7% in the sample), but there were equal proportions of men and women.

The income distribution of those interviewed about accidents was the same as for the sample as a whole, as was the educational profile of those suffering accidental injury (although there were slightly more with no qualifications).

A higher proportion of those interviewed about injury and ill-health were in full time employment and fewer in part-time employment than in the sample as a whole. Unsurprisingly a relatively high proportion were long-term sick or disabled (12% as compared with 6% in the sample), or retired (16% as compared with 9%) and fewer were looking after the home (5% as compared with 14% in the sample as a whole).

Problems with landlords

Difficulties with landlords was the most common type of justiciable problem reported by respondents to the screening survey who said that they had experienced a problem relating to living in rented accommodation. Given that only about one-third (32%) of households in England and Wales occupy rented accommodation (according to the General Household Survey for 1995), the proportion of the screening sample reporting such problems is notable.

Those reporting problems with landlords were more likely to be in the age range 25–34 than the sample as a whole (38% as compared with 29% in the sample as a whole), and were more likely to be looking after the home and family (30% of those with landlord problems as compared with 14% of the sample as a whole). Those who had experienced landlord problems were more likely than the sample as a whole to have low incomes (58% on incomes of less than £10,000 as compared with 37% of the sample as a whole) and less likely to have any higher educational qualifications (15% as compared with 30% of the sample as a whole), although the proportion with O or A level qualifications was similar to that of the sample as a whole.

In the sample as a whole about one-third of respondents were living in rented accommodation, with about two in five (43%) renting from the local authority and just over one in three (37%) renting from a private landlord. Among those reporting having experienced problems with landlords over half (58%) were renting from the local authority and one third (32%) were renting from a private landlord.

SUMMARY AND CONCLUSION

The screening survey has revealed a relatively high incidence of justiciable problems within the general population. Over a five year period about 40% of the general population experienced one or more problems or events for which a legal remedy is available. For most problem types, the mean number of problems experienced by respondents during the five year reference period was between 1.2 and 1.5, although certain types of problems seem to occur with considerable frequency, such as problems to do with living in rented accommodation. The problems that have the highest rate of occurrence in the population are those relating to faulty goods and services (about 153 problems per 1,000 adults over a five year period), money problems (about 138 problems per 1,000 adults over a five year period), problems with rented accommodation (about 124 problems per 1,000 adults over a five year period) and problems to do with home ownership (about 119 problems per 1,000 adults over a five year period).

Overall it was estimated that about 41,496,000 problems were experienced by 15,785,800 adults in England and Wales during the five year period covered by the survey. Applying a triviality criterion to reported justiciable problems produced few changes in the incidence of problems in the population, suggesting that respondents had either forgotten or chosen not to report most incidents that they regarded as trivial. The exception was accidental injury and work-related ill health in which a relatively high proportion of respondents said that no one was to blame for their injury.

Respondents who reported having experienced a justiciable problem in the previous five years often experienced a problem more than once *and* more than one type of problem. While 20% of the population reported having experienced only one non-trivial justiciable problem during the previous five years, a further 14% reported having experienced two or more problems during the five year period. Pairs of problems that commonly tend to cluster together are divorce and family matters; divorce and children; employment and money problems; problems with rented accommodation and money problems; employment problems and problems concerning ownership of property.

For most problem types respondents reported that they had taken some action to try and resolve the reported problem, most commonly talking or writing to the other side and seeking advice. When action had not been taken this was most often because of a belief that nothing could be done about the problem or because the problem was regarded as unimportant. This behaviour varied by problem type and is explored in detail in Chapters 3 and 4.

The findings of the screening survey demonstrate that the general public experiences a high volume of events for which the legal system could be mobilised. The workload of the civil justice system is the result of the cumulative choices of members of the public about whether to resort to legal proceedings in order to resolve such justiciable problems. An analysis of the behaviour of respondents reporting justiciable problems in relation to these issues, the influences on their choices, and their motivations for taking action or failing to take action are explored in the remainder of this book.

3

Strategies for Resolving Justiciable Problems

This chapter describes the approaches taken by the public to the resolution of justiciable problems. The information was obtained during full interviews with respondents identified during the screening survey as having been involved in a non-trivial justiciable problem during the survey period. When respondents had reported experiencing more than one problem during the previous five years, they were asked during the main interview only about the second most recent problem.

The chapter deals with broad patterns of behaviour in the whole sample: whether respondents took any action to try and resolve their problem; whether they handled problems themselves; whether they obtained advice about how to resolve the problem and where they went to get that advice. Attention is paid to barriers and pathways to advice in order to gain a better understanding of the circumstances under which advice is sought. The chapter also provides information about what members of the public were looking for from advisers, what help they received and how useful that help was found to be. Since the approach taken to problem resolution varied substantially depending on the type of problem being faced, a more detailed discussion of advice-seeking in relation to particular types of problem is provided in the next chapter[1].

OVERVIEW

The first step in dealing with a justiciable problem for the overwhelming majority of members of the public interviewed in the main survey

[1] Where the size of the subgroup permits this type of analysis. For the purpose of this and later analyses, problems were re-classified into narrower more consistent groupings than the broad categories used in the screening questionnaire (see discussion at end of Chapter 2).

was to try to resolve the problem directly themselves by contacting the other party or organisation involved in the problem. About two out of every three people experiencing non-trivial justiciable problems had made some contact directly with the other side in order to try to resolve the problem, whether or not they went on to obtain advice. Only when direct action failed to produce a result did many people go on to obtain advice about resolving the problem. A few went directly to advisers without first making contact with the other party to try and resolve the problem, and a small minority did nothing at all[2].

Overall about five percent of respondents did nothing ("the lumpers"), about one-third (35%) tried to resolve the problem without help ("the self-helpers") and about 60% tried to resolve the problem with advice or help from an outside adviser ("the advised") (Figure 3.1).

Among all respondents interviewed about a recent justiciable problem, about nine out of ten (91%) had received advice in the past from a wide range of advice sources to help resolve other matters, and about two out of three (68%) respondents interviewed said that they had taken legal advice at least once some time in the past, regardless of how the problem about which they were being interviewed had been dealt with. This demonstrates relatively high levels of use of advice sources and of lawyers within the population of respondents experiencing non-trivial justiciable problems in the previous five years.

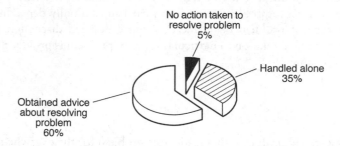

Figure 3.1. Broad strategy for dealing with justiciable problems. (Base = whole sample 1134 weighted)

---

[2] The full map of outcomes is presented at the beginning of Chapter 5.

"THE LUMPERS": NO ADVICE, NO CONTACT, NO ACTION

Among members of the public who had experienced non-trivial justiciable problems, only a very small proportion failed to take any kind of action to deal with their justiciable problems (one in twenty), despite the fact that the problems had been important enough to remember and to report during the screening survey.

Many people made efforts to deal with their problem by contacting the other side or by taking some other action, but eventually gave up without achieving any kind of resolution to the problem. These "self-helpers" have been distinguished from the few "lumpers" who did nothing at all about their problem.

This small group of "lumpers" is interesting and has some distinctive characteristics. First, those members of the public who took no action at all to try and resolve their problem were most likely to have experienced problems relating to money, accidental injury or work-related ill health, employment, clinical negligence, or unfair action by the police. They were significantly less likely to have obtained outside advice about any problem in the past than respondents who had taken some action to resolve their recent problem, with or without advice. Over half of those who failed to take action to resolve their problem had an annual income of less than £10,000 (52% compared with 35% of self-helpers and 31% of those taking action with advice), and were more likely to be living in rented accommodation than those who took action. Those who took no action were more likely to have no educational qualifications and much less likely to be educated to degree level than those who took action (14% of those taking no action had degree level qualifications as compared with about one third of those who took action). There were no significant differences, however, between those who took action to resolve their problem and those who took no action at all in relation to age or sex, although those who took no action were more likely to be looking after the home or family than those who took action. In fact over one in four (27%) of those who failed to take action to resolve their justiciable problem were looking after the home (as compared with 13% of those who took action).

The main reasons given by respondents for failing to take any action to resolve their problem were that the problem was over and done with (about one in four cases), or that there was nothing that could be done about the problem (about one in five cases). Those who said that there was nothing that could be done about the problem were, of course, making this judgement without the benefit of any advice.

Those who failed to take any action to resolve their problem generally adopted this strategy after weighing up the possibilities, rather than by default. There are, in fact, substantial similarities between this group and some of those who took relatively perfunctory steps to resolve their problem before abandoning the attempt without having achieved any kind of resolution to the problem. The reasons for failure to take action given by "lumpers" during the survey and in-depth qualitative interviews convey, on the whole, a rather negative and powerless quality. The problems dealt with during the survey had been defined by the respondents themselves as non-trivial and therefore something that they cared about. In this context the failure to take action was generally not "accidental", but the result of deliberate choice or a sense of helplessness. An example encapsulating many common concerns was provided by a couple struggling with the results of faulty building work:

> "We got a council grant to do work on the house, but the builders didn't do the work properly . . . But there was no question that we could take them to court because we didn't have the funds to do it. We had experience of trying to get legal aid before and it's such a long involved thing that we didn't bother . . . I thought "Can I really get anywhere with this?" So you kind of think "Well it's not really worth the trouble, I might as well just let it go" . . . If you can't afford to risk that money you've got to really be sure that you're going to win. And if you're not sure you're going to win then it's like a major gamble isn't it? And I think that's mainly why we didn't do it . . . An hour of a lawyer's time is expensive to get that advice. And the Citizens Advice Bureaux are usually very busy. It's very difficult to get any advice from there. . . . The reason I wanted to go through Citizens Advice Bureau was because maybe it would have a more formal approach from them rather than just from me. We were a bit intimidated by the builders. It was a gang of about six burly men and they weren't particularly friendly . . . They were quite difficult to deal with." (*No action taken about problem with building work*)

Other respondents who failed to take any action offered similar expressions of powerlessness, fear of becoming involved in acrimony, and concern about the cost of taking formal action. For example:

> "I didn't get advice because of having a baby really and anyway they will only tell me to take it up with the DSS anyway." (*No action taken about benefits problem*)

"Because of the helplessness of the ordinary citizens when they get entangled with problems. We would have to go to law to get justice and we cannot afford to do it." (*No action taken over dispute over incorrect bill*) "I haven't got enough power to make the local authority do what I want." (*No action taken following accident at work*) "I didn't want people phoning my landlord and I didn't want to take the risk of being asked to leave the flat." (*No action taken over problem with landlord*)

Some of the difficulties expressed by those who failed to take action to resolve their problem were very similar to explanations given by respondents who had tried to handle the problem themselves, but who would have liked advice and assistance in dealing with the problem.

There was also some evidence that negative experiences of the legal system or negative beliefs about legal processes gleaned from media stories contributed to decisions to take no steps to seek a remedy or resolution. This has a particularly marked effect in areas such as personal injury and medical negligence litigation where horror stories of long battles for compensation regularly make the newspapers. For example:

"I think I would have been just very obstructed. I think you'll get no help from the hospital. I just get the idea it's an uphill task. I suppose one can get very, very good barristers and whatever these days but it was something that I'd rather not be involved in. But I think from the point of view of having one bad year, a lot of bad feeling, a bit hurt and upset, then no, money would not have made a great deal of difference to that. **Where do you get your impressions about it being a long uphill struggle to pursue legal action?** Via the newspapers, journals. Well everyone hears of tales related to people who have tried it. I don't know anybody who has gone through legal action, but it's reading about deals in newspapers that you think it's taken years and years and years to actually come to any payout." (*Clinical negligence—no action taken*)

THE SELF-HELPERS: PROBLEMS HANDLED WITHOUT ANY ADVICE

Just over one-third of respondents (35%) experiencing a non-trivial justiciable problem tried to resolve their problem by handling the matter themselves, and without obtaining any advice. These self-helpers were most likely to have experienced a consumer problem, a problem to do with money or a problem with a landlord. Respondents were least likely to handle matters on their own when they were dealing with problems to do with divorce or separation. Although the majority of self-helpers had obtained advice in the past about some matter (81%), a higher proportion of self-helpers than those who obtained advice about their problem claimed *never* to have received outside advice in the past to deal with any matter (19% compared with one percent of the advised and 29% of "lumpers"). In disputes concerning a money remedy, a self-help strategy was much more likely to be adopted when the amount in dispute was less than £500 than when it was for a larger sum. In the small number of cases involving sums of more than £3,000 virtually no one chose to try and resolve the problem entirely without advice.

Self-helpers are to some extent distinct from those who took no action at all to resolve the problem, those who took some direct action to resolve the problem and then sought advice about how to continue, and also from those who went directly for advice without ever trying to resolve the problem directly themselves.

Within this group of self-helpers there were very different kinds of experiences. The most straightforward, and a typical sort of case, might involve a consumer problem where the individual took the matter up directly with the company concerned and obtained a satisfactory response without too much trouble. The following are two fairly representative examples:

"I bought an electronic organiser which went on the blink and they were actually very helpful. It involved sending it back—hence a long delay and a lot of inconvenience and each time it came back, on about three occasions, it still wasn't working properly because it was difficult to identify what had gone wrong and eventually I got fed up dealing with their services section and contacted their customer services who were actually very obliging and I just explained. And they just replaced the equipment, which is an example of a responsible company."

"[The car had been MOT'd] but driving it back it was making a noise. It was still driveable, but it felt dangerous. Basically it had been given back to me in an unsafe condition. . . . The biggest issue I had was getting [back to the garage] because it was a 45 minute journey, in an unsafe car . . . They actually took it back quickly, said 'Yeah, as soon as you can get it back to us we'll have a look at it.' What annoyed me was it had caused me expense and time delay because obviously it was a 60 mile round trip, in a dangerous car. My time was valuable when I was busy working."

There were also cases where a direct approach required rather more work and persistence in order to achieve the desired outcome. Some of these cases took quite a long time to resolve and the people involved had to show determination, confidence and sometimes rather creative strategies to achieve a satisfactory response. For example:

"I spoke to a sales assistant at first and then demanded to speak to her superior . . . I wrote letters to him and to the management centre. I spoke to them and wrote to them and they said there was really nothing they could do about it. They were not prepared to say why I had been refused credit. That annoyed me . . . By this stage I had been doing some research. I had phoned somebody in the DTI government department and they sent me a leaflet. I thought 'If it's the law then I must be given information—somebody must be able to tell me'. . . . The government leaflet was very helpful and they were very quick . . . The leaflet was very readable. There was no technical jargon, just facts. I don't think anybody would have problems with that. Having got the leaflet I then wrote to them again when I knew what I could be doing. I copied the document and highlighted all the bits that I thought were wrong and asked for them to be corrected. And about three months later—it took as long as that—they sent me a further copy showing me that they had marked my form to indicate that someone had been trying to impersonate me. It didn't mean I couldn't have credit, but that extra checks should be done . . . Had I been somebody who might have needed credit for various things, I think I would have been quite worried . . . I never considered seeking legal advice . . . It may sound a bit conceited but I think the information I got in the documents I got from the credit agency and the DTI were adequate. They gave me the guidance that I needed." [*GP wrongly refused credit*]

"It was the ventilator in the bathroom. First of all I phoned up [the Council]. A few weeks went by and nothing happened. So I put my shoes on and went down the office. They had the cheek to say to me that there's a three-month waiting list for repairs. I said, 'What in a bathroom where there's no windows and no ventilation? I think that's disgusting'. Well then she got on the phone to someone and said there's no other form of ventilation. And then I saw one of the estate officers, walking along, and I bet he wished he hadn't bashed into me! Because I told him exactly what I thought. And then soon after two chaps knocked on the door and they said, 'Oh Mr So and So asked us to call'. And with that it was done . . . I was annoyed that it wasn't working and no one would come to fix it. I own the flat and I pay a yearly rate for certain repairs, there's a lot of things that I have to do myself . . . I try to work things out myself, then if it doesn't work then I would take it further . . . There are some things that you have to go to lawyers for, such as the will and the buying of this place because they are things that you can't do yourself. . . . You have to know the ins and outs of it don't you? When my husband died I went to see the lawyer about the will."

These successful self-helpers were, however, in the minority. As will be discussed in the Chapter 5, fewer than half of those who tried to resolve their problem by handling the matter entirely alone succeeded in achieving a resolution by agreement. Whether or not a self-help strategy will be successful depends on the nature of the problem, the confidence, competence, and persistence of the complainant and the intransigence of the other party involved in the problem. The following extract from a respondent who suffered hearing problems after years working on a noisy machine provides an example of how self-help strategies can fail:

"I went to my boss and said 'Look this machine's really noisy'. And he laughed it off . . . That went on for ages. I did see someone else in the office, who was higher than him. She told me to go to Boots and buy earplugs, which I did, but I didn't think that was the right answer—just go out and buy a pair of disposable earplugs. They're uncomfortable and if someone was to pop in the room or the phone was to ring you couldn't hear it 'cause you had earplugs in your earholes. So in the end I just left it. They got rid of the machine last week. I had been working with that machine for about six years . . . **Did you think about approaching anyone outside of your organisation?** I didn't . . . I didn't know who to contact. There was another woman who was affected and we talked about it and I think we were just worried because there was a good atmosphere in the office with my bosses. We got on pretty well in the office and we didn't want to rock the boat, so we just put up with it. **Who do you think you would have gone to?** I suppose the only thing that sprung to mind was health and safety. But then we wouldn't know who to contact and then we thought if someone comes in off the street from health and safety and all of a sudden starts asking questions then it will probably look bad on us . . . I think perhaps because they didn't take us seriously we should have pushed the point that bit further. We were gutless really. We didn't do anything at all about it. Just in case it caused bad feeling between us and the boss. **What do you think the health and safety people might have done for you?** I don't know. You see there's nothing to look at like a guide. We haven't got no guides or nothing so you don't know . . . Perhaps in retrospect again we could have phoned up and enquired to find out, but we didn't know. We didn't have a clue basically. I felt that I'd done my bit. I'd said something. I should have pushed it further, but I thought 'Oh well I've tried to get something done', so I just let it die a death in the end." (*Young man with damaged hearing*)

The experiences recounted by respondents in dealing with their justiciable problems, suggest, therefore, that although it is possible to distinguish between those who take no action to try and resolve their problem and those who take some action but fail, the differences at the margin are fairly minor. Self-helpers cover a broad spectrum, ranging from those who make perhaps one rather ineffectual attempt to achieve a resolution and then give up, to those who take positive and sustained action only to be thwarted in the end, to those who take a relatively simple step and are rewarded with a remedy, and finally to those who battle on until they achieve a satisfactory outcome.

Although the "lumpers" are an interesting atypical group, in seeking to understand how the public responds to justiciable problems and why they respond in the way they do, an important question is less why a small minority of people do not even try to resolve the problem, but why the numerically much larger group of defeated self-helpers fails to obtain advice or assistance in trying to achieve a satisfactory resolution of the problem. Information shedding light on this question was obtained from survey responses and from qualitative interviews with self-helpers

BARRIERS TO ADVICE

In answers to the main survey questionnaire, only a small minority of respondents reported that they had actually attempted but failed to make contact with a chosen adviser. About five percent of all those interviewed said that they had unsuccessfully tried to contact one of the advice organisations—the most common being the CAB (31%), a trade union (15%), MP or local councillor (6%), welfare rights officer (4%) professional body (4%) or court staff (4%).

However, there was also evidence that a substantial minority of respondents (about one in five) experiencing justiciable problems had considered seeking advice, but in the event failed to take any steps to do so. The most common sources of advice *considered* but not contacted by respondents were solicitors (mentioned by about six percent of the sample as a whole) and CABx (mentioned by about 5% of the sample as a whole). The most common reasons for not making contact, even though consideration had been given to the possibility, was a belief that nothing could be done about the problem (21% of cases). Other common reasons for not trying to make contact with an advice source were that it would involve too much trouble, or that it would be too expensive. In some cases advisers were not contacted because the other side responded to demands before contact was made.

Accounts of behaviour given during qualitative interviews provided vivid insights into some of the anticipated and real barriers to advice-seeking among those who considered trying to get help with their problem, but in the end failed to do so. Factors that emerged from interviews as being important influences on decisions about what action to take were: inaccessibility of good quality advice about legal rights; fear of legal costs; previous negative experiences of legal advisers or legal processes; a sense of powerlessness about certain types of problem; and in some cases a sense of alienation from the legal system.

As far as obtaining advice was concerned, interviews suggest that while some people were unsure about where to go for advice, most respondents were aware of the existence of the Citizens Advice Bureaux. Indeed, just over half of all respondents to the main survey (57%) said that they had actually obtained advice from a CAB at some time in the past. The proportion was a little lower among self-helpers (50%) and somewhat higher among those who received advice for their second most recent problem (60%). Among those who had taken *no action* to deal with the problem about which they were being interviewed, just over half had obtained advice in the past from a CAB (56%).

Despite this general knowledge about the existence of CABx and other local advice centres, if they existed, it was also clear that the public often experienced problems in finding out about opening times, managing to get through on the telephone, and being forced to take time off work in order to visit a CAB because they were only open during working hours. All of these matters created barriers to advice-seeking, even among those who were relatively knowledgeable about sources of advice and might have used advisers in the past. There was also some evidence of a lack of confidence in the quality of advice provided by CABx.

Accessibility of Advice Agencies

Practical problems in obtaining advice from CABx and other advice agencies provided a regular explanation for the failure to obtain advice when self-help strategies had failed to achieve a resolution to the problem. Although there were some concerns about the quality of advice offered at CABx, rather more common complaints related to the limited opening hours of CABx, waiting times for an appointment, difficulty in making telephone contact to arrange an appointment and, occasionally the scruffiness of the physical surroundings of CABx. Some of those who had been quite determined about trying to resolve their problem were, in the end, defeated by lack of availability of free or low cost advice.

"I took the name of his solicitor and I thought I would do something about it, but actually in the end I didn't. I think because partly it would have involved taking time off work to go to the Citizens' Advice Bureau or somewhere to get advice to see what I could do and those agencies weren't open at times that I was free, in the evenings, not the ones that were local to me anyway, or at weekends. I didn't really feel I could justify taking time off work for that. One of my friends actually recommended the CAB, and I passed the Citizens' Advice on the way to work every morning anyway. So I think I did check out the times that they were open. I think I was a bit fed up then at that point because of the opening times of CABx and other legal centres . . . This Citizens' Advice Bureau, I think the opening hours were 11.00 'til 1.00, and then there was a closure, and then I think it was 2 'til 4, or 2 'til 3, not Monday to Friday, and definitely not the weekends and there wasn't any evening opening." (*Woman attacked by a dog*)

"Whenever I've been to the CAB they haven't really been able to advise me— just tell me places to go . . . It just seemed to be that everywhere I went people said 'No. You're not talking to the right person. Go to this person. No no we're not the right people, go to this person.' So I didn't actually seem to ever talk to anybody who actually knew what they were talking about. I think it would have been helpful if I could have just gone somewhere and sat down and they could have explained to me. Once I realised the legal situation it did help, but it took a long time to get that information and over the phone is not the best way. If I could have spoken to someone free of charge and they could have explained my legal situation and all the options and written things down and said 'Try this address' it would have helped". (*Tenant threatened with eviction*)

"I mean they kept relying on this Children's Act of 1989[sic], well I never saw a copy of that so I don't know what that's about, you know. **Should you have had access to that?** Yeah, to understand more. 'Cause I wanted to go to a library and look around and find out what rights he did have and I couldn't do that until I went to a solicitor. Or I wanted to go to the Citizens Advice but you'd have ring them up and it was always engaged, you just couldn't get through to a Citizens Advice Bureau. **You tried them?** Yeah, yeah. Especially when I was getting all the threatening letters about people wanting money and that, you know I really did need help. It was only when I got a solicitor that I went through everything, 'cause really she was just dealing with the children but she'd go back to different colleagues in her office and find out for me. So she was helpful." (*Contact problems and debt problems*)

"You've got to be prepared to go down there and queue up and not give in. You've got to get past that lady on the door at the CAB. And you've got to know the reason why you want to get past the lady on the door, so you've got to ask her a question which she can't possible answer! But people give up too easily I think, I find. You go down to the Citizens Advice Bureau and the lady says, 'No you can't see a solicitor'. So you come away and say 'They wouldn't let me, there's nobody I could see'. But I mean if you ask them a question which they can't possibly answer then they let you through the door!" (*Benefits dispute for husband who is blind*)

The common experience and expectation that obtaining free advice from a CAB is extremely difficult presents a policy challenge to the architects of the Community Legal Service. Knowledge of the existence of CABx is widespread, as is a general belief that useful guidance and assistance might be obtained from CABx. However, the evidence of the survey indicates a substantial unmet need for such advice and assistance. Prospective clients are discouraged as a result of limited opening times, unanswered telephones, full offices, and queues. These findings are consistent with previous studies. For example, an analysis of reasons for lack of representation at tribunals conducted ten years ago produced identical evidence about the problems of congestion in CABx[3].

Quality of advice

Although not an overwhelming concern, there were some respondents who were mistrustful of the sort of advice that might be offered by a CAB and some whose experience led them to feel that CABx could not provide good quality advice.

"I have once been to the CAB. I didn't find them over helpful really. Perhaps it wasn't a situation where they could have helped a great deal. They just gave me some addresses and that was it. I went to one of these Law Centres once. They were very helpful. But again you have got to be careful because if you are a house owner they don't particularly want to know you. They are only going to help people that are at the lowest low. I suppose they think if you've got a house you are not too poor. They are very good. They are qualified solicitors. They weren't out for the money. You didn't have to think to yourself 'God this is costing me an awful lot of money to sit here and talk to them.' It's important for anybody not to have to worry about that. You can

³ H Genn and Y Genn, *The Effectiveness of Representation at Tribunals*, Lord Chancellor's Department, 1989, pp. 223–224.

get a half hour free time if they practice under the legal aid, but other than that you have got to find the means." (*Pensioner involved in consumer problem*)

"I think if the CAB was spruced up and more people knew about exactly what they did do, I think they're sort of sitting in the bottom of the alleyway aren't they? They're down the end of the corridor, this little dark and dingy corridor and nobody really knows anything about them and you think what's the point of phoning them? They're not up to date I don't think. They need to be there, you know sort of trendy logo et cetera, and more spruced up and let people know what they're for and what they can do for you. I mean it's a free service isn't it?" (*Consumer dispute*)

There were, however, respondents whose experience of the CAB was good. They did not seem to complain of particular difficulty in obtaining advice and found the advice received, and sometimes a referral, helpful. For example:

"I think it was when I got the letter saying, 'You've got to pay or we'll take you to court' that I went to Citizens Advice Bureau and then got the recommendation of going to a free solicitor for a consultation with them. **Why did you decide to go to a Citizens Advice Bureau when you did?** Because I felt that I had a case to answer and therefore I could go to court. Well I just thought, it's independent and it's free and you can just go along there and sort of cry on their shoulder and they could say to you 'You've got no case or be off'." (*Defendant being pursued for money owed*)

"I went to the Citizens Advice Bureau 'cause I thought I needed to know how I stood about it and whether they could actually make me sell the house. **Why did you go to them first of all?** Probably 'cause I'd used them on odd occasions before where I wasn't sure how I stood, like after my divorce and different debts and things like that. **And had you found them helpful in the past?** Yeah, yeah. They had been quite helpful, they'd helped me out with a couple of things . . . They said that they couldn't make me sell the property. I think I just needed someone to sort of like say, 'Yes you're all right. You're within your rights to hang out.' I think sometimes you just need to feel someone backs you up a bit don't you? The main advice was that you needed to keep the building society informed. If you had got problems paying one month you should advise them and then really once they've accepted it they can't then turn round and say, 'Well you're not keeping to agreements' . . ." (*Householder threatened with possession proceedings*)

"Well last time I went [to the CAB] I went with my younger son 'cause he got carried away with his credit cards, like a lot of young people and was getting himself into financial difficulty so I yanked him into the CAB. I said 'Come along let's get this sorted out', and they were very good."

Cost of obtaining legal advice

There was a widespread feeling among many respondents that obtaining legal advice was simply not an option because of the cost. Most of those respondents to the survey who said that they had considered consulting a solicitor, but in the end had not done so, gave concern about cost as the reason for not making contact. Examples of the way in which these feelings were expressed in survey interviews were as follows:

> "Could not afford to do so. I thought I might get too involved in expensive discussions."
> "Once you start getting into that sort of area it costs. Better to just go for the best we could get."
> "Because I thought it would be expensive and litigious, and I ought to be able to solve my own problems. I didn't want the expense. I thought the process wouldn't achieve anything—it would add to the problem."
> "I was quoted between £50 and £200 for a consultation with a solicitor and considering that I was on the dole it was more than my weekly amount of money."

Respondents telling their stories during in-depth interviews often took the opportunity to explain in detail how legal advice seemed to be beyond their means and to express fear of the cost of becoming involved in legal proceedings. Those who had received legal advice in the past, as well as those who had not, expressed such fears. Fear of costs derives from assumptions about the absolute level of costs that might be incurred and the chances of obtaining a successful resolution of the problem, weighed against the seriousness of the threat or problem facing the individual. These considerations were neatly summed up by one respondent who had been troubled by neighbour noise for some time, had sought help from various sources, but would not consider becoming involved in legal proceedings because of fear of the likely cost, even though the respondent's son was a solicitor:

> "No if I was fighting something that I felt I really was going to be successful at, the expense wouldn't enter into it, I would go ahead and do it . . . In the case of the neighbour you'd be entering into an awful lot of expense an awful lot of heartache knowing at the end of the day that it was just going to carry on and continue. I think you have to look at it very, very carefully before you actually proceed to law. I think you have to be very convinced that you've got a water tight case."

Another respondent in financial difficulties was being threatened with repossession of his home. He suffered depression as a result, which affected his performance at work. During a relatively long period when he was struggling with these difficulties he felt unable to obtain legal advice from a solicitor because of fear of costs, and unable to get help from a CAB because of the practical obstacles:

"We sold our house and moved back to London. Then we bought another place, so all the money went. We had a large overdraft, which we had to pay back. We were getting letters and they were very unpleasant. After a while we suddenly got a summons against us. This all went on for about a year . . . I was getting very depressed and very anxious, more worried about my family than anything else, and it was showing in my work, affecting my job, so that's when they said go and see the counsellor. **In the period of 12 months when you were receiving letters and feeling quite stressed about it, did you think about turning to any advisors or organisations that offer help?** We didn't really know what to do. We'd never been in a situation where we couldn't repay a loan . . . where we were receiving threatening letters all the time and it was very unpleasant, demanding this and demanding that and threatening us. As far as advisors, we didn't really know what to do. **Did you think about going to a lawyer?** We couldn't afford to go to a lawyer. We thought about a solicitor, but to see a solicitor you have to have money. We'd seen a solicitor after buying the house and selling it, and it was very expensive. **Did you consider any other organisations?** I think the Citizens' Advice Bureau could help, but it's so hard to get to see the Citizens' Advice Bureau, because there aren't that many. I think the Citizens' Advice Bureau should be branched out so there is more. The population is so huge now, it's getting bigger and bigger each day. So to see a Citizens' Advice Bureau you need weeks and weeks to make an appointment . . . They are not open for long hours either, it's only a few hours each day . . . We tried and you phone them and keep phoning and there's never anyone there, so I think in the end we just gave up . . . They are open one or two days a week. I think if the Citizens' Advice Bureau were more available to the public on a working week and a working hour basis, like if they had a full time office with qualified counsellors, I don't think there would be half the problems. If you had somewhere you can go, just like a job centre, if you had somewhere you can go to just talk to, without waiting three weeks. Because most interviews would be over in ten minutes, all they would say is, 'They can't do this, this is what you need to do, don't worry'. That's all we wanted somebody to tell us, don't worry, you'll be OK."

In addition to concern about the cost of legal advice, there was also evidence that some respondents, lacking experience of obtaining legal advice felt unsure about how to go about finding a solicitor and were apprehensive about dealing with solicitors, although this situation was relatively rare:

"I haven't a clue about solicitors. If I walked in I would probably be quite frightened and not know. **Have you ever had any dealings with a solicitor at all in your lifetime?** Not once. **So why do you feel nervous of them?** For that reason. **Because they are unfamiliar?** Unfamiliar, I don't want to sound stupid. **Do you know how they operate?** Haven't a clue, no. I don't know anything about solicitors. I don't even know if I've met one . . . I always find solicitors shops and offices look like estate agents. It's a field where if you don't know it, I'm scared to walk in an estate agents, all the boards up, I don't know what all the abbreviations mean, it's a whole institution isn't it, estate agents, solicitors." (*Woman with employment problem—no advice obtained*)

Despite the concerns expressed about the cost of legal advice by those who *did not* go to a solicitor to seek assistance in resolving their problem, anxiety about cost clearly did not afflict everyone. As will be seen below, many respondents went directly to solicitors for legal advice about their problem, either because the matter was so serious that they were prepared to risk the cost, or because they knew, or were told by friends and relatives that they would be entitled to receive legal aid or a "fixed fee" interview with a solicitor. These experiences are discussed in the next section.

THE ADVISED: OBTAINING ADVICE ABOUT RESOLVING PROBLEMS

About six out of every ten people who had experienced a non-trivial justiciable problem obtained some kind of outside advice about how to resolve their problem. Although most people sought advice only after having tried first to resolve the problem by direct contact with the other side, a minority obtained advice directly and without any prior contact with their opponent. This kind of situation occurred typically in cases of violence against a spouse, other family matters, accidental injury and work-related ill health. It also occurred occasionally in relation to neighbour disputes.

Those experiencing justiciable problems used an extremely wide range of advice sources for their first port of call (Figure 3.2). The single most common first point of contact was a solicitor, with about one-quarter of those obtaining advice going first to solicitors (24%, representing 14% of all those experiencing a non-trivial justiciable

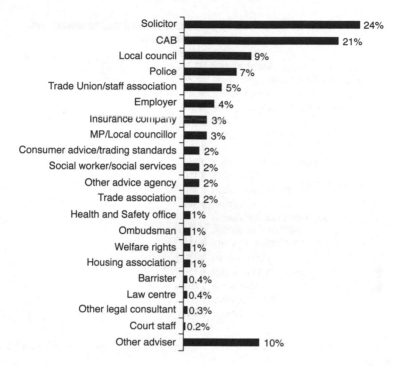

Figure 3.2. First source of advice. (Base = all those obtaining advice 682 weighted)

problem). The next most common first point of contact was a Citizens Advice Bureau with about one in five (21%) of those obtaining advice going first to the CAB (13% of all those with a non-trivial justiciable problem). Apart from these two major advice sources, the most common places to which respondents turned for advice were the local council (9% of advice seekers), the police (7% of advice seekers), trade unions or staff associations (5% of advice-seekers).

About half of all those respondents who obtained advice went to only one advice source (49%), but a similar proportion (42%) took advice from two or three sources. Only a tiny proportion of people went to more than three different advisers (9%).

The list of second advisers is almost as varied as the first, and again the most common second adviser was a solicitor in private practice (Figure 3.3).

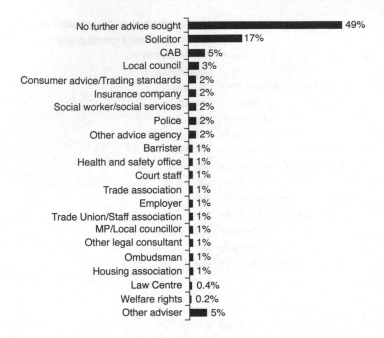

Figure 3.3. Second source of advice. (Base = all those obtaining advice 682 weighted)

In cases when more than one adviser was contacted, the most common, but by no means the only pattern, was for people to go first to a CAB and then to contact a solicitor for further advice. Of those respondents whose first contact was with a CAB about one in three took no further advice (35%) while another third (31%) took advice from a solicitor. About eight percent of those who went first to the CAB went on to take advice from a consumer advice centre, six percent went to the local council for further advice, four percent went to another advice agency, and four percent went on to a legal consultant of some kind for assistance.

Among those whose first source of advice was a solicitor, about two thirds (67%) took no further advice from any other source. About eight percent went on to take advice from a CAB, four percent went to another advice agency, four percent received subsequent advice from an insurance company, and the remaining handful took advice from such sources as trades unions, barristers, court staff, ombudsmen, MPs or local councillors and other legal consultants.

Taking into account *all* of the sources of advice contacted by the respondents while trying to resolve their justiciable problem, it appears that a little over one-quarter (27%) of members of the public who experienced a non-trivial justiciable problem obtained advice from a solicitor *at some point* about trying to resolve their problem (representing almost one-half of all those who obtained any advice). About 17% of members of the public *at some point* contacted a CAB about trying to resolve the problem, representing a little over one in four of all those who sought advice (29%) about their problem. However, as will be seen in the following sections, the choice of both first and subsequent advisers differed significantly depending upon the nature of the problem being faced and the extent to which respondents were able to call on friends and relatives who could offer professional advice.

Using friends and relatives with professional skills

About one in ten of all those who obtained advice turned first to a friend or relative who was also a professional adviser and this tendency varied considerably by type of professional advice skill. So, for example, among those who said that their first source of advice was a solicitor, over *one-fifth* (21%) said that the solicitor from whom they obtained initial advice was a friend or relative. About 14% percent of those who went first to the police and about 7% of those who went first to the local council said that the person they contacted was a friend or relative. On the other hand, people were less likely to turn initially to a friend who was a CAB adviser. In only two percent of cases when the CAB was the first source of advice did respondents report that the initial CAB contact was a friend or relative.

Choice of adviser: People type and problem type

An analysis of choice of adviser in relation to demographic characteristics shows some interesting patterns in relation to respondents' income, education, and age, although the patterns do not entirely conform to traditional assumptions about advice seeking. Pattern of advice-seeking in relation to income shows that in the choice of first adviser, respondents on incomes of under £10,000 were as likely to go directly to a solicitor as those on the highest incomes and in fact there was little difference between income bands in their choice of first adviser (Figure 3.4). This pattern holds true in relation to all advice obtained about trying to resolve the problem and not just in relation to first advisers. In analysing all sources of advice obtained to try and resolve the problem, Figure 3.5 suggests that there was *no* significant difference in the extent to which different income groups made use of solicitors as opposed to other advisers. Those on the lowest incomes who obtained any advice about resolving their problem were as likely to obtain advice from a solicitor at some point as those on higher incomes. This fact is important in that it suggests that the effect of existing legal aid provision is to make it possible for individuals on the lowest incomes to have access to legal advice with at least the same frequency as those on higher incomes (see discussion of results of multivariate analysis in Chapter 4 for further discussion).

Another interesting feature of the analysis of advice-seeking in relation to income is that, with the exception of those on the highest incomes, between one-fifth and one-quarter of all other income brackets used the CAB as their *initial* source of advice. Among those with

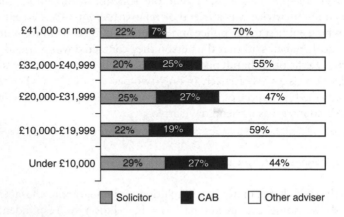

Figure 3.4. First adviser in relation to respondents' income. (Base = all who obtained advice 682 weighted)

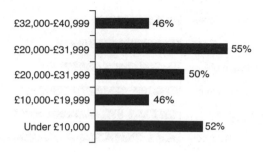

Figure 3.5. Advice obtained from a solicitor at any point while resolving problem in relation to respondents' income. (Base = all those who obtained advice 682 weighted)

incomes under £10,000 about one in three of those obtaining advice used the CAB at some point for advice about their problem. Among those with incomes of between £10,000–£19,999 about one in four of those obtaining advice used the CAB (28%); among those with incomes of between £20,000–£31,999 about one in three of those obtaining advice used the CAB at some point about the problem and the proportion is similar for those on incomes of between £32,000–£40,999. However, among respondents with incomes of £41,000 or more, only seven percent of those obtaining advice went to the CAB. These figures indicate the fact that there is a demand for free advice about justiciable matters among most income groups and that such advice is currently being made available and being used across a wide income spectrum.

Education did not appear to be significantly associated with either choice of first adviser or whether advice was obtained from a solicitor at any point about the problem, although as discussed above and in the next chapter, education was related to whether or not advice would be obtained *at all* about the problem.

The propensity to obtain advice from a solicitor or other adviser, however, did vary substantially between different problem types as is illustrated in Figure 3.6. As well as variation between problem types in the propensity to obtain advice at all, there were also immediately evident differences in the *type* of advisers to whom people turned when faced with certain problems. For example, solicitors and other legal

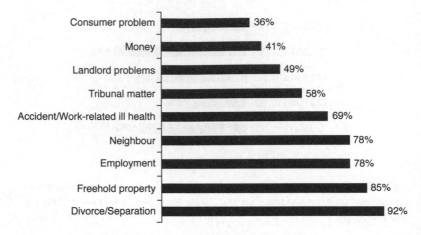

Figure 3.6. Percentage obtaining advice by problem type. (Base = All respondents 1134 weighted)

advisers were the most frequent first contact point for those with problems relating to divorce and other family matters, underlining the perceived importance of these problems to those who experience them and the current significance of legal advice in seeking to resolve such matters. Solicitors were also the most frequent first point of contact for respondents who suffered accidental injury or work-related health problems, again indicating the extent to which legal advice is important in seeking a remedy for these misfortunes.

The CAB was much more likely to be the first port of call for those with consumer problems, money problems, employment problems, or landlord and tenant problems. Some of this variation is displayed in Figures 3.7 and 3.8, and the approaches characteristic of different problem types is explored in detail later in the next chapter.

Delay before obtaining advice

All respondents were asked about how long after the problem started they contacted their first adviser. This had to be slightly modified for some problem types, such as divorce. There was quite a lot of variation in the length of time taken by respondents to obtain advice after the problem started or after they realised that there was a problem that

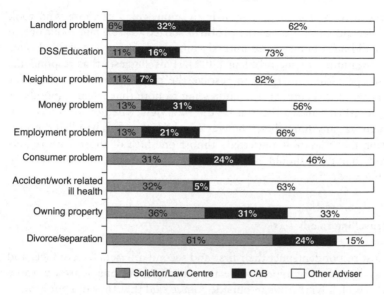

Figure 3.7. First adviser by problem type. (Base = all who obtained advice 682 weighted)

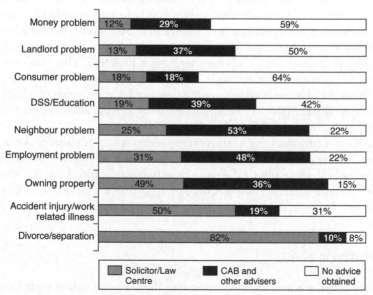

Figure 3.8. Advice from solicitors and other advisers at any time to resolve problem by type of problem. (Base = All respondents 1134 weighted)

needed to be sorted out. A little over one-third of those who took advice did so as soon as the problem started (39%), but about one in five did not obtain advice until six months or more had elapsed since the beginning of the problem (20%). This suggests that respondents had spent time in trying to resolve the problem before looking for advice. In this context it is interesting to note that when respondents were asked toward the end of the interview whether, on reflection, there was anything about the way in which they had handled the situation that they now regretted, almost one-fifth of those with regrets said that they should have taken action sooner (see discussion in Chapter 6).

Travelling to advisers

Most respondents met their first and second advisers face to face, and travelling did not appear to be a problem. About one quarter of those who took advice from an outside source said that they did not have to travel any distance to see their first adviser. Among those who did have to travel, most had a journey of *less* than five miles, although a small minority travelled considerable distances (about two percent of those who obtained advice had to travel more than 50 miles). This suggests that for most respondents using advisers at the time of the survey, geographical accessibility of advisers was not a problem. This was confirmed in qualitative interviews in which complaints about accessibility of free legal advice related to opening times and waiting times of advice agencies, and complaints about inaccessibility of legal advice related to cost, not to the availability of outlets.

All but a tiny minority of those respondents using advisers spoke to their adviser either in person or on the telephone. About half of those who spoke to their adviser did so once or twice only and about ten percent of those receiving advice spoke more than ten times to their first adviser. The pattern was very similar for second advisers.

Pathways to advice

When asked what made the respondent think of contacting their first adviser, the most frequent answers were that it was the respondent's own idea, or that it seemed obvious (41%); that it had been suggested by a friend/relative/work colleague (21%); or because the respondent had had experience of a similar situation (11%). Respondents' accounts of how they found their adviser varied depending on who the adviser was. Where CABx were concerned, respondents mostly seemed to know where they were located, although there was difficulty in establishing opening times and getting appointments. In the case of solicitors, respondents asked among friends and work colleagues, walked into the nearest office to where they lived or worked, or used the Yellow Pages. The following are typical examples of the path to advice:

Employment problem
"How did you decide what to do about the problem? Basically I just had to make up my own mind. But by talking to enough people, getting ideas, getting information from newspapers, radio, television, you do make up your own mind about things. Because I always find I need as much background information as possible on all subjects . . . Because you can never tell when you might need information. But also I think with the courses I've been on, you know a little bit about law as well, so you should never be afraid of using the law . . . My background's engineering and so at university I did just a general legal course to go with patent law, engineering law and so on. Then two or three years ago I did some course on accountancy and one of the module courses there was to do with law again . . . **How did you find a solicitor?** All I did I just went through the Yellow Pages and looked for one which gave a free interview initially." (*Employment problem*)

Contact and residence problem
"How did you decide what to do about the problem? I spoke to my family about it and they suggested a solicitor, so I went to see a solicitor. I discussed it with my family and I rung up that day but I had to wait a couple of weeks to get an appointment . . . I knew he had parental rights but in the situation . . . I was concerned about the children . . . I wanted it done properly. Visiting where and when, what times, how frequent and this, that and the other. **So, did you already have a solicitor?** No. No. **How did you set about finding one?** I looked in the Yellow Pages. My sister in law suggested I went to one that was to do with children, there's a special solicitor that deals specially with children, you know the situations with children, contact and that. **And did you find one of those?** Yeah, Yellow Pages. It also did legal aid as well, so I needed those two. **Did you know much about the legal system?** No, definitely not. No, No. **Had you ever had to use a solicitor before?** No. **Or go to law for anything?** No, never. **So you didn't have previous experience to call upon?** No. No. Not at all. **Apart from your family, did you turn to anybody else for advice at that stage?** No. **So you found a solicitor from . . .** Yeah . . . from the Yellow Pages." (*Family problem*)

Divorce Problem
"[Local authority officer. Husband had committed adultery for second time]. As soon as I picked myself up, a couple of days later, my mate said 'Jane, you've got to seek legal advice, you've got to. You've got your own property.' I thought it was sound advice. So I went to a solicitor near work. They did a fixed fee. I asked around at work where the nearest one was and they said 'There's one just up the High Street'. You could see them from the office window. But it's something I've never looked for before. Only for house purchase. I'd never used them in any other sense. So I rang them up and asked them did they do the fixed fee interview scheme and basically you get half an hour of a solicitor's time for a set fee. You can ask them anything you want . . . I didn't go back to them. I did ring the legal aid service for the run of the mill things e.g. where would I go to obtain a divorce. I understand I can do it for myself. So they advised me on those sort of things. I wasn't entitled to money [from legal aid] so I went down to the county court on the suggestion of my boss. They were very good. I asked them for the forms, which they gave me with explanatory notices. I got my Decree Nisi through the post. The Decree Absolute comes later."

Benefits problem
"Other people were getting [the higher benefits band] and they'd got good vision. I know they couldn't see that well but they'd got good vision compared with my husband. They weren't getting the problems he was getting . . . We did need the money because I wasn't working . . . I don't know that if I'd been working whether we would have gone through with it. We'd have probably felt a bit too guilty to go through with it then . . . I think at the back of my mind I thought I would win . . . Because I think from past experience I knew that if you can write good letters to the right people and you dig your heels in enough. I sent for the forms. I filled them in. And they said 'No'. They said you could reapply, so we reapplied. And they said 'No'. And then they tell you you can go to tribunal if you still feel strongly. So we did. **Was anyone advising during this period?** Not till it meant going to the tribunal. Then we realised. They said you could have help on the form and we thought, yes you do need help then. We went to the welfare rights people. There's two people we could have gone to, we found out from other people where they'd been for help. There's a very good welfare rights person in [. . .] or Action for Blind People were also very good . . . So we went to the local person because she's a friend of mine so I did know her. And I knew that she'd won a lot of battles and things so we thought we would use her."
[*Claiming benefits for disability*]

Property damage following car accident
"[The solicitor] just basically advised me on how to go about getting proceedings moving and he said if there were problems over whose fault it was

then obviously it would have to go to court . . . I was paid, 8 to 12 weeks later. He just told me how to go about it basically. **Did he charge you every time you phoned him?** No, he didn't. I was able to get legal aid. I only saw him I think twice. The first time was a consultation and that was just an initial meeting just to find out what the case was about and that was only £50 legal aid, that first meeting. **What was the process like for getting legal aid? How easy was it?** Right you have to be unemployed, which I was, well I was a student and I still am. You have to bring proof of that with you and that's basically it. They will take down personal details, date of birth, address, national insurance number, details like that, and that's basically about it. It's quite simple."

Repossession problem
"At a stage when I knew I couldn't cope with the situation any longer . . . when I knew that I couldn't pay the mortgage and that I would lose the property, I wanted to see if there was anything I could do. I just went to a solicitor. **Was it one you knew anyway?** No. I'd never been to one before in my life. **So was this the first experience you had?** Yeah. **So how did you pick one?** I walked into Catford and found one. **Did you talk to friends or anyone about doing this?** No. I'm a very independent person.

Another useful pathway to advice was by using friends and relatives whose job was the provision of advice. As discussed earlier in the chapter, a substantial proportion of professional first advisers were actually friends or relatives of the respondent. Interviews illustrated how those experiencing a problem might call up a friend or relative who was a solicitor or other adviser and pick their brains about how to deal with the matter. In some cases this resulted in the friend actually taking some action, such as writing a letter on the respondent's behalf without charge, or taking on the case with an understanding that only a minimal charge might be made. In this way respondents with easy access to legal or other professional advisers gained an advantage in being able to press their claim with more confidence and with less financial risk than if they had sought legal advice in another way. This was particularly useful in the kinds of cases, such as those extracted below, in which direct attempts to obtain redress had proved fruitless. When the same claim was pressed by means of a solicitor with the background threat of legal proceedings, a satisfactory response was forthcoming from the offending party or organisation.

"We'd asked for compensation and she denied it. She just denied that anything was wrong. She said there was nothing wrong with the ovens. She said 'It's nothing to do with me it's down to the caterer.' . . . We spoke to our

friend who's a solicitor. And he said, 'Well look I can write a letter for you.' **Did you speak to him just as friend at that stage?** As a friend at first, and then he suggested writing, and of course being a friend I thought 'Well he's not going to start charging us £100 just for having a conversation.' I think had we not mentioned it to him we probably would have just taken it into our own hands and done it ourselves. I mean we had no idea at that stage what would develop and whether it was worth our while even doing anything. I think had we not known a solicitor I don't think we would have even gone as far as that. We would have tried our best and thought 'Well just give it up as a loss'. Because to go looking for a solicitor, you know, by the time we've paid all the costs and everything we wouldn't have had much back."
(*Dispute over rebate of hire charge on hall where cooker faulty*)

The following extract illustrates how a competent and determined person facing a relatively intransigent opponent can become frustrated at being unable to secure redress by direct efforts. It also shows how the intervention of a professional adviser can yield results because opponents may not respond unless faced with a credible threat of legal action. Finally, the quote neatly conveys the advantages attaching to a social or business network that includes professional or legal advisers.

"I thought 'I'll write to them'. I didn't expect to get something immediately, but I thought I might have got some favourable reply back from them. But no, nothing like that. The first reply wasn't too brilliant. I thought 'They're just brushing it off 'cause they'll wait for something more', so I thought 'Well I will write back again and I'll give them the facts'. And that's when they started being negative and I thought 'It's not good enough. I've got broken chairs, and I've two or three of them going wobbly on me, what am I going to do? I've got nothing to sit on'. I got crosser. I got really angry. 'You think I'm going to drop this then? You're wrong, I'm not going anywhere until I've got exactly what I want.' They did write back and say they will replace the chairs but we had to pay a percentage or something, which amounted to the fact that we would have to actually buy one chair and they would replace the rest. And I thought 'This is ridiculous, we've already paid our money for the chairs'. A solicitor we know came into our shop out of the blue and we told him all about out it and showed the letters we'd had. And he had a look at it and said, 'Oh give that to me I'll sort them out for you. As a favour.' And that's how it started. 'Cause he just came in . . . And he wrote to them. He did it as a favour and in the end they agreed they would supply us with six new chairs." (*Dispute over faulty furniture*).

What is wanted from advisers

What people were looking for from advisers, initially at least, was advice about how to solve their problem (more than two in three respondents (68%) obtaining advice mentioned this) and to a lesser extent, advice about their legal rights (47% of respondents obtaining advice saying that this was what they wanted). About one in three were looking for advice about dealing with court procedures (34%) and about one in five were looking for advice about their financial position (20%). A small minority were looking for someone who could represent them in a court or tribunal hearing (12%). This pattern was repeated for second advisers as well. It therefore seems that although solving the problem is a priority, in seeking advice many people are looking specifically for information about their legal rights. As the discussion in Chapter 4 demonstrates, the requirement for information of a specifically legal nature varied substantially between different problem categories.

Advice received

In three-quarters of cases where advice was obtained (75%), the first adviser thought that something could be done about the problem. However, the effect of being told by a first adviser that nothing could be done about the problem, unsurprisingly, had a substantial impact on subsequent behaviour. Of those who were told that nothing could be done about their problem, almost two-thirds did *not* obtain any further advice (see Figure 5.1 Chapter 5). Among the one-third who did go on to obtain further advice, the majority went to solicitors and the police.

First advisers gave advice about procedures, for example how to deal with summonses or court procedures (55%), about legal rights (38%), and about the financial position of the respondent (21%). In one-third of cases, however, first advisers did not offer advice about any of these matters.

The type of advice received from the most common first sources varied depending on who was providing the advice. So, for example, the most common advice given by the CAB was to contact the other side involved in the problem (40%), or to obtain help from another organisation (36%). In only a minority of cases did the CAB suggest threatening the other side with legal action or taking legal proceedings.

Advice to go to mediation or an ombudsman occurred very rarely (3% of those taking advice from the CAB in each case).

The police as first advisers most often told people to seek advice from elsewhere (47%), or to contact the other side involved in the problem (24%). However, in about a fifth of cases the police advised respondents to go to court (19% of cases where advice taken from police). The most common advice given by local councils was to contact the other side (55%) or to seek advice from elsewhere (28%). Unsurprisingly, the most common advice given by solicitors was to contact the other side (34%), to threaten the other side with legal proceedings (30%) or to go to court (20%). Solicitors recommended trying mediation in about 2% of cases.

The very low rate at which either CABx or solicitors advised clients to consider mediation or other alternatives to traditional methods of dispute resolution demonstrates the very slight impact that these processes have had on the thinking of advisers and, therefore, on the strategies adopted by the public for dealing with disputes.

Referrals

Those who sought advice first from a CAB were referred on to a variety of second advisers. In about half the cases where CABx made a referral this was to a solicitor (49%). In a little under one in five cases, referral by the CAB was to the local authority (17%) and in 10% of referrals respondents were advised by the CAB to contact a consumer advice centre. Legal advisers were less likely than CABx to refer clients on, but when they did this was most often to an advice agency.

First advisers other than the CAB or solicitors were also quite likely to refer respondents on to other organisations. Most commonly other advisers suggested contacting a solicitor (32%), the local council (10%), the police (6%), a social worker (5%), or an insurance company (5%). In a few cases other advisers also suggested contacting a trade union or staff association (5%) or another advice agency (5%).

Assistance

Those respondents who had contacted an adviser were asked what kind of assistance they had received. For example, whether the adviser had contacted the other side involved in the problem on the respondent's behalf, whether the adviser had negotiated with the other side on the respondent's behalf, whether the adviser had made contact or helped to make contact with another organisation, or whether the adviser had accompanied the respondent to any kind of court or tribunal proceeding. In almost half of the cases, first advisers gave no assistance of this kind. The most common type of assistance provided by first advisers was to contact the other side on the respondent's behalf (33% of cases), to negotiate on the respondents behalf (20% of cases), to contact another person or organisation who might be able to provide help (13% of cases) or to help the respondent make contact with another person or organisation (11%). In about five percent of cases the first adviser accompanied the respondent to a court or tribunal.

Comparing the type of help offered by solicitors, CABx and all other types of advisers, it appears that CABx were *less likely* than solicitors or all other advisers together to provide these kinds of direct assistance (61% of those going first to a CAB received no help of this kind compared with 47% of those going to other advisers and 32% of those going to legal advisers). Legal advisers were much more likely than other types of advisers to contact the other side involved in the problem or negotiate with the other side. They were also much more likely to accompany respondents to a court or tribunal. When CABx gave assistance of this kind it was most frequently to help the respondent make contact with another person or organisation that might be able to assist in resolving the problem. Non-CAB non-legal advisers were also more likely than CABx to make contact with the other side on the respondent's behalf (this occurred in 33% of cases), to negotiate with the other side (18%) or to contact another person or organisation on the respondent's behalf (14%).

These findings indicating the kind of help that is currently available to members of the public with justiciable problems from the advice sector and from private legal practice has a direct bearing on policy discussions concerning the future scope of the Community Legal Service. The significance of the nature of help on offer is discussed more fully in Chapter 5 when the outcome of attempts to resolve justiciable problems is analysed in relation to the resolution strategy adopted and the nature of advice and assistance received. As will be seen in Chapter 5, the result of multivariate analysis indicates that the type of assistance provided by advisers is significantly associated with the outcome of cases. Members of the public were found to be more likely to achieve a resolution of their case when they received advice from a solicitor or from a non-solicitor adviser who provided assistance such as negotiating with the other side, arranging court/tribunal proceedings, or representing at proceedings, as compared with respondents who received no advice, or who received advice from non-solicitor advisers who did not provide such active assistance.

Helpfulness of advisers

Levels of satisfaction with first advisers were very similar among those who used CABx, solicitors, and trades unions or staff associations. Among first advisers, the greatest satisfaction expressed was with advice from trades unions or staff associations, with 59% of respondents who used them saying that they had been very helpful. Of those who sought advice first from solicitors, some 56% said that they had found the advice very helpful. CABx were rated as very helpful by 53% of those who had obtained initial advice from there. Initial advisers who received rather lower ratings were the Council (37% saying very helpful), the police (37% saying very helpful) and insurance companies (33% saying very helpful).

When asked whether they would recommend first advisers to others in a similar situation, respondents were generally quite positive. There were however some differences depending on the type of adviser. Among those whose first adviser was a solicitor or other legal adviser only seven percent said that they would probably or definitely not recommend others to seek advice from that source. Among those whose first adviser was a CAB about 14% said that they would probably or definitely not recommend the CAB as a source of advice. The highest level of dissatisfaction was with other non-legal advisers, in relation to whom 22% of those using such advisers said that they would probably or definitely not recommend the source to others.

Among second advisers, insurance companies, solicitors, the CAB and the police had roughly similar approval ratings ranging from 53% saying insurance companies had been very helpful to 46% saying that the police had been very helpful. When the Council was the second adviser fewer than one-quarter (23%) of those obtaining such advice felt that the Council had been very helpful.

The degree of satisfaction with advisers expressed by respondents appears to increase with the level of help offered by the adviser. When advisers contacted the other side on the respondent's behalf, this was felt to be helpful or very helpful in 82% of cases. When advisers negotiated on the respondent's behalf 87% thought this was helpful or very helpful (most saying very helpful) and similar levels of satisfaction were expressed when advisers contacted another person or organisation on the respondent's behalf. When advisers helped respondents to contact another organisation by making an appointment or giving a list of people to approach some 93% of respondents found this to be helpful or very helpful (mostly very helpful).

Levels of satisfaction were lower when advisers simply suggested that respondents contact the other side to resolve the problem (80% finding this helpful or very helpful) or that they seek advice from elsewhere (75% finding this helpful or very helpful). These findings are fleshed out in the next section, which offers additional information obtained from qualitative interviews.

Expectations of advisers

Information gathered during in-depth interviews fills in some of the detail on expectations of advisers and also goes some way to explain why many of those who received advice nonetheless failed to achieve a resolution of their problem. Although about six in ten respondents sought and obtained advice from at least one source in order to try and resolve their problem, it is also clear that almost half of those who obtained advice (46%) nonetheless failed to achieve a satisfactory resolution of their problem.

Obtaining advice does not in itself ensure any kind of success in dispute resolution either through legal or other procedures. A complicated mix of factors influences the outcome of different kinds of problems and disputes and this is explored in Chapter 5. However, depth interviews with respondents raised issues about the mismatch between public need for advice and assistance and what was sometimes on offer, in particular the perceived inadequacy of mere "advice". Several respondents explained the futility of being told to write letters or make telephone calls when they felt that they lacked the necessary confidence, vocabulary, and basic knowledge about rights and remedies. What people need when they go for advice will depend on the type of problem that they are experiencing and, importantly, their own personal competencies (e.g. confidence, verbal skills, literacy) as well as their emotional state. Many respondents who were relatively educated and knowledgeable felt a need for information about how to enforce their rights—where to go, who to write to and what exactly their rights were in certain situations. For those respondents the provision of information met their perceived needs. For many others, however, the provision of information and guidance about how to take a problem forward did not meet perceived needs. What was wanted was someone to take over and deal with the problem—to make difficult phone calls or to write difficult letters. Moreover, some respondents were so emotionally drained by the worry about the problem that even if they would normally feel competent and confident, at that particular time and in those particular circumstances they were not able to manage dealing with the problem. They did not want to be *empowered*, they wanted to be saved. When respondents commonly talk about abandoning or giving up because of "the hassle" involved in trying to deal with a problem, this simple colloquialism actually obscures what is in many cases an important form of paralysis. For example:

"There's a legal advice Centre in a church down the road, but they are only open on Wednesday mornings, so I am going down there next Wednesday and say to them 'What do I do?' . . . The Church runs it. Church volunteers. They are very helpful, very. It's been there for years. You don't even know it's there actually. . . . There's just a little sign outside about legal advice. It's free. I only know about it because I've got a friend who's in the Samaritans and they are down there as well and she told me about it. When I was being evicted I went to the CAB. They weren't very good. I don't know if it was the particular woman—but she just said 'Well you do this, this, this and this, goodbye.' . . . The place we really got help from was the Church. They bent over backwards to help me. The CAB in the same situation said 'Go away and write a letter'. The Church people got on the telephone to them themselves. . . . I felt I was getting a personal approach. Somebody was actually willing to deal with the particular problem whereas with the CAB I felt like I was just another person with a problem." (*Threatened with eviction*)

"I phoned up, actually I phoned up a CAB or something like that and I got some wording from them. They weren't over helpful, they didn't want to do too much for you, at least I didn't think they did . . . It's almost as if you've got too many corners to go round to get where you want to go. It's too many obstacles in the way, the way they describe things. She said 'You must do this and you must do that'. I thought 'Well I can't do this and I can't do that' . . . This is where I need somebody else to step in before I can do something else. It was full of obstacles or it seemed that way anyway." (*Consumer problem*)

The striking messages that emerges from interviews with members of the public about the need for advice and active assistance in dealing with justiciable problems has important implications for the new Community Legal Service.

SUMMARY AND CONCLUSION

The evidence of the survey is that the overwhelming majority of members of public tried to resolve their problem directly by contacting the other side involved in the problem or dispute. Those who went on to obtain advice generally did so only after having tried a direct approach. A very small minority of "lumpers" took no action whatsoever to resolve their problem. This group of people was significantly less likely than those who took action ever to have obtained advice about a problem in the past. The group also disproportionately comprised people on low incomes, with little education, living in rented accommodation. Reasons for failure to take any action at all reflected a sense of powerlessness, fear of becoming involved in acrimony and concern about the cost of taking formal action.

About one in three respondents adopted a self-help strategy. Self-helpers who attempted to resolve their problem without taking outside advice were often required to show determination and creativity in order to secure a satisfactory resolution. Self-help strategies were more common for matters involving sums of money less than £500 and self-helpers were less likely than those who took advice to have a history of advice-seeking for problems in the past. Self-help strategies ranged from brief attempts to achieve a resolution to sustained campaigns. Many were defeated in their attempts and gave up without ever seeking any assistance in their efforts. The experiences of self-helpers provide a wealth of information about barriers to obtaining advice such as inaccessibility of good quality free advice about legal rights; fear of legal costs and some negative experiences or beliefs about legal advisers and the legal system. Practical problems in obtaining advice from CABx and other advice agencies provided a regular explanation for failure to obtain advice when self-help strategies had failed, as did fear of the cost of seeking legal advice from solicitors.

About six in ten respondents obtained advice about resolving their problem and the majority generally did so after having first tried to resolve the problem by themselves. A minority went directly to advisers, for example, in cases concerning spousal violence and other family matters, accidental injury and also occasionally about problems with neighbours. About half went to only one adviser and most of the remainder went to two or three advisers. A very wide range of advisers was used but by far the most common were solicitors in private practice and CABx. About a fifth of those who reported taking initial advice from a solicitor had used a friend or relative. Taking into account all of the sources of advice contacted by respondents to the survey, about one-quarter of the sample took advice from a solicitor at some point to try and resolve their problem and about one in six had some contact with a CAB.

The propensity to obtain advice and the choice of advisers varied significantly depending on the type of problem being faced. Issues relating to divorce and family matters, and accidental injury were most commonly taken directly to solicitors while the CAB was used more commonly as an initial advice source for consumer, money and employment problems. These differences are explored in more detail in the next Chapter.

Analysis of choice of adviser showed that respondents on the lowest incomes were as likely to obtain advice from a solicitor as those on the highest incomes. There was no significant difference in the extent to which different income groups made use of solicitors as opposed to other advisers. This suggests that existing legal aid provision makes it possible for individuals on the lowest incomes to have access to legal advice with at least the same frequency as those on higher incomes. Indeed a striking fact that emerges from the discussion of pathways to advice, and that is relevant to the proposed changes to the public funding of legal advice, is the apparent ease with which those entitled to legal aid can currently access the legal system in order to resolve their problems. It is likely that proposed changes to eligibility for funding from the Community Legal Service Fund will make such access less straightforward in the future.

The results also indicate a very widespread feeling of ignorance about legal rights that exists across most social groups. Different levels of competence will affect what can be done with information and advice, but the need for easily accessible free or low cost advice is profound. There is a demand for free advice among most income groups and such advice is currently being made available and being used across a wide income spectrum. This fact is also important for policy decisions about the shape and scope of the new Community Legal Service.

The current level of demand for free advice clearly appears to exceed the resources available. The graphic accounts of difficulties in accessing free advice from CABx contrasts sharply with the ease with which advice can be obtained from solicitors if members of the public can afford to pay for such advice and are willing to do so.

Respondents reported few difficulties in knowing where to find advisers or in travelling to meet them. Most said that they either did not have to travel at all or had a journey of less than five miles. This is relevant to concerns about the impact of changes to legal aid funding on the number of solicitors who will be available to provide advice under the Community Legal Service. If the number of solicitor outlets is substantially decreased as a result of contracting, this will inevitably affect the apparent ease with which solicitors can currently be located.

Finally, interviews with respondents revealed the mismatch between the public need for free advice and assistance and what was sometimes on offer, in particular the perceived inadequacy of information and advice when what was needed was more positive assistance. CABx were less likely than solicitors or all other advisers to provide direct assistance such as contacting the other side or negotiating on the respondents' behalf. They were also extremely unlikely to recommend threatening the other side with legal action or taking legal proceedings. Given the behaviour and intransigence of some opponents described by respondents in this chapter, it is unsurprising that by the time members of the public seek help they feel a need for active assistance and sometimes for credible threats to be made. These matters are again relevant to the provision of advice and assistance under the Community Legal Service and are developed further in Chapter 5, which explores the impact of advice on the outcome of justiciable problems.

4

The Response to Problems of Different Types

As the discussion in the last Chapter indicated, the approach taken to problem resolution varied substantially depending on the type of problem being faced by respondents. The first section of this Chapter therefore provides a more detailed account of how respondents dealt with non-trivial justiciable problems of different types[1]. The results of these analyses highlight the extent to which the *type* of problem experienced heavily influences public approaches to resolution. The chapter concludes with a discussion of the results of multivariate analysis, which identified factors significantly associated with the likelihood that advice will be obtained about a justiciable problem, and the characteristics of the groups who were most and least likely to obtain advice.

The problem types discussed in this chapter are:

- consumer problems
- divorce and separation problems
- neighbour problems
- employment problems
- money problems (excluding benefits)
- accidental injury or work related ill health.
- problems with landlords

The discussion is limited to these specific groups because the number of respondents in the other problem type subgroups is rather too small for reliable analysis of those groups individually. However, some brief information is given at the end of the first section of the chapter about the approach to resolution of problems relating to benefits, schooling, clinical negligence, and actions against the police where the numbers of respondents were too small to conduct full analyses. In relation to each

---

[1] For the purpose of this and later analyses problems were re-classified into narrower more consistent groupings than the broad categories used in the screening questionnaire (see discussion at end of Chapter 2).

problem type there is a brief discussion of respondents' propensity to obtain advice, the purpose of advice seeking, advice received, and satisfaction with advice.

CONSUMER PROBLEMS (FAULTY GOODS AND SERVICES)

Consumer Problems: The Lumpers (No advice and no contact)

A relatively small minority of members of the public who experienced a non-trivial consumer problem failed to make direct contact with the other side to try and resolve the problem and took no advice about resolving the problem (4%). This figure can be compared with 13% of those experiencing accidental injury and two percent of those with neighbour problems. Moreover, when interviewed, all of those reporting on consumer problems who had not taken any action about the problem at the time of the interview said that they would definitely (83%) or probably (17%) not take any action in the future. The reasons given for not intending to take further action were that the dispute was no longer seen as a problem or that it was over and done with (one in three); that the problem sorted itself out (17%); that the respondent was sick of the case and no longer wanted to try and deal with it (17%) or a feeling that there was nothing that could be done or no prospect of succeeding (17%).

Consumer problems: Self-helpers

Consumer problems were the most likely of all problem types to be handled directly by respondents without obtaining any outside advice. About six in ten of all those interviewed about consumer problems said that they had dealt with the problem themselves. This figure can be compared with 50% of those who experienced money problems, 15% of those with employment problems and seven percent of those who had experienced divorce or separation problems.

The most common strategy adopted for consumer problems by self-helpers was for the respondent to contact the other side to seek to resolve the problem directly (73%). A small minority (8%) said that they had threatened the other side with legal action and 12% took some other kind of action. As will be seen in the next chapter these self-help strategies had a relatively high rate of success when members of the public were dealing with consumer problems.

Consumer problems: Obtaining advice

A little over one in three (36%) of those with non-trivial problems relating to consumer goods or services obtained outside advice about solving the problem. This is was the *lowest* rate of advice-seeking of all problem types. For example, 78% of those with employment problems obtained advice about resolving their problem, 92% of those with divorce or separation problems obtained advice, 69% of those suffering an accidental injury or work-related illness obtained advice, and 78% of those experiencing problems with neighbours obtained advice about trying to resolve the problem.

Most of those with consumer problems who took advice went to one source only (60%), although about one in three consulted two or three outside sources. Only a tiny minority took advice from four or more sources (5%).

The first point of contact for consumer problems was most often a CAB (30%), although about one in five of those with consumer problems who sought advice went directly to a solicitor for legal advice (21%). The next most frequent sources of advice were consumer advice agencies or trading standards offices (14%), insurance companies (8%), and trade associations (6%). In this context it is interesting to note that members of the public experiencing consumer problems demonstrated the highest propensity of all problem types to choose a first adviser who was also a friend or relative (27% of first advisers were friends or relatives as compared with 11% of first advisers for divorce and separation, 4% for problems with landlords, 10% for accidental injury, and 14% for neighbour problems).

When more than one adviser was contacted, the most common pattern was for the person experiencing the problem to go first to a CAB and then to a consumer advice centre/trading standards office or a solicitor.

Of all those interviewed who had experienced a consumer problem, about 18% obtained legal advice at some point about the problem, about 12% contacted a CAB, about 11% received advice from a consumer advice centre or trading standards department, about 4% contacted a trade association and about 2% of the group as a whole contacted an ombudsman.

Although a large proportion of respondents said that the idea of making contact with their first source of advice was their own (42%), around one-quarter said that the suggestion had come from a friend or relative (24%) and almost one in ten said that they had done the same on a previous similar occasion (9%).

Among people with consumer problems who took advice about dealing with the problem, four out of five had already either been in contact with the other side or tried unsuccessfully to contact them before obtaining advice. It seems then that the overwhelming majority of people with consumer problems attempt to resolve the problem directly before obtaining advice about how to proceed and only seek advice once their own efforts to obtain redress have failed.

This was borne out in qualitative interviews during which respondents explained the steps taken to resolve disputes. A common strategy was writing letters, telephoning, and entering into discussions to try and reach a settlement. Advice-seeking for consumer problems at least therefore appears most often to follow unsuccessful attempts to achieve settlement, or following unsatisfactory offers of settlement from the other side. For example:

> "When we got back (from the holiday) the first thing my husband did was phone the London office to make sure a report had been filed . . . They asked what the problem was, he told them briefly and they said put it in writing, which we then did. So we catalogued everything literally . . . We then got a letter, a courteous letter back in which they said they understood our problems and we would get £20 refund. . . . So of course that wasn't acceptable. At that point my husband spoke to somebody at ABTA that he deals with and said, 'Is this acceptable?' And even ABTA said no. They said it was a courtesy reply and they offered £20 in the hope that you'll take it. And if you were an 18 year old perhaps you would have done." (*Spoiled holiday*)

Advice was generally obtained fairly soon after the problem started with over half of those obtaining advice doing so within one to two weeks of the start of the problem.

Consumer problems: Advice needs

What members of the public experiencing consumer problems were looking for from advisers, initially at least, was advice about how to solve the problem (almost three in four (73%) mentioned this) and to a lesser extent, advice about their legal rights (47% of respondents with consumer problems saying that this was what they wanted). About one quarter were looking specifically for advice about dealing with court procedures (27%). A small number of people wanted someone to represent them in a court or tribunal hearing (5%).

Consumer problems: Advice received

Most people obtaining advice about a consumer problem were told that something could be done about the problem (82%) and the most common advice given was to contact the other side to try and resolve the problem (57%) or to obtain help from another organisation (32%). Almost one in four were told to threaten the other side with legal action (23%) and a small minority was advised to begin court proceedings (6%). In a handful of instances people were advised to take their case to an ombudsman (4%) or to mediation or conciliation (2%). The low rate of advice to take cases to mediation or conciliation demonstrates the slight impact that these alternatives to traditional methods of dispute resolution are currently having on advisers' thinking.

Consumer problems: Satisfaction with advice

Members of the public experiencing consumer problems expressed a relatively high degree of satisfaction with the advice received from their first point of contact. A little over half thought the advice had been very helpful (54%), about one in three thought the advice was fairly helpful (32%). The remainder thought that the advice was not very helpful (4%) or not helpful at all (10%).

EMPLOYMENT PROBLEMS

Employment problems: The Lumpers (No advice and no contact)

About seven percent of respondents interviewed about work problems in the main survey said that they had made no attempt to resolve the problem directly with their employer and had obtained no advice about trying to resolve the problem. Moreover, almost all employees in this group made no attempt to contact the other side and had no intention of taking action in the future. Their reasons for not taking action were most frequently that they had now left their job, that taking action would not be worth the trouble, a belief that nothing could be done to resolve the problem, and concern that it would cost too much to take action against the employer. There can also be a reluctance to be seen to be causing trouble as illustrated in the following extract from a qualitative interview, which provides a clear example of the reasoning behind a failure to take action in relation to a problem at work:

"When the new managing director came in lots of things changed. One of the things that changed was the contracts in the store. You only worked three and a half days a week, but you'd work long hours, you would work all day for three and half days and then get the rest off. 37½ hours, but more concentrated. What we were finding was that we would be working from seven to seven in a day for three days, and half a day would be seven until two, adding up to 37½ and having the rest of the days off. Although it sounds great, you've got 3½ days off a week, you would be so tired from those kind of shifts that what's the point, you just sleep, you wouldn't get anything done or enjoy it. We were told it's going to happen whether you like it or not, but we want you to sign to say you're happy with it. So it started off as everyone at the bottom saying 'No we're not going to sign it' then one person said 'Oh I wouldn't mind 3½ days off a week, I'm going to sign'. So gradually everyone started signing and saying yes to it and it was just implemented and that was how it is. . . . I never went for advice from anyone. Once everyone started signing I felt pressured into following. And then I tried to look at the positive side, maybe it could be a good thing, but in my heart I knew I wasn't going to be happy working seven 'til seven every day. I came home and moaned to my husband of course about it. He thought it was outrageous. **Did he suggest that you do anything at all?** No. That was it. He didn't try and encourage me to do anything about it. We are quite similar creatures in that way, we just tend to go with the bureaucracy. We are a bit afraid to do anything about it, don't know what our rights are and afraid to challenge. Probably due to money. Thinking things like this would cost something for us and we don't want to take that risk. Well first of all creating waves at work, didn't want to start anything there, plus I could get sacked or I could lose friends, I could lose respect from my managers. I don't want to be a troublemaker. Being a troublemaker at work is a bad thing. They might find a loop hole and get rid of me or put me in another department. I would be worried about losing my job and what people think of me."

Employment problems: Self-Helpers

About 15% of respondents who had experienced problems to do with employment said that they had attempted to reach a resolution of the problem without obtaining any outside advice. This figure is quite low by comparison, for example, with those experiencing consumer disputes. Among these self-helpers most (84%) did nothing other than attempt to contact the other side. A small minority (3%) threatened the other side with legal action; and about six percent said that they simply left their job in order to avoid the problem.

Employment problems: Obtaining advice

Almost eight out of ten respondents with problems relating to employment obtained advice about solving the problem (78%). This figure is relatively high and can be compared with 36% for consumer problems, 41% for money problems, 69% for accidents and work-illness, 78% for neighbour problems, and 92% for divorce and separation problems.

About half (53%) took advice from only one outside source and a further 40% consulted two or three outside sources. Only a small minority took advice from four or more sources (7%).

The first point of contact for those with employment problems was most often a Trade Union or staff association (27%), and the second most common initial source of advice was a CAB (23%). Solicitors were the first source of advice in 16% of cases concerning employment problems. Employers were also used as an initial source of advice (13%). About four percent of those with employment problems went directly to a Law Centre, which is high in comparison with other problem types. This undoubtedly reflects the specialist expertise of Law Centres in employment tribunal work.

When more than one adviser was contacted, the most common pattern was for the second adviser to be a solicitor, CAB, or trade union/staff association.

In just over one in ten employment cases where advice was obtained this first professional or outside source of advice was also a friend or relative (11%). Although a large proportion of respondents said that the idea of making contact with their first adviser was their own (42%), around one-fifth said that the suggestion had come from a friend or relative (20%), and about 14% said that they had used the same source of advice on a previous similar occasion.

Looking at the sample of those experiencing employment problems as a whole and at all sources of advice, just under one in three of those experiencing employment problems obtained legal advice at some point about the problem (31%) mostly from solicitors, although a small proportion went to Law Centres or some other type of legal consultant. This can be compared with 82% of those in divorce and separation cases obtaining legal advice, 13% of those with landlord problems, 8% of those with money problems, 25% of those with neighbour problems, 54% of those suffering accidental injury, and 15% of those with consumer problems. Furthermore about one quarter of all those with an employment problem at some time or another contacted a CAB (23%).

About three in five of those obtaining advice about employment problems had already had some contact with the other side prior to obtaining advice. Among those who had not had contact with the other side before obtaining advice, the vast majority had *not* tried to make contact (83%). This is somewhat different from, say, consumer problems where it appears that advice was generally obtained after attempts had been made to settle the problem directly. In employment cases, it seems that in a relatively high proportion of cases no attempt at resolution had been made prior to obtaining advice about the problem, nor apparently had the other side sought to make contact in order to resolve the problem (only 3% of cases).

This is borne out by qualitative interviews during which respondents explained the steps taken to resolve disputes.

"I found I was doing more and more and more of the work, and in the end I swore at a female colleague, told her she was fucking lazy. But instead of having a go back at me she didn't, she went to management and took out a harassment thing out against me and I was suspended from duty . . . The first I knew of it was when I came back from a week's holiday and one of the senior managers came round and told me not to report back to my station, but to report to the senior office manager at [another station] on my first day back, at midday and take a union rep with me and that I was suspended from duty. I was told not to communicate with anybody, if I did communicate with anybody at work or come near the work it'd be bad for me. Then I had a letter saying would I go for an interview with another senior manager to put my side of the story. So I went with the union rep to see another senior manager, and then it came to they were going to have a big hearing. But it never did come to a big hearing. It was more or less dropped and I got told I mustn't swear. But it was very harrowing being off, not knowing if you had a job to go back to. I mean I'd been on the job 19 years, coming up for 20 years . . . I must say I had a really good union rep 'cause he pulled their case to pieces." (*Ambulance man*)

In most cases advice was obtained fairly rapidly after the problem started. Around 42% obtained advice as soon as the problem started and a further 11% obtained advice within one to two weeks. A handful of people, however, waited more than six months before obtaining advice to solve the problem (7%).

Employment problems: Advice needs

What people were looking for from advisers initially at least was advice about legal rights (56% mentioning) and how to solve the problem (62% mentioning). About one third mentioned that they wanted advice about court procedures (34%) and a substantial minority mentioned that they wanted someone to represent them at a court or tribunal hearing (18%). Most people obtaining advice about an employment problem were told that something could be done about the problem (69%), although this figure is lower than in other problem areas (for example children 92%, consumer problems 81%, and money 80%).

Employment problems: Satisfaction with advice

Respondents with employment problems expressed a very *low degree of satisfaction* with the advice received from their first point of contact. Almost half of respondents obtaining advice about employment problems thought that the advice received from their first adviser was either not very helpful (21%) or not at all helpful (27%). Only 28% found the advice very helpful which is the lowest proportion of all problem types.

DIVORCE AND SEPARATION PROBLEMS

This category includes both cases relating to divorce proceedings and also other problems in relationships between partners, for example disputes over the division of property and child maintenance, disputes over contact with children and spousal violence. Among those included in this category some 42% were included in the main survey because they had been involved in divorce proceedings during the previous five years; 40% reported a dispute with their ex-partner in relation to family matters such as child maintenance, division of property or violence; and 16% were in dispute with their ex-partner in relation to children under the age of 18. Some two percent were in dispute with the Child Support Agency.

Divorce and Separation: The Lumpers (No advice and no contact)

Among those experiencing divorce or separation problems there were virtually *no* respondents who failed to take action to try and resolve the problems (1%). These kinds of problems clearly involve issues either that cannot be ignored, or the relationship between the parties is such that at least some kind of attempt is made to deal with the problem between the parties, whether or not advice is eventually obtained.

Divorce and Separation: Self-Helpers

There was a similarly small proportion of respondents with divorce or separation problems who sought to deal with the problem without taking advice at some point. Only seven percent of all those with divorce and separation problems said that they dealt with the problem without advice and this is the lowest proportion of self-helpers of all problem types (for example 60% of those involved in consumer problems attempted to handle the problem without advice and 49% of those with money problems did so).

Most of this very small group of self-helpers, had some contact with their partner or ex-partner to seek to resolve the problem. When there was no contact in this group it was generally because there had been no attempt to contact the partner. The strategy adopted among self-helpers was generally simply to contact their partner or ex-partner directly to seek to resolve the dispute. About a fifth also threatened legal action.

Divorce and separation: Obtaining advice

About nine out of ten (92%) of those who had been divorced or who had problems to do with partners or ex-partners obtained advice about dealing with the matter. This is the highest rate of advice-seeking among all problem types and compares with 36% for consumer problems, 49% for landlord problems, 78% for employment problems, and 69% for accidental injury.

About half took advice from only one outside source (52%) although about two in five consulted two or three outside sources (40%). Some eight percent of those involved in divorce and separation problems took advice from four or more sources.

The pattern of advice-seeking among divorcees and those with relationship problems was rather different from other problem types. A much more limited range of advice sources was used and there was a much greater concentration on legal advice. The first point of contact was most often a solicitor, with over three in five respondents going *directly* to obtain legal advice from a solicitor (61%). The next most common first contact was with the CAB, the first destination for one in four of those with divorce and separation problems. The only other source of advice contacted by a substantial proportion of those with divorce or separation problems was the police, who were the first point of contact for six percent of those experiencing divorce or relationship problems.

Looking at all of those members of the public who experienced divorce and separation problems, just over eight out of ten obtained advice at some time from a solicitor in private practice (82%). Just over one quarter (27%) contacted a CAB at some time and almost one in ten (9%) were in contact with the police at some time in connection with the divorce or separation problem. This group had the highest rate of contact with legal advisers of all problem types and can be compared with 27% in employment cases, 13% in landlord problems, 8% for money problems, 25% in neighbour problems, 54% in accidental injury cases, and 15% for consumer problems. As will be seen in the next chapter, a relatively high proportion of advice from solicitors about divorce and separation problems was supported by Legal Aid.

Most of those obtaining advice about divorce and separation problems had contacted their partner to try and resolve the problem before obtaining advice (60%), leaving a substantial proportion (40%) who apparently had made *no attempt* to resolve the problem before turning to outside advisers. Among those who had not contacted their partner or ex-partner about the problem most had made no attempt at contact. Examples of this kind of situation were provided in qualitative interviews. For example:

> "He gave me a beating and I just left with my daughter. I actually went to the police station that night I left and obviously they couldn't do nothing for me at that particular time because it was the early hours of the morning. So I had to find a friend to go and stay with that night, but they sorted it out like a place for me the next day . . . into a woman's refuge and then got put into B and B's after that. There was quite a few moves. We moved quite a few times because my husband kept on finding out where we were staying and at the time he was out to hurt so we had to keep on moving. When I went to the refuge they were really helpful. It was the worker actually got in contact with a solicitor for me and the solicitor was just brilliant. I mean once I'd made that step to go I had all the help I needed. It's hard but we got there." (*Family problem involving violence*)

> "I personally knew what I wanted so I thought 'I'm not going to waste my time', and I went straight to a solicitor." (*Divorcee in dispute with ex-husband over property*)

Although about half of those obtaining advice about divorce and separation problems did so within one month of the problem emerging, the other half of these respondents often took quite a long time before obtaining advice. About one in four waited for more than six months before obtaining advice.

Divorce and separation: Advice wanted

In seeking initial advice there was a heavy emphasis on wanting advice about legal rights (66% said that they wanted this, among other things, from their first adviser). In addition to wanting advice about legal rights, respondents experiencing divorce and separation problems also wanted advice about procedures (43% mentioned this), advice about ways to solve the problem (44%) and advice about their financial position (43%). About 17% were looking specifically for someone to represent them in court proceedings. The high demand for advice about legal rights and procedures underlines the significance of legal advice in the resolution of matters concerning divorce and separation referred to in the previous chapter. In practise, the law and lawyers are apparently fundamental to the resolution of disputes surrounding the breakdown of relationships as illustrated by this respondent who went directly to a solicitor as soon as she decided that she wanted to divorce her husband:

"I went to a solicitor because I wanted a divorce. And that was final. This time, there was going to be no going back on it, that was it. I mean how else do you get divorced? Where else do I go if I want to get divorced? Is there anywhere else?" (*Female divorcee*)

It also appears that use of traditional court-based solutions to these problems and disputes is fundamental. The kind of advice sought by the public about problems relating to divorce and separation highlights the very low levels of interest in or use of mediation as an approach to resolution, which is discussed further below and in the next chapter.

The fact that such a high proportion of those involved in divorce and separation matters obtained legal advice is a reflection of the seriousness with which such matters are regarded by the parties involved, the current availability of public funding of legal advice for disputes relating to the breakdown of relationships and arrangements over children and property for those without the resources to pay for legal advice, and the willingness of others to bear the cost of obtaining legal advice.

Divorce and separation: Advice obtained

Most people obtaining advice about divorce and separation problems were told by their first adviser that something could be done about the problem (72%) although this figure is lower than in some other problem areas (for example 85% for accidental injury, 81% for consumer problems, and 80% for money problems). The most common course of action recommended by first advisers was to go to court (suggested by first advisers to 45% of those receiving advice) or to threaten the other side with legal action (suggested by first advisers to 38% of those receiving advice). In less than one case in ten (9%) did a first adviser suggest that the respondent go to mediation or conciliation to try and seek a resolution of their divorce or separation problem. This figure confirms the limited impact that mediation has had on the approach of advisers to dealing with the problems that flow from divorce and separation, and accounts for the tiny proportion of the public responding to the survey who had experimented with alternative dispute resolution processes in the field of family disputes (see Chapter 5).

Divorce and separation: Satisfaction with advice

The level of satisfaction expressed with first advisers among respondents experiencing divorce and separation problems was *relatively* high by comparison with other problem types. Over eight in ten of those obtaining advice (81%) found the advice very helpful (53%) or fairly helpful (28%). Since the overwhelming majority of advisers were solicitors in private practice it is not possible to make comparisons with levels of satisfaction with solicitors as compared with other advisers among those seeking to resolve divorce and separation problems.

PROBLEMS WITH NEIGHBOURS

This category includes both owners of freehold property and those living in rented accommodation who reported having experienced a non-trivial problem with a neighbour during the survey period. Neighbour disputes represented the most common problem experienced by those reporting problems to do with owning property. This is interesting since the traditional stereotype might be more likely to anticipate that neighbour problems generally afflict those living in rented accommodation. Neighbour problems were, in fact, the second most common problem experienced by those reporting problems relating to living in rented accommodation (second only to the difficulty of getting landlords to carry out repairs to the premises).

Neighbour problems: The Lumpers (No advice and no contact)

Only a handful of respondents experiencing neighbour problems (about one in 50) took no action at all to try and deal with the problem. This is one of the lowest rates of "lumping" of all problem types (second only to divorce and separation problems), indicating that members of the public are not prepared to endure these problems without at least taking some kind of action, despite the fact that in reality neighbour problems are among the most difficult to resolve (see Chapter 5). The main reason given by respondents for not doing anything about a problem with a neighbour, and for not being likely to do anything in the future, was the belief that there was nothing that could be done about the problem.

Neighbour problems: Self-Helpers

About one in five of those who experienced a problem with a neighbour tried to handle the problem without advice, and this is a relatively low figure by comparison with other problem types. It suggests that those who try a self help strategy and fail are highly likely to enlist help in seeking a resolution rather than simply abandoning the attempt, underlining the seriousness with which the public regard these problems and the impact that they have on daily life. Most of those who adopted this strategy tried to resolve the problem simply by contacting their neighbour directly (60%), although about 12% said that they also threatened the neighbour with legal action.

Neighbour problems: Obtaining Advice

A little over three-quarters of those experiencing problems with neighbours obtained advice about solving the problem (78%) which is a relatively high rate of advice-seeking and compares with 40% for consumer problems, 78% for employment problems, 92% for divorce and separation problems, 69% for personal injury, and 41% for money problems. This demonstrates the difficulty of achieving a resolution of neighbour problems simply by adopting a self-help strategy.

About half of those with neighbour problems took advice from only one outside source (50%), and almost two in five consulted two or three outside sources (38%). About 12% took advice from four or more sources and this figure is rather higher than for other problem types. This indicates a substantial demand for advice among those with neighbour problems and highlights the extent to which the public will explore all avenues in order to achieve some sort of resolution.

The sources of initial advice used by those with neighbour problems were also somewhat different from other problem types. The most common first point of contact was the local council, with more than one in three of those obtaining advice going there first (36%). The second most common source of advice was the police, with almost *one-quarter* of advice-seekers going there first. Solicitors were also quite often the first source of advice (17% of advice-seekers' initial contact). The CAB was much *less frequently* the first choice for those with neighbour problems than for other types of problem (only 7% going first to a CAB). In 11% of neighbour disputes these first sources of advice were friends or relatives (most commonly solicitors, police, local council).

The local council was also the most common second source of advice for neighbour problems (38% of second advisers), which suggests that first advisers were frequently referring people on to the council. After the local council the most common second sources of advice were solicitors (17% of second advisers), the police (12% of second advisers), and MPs or local councillors (7% of second advisers).

Taking all of those experiencing neighbour problems as a whole, 45% contacted their local council at some time or another, 27% contacted the police, 25% contacted solicitors, and 25% contacted the CAB at some time about trying to resolve the problem with their neighbour.

The vast majority of people with neighbour problems attempted to resolve the problem directly before obtaining advice about how to proceed, although approaches were not always constructively received. Among respondents who obtained advice, almost three-quarters had either been in contact with the other side or tried unsuccessfully to contact them before obtaining advice (73%). For example:

> "They have built a hotel just behind my back wall . . . there is a fire door that they're supposed to keep shut but they don't, they have it open all the time for access to and from the car park. So of course you have the noise of the disco coming straight up, which is very loud. The hotel staff themselves are extremely rude. I used to phone them up and say 'Please could you turn it down or could you shut the door'. It's been a problem with the council now for a number of years, everybody has taken it on and tried to sort it out and nobody has succeeded. It's been going on for years . . . It's just a continual noise. They've got no consideration and when you've tried to speak to them politely they're just downright rude and they don't want to know . . . It's made me ill. I get very stressed out, I've started panic attacks. I can't cope with it because I'm a very light sleeper and I get very stressed. I've just fought so much and got absolutely nowhere."

Virtually all of those who had *not* been in contact with their neighbour prior to obtaining advice had made no attempt to contact their neighbour to sort out the problem. This potentially odd finding is borne out and explained by qualitative interviews during which respondents talked about the peculiar problems of dealing with neighbours. Continuing proximity and fears for personal safety make neighbour problems unusual. In some respects they have more in common with family problems than other types of disputes. Not everyone is prepared to have direct confrontation with neighbours before obtaining advice about the problem. For example, a woman of 80 living alone was tormented by noise from a neighbour, but was afraid to confront him:

"He started playing music from early in the evening until it was time for us to get up. I complained to the council. This went on for months and months and it was very loud. I wouldn't ask him to turn the music down. My neighbours did. I banged on the floor and he banged back. I phoned the local police first of all but they couldn't do anything. They said, 'You'll have to get on to the council'. Well I didn't get any satisfaction from them, so I went to the Citizens' Advice Bureau and they told me to get in touch with the council, so I did. So what they did was send me a form. I found out afterwards that I had been in touch with the wrong department, but they didn't tell me that. This went on for about two years. I got ear plugs. In the end one of my neighbours phoned Scotland Yard and said he thought there was a drug orgy going on in the flat. Anyway, they came down and since then it's been quiet."

Most people who obtained advice about neighbour problems did so quite rapidly after the problem started. About one-quarter (27%) obtained advice as soon as the problem started, and about another quarter took advice within four weeks of the problem starting (24%). However, a sizeable proportion of those with neighbour problems waited quite a long time before obtaining advice. Around one in five waited for more than six months before taking advice.

Neighbour problems: Advice wanted

What people involved in neighbour problems were looking for over-whelmingly was advice on how to solve the problem (78% of those with neighbour problems were looking for this kind of advice). Only one in three mentioned wanting advice about their legal rights (a considerably lower proportion than in some other problem types) and only one in five mentioned wanting advice about court procedures (20%), again a lower figure than in other problem types.

Neighbour problems: Advice obtained

Although the majority of those experiencing neighbour problems were told by their first adviser that something could be done about the problem, the proportion was among the lowest percentage of all problem types (64%). For example, the figure can be compared with 85% of those suffering accidental injury or work-related ill health who were told that something could be done about their problem, and with consumer problems when 82% were told by their first adviser that something could be done to resolve the problem. The most common advice given by first advisers to those with neighbour problems was to contact the other side to try and resolve the problem (37%), seek help from another person (23%), take the case to court (12%). Second advisers were less likely to suggest contacting the neighbour to reach a resolution and slightly more likely to recommend taking the case to court. In no case did a first or second adviser suggest that the respondent try mediation to resolve the problem with their neighbour. Indeed this suggestion was made in only *one case* of a neighbour dispute, and that was by the third adviser from whom the respondent had sought help.

Neighbour problems: Satisfaction with advice

On the whole members of the public experiencing problems with neighbours expressed a *low* level of satisfaction with their first advisers. About half said that they thought the advice very helpful or helpful, but the remainder thought that the advice had been not very helpful (34%) or not helpful at all (13%). This is among the highest level of dissatisfaction with first advisers, other than for employment disputes, where 47% thought that their first adviser had not been helpful. This high level of dissatisfaction reflects the intractability of neighbour problems and the limited extent to which the law is able to offer a remedy to those locked into disputes with their neighbours. Neighbour problems have some characteristics in common with employment problems and divorce and separation problems in that the protagonists are often caught in an unhappy relationship from which it is difficult to escape and for which the possibilities of reaching a satisfactory resolution are slim.

This category excludes respondents who were involved in disputes over social security benefits, but covers matters to do with disputed bills, disputed tax demands, problems with pensions, or loans. Disputes relating to money (not including benefits) were one of the most common problems experienced by the public. About thirteen percent of those interviewed about money problems said that action was being taken against them, rather than the respondent being the person initiating action.

Money problems: The Lumpers (No advice and no contact)

About ten percent of those with money problems took no advice about resolving their dispute and made no attempt to contact the other side. This is a relatively high proportion by comparison with other problem types (for example one percent among divorce and separation problems, four percent for consumer disputes, two percent for neighbour disputes, and four percent for disputes with landlords). Of those respondents who said that they had taken no action to resolve the problem at the time of the interview, most had little or no intention of doing anything in the future. The reasons given for not intending to do anything else were rather diverse although about one quarter said that the problem had somehow or other resolved itself.

Money problems: Self-Helpers

Almost half of all those experiencing money problems took action to resolve the problem without obtaining any advice about how to resolve the problem (49% of all those with money problems). This is one of the highest proportions of self-helpers among all problem types (for example 20% in neighbour disputes, 15% in employment disputes, 18% for accidental injury cases). The most common strategy adopted was simply to contact the other side involved in the problem (76%), although in about 3% of cases the respondent threatened the other side with legal action.

Money problems: Obtaining advice

Among those with money problems about two in five obtained outside advice about dealing with the problem (41%). This figure is relatively low and can be compared with 36% obtaining advice for consumer problems, 78% for employment problems, 78% for neighbour problems, 92% for divorce and separation problems, and 69% for personal injury. Around three in five of those with money problems took advice from just one outside source (62%), with most of the remainder consulting two or three advisers (34%).

The most common first point of contact for those with money problems was the CAB (31% going there first). The next most common source of advice was a solicitor (13%). However, the range of advisers used by those experiencing money problems was very large indeed and there were few identifiable clusters. The range of second advisers was similarly large.

When people with money problems obtained advice to find a way of resolving the problems, the first adviser, although a formal outside source of advice, was actually a friend or relative of the respondent in 9% of cases.

Taking all of those with money problems as a whole, around 15% obtained advice at some time from a CAB about dealing with the problem, about 12% obtained advice from a solicitor and about 3% obtained advice from an ombudsman. This spread of advice is rather different from other problem types in that a rather *lower* proportion of those with money problems obtained advice from solicitors and a relatively high proportion of those obtaining advice (30%) went to a CAB.

Although a large proportion of respondents with money problems said that the idea of making contact with their first source of advice was their own (41%), around 28% said that the suggestion had come from a friend or relative. A lower proportion than average said that they had gone to the same source of advice on a previous similar occasion (6%).

The majority of respondents (about two in three) with money problems said that they had made contact with the other side before obtaining outside advice (66%) and another 9% of advice seekers had unsuccessfully tried to make contact with the other side before obtaining advice. Thus about three-quarters of those with money problems who obtained advice had either been in contact or tried to make contact with the other side prior to obtaining advice.

Among those respondents with money problems who were potential defendants, most had *not* obtained any advice although they had been in contact with the other side. This indicates that people who are being pursued in relation to money matters are frequently not obtaining advice or assistance that might help in resisting disputed claims. This is an important issue since cases involving potential defendants had a relatively high propensity to end in court proceedings (see next Chapter).

Most people who obtained advice about money problems did so quite quickly. About one in three said that they obtained advice as soon as the problem started (33%). About one in five said that they obtained advice within four weeks. However, almost one-quarter waited more than six months before obtaining advice.

Money problems: Advice wanted

The vast majority of those with money problems were unsurprisingly seeking advice about how to solve the problem from their first adviser (74% of respondents with money problems mentioned this). Just over one-third said that they wanted advice about their legal position (37%) and just over one-quarter said that they wanted to be advised about their financial position (27%). Only about one in five mentioned wanting advice about court procedures and only a handful were looking for representation in legal proceedings (2%).

Money problems: Advice obtained

About three-quarters of those with money problems who sought advice were told by their first adviser that something could be done about the problem. This was about average and compares well with neighbour disputes and employment disputes, which had the lowest levels of positive advice. The most common advice given by first advisers was to contact the other side to try and resolve the problem (45%) or to seek help from another person or organisation (28%). In a little over one in ten cases (11%) respondents were advised to go to court and in three percent of cases respondents were advised to take the case to an ombudsman.

Money problems: Satisfaction with advice

On the whole those with money problems were fairly satisfied with the advice received from their first contact. About three quarters thought that the advice had been very or fairly helpful, with the remainder split on whether the advice had been not very helpful or not at all helpful. This represents a slightly higher degree of dissatisfaction than, say among respondents who had suffered personal injury (nine percent saying not helpful), but a lower degree of dissatisfaction than among those experiencing neighbour problems.

ACCIDENTAL INJURY AND WORK-RELATED ILL-HEALTH

About eight percent of the surveyed population reported having had one or more injury or health problem in the last five years that resulted from an accident, or from poor working conditions and which necessitated a visit to a doctor or hospital.

Accidental Injury: The Lumpers (No advice and no contact)

About 15% of those who experienced an accidental injury or work related illness requiring medical treatment had taken no advice, made no direct contact with the other side and had not attempted to contact the other side. About half of this group reported that they would definitely or probably not take any action in the future. This is the highest proportion of "lumpers" in any of the types of justiciable problem included in the study. Qualitative interviews provided some graphic examples of the reasoning behind this failure to take action, which included an unwillingness to undergo the anticipated strain of litigation. For example

> "[*53 year old women tripped on paving stone and broke hip. Looked after by mother aged 81*] I sent for the doctor immediately and I was going to send for an ambulance, and take her to the X-ray, and he said no it wasn't necessary. He didn't think she'd broken any bones or anything, it was just a very bad sort of strain, you know. So he gave her some tablets and ointment to rub in. And so we left it at that. But she didn't seem to get any better and I was awfully worried. So we waited about a week with her in pain and then

I sent for another doctor. And the other doctor came and sent her to the hospital . . . And she had an X-ray and they came out and said, 'Oh you know your daughter needs an operation, she's got a broken hip'. . . . Well I know people do take action but sometimes they get something and sometimes they don't and I was in such a state of bad health myself at the time . . . I thought you would probably have to have a witness, would you? Or something. You know. How can we prove that she did that the way she did it? I never took any advice. I didn't think I would bother . . . because of the stress and the hassle and to be perfectly honest I don't really like going to solicitors. I had a solicitor when my husband died and that wasn't very successful. Just had to pay a hell of a lot of money for nothing really it seems to me. We finished doing everything ourselves. So I thought, 'Oh that's finished me with solicitors'."

In one case where a qualitative interview was carried out the chief reason for failing to take action in respect of injury resulting from defective medical treatment was the embarrassment that would be caused by bringing a complaint against a spouse's work colleague:

"I considered taking action up to about three years afterwards. But my husband was always very against it. His attitude very much was, would £1,000 make you feel better? And I said, no. So he said, why do it? He actually sees the consultant regularly at work because they work in the same hospital . . . And I tried to say, 'Well I'm not after the money'. And I wasn't, but I was angry and wanted to make a point that it wasn't acceptable. I considered action for a long, long time afterwards . . . a formal complaint . . . [I wanted] I suppose an explanation . . . I think I would have just liked someone to say, 'Yes we appreciate we didn't really do right by you' . . . I wanted the people involved to acknowledge that they did give a shortfall in their care . . . I felt there possibly was a legal case that I could have won. My husband was never so sure about this because he said, 'Well you have to actually prove that these guys were negligent and at the end of the day you didn't die'. I suppose the other thing that he put to me a few times was if you start anything it's going to take you years and years and years to see it through, and do you really want your life to be wrapped up in this for years and years?" [*Damage to bladder during hysterectomy operation*]

Accidental Injury: Self-Helpers

Rather few victims of accidental injury or work-related ill-health tried to take action to obtain redress on their own. On the whole, this group of respondents either did nothing at all or sought advice about taking action. About 18% of all those interviewed about injury said that they had tried to handle the matter on their own. In general this amounted to little more than making contact with the other side. They do not appear to have threatened legal action or done anything else. The relatively modest success of self-help strategies where personal injury claims are involved is discussed in Chapter 5.

Accidental Injury: Obtaining Advice

About seven out of ten (69%) respondents suffering accidents or work related health problems obtained advice about the problem. This is a relatively high rate of advice seeking by comparison with other problems, but by no means the highest (for example it can be compared with 36% for consumer problems, 78% for employment problems, 92% for divorce and separation problems, and 78% for neighbour problems).

Respondents were fairly evenly divided between those who obtained advice from just one source (43%) and those who went to two or three advisers (51%). A handful (7%) went to four or more advisers.

The first point of contact for respondents who suffered injury or work-related illness was most often a solicitor, with about one in three of those seeking advice going directly to a solicitor (32%). The next most common initial contact was with trades unions (18% of first advisers), insurance companies (15%), and the police (15%). Unlike other problem types, CABx were only used as an initial source of advice by a small minority of accident victims (5% of first advisers).

Among those seeking a remedy for accidental injury or work-related illness, the first source of advice was a friend or relative in about 10% of cases.

Although a large proportion of respondents said that the idea of making contact with their first source of advice was their own (40%), around one-fifth said that the suggestion had come from a friend or relative (19%), almost one in ten said that they had done the same on a previous similar occasion (8%), and 6% said that they had seen an advertisement for the adviser. The second source of advice was also most often a solicitor (50% of second advisers) or an insurance company (15%).

Among all victims of accidental injury and work-related illness in the sample, about half contacted a solicitor at some time to obtain advice about the problem.

In two out of three cases (67%) where advice was obtained about compensation for injury or illness, the respondent had *not* been in contact with the other side before seeking advice, nor had they generally tried to make contact with the other side. This suggests that respondents are aware that if they are going to seek any kind of remedy against the person responsible for the injury or illness, success will depend on more than direct negotiations or other self-help remedies.

Advice was generally obtained very rapidly after the accident or illness. Over half of those who obtained advice said that they did so immediately (56%). An additional one-quarter (24%) obtained advice within four weeks. About one in ten respondents (9%) waited more than six months before seeking advice about their accident or illness.

Accidental injury: Advice wanted

What respondents were looking for from advisers, at least initially, was advice about legal rights (41% of respondents mentioning this), advice about procedures (37% mentioning), and advice about how to solve the problem (42%). Around 16% of accident victims wanted their first adviser to represent them in court.

Accidental Injury: Advice obtained

A very high proportion of those obtaining advice about an accident or work-related illness were told that something could be done about the problem (81%). This figure can be compared with the relatively low figure of 56% for neighbour problems and 49% for employment problems. The most common advice given by first advisers was to seek advice or help from another person (28%), to contact the other side to try and resolve the problem (19%) and to threaten the other side with legal action (18%). In one case a first adviser suggested going to mediation.

Accidental Injury: Satisfaction with advice

Respondents with injury and health problems expressed a high degree of satisfaction with the advice received from their first point of contact. About three in five (61%) said that the advice had been very helpful and a further 30% said that the advice was fairly helpful. Less than one in ten (9%) thought that the advice was not very or not at all helpful.

About 3 percent of the surveyed population reported having had one or more problems relating to getting landlords to do repairs during the previous five years. Most of these were living in local authority housing (52%), although one third were in private rented property (35%). About 10% of those with problems with landlords were renting from housing associations.

Landlord problems: The Lumpers (No advice and no contact)

Most respondents who had experienced problems with landlords had tried to do something about the problem. Only four percent of those experiencing problems with their landlord failed to take any action at all to try and resolve the problem. Moreover, almost all of this group reported that they would definitely or probably not take any action in the future because the respondent did not think that anything could be done to resolve the problem, or because the problem was over and done with by the time of the interview.

Landlord Problems: Self-Helpers

Quite a high proportion of those with landlord problems tried to resolve the problem without obtaining any advice (46%) but the overwhelming majority of self-helpers did nothing much else other than make contact with the other side to try and achieve some sort of resolution to the problem. They do not appear to have threatened legal action or done anything else. As will be seen in the next chapter, these self-help strategies had a relatively low rate of success.

Landlord Problems: Obtaining Advice

About half of those interviewed who had experienced problems with landlords (49%) sought advice about the problem. This compares with

78% for neighbour problems, 36% for consumer problems, 78% for employment problems, and 92% for divorce and separation problems. Almost two out of every three of those with landlord problems who sought advice went to only one adviser (64%).

The first point of contact for those experiencing problems with their landlord was most often the local authority (29%) or a CAB (32%). Only six percent of those with problems to do with landlords went first to a solicitor. In only about four percent of cases was the first adviser a friend or relative of the respondent. Where a second adviser was contacted this was most often a solicitor (27% of second advisers), a CAB (20%), or the local council (20%).

Among those experiencing landlord problems as a whole, 18% contacted the local council and about 20% were in contact with a CAB at some time for advice about dealing with the problem. Only 13% of this group sought advice from a solicitor at any point about trying to resolve the problem with the landlord.

In four out of five cases where advice was sought about problems with landlords the respondent had been in contact with the landlord about the problem before obtaining advice (81%). Advice was sought mostly very soon after the problem started, although about 17% of those with landlord problems waited for more than six months after the problem began before obtaining advice.

Landlord Problems: Advice Wanted

What people were looking for from advisers initially at least was advice about how to solve the problem (84% of those obtaining advice) and advice about legal rights (30% mentioning this). Quite a high proportion were also looking for advice about procedures (27%). About 12% wanted advice about their financial position, but virtually none were looking for someone to represent them in court proceedings.

Landlord Problems: Advice obtained

A very high proportion of those obtaining advice about problems with their landlord were told that something could be done about the problem (74%). This figure can be compared with the lower figures for example in neighbour disputes (56%) and employment disputes (49%).

The most common advice received from first advisers was to contact the other side to try and resolve the problem (52%), or to seek advice or help from another person (26%). In eight percent of cases respondents were advised to go to court. Interestingly, in about three percent of cases involving problems with landlords first advisers suggested that the respondent try to seek a resolution through mediation.

Landlord Problems: Satisfaction with Advice

Respondents who were interviewed about their approach to resolving problems with landlords expressed only moderate satisfaction with the advice received from their first point of contact. About one in three (32%) said that the advice had been very helpful, although a further 48% said that the advice was fairly helpful. About one-fifth overall said that the advice was not very or not at all helpful.

OTHER PROBLEMS

There were several other types of problems that respondents reported during the screening survey and about which they were interviewed in the main survey. However, because of the relative rarity of these types of problems the number of cases about which information is available is small, making full analysis unreliable. The following information is presented as indicative, however, of the approaches taken by those experiencing these rather less common problems. In general unweighted numbers have been given rather than percentages.

Problems about receiving benefits

Some 39 respondents to the main survey were interviewed about problems to do with receiving benefits. Of this number there were none at all who failed to take any action to try and deal with the problem. Everyone did something. The majority obtained advice about trying to resolve the problem (27 out of 39) and of these all but six obtained advice from a CAB or other non-solicitor advice source.

Unfair treatment by the police

Of the fourteen respondents interviewed about a problem relating to unfair treatment by the police most took some action to deal with the problem, although a relatively high proportion in comparison with other problem types did nothing (two out of the fourteen). Of those who took action the majority obtained some advice (nine of the twelve respondents) and most of these obtained legal advice (seven of the nine). Of those who took advice, seven were advised that something could be done about their complaint.

Clinical negligence

Nineteen respondents were interviewed about a problem relating to negligent medical or dental treatment. Only two of these took no action at all to try and resolve the problem, but on the other hand a very low proportion obtained any advice about the problem. Of the seventeen respondents who took action as a result of clinical negligence only two obtained any advice, both of whom were advised to pursue the case. The remainder handled the problem themselves. No respondents obtained any legal advice from a solicitor.

Problems with schooling

In nineteen cases respondents were interviewed about a problem to do with schooling for children under 18. Within this group of respondents there was none that said that had taken no action at all to deal with the problem. Everyone tried something and a majority of respondents obtained advice. Ten of the nineteen obtained advice, but only two sought advice from a solicitor. In most cases advisers said that something could be done about the problem (seven out of ten cases).

SECTION 2: EXPLAINING ADVICE-SEEKING

In order to try and understand more fully the factors associated with the likelihood that respondents would obtain advice about trying to resolve a justiciable dispute a multiple regression analysis was conducted. Using this type of analysis it is possible to identify factors that are significantly associated with the likelihood that advice will be obtained when members of the public are faced with different types of justiciable problems, and to estimate whether certain groups are more or less likely than average to obtain advice[2].

The purpose of the analysis was to try and isolate factors associated with *any* kind of advice-seeking and no distinction was made at this point between different types of adviser. The factors included in the analysis of whether or not advice would be obtained, on the basis of the results of earlier cross classification of variables were: the type of problem being experienced by the respondent and the type of remedy being sought, and whether the respondent was taking action or having action taken against them; the respondent's age, sex, social class, education, employment status, and income; and finally an indicator of the extent to which respondents reported having suffered negative effects from dealing with their problems, and an indicator of respondents' attitude to the legal system (i.e. whether they would be confident of receiving a fair hearing if they had to go to court).

Taking all of these factors into account, the results of the multiple regression analysis indicated that the factors that were *not* found to be significantly associated with the likelihood that advice would be obtained to resolve justiciable problems were:

- respondent's social class
- respondent's employment status.

Factors that were found to be significantly associated with the likelihood that advice would be obtained to resolve the problem were:

- type of justiciable problem experienced
- respondent's educational qualifications
- respondent's age
- respondent's income
- type of remedy being sought
- attitude to legal system (i.e. whether confident of a fair hearing)
- whether the respondent was taking action or the subject of action
- respondent's gender.

Of these eight factors found to be significantly associated with whether or not advice would be obtained about the problem, the factors show-

---

[2] The full results of the regression analysis are presented in Appendix B.

ing by far the strongest correlation were *problem type*, followed by *respondent's educational qualifications*, and *respondent's age*. This means that much of the variation noted in advice-seeking is accounted for by these three factors.

Type of justiciable problem

Employment problems, neighbour problems, divorce or separation, and problems to do with owning residential property were all associated with an *increased* likelihood that respondents experiencing those problems would obtain advice about resolving the problem. For example, if the problem facing the respondent resulted from divorce or separation, then the odds of a respondent obtaining advice were 489% *higher* than average. Respondents experiencing problems to do with owning residential property were about 189% more likely to obtain advice about the problem than average.

On the other hand, money problems, landlord and tenant problems, and consumer problems were associated with *decreased* odds of obtaining advice. For example, respondents experiencing consumer problems were 79% less likely to obtain advice than average, and respondents experiencing money problems were about 70% less likely than the average respondent to obtain advice.

Education

The respondent's level of education was also strongly correlated with obtaining advice. Respondents with no educational qualifications were about 36% *less* likely to obtain advice than average, while respondents with A levels were about 89% *more* likely than average to obtain advice about a justiciable problem. Those with qualifications equivalent to GCSE only were about 21% less likely than the average respondent to obtain advice about resolving their justiciable problem.

Age

Younger people (between 18–34 years old) were *less likely* to obtain advice, while older people (between 45–64) were *more likely* to obtain advice when compared with the average respondent in the dataset. In fact respondents between 55–64 years old were about 115% more likely to obtain advice compared with respondents aged between 18–24 years old.

Other factors also found to be significantly associated with the likelihood that advice would be obtained about a justiciable problem were income, claim value, gender and a measure of attitude to the judicial system, although these factors were less strongly correlated with advice-seeking than problem, education or age.

Income

Respondents with an annual income in excess of £29,000 were about 27% *more likely* than the average respondent to obtain advice about their justiciable problem.

Remedy sought

For the purpose of this analysis respondents were categorised according to whether their problem involved a claim for a lump sum of money, regular payments of money, or a remedy that did not involve the payment of money. Claims involving a lump sum were divided between amounts under and over £500[3]. The results of the analysis show that the value of the claim was associated with obtaining advice. Larger lump sums were associated with increasing odds that advice would be obtained about the problem. The odds of a respondent obtaining advice were 110% higher if she or he was seeking more than £500 compared with the average. On the other hand, when respondents were seeking a remedy other than money they were 23% *less* likely than average to obtain advice. This suggests that the tendency to seek advice is greater if respondents are seeking to obtain a lump sum in compensation.

Attitude to judicial system

As will be seen in Chapter 7, during the survey respondents were questioned about their attitudes to the courts, judiciary, and the legal

---

[3] This categorisation was chosen because, as will be seen in Chapter 6, the amounts of money at issue were generally quite low, with a high proportion under £500.

profession and the results are discussed in full in that chapter. For the purpose of the analysis of advice-seeking, one of these attitude questions was used as an indicator of broadly positive or negative assessments of the judicial system as a whole and was included in the multiple regression analysis. The question used was: *"If I went to court with a problem, I am confident that I would get a fair hearing."* Respondents were invited to agree or disagree with the statement. This factor was found to be significantly associated with the likelihood that respondents would obtain advice in that those expressing a *positive* view of the judicial system were somewhat more likely than those expressing a negative view to obtain advice. However, this is difficult to interpret since the positive or negative attitudes to the legal system were being assessed at the time of the interview and not at the time that advice was sought.

Whether respondent was taking action or was the subject of action

Respondents were divided broadly between those who reported that they were initiating action against another person or organisations (potential claimant) or whether their problem involved another person or organisation taking action against them (potential defendant). Although this factor was significantly associated with the likelihood that advice would be sought, it was one of the weaker correlations. However, the results of the analysis show that those who were the subject of action were about 15% *less* likely than the average respondent to obtain advice about trying to resolve their problem.

Gender

The results of the multiple regression analysis indicate that women were about 21% *more* likely than men to obtain advice about a justiciable dispute.

THE INTERACTION OF FACTORS ASSOCIATED WITH ADVICE SEEKING

The analysis thus far has identified a number of factors that are associated with the likelihood that advice would be obtained in order to try and resolve a justiciable problem. It is not clear, however, how these various factors interact. To address this question a further analysis was undertaken[4] in order to identify the characteristics of subgroups of respondents which differed in terms of their propensity to seek advice about their justiciable problem. The analysis produced twelve different (mutually exclusive and exhaustive) groups for which the percentage of cases obtaining advice about a justiciable problem varied from 20% to 92%. The characteristics of these groups are discussed below.

Groups with low propensity to obtain outside advice

The analysis suggests that the group of respondents in the sample *least* likely of all to obtain advice about dealing with a justiciable dispute had the following characteristics:

• Experiencing a money or a consumer problem
• Respondent's income up to £29,000
• Remedy sought by respondent did not have a money value.

Some 20% of this group obtained advice about the problem and the group represented seven percent of the total sample of respondents interviewed in the main survey.

The group with the next lowest propensity to obtain advice about resolving their justiciable problem had the following characteristics:

• Experiencing a money or a consumer problem
• Respondent had no educational qualifications or O levels only
• Respondent's income up to £29,000
• Money remedy sought.

Among this group about 28% obtained advice about the problem and the group represented about nine percent of the sample as a whole.

Another group with a similarly low propensity to obtain advice was characterised by:

• Experiencing a problem with a landlord, or a tribunal problem about benefits or schooling for children
• Respondent had no educational qualifications or O levels only
• Respondent expressed a negative attitude to the legal system.

---

[4] The CHAID (Chi-squared Automatic Interaction Detector) module within SPSS. The full results of the CHAID analysis are given in Appendix B.

About 31% of this group obtained outside advice about their problem and the group represented about five percent of the sample as a whole.

Average propensity to obtain outside advice

There were three groups with an about average propensity to obtain advice. The first of these had the following two characteristics:

• Experiencing a money or consumer problems
• Respondent earning more than £29,000 per year.

The rate at which advice was obtained among this group was 51% and the group itself represented eight percent of the total sample of respondents.

The second group with about average propensity to obtain advice about a justiciable problem had the following characteristics:

• Landlord and tenant problem, tribunal matter concerning benefits or child's schooling
• Respondent had no qualifications or O levels only
• Respondent expressed a positive or neutral attitude to judicial system.

About 54% of this group obtained outside advice about their justiciable problem and the group represented about twelve percent of the sample as a whole.

The third group of cases showing a roughly average propensity to obtain advice about a justiciable problem had the following characteristics:

• Money or consumer problem
• Respondent earning up to £29,000 per year
• Respondent had obtained A level qualifications or degree level qualifications

Among this group the percentage obtaining advice about their justiciable problem was 59%, although the group was fairly small representing about five percent of the total sample.

High propensity to obtain outside advice

There were several groups with a high propensity to obtain advice about their justiciable problem.

The first group with a high propensity to obtain advice about their justiciable problem had the following characteristics:

- Problem with landlord, tribunal matter concerning benefits or child's schooling
- Respondent had A level qualifications or degree level qualifications.

Among this group the rate at which advice was obtained was 68% and the group represented 16% of the sample.

A group with a single identifying characteristic was those suffering from accidental injury or work related illness. The rate at which advice was obtained among this group was 69% and the group represented about seven percent of the total sample.

Another group with a high propensity to seek advice had the following characteristics:

- Employment problem, neighbour problem, problem to do with residential property
- Respondent earning less than £15,000 per year.

The highest levels of advice seeking were found in two specific groups. The first had the following characteristics:

- Problem to do with employment, neighbours, owning residential property
- The respondent's income was more than £15,000 and less than £29,000 per year.

The rate at which advice was obtained among this group was 90% and the group represented about six percent of the sample as a whole.

The group with the highest rate of advice-seeking had one characteristic only and that was that the justiciable problem concerned divorce or separation problems. In this group the rate at which advice was obtained was 92% and the group represented ten percent of the sample as a whole.

The results of the CHAID analysis show the way in which the factors associated with advice-seeking tend to interact. What emerges is the extent to which problem type largely determines whether or not advice will be obtained about a problem, but it also clearly illustrates the extent to which education is important in determining whether or not advice will be obtained. Income has a rather patchy influence, although a low income is among the characteristics defining one of the groups with the *highest* propensity to obtain advice about their justiciable problem. It can also be seen clearly that divorce and separation problems represent a class on their own as far as advice-seeking is concerned.

CONCLUSION

The chapter has built on the discussion in Chapter 3 presenting a wealth of data about how members of the public faced with particular kinds of justiciable disputes sought to deal with those problems. As discussed in the previous chapter, it appears that the overwhelming majority of respondents who perceived and defined a problem as being more than trivial, took steps to do something about it. Among the few who did absolutely nothing, the failure to take action was not the result of inadvertence, but generally seemed to flow from fairly careful weighing of options.

Among those who took steps to resolve the problem most tried first to deal with the matter themselves and only resorted to advice when their efforts proved fruitless. The exceptions to this rule were some divorce and separation problems, some neighbour problems and some accidental injuries, when respondents went directly to seek advice, rather than attempting to deal directly with their opponent as a result of fear of the consequences, a total breakdown of communication or a sense that a direct approach would be fruitless.

It is also clear that whether members of the public obtain advice, where they go for advice, and whether they are prepared to pay for that advice is greatly influenced by the nature of the problem. The results of the multivariate analysis confirm that problem type tends to swamp other considerations, although they also confirm that some personal factors, such as level of education, are important.

The problems about which advice is most likely to be sought are divorce and separation problems, employment problems, neighbour problems, and problems relating to the ownership of residential property. What most of these problem types have in common is the likely importance of the matters to the parties and the relative intractability of the issues that might be involved. For example, in employment problems, neighbour problems and divorce and separation problems the parties have been in a relationship. Where neighbour problems and divorce and separation problems are concerned, the parties may still be locked into a continuing relationship. These are problems that cannot be solved by a simple transfer of money. In employment cases an employee may be struggling to hold on to a job, or may be hoping to improve or preserve the conditions under which he or she is working. The increased propensity to obtain advice for these problems is a reflection of the complexity of the issues and the difficulty of achieving a resolution by means of self-help strategies.

Those problems about which advice is less likely to be obtained are consumer problems, money problems and problems with landlords reflecting, possibly, that the issues involved may be relatively uncomplicated and have less serious implications. As a result respondents may feel less inclined to go to the trouble and potential expense of obtaining advice.

Some demographic factors are also important in explaining advice seeking. Respondents with the lowest levels of education were less likely to seek advice than those with higher levels of education, perhaps because they do not realise that advice might help or perhaps because a certain level of education and awareness is necessary in order to be able to access advice. If this is the case it is possible that as the proportion of the population achieving higher educational qualifications increases, so will their levels of knowledge and confidence about dealing with justiciable problems and so will the demand for advice. The implications for future litigation rates of this are unclear. Increased competence might lead to a greater capacity for avoiding disputes or for effectively achieving a resolution. However, it may also mean that the public, armed with greater knowledge and understanding of their rights and of the obligations of others, may be more prepared to take their cases to court.

Other demographic factors associated with a differential propensity to seek advice were age, income and gender. Younger respondents were less likely to obtain advice than older respondents suggesting lower levels of knowledge about how to obtain advice or simply less determination to achieve a resolution of their problem. Respondents with higher incomes were more likely to obtain advice than those on the lowest incomes; and women were more likely than men to obtain advice about a justiciable problem.

Despite the range of factors found to be correlated with advice-seeking, the nature of the problem experienced explains much of the variation in advice seeking and this was graphically illustrated in respondents' accounts of their approach to the resolution of problems of different types. It seems clear that very few members of the public would remain supine in the face of *any* justiciable problem. But decisions about whether to take action, what action to take, and when to give up, are also influenced by respondents' own competence and resources, and by the character of the opposition in the context of the severity of the problem.

Table 4.1 below suggests the combination of factors that seem to influence the extent to which members of the public faced with a justiciable problem will be able to resolve that problem alone and whether they are likely to need help. The level of need for advice and assistance will depend on the competence and resources of the party facing the problem, the importance of the problem to that party, and the intransigence of the opponent. Thus those members of the public with low levels of competence in terms of education, income, confidence, verbal skill, literacy skill, and emotional fortitude are likely to need some help in resolving justiciable problems no matter what the importance of the problem and no matter how intransigent or accommodating the opposition, although this need will increase as problem severity and opponent intransigence increases.

Table 4.1. Factors determining need for advice.

Level of Need	Competence/ Resources of Party	Importance of Problem	Intransigence of Opponent
HIGH	LOW	LOW/MEDIUM/HIGH	LOW/MEDIUM/HIGH
HIGH	MEDIUM/HIGH	HIGH	HIGH
MEDIUM	MEDIUM/HIGH	LOW	HIGH
LOW	MEDIUM/HIGH	LOW/MEDIUM/HIGH	LOW

A high level of need for advice might also be experienced by members of the public with medium to high levels of the necessary competencies, when faced with a problem of great importance or severity and an opponent who is intransigent. Examples here might be some divorce and separation problems, repossession of homes when people fall on hard times, accidental injury, and serious problems with neighbours.

A relatively low need for assistance, but a need nonetheless, might exist among those with medium to high levels of confidence, but who lack the specific knowledge about rights and procedures to mount a credible attack on an opponent or to present a convincing defence.

The question of whether or not people are willing to pay for advice involves another set of considerations that have to be overlaid on the suggested matrix. Does the problem involve some kind of immediate threat? Examples might be contact and residence cases, violent spouses, money being demanded, and employment problems. These are matters about which there might be a tangible threat of harm leading to an imperative for action. In these cases individuals might be prepared, if they must, to pay whatever it costs to avert the threat of harm or mitigate the damage.

Those situations can be distinguished from cases concerning recompense for harm already suffered, such as consumer problems, wrangles with insurance companies and accidental injury. In such cases what is being sought is a possible financial gain set against an uncertain outcome and the decision as to whether or not it is worth investing money in that doubtful outcome may lead to hesitation. One respondent in a qualitative interview neatly summed up this dilemma:

> "What you do about something depends on many things. Do you feel 'Well I've stood enough. I've finally stood enough!' In this day and age—a whole variety of things that are irksome or downright damaging roll by. Most of them just roll by, because there are other things to do. There's your life to get on with. In the last year and a half we had the outside of the house painted [caused damage to windows]. If I had the time and if I had the inclination I would do something about that, but I didn't. One of the things I sense is that it is quite difficult to know what is the best thing to do. Do you phone up and say 'Hey. You screwed up and have been bloody careless, unprofessional etc' and what then? They are obviously going to disagree and then there is the whole succession of steps that have to be gone through to possibly get nothing out of it. And then the overall cost of doing it. And what can be recovered—and that's a lot of hassle too. Repainting it with possibly another bunch of cowboys. It's one thing to complain to a large organisation which has got something to defend, but it is quite another thing to try and complain to a small company or one man band. It's much more difficult."

5

Outcomes

The previous chapter looked in detail at the various approaches taken by respondents to the resolution of problems of different types. This chapter focuses more directly on the outcomes that were achieved by those trying to resolve their problem, and considers these outcomes in relation to the strategy adopted. The chief outcome with which the chapter is concerned is whether any resolution to the problem was achieved. In this context "resolution" is taken as meaning either that an agreement was reached to end or settle the problem (with or without the commencement of legal proceedings) ("agreement"), or that the matter ended with a court, tribunal or ombudsman's decision or order ("adjudication"). No judgement is made about whether agreements were good or bad or whether respondents were happy with the terms. The term resolution also includes cases where the respondent lost their case in court. "Unresolved" cases are those where action was taken to seek a resolution of the case but no agreement was ever reached to settle the matter and no court, tribunal or ombudsman's decision or order was ever obtained. These are, in effect, cases in which attempts to obtain a resolution were tried and then abandoned.

The first section of the chapter describes what happened when respondents handled the problem entirely alone, when they handled the problem with help from advisers, and when they turned to the legal system to achieve a resolution. The second section of the chapter presents information about the extent to which agreements and court decisions led to genuine resolution of problems and about some of the financial costs incurred by respondents in the process of trying to resolve their justiciable problems. The final section uses the results of multivariate analysis to try and explain the way in which certain characteristics of respondents and certain problem types are associated with different outcomes to justiciable problems

There is a wide range of possible outcomes to justiciable problems and the paths to those outcomes can be labyrinthine. Figure 5.1 displays the primary pathways that were followed by various groups of respondents interviewed in the main survey in order to try and achieve a resolution to their justiciable problem. Reconstructing behaviour from respondents' accounts of what happened is difficult because sometimes there is a lack of fine detail about deviations from primary routes, and because sometimes survey respondents give logically incompatible answers. This was not unexpected and reflects the confusion that many ordinary people feel in relation to legal and other dispute resolution processes that they do not fully understand and that are not adequately explained.

As Figure 5.1 shows, it is possible to resolve a dispute by handling it in a number of different ways: respondents could deal with the problem completely alone; they could obtain some advice and then continue alone; or they could obtain advice and then move toward a resolution with the aid of an adviser or representative. Even if legal proceedings had been started by the respondent, or against the respondent, a resolution could have been reached without a legal decision, or the case might have been abandoned. Thus the primary outcomes of agreement, adjudication or abandonment can be reached by a number of routes.

OUTCOMES ACHIEVED

The Lumpers: No action, no resolution

Among all those interviewed in the main survey who had experienced a non-trivial justiciable problem, some five percent of respondents took no action to try and resolve the matter. This means that they did not contact the other side in the dispute or any other party or organisation, effectively eschewing the possibility of any resolution or remedy, despite the fact that these respondents all regarded their problem as non-trivial[1].

---

[1] See discussion in Chapter 3 for details of characteristics of this group.

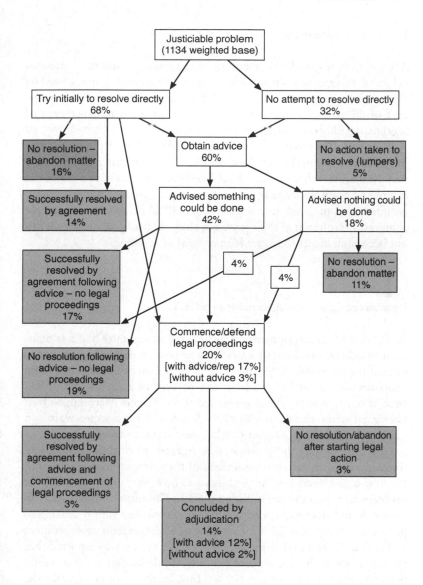

Figure 5.1. Paths and outcomes following non-trivial justiciable problem. (All percentages given are of total sample 1134—shaded boxes are final outcomes)

Resolved by agreement

According to respondents' accounts of their actions and the outcomes achieved, it seems that justiciable problems were eventually resolved *by agreement* in one-third of all cases (35%), and that in about three percent of all cases agreement was reached after the commencement of legal proceedings (see Figure 5.1).

Figure 5.1 also reveals that the proportions of the sample succeeding in reaching a resolution of their problem by means of agreement are very similar, whether or not advice had been taken. About 14% of the sample as a whole managed to resolve their problem by agreement, without obtaining advice, while about 17% of the whole sample achieved a resolution of their problem after obtaining advice, but without becoming involved in any formal legal proceedings.

Unresolved Cases: No agreement or adjudication

About *half* of all respondents to the main questionnaire had not managed to achieve any kind of agreement to resolve their problem by the time of the interview (51%), nor had the problem been the subject of a court decision or order. In about five percent of cases no action had been taken to resolve the dispute and three percent were unresolved after legal action had been commenced. A few of these were awaiting a court hearing, particularly among accidental injury cases.

However, despite the absence of an agreement or decision to bring the problem to an end, just under half of these respondents said that at the time of the interview the problem was no longer ongoing—that the problem had in some sense ended (46%). The most common way in which the problem had ended was by the respondent simply ceasing to pursue the complaint (26% of cases where respondents said problem had ended). In just under one in five of these cases, it was reported that the other side in the dispute had promised to do something that would bring the problem to an end (19%). In a small minority of cases the "resolution" of the problem was achieved by the respondent or the other side taking fairly drastic action. Among those respondents who said that the problem had ended, despite the absence of an agreement, in just over one in ten cases this was achieved by the respondent moving to a new house or area (11%). About 7% of respondents said that the problem ended when the respondent moved to another job. Some respondents who had been the subject of a complaint said that the problem had ended by the other side withdrawing or stopping pursuit of the respondent (9% of those saying that the problem had ended) or by the other side moving to a new house (4%).

In just over half the cases in which there had been no agreement or adjudication the problem was still ongoing (54%) and in most of these cases respondents had no intention of taking any action to try and resolve the problem in the future. The most common reasons for not intending to take any further action were either that the respondent was waiting to see what might happen next (23%), or that the respondent felt there was nothing else that they could do to resolve the problem (22%). Other common reasons for giving up were that it would cost too much to do anything else (7%), that the respondent was fed up with the problem or had had enough of trying to sort it out (7%), or that it was not worth the hassle to continue (5%). Typical examples of reasons taken from survey questionnaires are as follows:

"No point in it [going on with action]. My son and daughter in law are now doing the work for us and the paint alone has cost us £50." (*Female over 65, local council failure to do repairs to rented property*)

"I haven't got enough power to make the local authority do what I want." (*Female aged 35–44, suffered accident at work*)

"Because of the pain and distress of what has gone on." (*Female 45–54, problem involving another family member*)

"Several families have complained to the Council. I'm not the only one, but they are still smashing windows, destroying gardens, and doing 'moonies' outside our windows. If I complain again I don't know what they may do next. The police can't do anything unless they actually catch them cutting the tops off the flowers." (*Male aged 55–64, problem with neighbours living in rented accommodation*)

"Because of the helplessness of the ordinary citizen when they get entangled with problems where we would have to go to law to get justice and cannot afford to do it." (*Male, problem involving money, dispute with utility company*).

"The hospital have told me it's only asthma. The union rep told me I only qualify for compensation if I've worked underground for 20 years and I've worked above ground." (*Male 45–55, work related ill-health*)

"I don't have enough legal rights to stand on at present. This was advised by my solicitor. The quote did not specify enough. It is not a legally binding document." *(Female 25–30 in dispute with tradesman over performance of services)*

Legal proceedings and adjudication

In only about 14% of all cases of non-trivial justiciable problems was the matter concluded on the basis of a court, tribunal or ombudsman's adjudication, although the proportion of the sample involved in legal proceedings was rather higher at about 20%. This suggests that court and other legal proceedings play a very minor role in the resolution of justiciable problems afflicting ordinary members of the public as private individuals. This low level of use is even more extreme when considering individual problem types, as will be seen later in the chapter.

As Figure 5.2 shows, involvement in legal proceedings was most common in cases concerning divorce and separation (62%), DSS and education tribunal matters (38%) owning property (37%), employment problems (21%), and accidental injury (14%). Involvement in

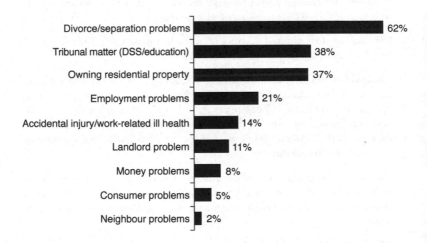

Figure 5.2. Involvement in formal legal proceedings by problem type. (Weighted base = 1134)

legal proceedings was least common in neighbour disputes (2%) and consumer problems (5%).

Moreover, as far as private individuals are concerned, it appears that their exposure to legal proceedings is more likely to be as a defendant than as a plaintiff. Those respondents who were having action taken *against* them were far more likely to be involved in court proceedings than those respondents who had initiated action (see further below). Among those respondents who reported that they were having action taken against them, two in three (69%) reported that they had been involved in legal proceedings in the course of resolving their problem. Among respondents who were *initiating* action to try and resolve the justiciable problem, on the other hand, only 13% reported having been involved in legal proceedings. The experience of defendants and plaintiffs diverge even further when looking at the distribution of court hearings. The proportion of respondents who reported that a hearing had taken place in connection with their case was about 14% over the sample as a whole. Among respondents having action taken against them, however, over half (56%) said that their case had been decided on the basis of a decision by a court, tribunal or ombudsman as compared with only nine percent of those respondents who initiated action.

A further 12 respondents said that their case had come before an ombudsman. These cases concerned disputes over money involving insurance companies, utility companies, and pension companies. A couple of cases resulted from consumer problems over goods and services and in two cases the matter related to ownership of property.

According to respondents their cases went to a variety of courts or tribunals, most commonly the county courts, followed by the magistrates courts, and tribunals (Figure 5.3). A very small minority of those involved in court proceedings said that their case had been dealt with in the High Court. The information regarding courts does not appear to be wholly reliable. Some of the types of courts mentioned seem rather unlikely given the nature of the case in which the respondent was involved. A relatively small proportion of respondents mentioned the small claims procedure in the county court, although it is highly likely, given the amount of money at stake, that a greater proportion of cases were actually dealt with through that procedure. Although this lack of understanding raises minor difficulties for the interpretation of the findings, it helpfully demonstrates the extent to which members of the public can be heavily involved in legal proceedings and yet have little understanding of those processes or the terminology.

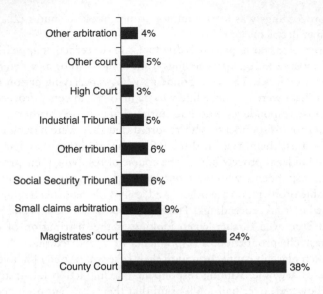

Figure 5.3. Respondents' reports of type of court/tribunal dealing with problem. (Base = all those involved in court proceedings 172 weighted)

"Defendants": Those having action taken against them

The experience of potential defendants (i.e. those who said that their justiciable problem involved having action taken against them), was significantly and predictably different from those respondents who were themselves the complainant or initiator of action. About twelve percent of the sample reported that their justiciable problem involved them being the subject of action rather than the initiator of action. The kinds of problems in which these respondents were involved predominantly concerned divorce or separation problems (one in three potential defendants 33%), money problems (one in five 19%), disputes concerning freehold property (17%), and problems with landlords (11%). Those respondents who said that their problem involved having action taken against them were more likely than others to have incomes of under £10,000 (41% as compared with 32% of others), and slightly less likely than others to be over the age of 55 (7% compared with 15% of others). They were also more likely to have received legal advice at some time in the past (77% as compared with 67% of others), more likely to have obtained legal advice about the problem being discussed in the interview (45% compared with 28% of others) and much more likely to have become involved in legal proceedings during the resolution of the problem about which they were being interviewed (69% as compared with 13% of others).

A higher proportion of those who were having action taken against them reported that the problem had reached some sort of resolution (81% as compared with 45% among those who were initiating action). Only about 17% of all those who had action taken against them said that the problem had not been resolved by agreement or adjudication at the time of the interview (as compared with over half of those cases in which the respondent was initiating action (55%)). It is also notable that in those cases in which the respondent was the subject of action, the outcome of the case was much more likely to be a court or tribunal decision than among those who were taking action (56% as compared with 9% of others). Of those respondents whose cases ended in a hearing in the county court, nearly two in three were defendants (and among those who said that their case was dealt with in a small claims hearing almost all were defendants).

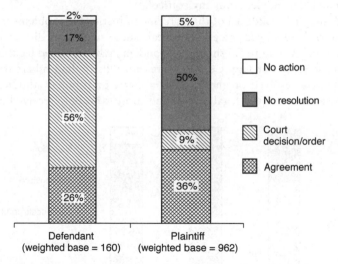

Figure 5.4. Outcome of justiciable problems—plaintiffs and defendants compared. (Weighted base = 1134)

---

[2] In the multivariate analysis in the final section of this chapter these definitions were further refined to distinguish between "other advisers" who provided positive assistance or representation and those who simply offered information and advice.

A comparison of plaintiffs and defendants in relation to the outcome of justiciable problems (Figure 5.4) shows that in the case of defendants, problems are far more likely to be concluded on the basis of a court decision or order than in the case of plaintiffs (56% as compared with 9%), and far less likely to remain unresolved (17% unresolved as compared with 50%). This is hardly surprising since defendants are in the position of being pursued.

The significance of advice in outcome

In order to assess the influence of advice on the outcome of justiciable problems advice was initially divided into three categories: "legal advice", which was overwhelmingly advice from a solicitor in private practice with the odd case involving advice from a law centre; "other advice" which covered advice from a CAB and all other sources of advice from advice agencies and other sources identified in Chapter 3; and "no advice", where respondents reported that they had not obtained any advice from any source[2].

A simple breakdown of the outcome of justiciable problems in relation to these advice categories reveals some significant differences in outcome. As Figure 5.5 shows, respondents who obtained legal advice from solicitors or Law Centres were *more* likely than others to have their case resolved on the basis of a court or tribunal adjudication. Those who received legal advice and those who only received advice

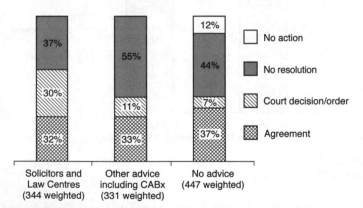

Figure 5.5. Outcome in relation to advice. (Base = whole sample 1134 weighted)

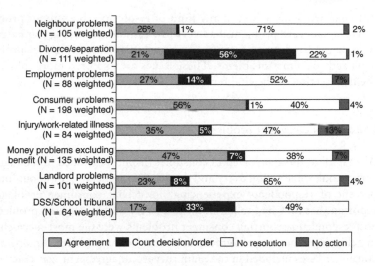

Figure 5.6. Final outcome of different problem types.

from other advisers achieved fairly similar rates of agreement, although among those who obtained other advice the proportion of cases in which no resolution was achieved was higher than among those obtaining legal advice. Among self-helpers who took action, the rates of agreement were slightly higher overall than among those who took advice (43% of self-helpers achieving an agreement compared with 32% of those who received legal advice and 33% of those who obtained other advice), but more problems remained unresolved than among those who received legal advice. These issues are, however, complicated and the role of advice is considered in more detail below in the analysis of outcome between problems of different types, and again in the final section in the explanation of outcome based on multivariate analysis.

OUTCOMES ACHIEVED FOR DIFFERENT PROBLEM TYPES

Just as there were substantial differences in the approaches taken to strategies for resolving disputes depending on the type of problem, so there appear to be substantial differences in the types of outcome achieved. From Figure 5.6 it can be seen clearly that there was considerable variation in the extent to which respondents experiencing different problems achieved any kind of resolution. Neighbour problems and landlord problems had very low resolution rates as compared with divorce and separation problems, tribunal matters, money problems and consumer problems. These issues are explored more fully in the final section of the chapter.

Outcome of consumer problems

Almost all of those involved in consumer disputes included in the main survey took some action to try and resolve the problem. Only about four percent of respondents experiencing non-trivial consumer problems reported that they had taken no action to try and resolve the problem and respondents reporting consumer problems were the most successful in achieving some sort of agreement to resolve the problem. Among all consumer cases included in the main survey, an agreement was reached to resolve the problem in over half the cases (56%). This can be compared with an overall agreement rate for example in employment cases of 27%, accidental injury 35%, divorce/separation, 21% and neighbour disputes 26%.

The overall picture of the outcome of consumer problems is interesting. In a moderately high proportion of cases (40%) no resolution to the problem was ever achieved. This can be compared with only 22% in divorce/separation cases (which had the lowest rate of "non-resolution") and 71% in neighbour problems (which had the highest rate of non-resolution of all problem types). Courts and ombudsmen seemed to play in minimal role in the resolution of consumer disputes. Among all consumer cases, less than 1% ended in any kind of court hearing and in a very small proportion of cases proceedings had been started (3%) although the case did not come to a hearing. Of those that went to a hearing, most were dealt with in the small claims procedure and the remainder in the county court[3]. In half of the hearings the respondent was the plaintiff and in half the respondent was the defendant.

Looking at outcomes of consumer problems in relation to advice-seeking, it appears that those who did *not* obtain advice about solving their consumer problem were, on the whole, quite successful in achieving an agreement. About 57% of those who took action without advice

---

[3] However, it is possible that parties were unclear of the precise name of the procedure. Small claims hearings are held within the county court.

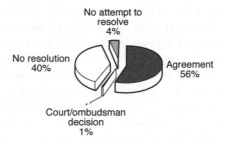

Figure 5.7. Outcome of consumer problems. (Base = all consumer problems 196 weighted)

succeeded in reaching some sort of agreement with the other side, which compared favourably with those who obtained advice about their consumer problem, of whom 58% succeeded in reaching an agreement with the other side. This finding may simply reflect the fact that advice was largely obtained once it was clear that a direct self-help approach had failed. It is interesting to note that there were no consumer cases that went to court without advice first being obtained.

Those who were advised and those who handled their consumer cases alone also had identical rates of non-resolution (41%). It therefore seems that if a direct approach fails, considerable effort is needed to achieve a resolution. This reflects the argument in Chapter 3 that outcome depends on the person, the problem and the opponent.

Outcome of employment problems

Among all employment cases included in the main survey, about 7% of respondents took no action to resolve their problem, about 27% resolved the problem by means of an agreement with their employer and about 14% ended with a court or tribunal decision. In just over half of the employment problems reported (52%), no agreement was reached and no formal resolution to the problem was achieved, although in six percent of all cases employees said that the problem had resolved itself. Of those employment cases that went to a hearing, two-thirds were heard in industrial tribunals and one third of cases went to the county court (the industrial tribunals were renamed "Employment Tribunals" after the fieldwork had been completed). In cases where a decision was given at the end of a hearing 60% of employees said that they had won and 40% said that they had lost their case.

Comparing outcomes of cases in relation to advice-seeking, we find that all of those who became involved in court or tribunal proceedings obtained advice about resolving the employment problem from an outside advice source. In fact employment cases where advice was obtained were more likely to end in a tribunal hearing than an agreement, although 40% of employees lost their case at the tribunal hearing. Although the number of respondents with employment problems who failed to obtain advice is rather small, the indication from the analysis is that one in three of these self-helpers achieved an agreement to resolve the problem (38%). However, the remaining 62% of self-helpers failed to achieve a resolution by agreement or by means of adjudication. Whether or not advice was obtained about resolving employment problems, in over *one half* of all employment cases no resolution to the problem was achieved by agreement or legal decision.

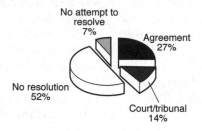

Figure 5.8. Outcome of employment problems. (Weighted base = 88)

Outcome of divorce and separation problems

There were virtually no cases of divorce and separation problems where the respondent claimed that no action had been taken to resolve the problem (1%). Over half of all divorce and separation problems ended with a court decision or court order (56%) and a further two percent were waiting for a hearing date at the time of the interview. This is a much higher rate of involvement in court proceedings than for any other category of problem. One in five cases (21%) had been resolved by means of agreement (in a handful of cases as a result of mediation).

At the time of the interview there had been no agreement to resolve the problem in about one in five cases (22%) although in about 1% of those cases the respondent said that the problem had resolved itself. The proportion of divorce/separation problems in which the respondent reported that there had been no resolution was the *lowest* of all problem types.

It is not possible to make a comparison between the outcome of divorce cases where advice was received and those where it was not received, since the number of respondents falling into the latter category is rather small. It is worth noting, however, that there were no cases involving divorce or separation problems that ended in a court hearing without the respondent having received advice.

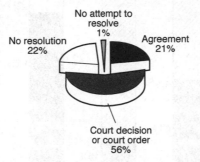

No attempt to
resolve
1%

No resolution
22%

Agreement
21%

Court decision
or court order
56%

Figure 5.9. Outcome of divorce and separation problems. (Weighted base = 111)

Outcome of neighbour problems

Almost all of those respondents who had experienced a problem with a neighbour had taken some kind of action to try and resolve the problem, but as Figure 5.10 shows, neighbour disputes had a very low resolution rate. In about seven out of ten neighbour disputes no agreement was reached to resolve the dispute (71%), although about 16% of this group said that the problem eventually resolved itself—in some cases by the complainant moving house. In just over a quarter of cases (26%) some kind of agreement was reached to resolve the dispute (1% after the issue of court proceedings) and in a very small minority of cases the neighbour dispute ended in a court hearing (1%).

Most respondents experiencing a problem with a neighbour had obtained advice about trying to resolve the problem (77%) and it seems clear that obtaining legal advice from a solicitor or Law Centre has an influence on outcome. As can be seen from Figure 5.10, respondents who obtained advice from a solicitor or Law Centre achieved some sort of agreement in 48% of cases as compared with only 15% of cases where other advice was obtained and 30% of cases where no advice was obtained. The non-resolution rate among neighbour cases was the highest of all problem types and this is explored further in the final section of the chapter. In all of the neighbour cases that went to court, the respondent had received advice about resolving the problem.

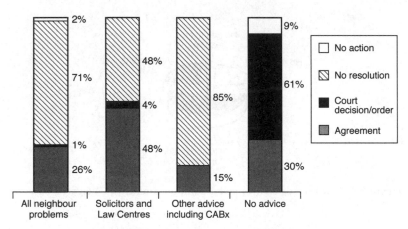

Figure 5.10. Outcome of neighbour problems in relation to advice. (Weighted base = 105)

Outcome of money problems

About seven percent of respondents who had experienced non-trivial money problems (excluding benefits issues) had failed to take any action to try and resolve the problem and the same percentage of cases involving money problems ended with a court decision or decision by an ombudsman. In *all money cases* where there was a court hearing the respondent had been the *defendant* in the case, reinforcing the view of the courts being used more by institutional plaintiffs than private plaintiffs—at least in the context of matters to do with money and finances.

A little under half (47%) of all of money problems ended with some agreement being reached between the parties (none of which followed the issue of court proceedings). In around two in five of money cases (38%) there had been no resolution of the problem, although a very small minority of these said that the problem had somehow resolved itself (3%).

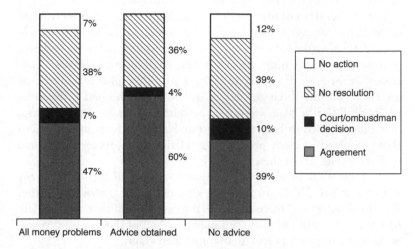

Figure 5.11. Outcome of money problems in relation to advice. (Weighted base = 135)

Figure 5.11 provides a comparison of the outcomes of cases involving money problems in relation to whether advice was obtained. The Figure indicates that those respondents who had sought advice about their money problem were significantly more likely to reach an agreement to resolve the problem than those who did not seek advice. It is notable that a relatively large proportion of those respondents whose cases went to a court hearing had *not* obtained any advice about their money problem.

Outcome of accidental injury and work-related ill health cases

In about 13% of cases included in the main survey where respondents had suffered accidental injury or work-related ill health that required medical treatment, no action was taken to seek any compensation or other remedy. This was the largest proportion of respondents taking no action of any problem type. Among those accident and ill-health victims who took some action to obtain redress, only a very small proportion tried to handle the problem themselves without first taking some advice (about 14%). However, of the small number who did take some action without advice, about one in three said that they had succeeded in settling the claim by agreement with the other side.

In a further third of the cases (35%) an agreement had been reached between the parties to settle the claim after receiving advice (about 6% apparently after the issue of court proceedings). A relatively small proportion of personal injury and work-related ill health cases were concluded on the basis of a court decision (5%), although at the time of the interview another three percent of respondents who had suffered an injury or ill health were waiting for a court hearing. In all of the cases that ended in a court hearing the respondent won their case and all of those involved in court proceedings relating to injury or illness had received advice about their claim.

In about 47% of all injury and work-related ill health cases the respondent had failed to reach any kind of agreement with the other side. In about 8% of these cases the respondent said that the problem had somehow resolved itself, but in almost half of these cases this was because the respondent had abandoned their claim.

It is impossible to analyse the outcome of personal injury cases in relation to advice since so few respondents took any action to resolve the problem without obtaining advice. Accident victims appear either to do nothing, or to take action with the benefit of advice, usually from a legal adviser (see previous discussion in Chapter 3).

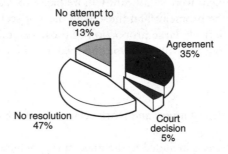

Figure 5.12. Outcome of accidental injury and work related ill-health. (Weighted base = 84 weighted)

Outcome of landlord problems

In almost all cases included in the main survey involving problems relating to landlords, respondents took some action to try and resolve the difficulty. In only four percent of cases did respondents say that they had taken no advice or any other kind of action to deal with the problem. As compared with other categories of problem, difficulties with landlords appeared to be rather difficult to resolve. Almost two in three of all landlord cases (65%) remained unresolved at the time of the interview. About one quarter of cases had been resolved on the basis of an agreement (23% with about 4% being agreed after the issue of court proceedings) and about eight percent ended following a court decision.

The analysis of the outcome of problems to do with landlords in relation to advice shows that there was little difference in outcome whether or not advice was taken, except that respondents who had obtained advice were much more likely to be involved in a court hearing than those who did not take any advice. This was especially true for the small minority who obtained legal advice.

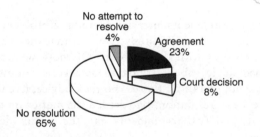

Figure 5.13. Outcome of problems with landlords. (Weighted base = 101 weighted)

Outcome of benefits problems

None of the respondents interviewed in the main survey about problems to do with receiving benefits said that they had taken no action to deal with the problem. In a very high proportion of cases, by comparison with other problem types, problems to do with receiving benefits were resolved on the basis of an adjudication, although this is not surprising since benefits matters can only be heard in tribunals and any action taken by a respondent to challenge a decision about a benefit will automatically lead to a tribunal hearing. Of the 39 (unweighted) respondents interviewed in the main survey about problems relating to benefits, nine reported that their case had been decided at a tribunal hearing. Eight respondents reported that the problem had been resolved by reaching an agreement with the other side, but in over half of the cases (22 out of 39) respondents said that there had been no resolution of the problem.

Most respondents with benefit problems had obtained advice about their problem (22 out of 39) and where advice had been obtained, the rate of resolution was relatively high. Of those respondents who tried to deal with the problem without advice, nine out of twelve reported that they had not achieved any resolution of the problem. Among those who did receive advice, five out of the 27 succeeded in settling the matter by agreement and nine respondents had the matter decided by a tribunal. Of those who had received advice, therefore, under half said that there had been no resolution of the matter.

Outcome of problems to do with unfair treatment by the police

Of the fourteen respondents interviewed about a problem to do with unfair treatment by the police, only two said that they had taken no action at all to deal with the problem. Of those who took action most obtained advice about trying to achieve a resolution of the problem (nine out of 14). Of those who took advice, five did not succeed in achieving a resolution, two settled the matter on the basis of an agreement, and two respondents had the matter decided at a court hearing.

Outcome of clinical negligence problems

Of the nineteen respondents interviewed about clinical negligence, two reported that they had taken no action to try and obtain a remedy. Of the seventeen respondents who said that they had taken some action, only two had actually obtained advice and neither of these achieved any kind of resolution of the problem. Of the fifteen self-helpers who took action following clinical negligence, six respondents said that they had succeeded in resolving the problem on the basis of an agreement with the other side and nine said that they had achieved no resolution of the problem.

Outcome of problems with schooling of children

There were about 19 cases in which respondents had been involved in a problem to do with their child's schooling. In *none* of these cases did the respondent say that they had taken no action at all to try and resolve the problem and over half obtained advice about resolving the problem. A relatively high proportion of these cases concerning schooling were resolved on the basis of an adjudication by an education appeal committee (six out of the nineteen). As is the case with benefits problems, the only forum for the resolution of the problem is a tribunal. Six respondents said that they had managed to resolve the problem by reaching an agreement with the other side and seven respondents reported that there had been no resolution of the problem. Those respondents who had obtained advice about the problem were more likely to have resolved the problem on the basis of an agreement than those who had taken no advice (half of those taking advice compared with one out of nine not taking advice).

Dispute resolution?

In the vast majority of cases where an agreement had been reached between the parties or a where a court or tribunal decision had been given, this effectively ended the dispute between the respondent and their opponent. In nine out of ten cases the respondent said that the agreement or decision had completely or partly ended the dispute between the two sides, although in nine percent of these cases the respondent said that the dispute had only been partly ended. Comparing agreements and court decisions it is clear that agreements appear to bring disputes to an end more completely than do court decisions. Among cases where the respondent reported that the matter had been resolved by agreement, 84% of those respondents said that the agreement had completely ended the dispute and nine percent said that it had partly ended the dispute. Only seven percent of those who had reached an agreement with the other side said that the agreement had failed to end the dispute.

By contrast, those respondents whose cases had been resolved on the basis of a court, ombudsman, or tribunal adjudication were considerably *more* likely to say that the decision had *not* brought the dispute to an end. Some 16% of respondents whose cases ended with a court hearing said that the decision had not ended the problem. A further nine percent said that the decision had only partly ended the dispute. In two-thirds of cases where agreements or court decisions had not wholly ended the dispute, the problem was reported to be still on-going. These findings together with evidence about abandoned cases suggest that in a high level of cases no resolution to problems is achieved and that simply taking advice does not necessarily lead to an agreement to resolve the problem. This reflects some of the problems with the kind of advice available to respondents, discussed in Chapter 3. The relationship between advice and outcome is explored further through multivariate analysis in section three below.

SECTION 2. THE FINANCIAL COST OF PURSUING A RESOLUTION TO
JUSTICIABLE DISPUTES

Legal Costs

Among those cases where legal advice had been obtained or a decision given by a court, tribunal or ombudsman, 14% of respondents said that they had incurred no legal costs; 16% said that their legal costs had been paid by their opponent; and the remaining 70% said that their opponent did not pay their legal costs, suggesting that the majority of people involved in legal proceedings were responsible for their own costs[4].

Just over one in four of those respondents who had incurred legal costs had been offered legal aid (27%) and of these, two percent refused the offer of legal aid. By far the greatest use of legal aid was among

---

[4] It has to be borne in mind, however, that previous research seeking to ascertain information about legal costs has shown that respondents are notoriously vague about costs and responsibility for dealing with them. See Law Commission study on personal injury claims and Oxford survey of personal injury litigation op cit. See also John Baldwin, *Monitoring the Rise of the Small Claims Limit: Litigants' Experiences of Different Forms of Adjudication*, London, Lord Chancellor's Department, Research Series No 1/97, 1997. Baldwin comments, "Most of the people who were interviewed were surprisingly vague about how much they had actually expended on the litigation . . . an attempt to estimate the scale of expenses incurred in pursuing an action in the county courts had to be abandoned as it would have been too crude and inaccurate to be worthwhile", p 30.

those experiencing divorce and separation problems, where a little over half of those incurring legal costs received legal aid. Those experiencing other kinds of justiciable problem who incurred legal costs were far less likely to have received legal aid. For example, among those who incurred legal costs in the course of dealing with a dispute with their landlord about one in three had obtained legal aid; a little under one in five of those with employment problems incurring legal costs obtained legal aid; and about one in ten of those bringing personal injury claims who incurred legal costs had received legal aid. There were also small proportions of neighbour problems, consumer problems, and money problems where legal costs had been incurred and legal aid had been obtained (Figure 5.14).

About three percent of respondents with legal costs had been supported by legal expenses insurance, and a trade union or staff association backed another three percent. About two percent of those incurring legal costs said that they had been offered a conditional fee arrangement and this had been offered by a solicitor in 80% of cases and by another sort of legal consultant in the remaining cases. Two-thirds of conditional fee arrangements were in the form of written agreements. Finally, about four percent of respondents who incurred legal costs said that they had been offered free legal advice, generally by a solicitor or friend or relative.

Not all respondents who incurred legal costs were, according to their reports, involved in formal legal proceedings. Among those who said that proceedings had been issued or a hearing held, one-quarter had legal aid, two percent had legal expenses insurance, three percent were backed by a trade union or staff association, and one percent said that they had received free legal advice. This leaves over two thirds (68%) of those involved in formal legal proceedings apparently responsible personally for their own legal costs.

Of all those respondents who incurred some legal costs, whether or not legal proceedings were commenced, about one in three said that they had paid some of those costs personally and a further four percent said that they expected to have to pay some money in legal costs. Among those who had paid some legal costs themselves, the median amount paid was £198 (mean £829, range £5–£8500). One-quarter of all those who paid some legal costs themselves said that they paid less than £50. Half of all those who had to pay legal costs paid less than £200. Three-quarters of those who paid their own legal costs said that they paid less than £950, and one quarter paid more than £950. If these figures are correct, then the fears expressed by respondents in Chapter 3, and those vividly expressed in Chapter 6 may be somewhat exaggerated, although for many people in difficult circumstances even £50 is an unaffordable amount of money to obtain redress. Moreover, among the group of respondents who reported that they had paid some legal costs, about one-fifth said that they had *not* expected to have to pay anything in legal costs.

About one in ten of those incurring legal costs had been worried about having to pay their own legal costs; about one percent had been worried about paying the other side's legal costs and about five percent had been worried about paying both their own and their opponent's costs. However, some 84% of respondents who had incurred legal costs said that they *had not been worried* at any stage about having to pay legal costs. This is difficult to interpret and may simply suggest that those who were likely to be concerned about legal costs simply either did not seek legal advice or did not begin legal proceedings.

An analysis of sources of financing legal advice and action within problem types suggests that divorce matters and actions relating to tenancy problems were the most likely to have been dealt with by means of legal aid funding (Figure 5.14). Conditional fees were occasionally used for personal injury and employment problems, and trade union support was used for accidents and employment problems. In most of the problem types, however, it appears that a large proportion of respondents sought legal advice or began legal proceedings without any type of insurance against legal costs. This was most often the case for problems relating to ownership of property, consumer problems, and money problems. For divorce and separation problems, consumer problems, landlord and tenant problems and problems relating to ownership of residential property, the only form of assistance with legal costs was through legal aid, other than in the odd instance when free legal advice had been given.

Other costs

About 60% of *all* respondents to the main questionnaire reported that they had incurred other costs in sorting out their justiciable problem. These costs were most often telephone calls, travelling costs and, less often, loss of earnings. In about one-half of cases these costs did not exceed £10 and in a further one-fifth of cases the costs did not exceed

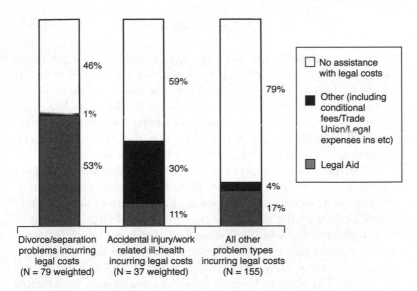

Figure 5.14. Financing of legal action by problem type. (Base = Legal costs incurred 348 weighted)

£50. In about three percent of cases, however, the cost of sorting out the problem was said to have been more than £10,000 (Figure 5.15). About 15% of respondents said that they had taken time off work or used annual leave to sort out the problem.

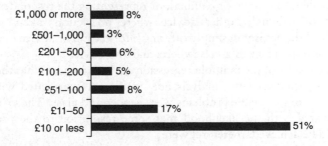

Figure 5.15. Cost of resolving dispute excluding legal costs. (Base = all those with costs 612 weighted)

SECTION 3. EXPLAINING OUTCOME

In order to identify factors that were significantly associated with the outcome of cases, a multiple regression analysis, similar to that undertaken for advice-seeking, was carried out. The analysis of outcome distinguished between cases in which a resolution had been reached either through agreement, or court decision or order, tribunal or ombudsman's adjudication (resolved), and those cases where there had been no agreement or adjudication or court order (not resolved).

The purpose of the analysis was to try and estimate the distinct contribution to different outcomes made by particular factors and to say whether respondents with specific characteristics might be more or less likely than the average respondent to achieve a resolution of their justiciable problem. The factors included in the multiple-regression analysis of outcome were demographic factors such as age, sex, education, income, class, employment status, as well as other factors hypothesised as likely to have an influence on outcome; for example the type of problem experienced, the type of remedy sought by the respondent; and whether the respondent was initiating the action or was the subject of action. The analysis also included a variable concerning whether any advice had been obtained and the source of that advice. For the purpose of this analysis the definitions of advice used in the first section of the chapter were further refined as follows: "legal advice" involving advice from a solicitor (and very occasionally a law centre); "other advice where action taken" which involved the adviser taking positive steps to assist in the resolution of the problem by contacting the other side, negotiating with the other side, contacting another person to try and resolve the problem, accompanying the respondent to a court or tribunal, or representing the respondent at a court or tribunal; "other advice where no action taken" which involved the adviser in simply offering information or advice or advising the respondent to go elsewhere; and "no advice".

The results of the multiple regression analysis indicate that the only factors included in the analysis *not* significantly correlated with the outcome of justiciable problems were gender and class. Those factors associated with the likelihood that some resolution to the problem would be achieved, therefore, were:

• the type of justiciable problem experienced
• the remedy desired (money or non-money remedy)

- the type of advice obtained
- the respondent's age
- the respondent's income
- the respondent's educational qualifications
- whether the respondent was the plaintiff or the defendant.

Of these important factors, the four most strongly correlated with the likelihood that the problem would be resolved were, the type of justiciable problem experienced, the remedy desired by the respondent (money or non-money), whether the respondent was a plaintiff or a defendant, and the type of advice received by the respondent.

Type of justiciable problem

The analysis revealed that respondents with employment problems, neighbour problems, or problems with their landlord were *less* likely to achieve a resolution of the problem than average respondents. For example, respondents with neighbour problems were about 49% *less* likely than average to achieve a resolution of the problem; respondents with landlord and tenant problems were 37% *less* likely than average to achieve a resolution of their problem; and respondents with employment problems were about 31% *less* likely than average to achieve a resolution of the problem.

On the other hand, respondents experiencing consumer problems were about 84% *more* likely than the average respondent to achieve a resolution of the problem; those with divorce and separation problems were about 68% *more* likely than average to achieve a resolution of the problem; and those with money problems (excluding matters to do with benefits) were about 65% *more* likely than the average respondent to have the case resolved.

Type of remedy desired

For the purposes of this analysis respondents were divided between those seeking a non-money remedy, those seeking a lump sum of money and those seeking regular payments of money. The analysis indicates that when the desired remedy did not involve money, the likelihood of achieving a resolution of the problem was about 18% *lower* than average. If a lump sum was the desired remedy, those seeking less than £500 were about 61% less likely to achieve a resolution than those seeking more than £500. Respondents seeking regular payments of money were also more likely to achieve a resolution than those seeking a non-money remedy, with the odds of resolution estimated at about 41% higher.

Whether the respondent was the plaintiff or the defendant

The results of the analysis suggest that after controlling for the factors included in the analysis, cases were about 57% more likely to be resolved when the respondent was a defendant than when the respondent was a plaintiff. This finding is unsurprising since "resolution" includes matters ending in court proceedings and the analysis in the first part of the chapter described the greater extent to which those having action taken against them were involved in legal proceedings and in court hearings.

Type of advice obtained

On the basis of the redefinition of legal advice described above, the multivariate analysis shows that, after controlling for the factors included in the analysis, cases in which no advice at all was obtained were 45% less likely to be resolved than those cases were advice was obtained from a solicitor or law centre. Cases in which advice was obtained only from other advice sources (including from CABx), and where the help given was limited to the provision of information and advice, were 30% *less* likely to be resolved than where advice had been obtained from a solicitor or law centre. When advice was obtained from other advice sources (including CABx) and active assistance was provided, the results were not significantly different from those when advice was obtained from a solicitor or law centre.

The similarity in resolution rates between cases obtaining legal advice and those obtaining other advice with active assistance reflects the discussion in Chapter 3 about the extent to which the provision of mere information or advice may be inadequate for certain kinds of cases and certain kinds of respondents. The results of the multivariate analysis show that when controlling for a wide range of factors, the type of advice and assistance obtained is significantly correlated with outcome.

Other factors found to be significantly, but less strongly correlated with the outcome of justiciable problems were education, income, age and employment status[5].

Respondent's educational qualifications

Respondents with no educational qualifications were *less* likely than average to achieve a resolution of their dispute while those with A levels were more likely than average to achieve a resolution[6].

Respondent's income

Respondents with an annual income of less than £8,000 were about 25% *less* likely than average to achieve a resolution of their dispute while those with an annual salary of more than £29,000 were about 44% *more* likely than average to achieve a resolution of their problem.

Respondent's age

Younger respondents between the ages of 25 and 34 were about 32% *more* likely than average to achieve a resolution of their problem. On the other hand, older respondents of age 65 or more were about 37% *less* likely than average to resolve their problem.

Interaction of factors associated with outcome

The analysis in this section so far has identified several factors that appear to be associated with the likelihood that a resolution of the justiciable problem would be achieved. It is not evident, however, how these various factors interact. To address this question an analysis similar to that carried out for advice-seeking was undertaken[7] and the

---

[5] Although employment status was significantly correlated with outcome, the correlation is fairly weak and the results for different categories were all on the borderline of significance.

[6] The results for those with degree level qualifications were on the borderline of significance.

[7] The CHAID (Chi-squared Automatic Interaction Detector) module within SPSS. The full results of the CHAID analysis are given in Appendix B.

results make it possible to identify a number of subgroups of respondents with similar characteristics and with varying propensity to achieve a resolution of their justiciable problem. The analysis produced nine different (mutually exclusive and exhaustive) groups for which the percentage of cases achieving a resolution of the problem varied from 17% to 66%. The characteristics of these groups are discussed below.

Low propensity for cases to be resolved

The analysis suggests that the group of respondents *least* likely of all to achieve a resolution of their problem had only two characteristics:

• A problem to do with neighbours or landlord
• Respondent had no educational qualifications.

The rate at which this group achieved a resolution of their problem was about 17 per 100 and the group was relatively small, comprising only 5% of all respondents interviewed in the main survey.

The group with the next lowest propensity to achieve a resolution of their problem had the following characteristics:

• A problem concerning divorce or separation, money, consumer problem, tribunal matter (benefits or schooling), owning property
• The respondent was over the age of 65.

The resolution rate among this group was about 23 per hundred and the group was the smallest of all those produced by the analysis, comprising about four percent of the sample as a whole.

A third group with a relatively low propensity to achieve a resolution of the problem had the following characteristics:

• A problem relating to employment or accidental injury
• The respondent did not obtain advice, or obtained "other" advice (including CABx) where no active assistance was provided by the adviser.

Among this group the rate at which problems were resolved was about 23 per hundred and the group represented about six percent of the total sample.

Another group with a relatively low propensity to achieve a resolution to their problem had the following characteristics:

- A problem with neighbours or with a landlord
- The respondent had a degree, A level or O level qualification.

This relatively large group of respondents had a resolution rate of 33% and comprised about 14% of the sample.

Average propensity for cases to be resolved

A group with about average propensity to achieve a resolution of their problem had somewhat different characteristics. These were:

- A problem relating employment or accidental injury
- Respondent obtained advice from a solicitor/law centre, or from an "other" adviser (including CAB) who provided active assistance.

About 47% of this group succeeded in achieving a resolution of their problem either by agreement or adjudication and the group comprised about 9% of the sample as a whole.

High propensity for cases to be resolved

There were two identifiable groups with a higher than average propensity to achieve a resolution of their dispute and they appear to have several common defining characteristics. The first of these was very large and comprised over one third of the sample. The characteristics were:

- Problem concerning divorce or separation, money problem, consumer problem, owning property, or DSS/education tribunal matter
- Respondent under 65 years of age
- Remedy sought either non-money or less than £500.

The rate at which problems were resolved among this group either by agreement or on the basis of a court decision or court order was 56%.

The group among whom problems had the greatest propensity to be resolved is identical to the previous group except in respect of the remedy being sought. The characteristics are as follows:

- A problem relating to divorce or separation, money, consumer matters, owning property, or DSS/education tribunal matter
- The respondent was under 65 years of age
- The desired remedy was regular payments of money or a lump sum of *more than* £500.

This group represented about ten percent of the total sample and had a resolution rate of about 66 per hundred.

The results of the analysis of the interaction of factors associated with the outcome of justiciable problems confirm some of the analyses in earlier chapters. What emerges again is the extent to which certain problem types appear to be more intractable than others, the effect of certain demographic factors such as education and age on the likelihood that problems will be resolved, and the influence of different kinds of advice and assistance on the likelihood that problems can be resolved.

Conclusion

The discussion in this chapter has focused on the outcome of justiciable problems. The chief outcome with which the chapter has been concerned is whether or not the justiciable problems experienced by members of the public had been resolved. "Resolution" has been defined as an agreement to end or settle the problem (with or without the commencement of legal proceedings) ("agreement"), or the conclusion of the matter by means of a court, tribunal or ombudsman's decision or order ("adjudication"). No judgement has been made about the quality of agreements or respondents' satisfaction with the terms of agreements. "Resolution" also includes cases where the respondent won their case in court and where they lost their case in court. "Unresolved" cases are those that were in effect abandoned after action was taken, but in the absence of any settlement or adjudication.

The analysis has shown that about half of all members of the public who experience non-trivial justiciable problems fail to achieve any resolution to those problems, whether or not they seek advice. Fifty percent of self-helpers failed to achieve any kind of resolution of their problem, but so did a similar proportion of those who obtained advice at some point about their problem (46%). However, these figures obscure two important facts. First, that the vast majority of those who sought advice had already tried to resolve their problem alone. This means that cases in which advice was sought are almost by definition the more serious or more intractable. Second, it obscures differences in the degree of assistance obtained from advisers.

A proportion of those who received advice were told that it was not worth pursuing the case and most respondents who received this advice took it. In this way the availability of good quality advice can filter weak cases out of the system and save individuals the time, expense and heartache that they might otherwise have spent in pursuing a fruitless cause. On the other hand, the relatively low level of advice to abandon cases that was actually given by advisers (discussed in the previous chapter) suggests that those taking the step of seeking advice had persevered with some justification. In those circumstances the very high failure rate is notable.

An important fact emerging clearly from the analysis in this chapter is the very limited use made by the public of formal legal proceedings to resolve justiciable problems. In about eight out of ten problems no legal proceedings were commenced, no ombudsman was contacted and no ADR process was used. This is despite the fact that about three in five members of the public took some advice about trying to resolve their problem, and that of those, about half received advice from a solicitor at some point about their problem[8]. Involvement in legal proceedings was most common in cases concerning divorce and separation, DSS and education tribunal matters, ownership of residential property, employment disputes, and accidental injury. Involvement in legal proceedings was least common in neighbour disputes, and consumer disputes.

Only a very small proportion of cases ended on the basis of a court order or tribunal adjudication, and those members of the sample whose problem was resolved by adjudication were disproportionately members of the public who were being *pursued* via legal proceedings rather than those who were *initiating* action. In the case of defendants, problems were far more likely to be concluded on the basis of a court decision or order than in the case of plaintiffs, and far less likely to remain unresolved. This demonstrates the reluctance voluntarily to become involved in legal proceedings that was so graphically described by respondents in Chapter 3.

According to respondents' reports, the majority of people involved in legal proceedings and who incurred legal costs were responsible for their own costs. About one in four respondents incurring legal costs received legal aid. By far the greatest use of legal aid was among those experiencing divorce and separation problems, where a little over half of those incurring legal costs received legal aid. Legal expenses insurance was used by a handful of respondents who incurred legal costs, as were conditional fee arrangements. A rather larger handful of those

---

[8] See discussion in Chapter 3.

who incurred legal costs had received free legal advice from a solicitor, friend or relative.

On the whole the amounts of money reported to have been paid out by respondents by way of legal costs were relatively modest, although the information provided by respondents about their costs might be unreliable. Other costs were incurred in the course of trying to resolve justiciable problems, such as telephone calls, travelling costs and taking time off work to sort out problems.

The results of multivariate analysis again confirm that problem type is enormously important in the outcome of justiciable problems, although factors such as the type of remedy desired, whether the respondent was a plaintiff or a defendant, and the type of advice and assistance obtained also help to explain different outcomes. Some problems appear to have a generally low rate of resolution, for example employment problems, neighbour problems and problems with landlords. Those with higher rates of resolution are divorce and separation problems, money problems, and consumer problems. The analysis shows that when legal advice is obtained from solicitors or law centres, or when agencies or other advisers provide active assistance, the likelihood that a case will end in an agreement, adjudication, or court order is increased. For example, an employment problem or personal injury problem with the benefit of advice from a solicitor or active assistance from another adviser will have an above average rate of resolution. However, the same types of problems without advice from solicitors or active assistance from other advisers have a lower than average rate of resolution. This seems to bear out the judgements made by some respondents and reported in Chapter 3 that going to a CAB and being given a list of people to telephone is not comparable with an adviser making the telephone calls, or offering credible threats of legal action to an intransigent opponent. The implications of these findings for the Community Legal Service are discussed in Chapter 8.

Problems were more likely to reach some kind of resolution when a money remedy was being sought by or from the respondent, than when the remedy required was some change in behaviour. Using the law to change behaviour can be tortuous, expensive, and potentially damaging, but the use of alternative dispute resolution processes such as mediation among the sample of respondents dealing with justiciable problems was negligible. This fact is notable when considered in relation to the finding reported in this chapter that agreements appear to bring disputes to an end more completely than do court decisions.

6
Fulfilling Objectives?

This chapter focuses on respondents' reported motivation for taking action to try and resolve their justiciable problem, and the extent to which those objectives were achieved during the course of trying to resolve the problem. The discussion also describes some of the effects of trying to achieve those objectives and the extent to which the outcomes achieved were regarded as fair. In the second section of the chapter the results of multivariate analysis are used to explain further the factors that are associated with the achievement of objectives and perceptions of the fairness of outcomes.

IDENTIFYING OBJECTIVES

The approach taken to the identification of objectives in the survey was quite deliberate. Anticipating a complex and subtle mix of objectives and the possibility that objectives might develop and change over time, an elaborate series of questions was posed to respondents. Rather than suggesting a range of possible objectives or motivations to respondents as has been the practice in other recent surveys[1], completely open questions were asked about objectives. This was done to avoid influencing response by implying any expectation of altruism.

First, respondents were asked about their initial main objective (*"Thinking back to when you first decided to do something about [the problem] what was the main thing you wanted to achieve?"*). This was followed by supplementary questions designed to elicit additional objectives (*"At that stage, were there any other things that you hoped*

---

[1] For example the NCC survey in 1995, and the SCC survey in 1997. The approach adopted in these surveys was to ask "What do/did you most want the law to help you to achieve?" Respondents were then asked to choose, from eight different outcomes, the one that was most important to them. The outcomes were: "Financial compensation; Prevent it happening again to me; Prevent it happening to someone else in future; An apology; Judgment about who is to blame; Clearing my name; An explanation; Public exposure of the cuplrit."

to achieve?"); this question was repeated until all of the respondent's objectives had been identified. In addition to the questions about initial objectives, further questions were asked in order to capture any changes that might have occurred in respondents' objectives during the course of trying to resolve their problem (*"You've now told me about what you wanted to achieve initially. During the course of trying to sort out [the problem] did you change your mind at any time about what you wanted to achieve?"*). For each initial and subsequent objective recorded, respondents were asked to say whether they had achieved their objective completely, partly, or not at all. As will be seen in later discussion, the time taken in probing objectives and trying to capture changes in objectives yielded rather less than had been anticipated since respondents generally had only one driving motivation and that was very specifically calibrated to the nature of the problem.

INITIAL PRIMARY OBJECTIVES

In response to the open question asked about main objectives, the single most common objective offered by respondents for taking action to resolve their problem was money or property related. Over half of all respondents said that their main aim in taking action was money or property related (51% of all main aims), which is unsurprising given the balance of problem types in the sample (Figure 6.1). Examples of the kinds of money or property related aims mentioned by respondents to the survey were as follows:

"I wanted them to pay for my physiotherapy treatment."
"Get money for my car which was a write-off."
"To pay a fair price for the work carried out."
"To stop the debt collector claiming money from us".
"To get the money back I had lost through bad advice."
"To recover my loss of earnings".
"To get the goods repaired."

The next most common motivation for taking action was to obtain a separation or divorce, or to deal with property following divorce or separation, or to deal with matters relating to children as a result of a divorce or separation (about eight percent of respondents taking action). For example:

"I didn't want my ex-partner to have any rights of access."

"To get back together with my wife".

"To remain in contact with my son".

"I wanted secretly to come back—a reconciliation."

"I wanted a divorce as quick as possible. I wanted to be rehoused. And I just wanted to get my family back, which meant I knew I had to go to court to get an injunction out of my ex-husband with power of arrest. I knew I'd have to go through that because I knew what my husband was like. **How did you know about that sort of procedure?** It's just general talk that you pick up on your TV and stuff like that . . ." (*Divorced woman, subjected to violence*)

About seven percent of respondents said that their primary aim for taking action was to achieve a change in the behaviour of the other party involved in the problem. Examples were to achieve a reduction in noise or to get some peace and quiet; to keep the other person away from the respondent or the respondent's family; to stop the hassle or aggravation being perpetrated by the other person involved in the problem or dispute. For example:

"To be left alone to live as a family without hassle from an unreasonable neighbour".

"I just wanted communication with my neighbour regarding the problem."

"To get him to have some respect for his neighbours".

"To get them to train their dogs. Not to see us an enemies".

"I wanted to stop him from threatening us."

"I would like to shoot the neighbour."

"All I wanted was some peace and quiet. You'd get into bed sometimes and then it would start up. You see I am right over the top of him. The others used to moan but I'm right over the top of him. I'm not exaggerating; sometimes it was all night."

A small group of respondents said that their main objective was work-related (6%). For example:

"I just wanted my employer to know that I could not be treated in that way."

"To have my contract validated."

"Not to be made redundant".

"Just to find out for the future if the chemicals were dangerous."

"Maintain the terms and conditions that had been guaranteed."

"I wanted to clarify the situation with regard to my employment rights."

"To get the manager sacked".

"Recognition for workers who have to deal with people who are known to be violent."

"To get the time off work that I needed".

"To prove that the manager was wrong about me and my work".

About three percent of respondents wanted to prove their own innocence or to prove that the other side was in the wrong, and about another one percent said that their primary aim was to enforce their rights. In just over one percent of cases, respondents said that that they wanted to prevent the same thing from happening to others, and in less than one percent of cases respondents said that their primary objective in taking action was to achieve an apology.

In a substantial number of cases the main objective given was either so broad or so specific to the particular problem being experienced that it was difficult to code the responses into a common category. Occasionally this was because people simply said that they wanted "justice", but in other cases their objective was a very specific description of how they wanted their problem to be resolved.

Rather few respondents were able to specify more than one objective in taking action, which shows a high degree of single-mindedness and rather defeated the subtlety of questioning. In all, three quarters of the sample said that they only had one objective in taking action. When respondents did mention a second objective, this tended to follow the pattern of first objectives, in that respondents predominantly mentioned money or property-related objectives, objectives relating to divorce or separation, and job-related objectives. Respondents occasionally mentioned as a second objective the desire to obtain an apology or to prevent the same thing from happening to others in a similar situation, but these were a very small minority. The following extract from a qualitative interview provides an example of the way in which a respondent explained, for example, the relationship between the desire for justice, for an apology and the desire for financial recompense.

> "I think when she started denying it we started getting very frustrated. We had hoped originally when we first set about writing to her and complaining, or telling her what had happened, that she would say, 'Look I'm very sorry. Please accept a refund, and x amount for the inconvenience' . . . We then got a denial not an apology. And she was adamant nothing was wrong with it and we were in the wrong for even suggesting it. We wanted compensation. A full refund and something to cover the whole inconvenience. We wanted justice. We felt we'd paid for something that didn't work. What is a measure of justice? Is it somebody turning round and apologising to you or can you measure it monetary terms? . . . An apology would have been nice I think. She didn't apologise. It was denial all the way. **Would an apology have been enough?** If she'd given us an apology without monetary reward I

don't think we would have been satisfied with that . . . In the end we didn't get an apology, but we got some money, and although there was no apology and they still didn't admit liability, as far as we're concerned by paying us some money back it was liability admitted, whatever they say." (*Consumer dispute*)

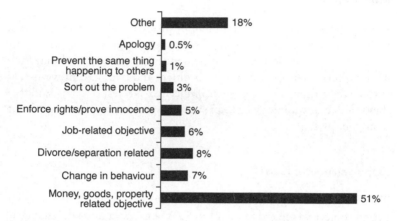

Figure 6.1. Main objectives in taking action. (Base all who took action = 1061 weighted)

The type of objective desired by respondents naturally varied substantially by problem type. Although many respondents gave objectives that were so specific that they could not be properly categorised, varying patterns of motivation emerge between different problem types that reflect the nature of the problem and the range of possible remedies.

Consumer problems

Three quarters of those with consumer problems said that their main objective was money or property related (e.g. to get my money back or a refund, compensation, to get the property or goods repaired or maintained, to have the goods replaced); about three percent said that they wanted to sort out the problem; and two percent said that they wanted to prove that the other side was in the wrong. Three percent of those with consumer problems said that their main objective in taking action

... to prevent the same thing from happening to someone else and less than one percent said that their primary motive in taking action was to receive an apology.

Money problems

Among those interviewed about money problems about 85% said that their main objective was money or property related (e.g. to get my money back, reduction of bill or demand); five percent said that their main objective was to sort out the problem and two percent wanted to enforce their rights or prove their innocence. No respondents said that they wanted any apology or to prevent the same thing from happening to anyone else.

Employment problems

Those experiencing employment problems most often mentioned a specific objective related to their job 51% (e.g. reinstatement, change in conditions). About 17% mentioned money-related objectives such as getting money back or receiving payments that they were owed; eight percent said that they wanted to prove their innocence. About seven percent of those with employment problems said that their primary motive was to receive an apology, which is about the highest proportion of any problem type, and two percent said that they wanted to prevent the same thing from happening to others.

Divorce and separation

The most commonly cited primary objective of those experiencing divorce and separation problems was to obtain a divorce or separation (19%) or to obtain a fair split of assets or property after separation or divorce (18%). A large proportion offered family-related objectives to do with children (38%). About six percent said that they wanted to get the other side to pay child support; and about two percent said that they wanted to keep the other side away from them or their house. None of those involved in divorce or separation problems said that a primary objective was to receive an apology or to prevent the same thing from happening to others.

Neighbour problems

The most common objective among those experiencing problems with neighbours was to achieve a change in the behaviour of the other side (57%), for example noise reduction, to keep the other side away from the respondent's home, to bring an end to hassle and aggravation. About six percent said that they wanted to prove that the other side was wrong or to prove their own innocence and about four percent said that they just wanted to sort out the problem. No respondents involved in neighbour disputes said that their primary objective was to receive an apology or to prevent the same thing from happening to others.

Accidental injury

Compensation was the most common motive for taking action among those suffering injury or work-related ill-health (37%); about eleven percent mentioned a motive that was job-related and about four percent said that they just wanted to sort out the problem. Not a single respondent experiencing accidental injury said that their primary motive in taking action was to receive an apology from the other side, despite the fact that this is often cited as a motivation for litigating. About six percent, however, said that their main objective in taking action was to prevent the same thing from happening to someone else. This may reflect the high number of work accidents and work-related illnesses in the sample.

Problems with landlords

Among those experiencing problems with landlords the most common reason for taking action was to get the property maintained (49%) or to get money back (11%). About four percent of respondents said that they just wanted to get the problem sorted out. No respondents experiencing problems with landlords said that their objective in taking action was to obtain an apology or to prevent the same thing from happening to others.

Changing objectives?

In order to gauge the extent to which respondents' objectives might have developed or changed over time, all were asked whether during the course of trying to sort out their problem, they had changed their mind at any time about what they wanted to achieve. Only about one in ten respondents said that there had been any change in what they had been wanting to achieve (12%), but even when this occurred there was little change between broad categories of objectives. So a respondent who had mentioned a money or property related objective as their initial primary objective would be most likely, if they reported having changed their mind about what they wanted, to mention another money related objective as their new objective. For example, some respondents began by wanting an object replaced or repaired and then changed to simply wanting a refund of the money paid out. Alternatively, some initially wanted a repair and then decided that they wanted compensation for the inconvenience suffered. There were also one or two people whose initial objective was to enforce their rights or prove their innocence, but who subsequently decided that they wanted compensation. Similarly, a small number of people who began by wanting to prevent the same thing from happening to others changed their objective to wanting compensation.

Money claimed and owed

One in four respondents was seeking to obtain some money from the other person or organisation involved in their problem (26%); about eleven percent of respondents wanted the other person or organisation to *reduce* the amount of money they were demanding from the respondent; the remaining 63% of respondents were seeking some other kind of outcome to their problem. This means that nearly two in three people were seeking a remedy *other* than direct payment of money. Among those respondents who were trying to get a reduction in the amount of money being demanded by their opponent about two-thirds (63%) were hoping to get a bill reduced, and about one third (36%) were trying to get a reduction in regular payments that they were making or being asked to make.

Most of those who were trying to obtain money from their opponent in the dispute were hoping for a lump sum (72%) and most of the remainder wanted regular payments (although 3% wanted both). The amount of money being sought (or the amount by which the respondent wanted a bill reduced) was in the majority of cases relatively modest (Figure 6.2). Almost three quarters of respondents wanted no more than £1000 (and most of those wanted no more than £500); about 18% of respondents wanted between £1000 and £5000; about six percent wanted between £5000 and £15000; and the remaining five percent were seeking over £15000.

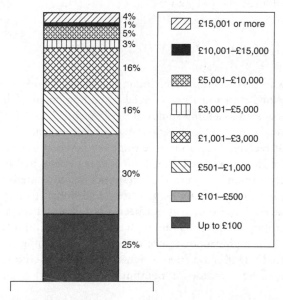

Figure 6.2. Amount of claim where respondent seeking lump sum. (Base = 282 weighted all those seeking lump sum)

The handful of cases where the amount of money at stake exceeded £15,000 comprised mainly divorce or separation cases, and one or two accidental injury cases, employment cases and money problems.

How expectations were formed

According to respondents, in over half the cases in which a sum of money was being claimed (54%), the sum being claimed was the respondent's *own* calculation of the amount he or she was entitled to.

In other cases, respondents said that the figure had been suggested by a friend or work colleague (13%) or by another organisation (10%) or by a solicitor (7%). In four percent of cases respondents arrived at their assessment of the value of the claim on the basis of previous experience; and in three percent of cases respondents said explicitly that they had based their assumption about the value of the claim on media reports of similar cases. Expectations were thus rarely based on advice and this has implications for the extent to which respondents might feel that they had achieved their objectives.

Amounts recovered

Of those who succeeded in receiving money from the other side, 90% received a lump sum and 10% received regular payments. The median amount recovered as a lump sum was £431 (mean £2,883) with a range of £6–£100,000. Although about one-half of respondents thought that the amount received was about the same as they had been expecting, about one-fifth received *much* or a *bit* less than they had hoped for. Interestingly, about a quarter of respondents said that they had received a little or much *more* than they had hoped for. Since most respondents said that they had not been advised about the amount of money that they should be claiming, but had worked it out largely for themselves, the high proportion of respondents obtaining the amount they expected might be taken as a sign of success. Indeed it seems that the majority who succeeded in obtaining a money settlement or court

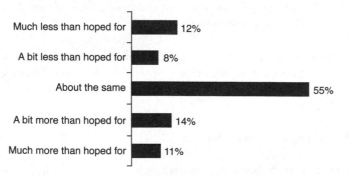

Figure 6.3. "Was this more, less or about the same amount of money as you had hoped for?" (Base = 151 weighted)

award achieved what they were hoping for or a bit more. Only one in five were disappointed in the amount obtained and they were generally respondents involved in consumer disputes, money problems, or divorce and separation. A handful of those injured in accidents or at work had received *more* than they had expected. Those who said that they had received less than they had expected were most likely to be respondents who had calculated the sum themselves or had been advised by friends or relatives. When respondents had been advised by a solicitor or other adviser they were *more* likely than others to obtain the amount they had expected, or slightly more. This underlines the role of advisers in shaping or moderating expectations.

Amounts paid out

About eight percent of respondents said that they had had to pay some of their opponent's legal costs and some 12% paid money by way of settlement to their opponent (about one-half paying lump sums and the other half making regular payments). The median lump sum paid by respondents to their opponent was £434 (mean £2,559, range £1–£30,000). Those respondents who had to pay money by way of a settlement were primarily those involved in divorce and separation problems (36% of those paying money to the other side), respondents experiencing money problems (32% of those paying money to the other side), those having problems with landlords (15%) and those involved in problems relating to residential property (8%).

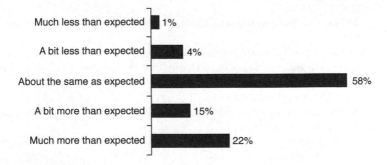

Figure 6.4. "Was this more, less or about the same amount of money as you had expected to pay?" (Base = 53)

Again, about one-half of those who had to pay something to the other side said that they paid out about the amount of money they had been expecting to pay. On the other hand, *over a third* said that they had had to pay a *little more* or *much more* than they had been expecting. About one in twenty said that they had paid less than they had expected.

OTHER AGREEMENTS—NO PAYMENT OF MONEY

In about 18% of all cases in the sample, respondents made agreements involving terms other than the direct payment of money to or by the respondent. Of the cases where a non-money agreement had been reached, the agreement nonetheless most often involved an agreement that related to money or to property. About 28% of agreements that did not directly involve the payment of money were money-related and about 46% of those agreements were to do with the repair, replacement, or maintenance of goods or property. Examples of agreements relating to money, but not involving the payment of money were as follows:

"They would convert my private pension with my company pension."

"We decided that my husband's stepmother would not get the will. She would get some money from a trust. She would get the interest while she was alive and my husband would get the money when she died."

"The bank sent a letter apologising for the inconvenience and they immediately credited the correct account."

"The council would stop sending me rent demands and eviction letters and would not contact my ex-husband about this house."

"The landlady would stop trying to get me to pay rent for remainder of the year."

"The Gas Company would stop sending me bills for gas they had not supplied."

"We agreed that he would give me a rise annually when he got a rise. We agreed that it was a clean break and I wouldn't claim on his pension or if he won the lottery or anything."

"The dentist would redo the tooth."

"The bank agreed we could continue to live in the house for an unspecified time, pending sale of property."

"That the County Council would pay for a full time ancillary worker to help my son in his education at school."

About a third of agreements that did not involve the payment of money concerned changes in the respondent's behaviour or in the behaviour of the other side. For example, keeping noise down, keeping away from the respondent or the respondent keeping away from the other side, or changes in working conditions. Examples of the kinds of agreements reached concerning behaviour were as follows:

"Contact to be made with the children during school holidays and half term."

"That I would make sure that the builders stayed as much as possible on my side of the boundary. That the builders would ensure the neighbour's garden was always secure and their dog wouldn't get loose."

"The person was demoted and removed from my immediate office and responsibility."

"It was agreed that I should have the time off work that I needed."

"I would take voluntary redundancy."

"I agreed to do more housework/ironing/cleaning/hoovering etc, and I agreed to stop going to the pub as much, and when we go out we now go out together."

"That my ex-husband would stop all contact with my son until such time that my son wished it."

"Ex-wife has to allow me regular access visits with my daughter."

"He agreed not to build the garage so that our access was maintained."

"I would restrict the playing of the drums to 3.30 p.m. to 6 p.m. on weekdays."

IMPACT OF SORTING OUT PROBLEMS

All respondents who took any action were asked whether there had been any impact on their work or personal life as a result of trying to resolve their problem. Of the two-thirds of respondents who were in paid work during the course of sorting out the dispute, only one in four reported that there had been a negative impact on their working life. The most common negative effects on working life were that the respondent had had to take time off work as a result of stress (24% of those reporting negative effects on work) or that relationships with colleagues had suffered (23% reporting). About 17% of respondents reporting negative effects on work said that they had had to move to another job or leave their place of work, and about one in ten said that their chances of promotion had been badly affected.

Such effects tended to be experienced *most often* by respondents whose problem involved employment disputes, accidental injury, and divorce or separation problems. This suggests that respondents were probably referring as much to the impact of the problem itself as to the impact of trying to sort out the problem. Respondents who were *least likely* to report negative effects on their work were those who had been involved in consumer disputes, neighbour disputes, and disputes with landlords.

All respondents who took action to resolve their problem, whether working or not, were asked whether they had experienced a range of both positive and negative feelings or situations listed on a show card (see below Table 6.1). Three out of four respondents (77%) reported having experienced one or more of the feelings or situations listed.

On the negative side almost two thirds of those reporting some impact said that they had found the experience of trying to sort out the problem stressful. Over one-quarter said that they had had difficulty

Table 6.1: Negative and positive effects of sorting out problem. (Base = all who took action 1061 weighted)

Effects of sorting out the problem	% respondents taking action	% respondents experiencing effects
None of these effects	23	
Negative effects:		
I have found the experience of trying to sort out the problem stressful	49	63
I have had difficulty sleeping	22	28
My health has suffered	22	29
My relationships with family and friends have suffered	15	20
I have had to move to another house/flat	9	11
I have had to move to another area	2	3
Positive effects:		
The experience has made me feel that I have some control over my situation	24	31
I am glad to have enforced my rights	24	31
I am glad to have cleared my name	5	6
Life is more peaceful now that I have sorted it out	*	*
Other effect on life	9	12

sleeping as a result of trying to sort out the problem (28% of cases)[2] and a similar proportion said that their health had suffered (29%). About one in five of those reporting some impact said that their relationships with family and friends had suffered (20%). About one in ten (11%) said that they had had to move to another house or flat as a result of trying to sort out the problem, and about three percent said that they had had to move to another area.

On the positive side, about one in three respondents reported that the experience had given them a sense of empowerment (31%) and an identical proportion said that they were pleased to have been able to enforce their rights (31%). About six percent said that they were glad to have been able to clear their name, and a handful said that their life had become more peaceful and less stressful as a result of sorting out the problem.

Impact and problem type

Unsurprisingly, reports of impacts experienced by respondents varied between problem types. Those most likely to say that they had experienced *none* of the listed effects, either positive or negative, were those suffering accidental injury (38% saying no effect) and those involved in disputes with their landlord (35% saying no effect). Those most likely to have experienced one or more effect were those involved in divorce and separation problems (only eight percent saying none of the effects experienced) and those involved in employment disputes (14% saying no effects experienced).

Those respondents most likely to say that they had found the experience of sorting out the problem stressful were those involved in employment disputes (80%), divorce and separation problems (77%), benefits or education tribunals (75%) and money problems (67%). Those least likely to say that they had found the experience stressful were those involved in consumer problems (40%) and accidental injury claims (42%). Over half of those experiencing divorce and separation problems said that they had had difficulty sleeping as a result of trying to sort out the problem (52%), as did about a third of those with neighbour problems (37%) and employment problems (37%).

---

[2] The figures add up to more than 100% because respondents were able to refer to as many items as they had experienced.

Those most likely to say that they were glad to have been able to enforce their legal rights were those involved in consumer disputes (46%), and those making a claim for accidental injury or work-related ill health (44%). Those involved in consumer disputes were also the most likely to say that they had felt empowered by sorting out the problem (48%), although over a third of those with money problems also felt empowered by sorting out the problem (37%).

The problems that appeared to have the most negative effects were employment, divorce, money problems, problems with landlords and to a lesser extent neighbour problems.

In the minority of cases where respondents said that they had had to move house or to another area as a result of the problem, this rather drastic outcome affected primarily those involved in neighbour disputes, matters to do with owning property and those dealing with divorce and separation issues. Occasionally those involved in employment disputes said that they had had to move house or to another area.

Impact and outcome

When comparing self-helpers with those who received advice about their problem it appears that those who received advice were *more* likely to report negative impacts than those who handled their problems alone. This is likely, however, to be a reflection of the seriousness of the matter and possibly the degree of difficulty experienced in achieving a resolution.

There were, however, significant differences in impact depending on the means by which the problem was resolved. Those respondents who resolved their problem by agreement were the *least likely* to say that they had found the experience of sorting out the problem stressful (38%) and the most likely to say that the experience had made them feel in control of the situation (36%) or that they were glad to be enforcing their rights (32%). Respondents whose problem had led to a court or tribunal adjudication were the most likely to say that the experience of resolving the problem had been stressful (68%) and that they had had difficulty sleeping (37%) and that their health had suffered (39%). Respondents who had failed to resolve their problem but who had taken some action to do so were also more likely than those who had reached an agreement to say that they had found the whole business stressful (50%) and that their health had suffered (22%) (Figure 6.5).

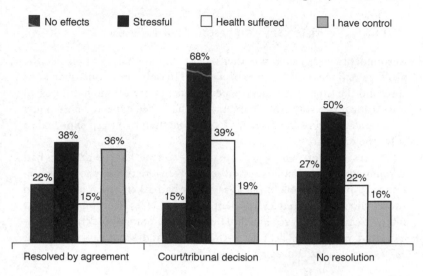

Figure 6.5. Impact of sorting out problem in relation to outcome. (Base = all those who took action 1016 weighted)

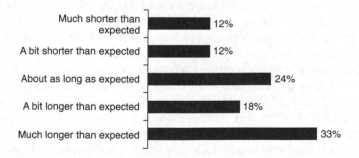

Figure 6.6. "Did solving this problem taken a shorter time than expected, about as long as expected, or a longer time than you expected?". (Base = resolved problems 520 weighted)

TIME TAKEN TO RESOLVE THE PROBLEM

Respondents were asked whether or not the time taken to resolve the problem had met with their expectations. In only about one-quarter of cases did the time taken meet expectations. In about one-half of cases it took longer to solve the problem than had been expected and in just under one-quarter of cases it look *less time* than had been expected to solve the problem.

The respondents who were most likely to feel that the problem had taken much longer than expected to resolve were those who had experienced a money problem (48% saying it had taken much longer) and those who had suffered an accidental injury (32%). Respondents most likely to say that the problem had been resolved more quickly than they expected were those dealing with divorce and separation problems (27% saying it had taken much less time).

ACHIEVING OBJECTIVES?

For each objective that had been identified, respondents were asked whether they had achieved their main objective completely or partly. Among all respondents interviewed about their objectives in taking action, fewer than half said that their main objectives had been achieved completely (41%); about 15% thought that the aim had been partly achieved; and one-third (34%) thought that the aim had not been achieved. A further ten percent said that it was too early to say whether or not they would achieve their objective. The results for the achievement of secondary aims were very similar.

Interestingly, there was no significant difference between plaintiffs and defendants in the extent to which they said that they had achieved their main objective either completely or partly. On the other hand there was a significant difference in the extent to which respondents felt that they had achieved their objectives depending on whether their case had been resolved on the basis of an agreement or court or tribunal decision. While 86% of those who resolved their problem by agreement said that they had completely or partly achieved their main objective, only 68% of those whose problem was dealt with in a court or tribunal said that they had achieved their main objective either completely or partly.

The objectives that were most likely to be achieved were objectives relating to enforcing rights or proving innocence (58% achieved completely), divorce or separation problems (51% achieved completely), and money or property related objectives (40%). The objectives least likely to be achieved were obtaining a change in behaviour from the other party involved in the dispute (22% achieved completely), or a job related aim (14% achieved completely). The numbers for preventing the problem from happening to others and receiving an apology are too small to analyse.

When respondents reported that their main objective had changed during the course of trying to resolve the problem they were asked whether they had achieved their new objective. The pattern here was similar to that for main objectives. About 44% of those whose objectives changed said that their new objective had been achieved completely and another six percent said that it had been achieved partly. About one in three (31%) said that they had not achieved their new objective and a little under one in five (18%) said that it was too early to say whether or not their changed objective would be achieved.

The achievement of objectives varied substantially between problem types. Those respondents most likely to have completely or partly achieved their objectives were accident victims (for whom compensation was the primary objective of taking action to resolve the justiciable problem). Those least likely to have achieved their objectives were tenants seeking remedies from landlords, those seeking to resolve a problem at work, and those dealing with neighbour problems (Figure 6.7).

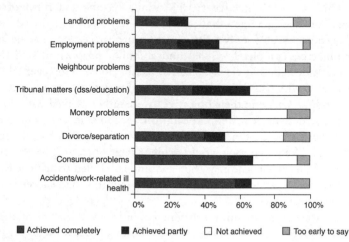

Figure 6.7. Achievement of main objectives by problem type. (Base = all who took action 1061)

Expectations of fulfilling objectives

Although it is rather difficult to ask people after the event what their expectations had been when beginning to deal with a problem, respondents were all asked how likely they had thought it would be that they would achieve what they wanted when they first took action. On the whole, respondents claimed to have been fairly optimistic about the possibility of achieving their objectives when they had first taken action. About three-quarters said that they had thought it very likely or fairly likely that they would achieve their objective (73%). Of the one-quarter who reported that they had been less optimistic at the time they took action to deal with the problem, the main reasons for pessimism were: the past behaviour of the other side (28%); feeling of powerlessness (11%); general pessimism (12%); expectations of how the other side would respond (15%); that their own legal position seemed weak (5%); conflict of views with other side (4%); lack of knowledge about this sort of problem (6%); communication difficulties (4%).

In general there was something of a mismatch between expectations and outcomes. For example, about two in five (40%) of all respondents had thought it very likely that they would achieve their main objectives, but among this group only half said that they had in the end achieved their objective completely (51%) and about one third said that they had *not* achieved their objective (30%). Similarly, about a third of all respondents had imagined that they were fairly likely to achieve their original objective, but only a little over a third succeeded in achieving their objective completely (38%) and a similar proportion said that they had not achieved their objective at all (30%). However, those respondents who claimed to have been pessimistic all along about the likelihood of achieving their objectives were either proved correct, or had adjusted their reported expectation to coincide with outcome. Only about six percent of respondents reported that they had thought it not at all likely that they would achieve their objective. Nearly two in three of this group said that they had, indeed, failed to achieve their objective (60%), although 16% said that in fact they had succeeded in achieving their objective.

There were some significant differences in levels of optimism about achieving objectives depending on the type of problem involved. For example, respondents who were most optimistic about the likelihood of achieving their main objective were those who had suffered an accidental injury or work-related illness (82% reported thinking that they would be very likely or fairly likely to achieve their main objective when they first took action), those experiencing consumer problems (79%), and those experiencing money problems (79%).

Those who were most pessimistic about achieving objectives were those experiencing employment problems (40% thinking it unlikely or very unlikely that they would achieve their objective), problems with landlords (39%) and those with tribunal matters relating to benefits or education of children (31%). Interestingly, respondents with neighbour problems were relatively optimistic about the possibility of achieving their objectives, despite the fact that those cases had a relatively low-resolution rate. Respondents were also more optimistic about achieving aims related to money or property than to obtaining a change in behaviour, or an aim related to their job.

OUTCOME AND ACHIEVEMENT OF OBJECTIVES

Whether or not people reported that they had achieved their objectives differed depending on the nature of the outcome. Among those who had resolved their problem by agreement nearly two in three maintained that they had completely achieved their main objective in taking action and a further 21% said that they had partly achieved their objective (86% saying completely or partly achieved main objective). Only about one in ten (11%) of those respondents who had resolved their problem on the basis of an agreement said that they had *not* achieved their main objective.

Among those whose problem was resolved on the basis of a court or ombudsman's decision, a little over half said that they had achieved their main objective (55%), but about one in three (30%) said that they had not achieved their main objective.

FAIRNESS OF OUTCOME

"It's not to do with fairness, it's to do with law—which is different."

All respondents whose problems were resolved by agreement or adjudication were asked whether, taking everything into consideration, they believed that the decision or agreement that brought the problem to an end was fair. Among all those asked the question, the vast majority said that they believed the outcome was fair (76%), and there was no significant difference of view within the sample as a whole depending on whether the dispute was resolved by adjudication or by agreement (71% of adjudicated cases saying they thought the decision was fair and 78% of those reaching agreements saying that the agreement was fair). There were, however, some differences in perception depending upon a number of factors.

Fairness of agreements

Among those assessing the fairness of agreements there were some significant differences in perception based both on characteristics of respondents and type of problem. For example, respondents involved in divorce/separation problems and employment problems were significantly more likely than those interviewed about other types of problems to say that they thought the agreement reached was *unfair* (32% of those involved in divorce and separation problems and 48% of those with an employment problem). On the other hand, respondents who reached agreements concerning neighbours all thought that the agreement was *fair*, and respondents who reached agreements concerning accidental injury were also very likely to think that the agreement had been fair (only 10% saying not fair).

There was a small difference in perception between men and women in relation to agreements, with men being more likely to view the agreement as somehow unfair (26% of men saying agreement unfair compared with 19% of women). Respondents over 65 were the least likely of all age groups to feel that the agreement reached had been unfair (4% saying unfair compared with 36% of those aged 45–54). There was also a difference in perception depending on respondent's income. The highest earning respondents were the most likely of all income groups to feel that agreements had been *unfair* (67% of those earning more than £41,000 compared with 13% of those earning between £10,000 and £20,000).

There was some difference in perception of the fairness of agreements between those taking action and those who had been the subject of action. Those who were the subject of action (potential defendants) were more likely than those taking action to think that the agreement was unfair (32% of those having action taken against them thought the agreement unfair as compared with 21% of those taking action).

Respondents who said that they thought their agreement was unfair were asked in what ways the agreement was unfair. The most common complaint was that the amount of money received as part of the agreement was not enough (19% of those saying agreement unfair). Another ten percent said that the agreement was unfair because the other side had not honoured a previous agreement, and eight percent felt the agreement was unfair because the problem had not been their fault. About five percent thought that they should have received compensation for some other item or matter and about three percent said that the agreement was unfair because it was not reasonable to expect people in their position to have to pay out money. There was also a relatively long list of more specific complaints relating to the unfairness of the agreement and the following are examples of the explanations given:

> "[The agreement] was not fully representative of the situation. It didn't give a full picture of the state of the central heating system at the time."
>
> "It cost us a lot of money. We had already done the work and had to do it again because of the council's incompetence."
>
> "I still feel I should not be paying anything because my children were taken away from me and I am paying for the privilege."
>
> "I felt that in the circumstances I should have been made redundant instead of attempts firstly to pressurise me out of the job and secondly threats of dismissal for unsatisfactory performances on an artificial plane of judgement that had been introduced."
>
> "I have accepted an offer before I really know how I may be affected in the future."
>
> "The boss did not get disciplined at all. He just got away with it."
>
> "The site foreman should have been made to apologise to me for not following the correct procedure. His part was swept under the carpet and forgotten about. While I was suspended he was allowed to carry on at work."

All those who said that they felt the agreement was unfair were asked why they had agreed to settle the case if they did not feel it was fair. The most common reason given for submitting to what was seen as an unfair agreement was to avoid any further disputes with the other side involved in the problem (21% of those who thought the agreement was unfair). The next most common reason mentioned was the belief that there was no prospect of the respondent getting what they wanted from the other side (19%). Other common reasons for agreeing to unfair settlements were that the respondent wanted to avoid more bother, trouble, and inconvenience—in effect to get the problem over with

(14%)[3]. There was also, among a few, a sense of powerlessness (6%) that led to making what was seen as an unfair agreement.

Fairness of court or tribunal decisions

Nearly three-quarters of those whose problems ended in some kind of adjudication (mostly court decisions) said that they felt the decision was fair (74%), but as with agreements, there were some differences in perception of adjudicated decisions. Most of the adjudicated decisions occurred in relation to divorce or separation problems, disputes over freehold land, money problems, or tribunal decisions relating to employment, benefits, or schools and there were no significant differences in perception of fairness of adjudicated decision simply related to problem type. There was also no significant difference in perception depending on whether the respondent had been taking action or was the subject of court action. However, unsurprisingly there was a significant difference in perception of the fairness of court or tribunal decisions depending upon whether or not the respondent had won at his or her hearing (Figure 6.8). Among respondents who said that they had won at the hearing, almost all thought that the decision was fair,

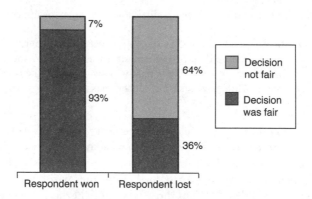

Figure 6.8. Perceptions of fairness of adjudication among those who won and lost. (Base = 150 hearings)

---

[3] These findings are consistent with other investigations of litigants' reasons for agreeing to settlements perceived to be unfair. See Harris et al (1984) op. cit.; Law Commission Report (1994) op. cit.

although an interesting group of about 7% of those who won were actually prepared to say that they thought the decision was *unfair*. Among those who lost at their hearing about two in three thought that the decision had been unfair, although about one in three of losers was prepared to say that the decision was fair.

Another factor that appeared to affect perceptions of the fairness of court and tribunal decisions was whether or not respondents had received any advice about their problem. Although the group of self-helpers who went as far as an adjudicated decision is relatively small, a higher proportion of self-helpers perceived their decision as unfair, when compared with those who received advice (41% of self-helpers said the decision was unfair compared with 25% of those who had advice). This suggests either that respondents who were advised received better outcomes, or that their advisers helped to shape or moderate their expectations and to make the decision acceptable.

Among respondents who received a court, tribunal or ombudsman's decision, the most common reason for thinking that the decision was unfair was the respondent's belief that they should have won at the hearing (6% of those saying unfair). Other reasons given were that the money awarded by the court or tribunal was insufficient, that it was unfair to expect a person in the respondent's position to have to pay out money, or that the problem was not the respondent's fault. In addition there was a relatively long list of very specific reasons given as to why decisions had been unfair that related directly to the circumstances of the problem or the practical effect of the decision. For example:

"Because they left me homeless and I had an hour to pack and get out".

"They didn't accept that what went on actually happened. The other parties lied under oath."

"We didn't have long to prepare for the case. It was rushed. I felt the judge favoured the social services."

"My ex-husband had threatened to sue over breach of confidentiality because they had copied everything over to me. I felt they were pandering to his whims as a result."

"They didn't look into the case. They didn't visit the site. They refused to understand what the dispute was about. They only seemed interested in proving that the Council wasn't guilty of anything."

"I believed that I was entitled to the benefit and I didn't get it. Everyone had said that I was entitled."

"It wasn't fair because we did not know why we were turned down. They didn't give us specific reasons."

Virtually none of those stating that the decision was unfair made reference to aspects of the court process, although the question was directed specifically at the fairness of the decision, rather than the fairness by which the decision was reached.

REGRETS

All respondents were asked whether, looking back over the experience of trying to sort out their problem, there was anything that they regretted about the way in which they had handled the situation. A little over two-thirds of respondents (70%) said that they did not regret anything about their handling of the problem. Among the third who did have some regrets, the most common regret was not having been more persistent or assertive (about a quarter regretted this); about 15% wished that they had taken action sooner; about four percent said that they should have consulted a solicitor and about three percent said that they should have consulted an advice agency. A few people said that they should have consulted an ombudsman, or obtained a second opinion from another adviser. There were also some respondents who regretted seeking advice from solicitors or advice agencies.

There were some differences between problem types in the proportion of respondents admitting that they regretted the way they had handled their problem. The problem types with the highest proportion of respondents saying that they had regrets were divorce and separation problems, problems with landlords and employment disputes. Those with the fewest regrets were neighbour problems and money problems. This is interesting since neighbour problems had a low-resolution rate, and divorce and separation problems had a high-resolution rate.

The most common regrets among those experiencing divorce and separation problems were not having been sufficiently assertive or persistent, and a few regrets about having consulted a solicitor, primarily because of the cost. The most common regret among those with employment problems was not having taken advice sooner. Those respondents who were most likely to say that they wished they had gone to a solicitor were those experiencing consumer problems and those experiencing problems with landlords.

In expressing their regrets respondents' reasons tended to divide between regrets about having become involved in the problem in the first place, regrets about not handling the problem better, and regrets about specific actions taken. The following are typical examples of each of these categories taken from open question responses on the main survey questionnaire.

Regrets about how the problem arose

The regrets expressed often related to the way in which the problem arose and how it might have been avoided. Several respondents felt with hindsight that had they obtained advice before taking action the problem might never have arisen.

"The fact that I filled in the forms myself to begin with. The WRO said they would have filled them in better for me. They picked holes in them."
"We should have sought advice from a trade association before appointing the builder."
"I wish I'd spoken to my next door neighbour at the beginning to try to make him understand."
"I should have had more contact with the neighbour before the job was started. To make sure they knew what was going to happen and what was going on."
"I wish I had tried to sort out a proper legal contract with the builder as I was spending £20,000."

Method of resolution

Most commonly those who regretted the way in which they had handled the resolution of their problem felt that they should have taken *more* formal action. Several specifically said that they regretted not having taken legal action at the time of dealing with the problem, not being more robust in their approach, and sometimes regret at not having had the money to pursue their claim further.

"I was too willing to offer my own solution. I should have possibly gone for advice or arbitration."
"I should have gone to social services and got them to speak to the council."
"I think I should have gone to the union, but I hate to make a fuss. It was internal, to do with work."
"Regret not following it through with legal action or at least finding out more about my legal position."
"If I was fitter I would have pushed for more money—gone to court perhaps."

"I should have gone to the arbitrators for the motor industry."

"There are times I wish I'd taken it to a tribunal, but that is now when I am away from them."

"Basically being very clear in the beginning of what I wanted because I went into the shop to complain, but I didn't insist on a replacement there and then."

"I should have gone to a small claims court. I think it would have been better as the resolution would have brought an end to the problem. Even if I had had no money out of it, it would have made [the landlord] face up to his responsibilities."

"I should have started court proceedings instantly. I gave them too much trust that they would sort it out".

"I should have gone for compensation for loss of earnings and the only reason I didn't was I didn't think I had the financial strength to deal with it".

"I wish I'd had enough money to pay a solicitor to sue them."

"I wish I had written because I was so ineffectual on the telephone."

"I just wish I'd gone to court. I still feel they treated me badly. I've since heard they do this sort of thing a lot. It might have changed their ways."

"I think I would have felt better personally if I'd have had my say in court but it all seems so petty now that I don't know if it would have been worth the hassle."

"Having to represent myself at the tribunal as it put me at a disadvantage as I found difficulty in knowing which questions to ask."

Regrets about adviser

A small proportion regretted taking certain kinds of advice, particularly when it had involved them in more costs than they had expected.

"I wouldn't go to a solicitor again. I would go straight to my MP. The solicitor was a waste of money."

"I regret that we ever started it. I felt like packing it in but I've been paying for four years and then we wouldn't get out legal aid money back".

"Having to use a solicitor to solve the problem. The cost was terrible."

SECTION 2. EXPLAINING FULFILMENT OF OBJECTIVES AND PERCEPTIONS
OF FAIRNESS

In order to explore in a little more depth the factors that appear to be associated with the fulfilment of respondents' main objective in trying to resolve the problem and their perceptions of the fairness of the outcomes that they achieved, two further multiple regression analyses were conducted, similar to those carried out for advice-seeking and outcome of problem. Following the previous procedures, a number of factors likely to be associated with the achievement of objectives and perceptions of fairness of outcome were included in the analyses. These included: type of problem being experienced by the respondent and the type of remedy being sought, and whether the respondent was taking action or having action taken against them; whether the respondent had obtained advice; the respondent's age, sex, social class, education, employment status, and income; and finally an indicator of the extent to which respondents reported having suffered negative effects from dealing with their problems.

ACHIEVEMENT OF MAIN OBJECTIVES

The results of the multiple regression analysis for achievement of objectives found that all of the factors included in the analysis were significantly correlated with the achievement of respondents' main objectives. However, those factors found to be most strongly correlated with whether or not respondents' main objectives would be achieved were: the type of problem experienced, the respondent's age, whether the respondent had reported negative effects from dealing with their problem, and whether the respondent was taking action or was having action taken against them.

Type of problem

Respondents who had made claims for accidental injury or work-related ill health, those involved in consumer problems, and those dealing with DSS or education tribunal matters were more likely than the average respondent to feel that they had achieved their main objectives. For example, the odds of achieving objectives if the dispute concerned injury or work related ill-health were 90% higher than average. For consumer problems the odds were about 55% higher than average and for DSS/education tribunal matters the odds were about 72% higher than average that the respondent would achieve their main objective. However, respondents dealing with landlord problems were about 68% less likely than average to achieve their main objective and those struggling with neighbour problems were about 29% less likely than average to achieve their main objective. Respondents involved in problems to do with divorce were about 17% less likely than average to feel that they had achieved their objectives and those involved in employment problems were about 24% less likely to achieve their objectives.[4]

Age

Younger respondents were more likely than average to say that they had achieved their main objective. The odds of a respondent between 55–64 achieving their main objective was 78% *lower* than those for respondents between the ages of 25–34.

Negative effects of taking action

Unsurprisingly, respondents who reported having suffered negative effects as a result of sorting out their problem such as damaged health or stress were about 27% less likely than average to say that they had achieved their objectives.

Whether or not respondent was subject of action

Respondents whose problem involved another person taking action against them were, interestingly, *more* likely than average to say that they had achieved their main objective. The estimate suggests that they were about 32% more likely than average achieve their main objective.

Other factors found to be correlated with whether or not respondents achieved their objective included gender, with women about 19% *less* likely than men to say that they had achieved their objectives; the remedy sought, with those seeking a money sum over £500 *more* likely than average to say that they had achieved their objectives; and income, those on incomes of between £8,000 and £15,000 about 28% *more* likely than average to achieve their objectives, while those on the highest incomes (over £29,000) were about 30% *less* likely than average to say that they had achieved their main objective.

---

[4] Although the results for these two problem types are on the borderline of significance.

As far as advice was concerned, those who obtained advice from sources other than a solicitor or law centre were about 17% more likely than average to say that they had achieved their objectives, although this result is on the borderline of significance.

The results of the analysis show, yet again, that problem type was a key factor in explaining whether or not respondents' main objectives in taking action to deal with justiciable problems had been achieved. It is also clear that several of the factors that were significant in explaining outcome are also significant in explaining whether or not respondents had achieved their objectives. So for example, older respondents were less likely to resolve their disputes and less likely to say that they had achieved their main objective.

EXPLAINING PERCEPTIONS OF FAIRNESS

A final multivariate analysis was carried out to explore the factors associated with respondents' perception of the fairness of the outcome that they achieved. During the main survey respondents whose problem was concluded on the basis of an agreed settlement were asked whether or not they thought that the agreement reached was fair. Those respondents whose case was ended on the basis of a court order or court, tribunal or ombudsman's decision were asked whether they thought that the decision had been fair.

The factors included in the analysis were: the type of problem being experienced by the respondent and the type of remedy being sought, and whether the respondent was taking action or having action taken against them; whether or not the respondent had obtained advice from a solicitor or law centre; the respondent's age, sex, social class, education, employment status, and income; indicators of the extent to which respondents reported having suffered negative effects from dealing with their problems; and finally, attitude to the legal system (whether they were confident of a fair hearing if they went to court).

The results of the analysis indicate that a large number of factors appear to be associated with perceived fairness of outcome, although three factors were not associated with perception of fairness. These were age, social class, and education.

The factors found to be significantly associated with perceived fairness of outcome were:

- problem type
- type of remedy sought
- respondent's income
- employment status
- gender
- whether respondent was taking action or the subject of action
- whether any negative effects were experienced while sorting out problem.
- whether the respondent obtained legal advice
- attitude to law (whether confident of a fair hearing).

However, those factors *most strongly* correlated with perception of fairness were: an indicator of the respondent's attitude to the legal system (i.e. whether they believed that they would receive a fair hearing if they went to court); the remedy being sought; and the type of problem experienced.

Attitude to legal system

This factor was the most strongly correlated with perceptions of fairness. If respondents said that they were confident of a fair hearing if they had to go to court, then the odds of thinking that the outcome of the problem was fair were 87% *higher* than average. On the other hand, if respondents were not confident of a fair hearing, then the odds of them perceiving the outcome as fair were 44% *lower* than average.

Type of problem

On the whole there appeared to be *little variation* between problem types in terms of perceptions of fairness of the outcome, although employment problems were associated with decreased odds of perceived fairness of outcome.

Remedy sought

When respondents were seeking a remedy other than money, the odds of perceiving the outcome as fair were 102% higher than average. On the other hand if respondents were seeking a sum of money greater than

£500 the odds of perceiving the outcome as fair were 37% *lower* than average. When the remedy being sought was regular payments of money, the odds of perceiving the outcome as fair were 47% *lower* than average.

Legal advice

If respondents obtained legal advice from a solicitor or Law Centre in the course of resolving their problem, then the likelihood that the agreement or court decision would be regarded as fair was 56% *higher* than average.

Negative effects of resolving problem

The odds of perceiving the outcome as fair for those who experienced any negative effects while sorting out their problem were 38% *lower* than average.

Income

Respondents earning more than £29,000 per year were 51% *less* likely than the average respondent to perceive the outcome of their problem as fair.

Sex

Men were about 35% *less* likely than women to perceive the outcome of their problem as fair.

Conclusions

The examination of respondents' objectives in taking action to deal with their justiciable problems has revealed some relatively simple truths. First, that the primary concern for most people is simply to solve the problem. How that is achieved depends on the nature of the problem. In some cases respondents wanted to prevent something dreadful from occurring. In other cases they just wanted to clear up a muddle. In other cases they simply wanted to get a piece of expensive equipment fixed, to obtain a refund for faulty goods, or to obtain compensation for harm suffered. There were also situations in which respondents passionately wanted to change the behaviour of someone who was making their life miserable. Most respondents had a clear sense of what would constitute a right, or fair, or proper outcome to the problem, and achieving that outcome would amount to obtaining justice.

The single most common objective for taking action to resolve justiciable problems was money or property related. Only a tiny proportion were interested in apologies or preventing the problem from happening to others. Very few respondents were able to specify more than one objective. Objectives varied depending on problem type in rather predictable ways, with money-related objectives being the most important in consumer, money, and personal injury problems. Those experiencing divorce and relationship problems were often motivated by the need to make arrangements about children and property, while those experiencing neighbour problems predictably wanted to achieve a change in the behaviour of the person with whom they were in conflict.

Fewer than half of all respondents said that they had achieved their main objective completely and about one in three said that they had not achieved their main objective. Those respondents who had resolved their problem on the basis of an agreement were more likely to say that they had achieved their objectives than those whose problem was concluded by a court or tribunal hearing or a court order.

The most common complaint about unfairness of agreements was that the amount of money received had been too low. When cases ended on the basis of a court or tribunal decision there was a significant difference in perception of fairness of outcome depending on whether or not the respondent had won at his or her hearing. Among those who lost their case at a hearing about two in three said that the outcome was unfair.

In the absence of education or advice about rights and obligations, information absorbed via the media plays an important part in forming beliefs about legal rights and understandings of entitlement as a consumer, as a spouse, as a parent, as a victim. Such informal sources of information also influence expectations of how easy or difficult it might be to secure the desired outcome. Advisers can help to make expectations realistic and outcomes more acceptable.

The process of attempting to achieve a resolution of justiciable problems appears to take quite a toll on members of the public, and the negative effects of being involved in dealing with a problem are greatest for those who fail to achieve a resolution and those who find themselves involved in court or tribunal proceedings. According to respondents, problems to do with employment, divorce and separation, money, landlords and neighbours all have a substantial impact on health. On the other hand, only a minority of respondents were prepared to say that they regretted the way that they had dealt with their problem and about a quarter of those who took some action to resolve their problem were glad to have enforced their rights or gained control over their situation.

The results of the multivariate analyses on the achievement of objectives and perceptions of fairness are somewhat more difficult to interpret than those relating to advice-seeking and outcome. The problem may derive from the fact that both perceptions of fulfilling objectives and perceptions of fairness are rather "soft" variables and that these evaluations and judgements were often being made at some distance from the event being described. Without doubt the issues of fulfilment of objectives and understandings of fairness require more detailed and specifically focused investigation. However, those findings that seem to emerge fairly clearly are that problem type is, as always, an important factor in explaining the achievement of objectives. The highest levels of achievement of objectives were found among personal injury cases, consumer problems and DSS or education tribunal matters. The most important demographic factor related to achievement of objectives was age, with younger respondents being more likely than average to feel that they had achieved their main objective. When respondents had experienced negative effects such as stress and ill health as a result of trying to resolve their problem, they were less likely to say that they had achieved their objectives. Finally, defendants were more likely than plaintiffs to have achieved their objectives, which reflects the difficulties inherent in the civil justice system for those who seek to press claims.

The type of problem experienced by respondents was less significant for perceptions of fairness than for the achievement of objectives. However several demographic variables appear to be associated with perception of the fairness of outcome, for example gender and income. Men were less likely than women to think that the resolution of their problem was fair and those on higher incomes were less likely than average to perceive the outcome of their problem as fair.

Another notable finding emerging from the multivariate analysis of perception of fairness was that the outcome of a justiciable problem had a higher than average likelihood of being perceived as fair if the respondent had obtained help from a solicitor or law centre in order to resolve the problem.

However, the factor most strongly associated with perceptions of fairness was confidence in the judicial system. Those respondents who expressed confidence in the judicial system were 87% more likely than average to perceive the outcome of their problem as fair. This fact is important in the context of the findings discussed in the next chapter about perceptions of the judicial system and levels of confidence in it.

7

Experiences and Perceptions of The Legal System

This chapter examines experiences of legal proceedings and attitudes to the legal system. In the first part of the chapter the experiences of respondents who were involved in court or alternative dispute resolution processes are described. Only a minority of respondents experiencing justiciable disputes had been involved in legal proceedings at all (about 20% see Chapter 5) and an even smaller proportion actually attended a court or tribunal hearing or a mediation session. Nonetheless, the experiences of these respondents are valuable for providing insights into the way in which the public experiences and responds to legal proceedings. The chapter begins with a description of the experiences of the handful of respondents who were involved in mediations and then goes on to describe the experiences of those involved in court and tribunal proceedings. The second section of the chapter looks more broadly at respondents' attitudes towards the courts, judiciary, and legal profession, including those respondents who had taken action to resolve their problem and those who had done nothing. These attitudes to the legal system provide useful contextual information that contributes to our understanding of the influences on the public when they make decisions about what to do in the face of a justiciable problem.

EXPERIENCES OF MEDIATION

Of all respondents to the main questionnaire only twenty stated that they had had any involvement with a mediation or conciliation organisation. A further two respondents said that a mediation or conciliation session was planned for the future. This represents two percent of all respondents to the main survey and reflects the trivial impact that ADR has had to date on dispute resolution processes in England and Wales.

Moreover, of the twenty people who had been involved in a mediation or conciliation, seven had used ACAS in the course of dealing with an employment problem, which is a statutory conciliation service rather than a voluntary ADR process. Other organisations used included the National Family Mediation Service (one respondent) and the Family Mediators Association (two respondents). The remaining eight respondents mentioned other organisations.

Respondents who had contact with mediation organisations were primarily those experiencing employment problems, divorce proceedings, matters to do with children following separation and divorce, and accidents or ill health at work. Those who went to a mediation or conciliation session were roughly equally divided between men and women (nine men and eleven women) and were all between the ages of 25 and 64 (the majority between 25 and 54). Fifteen of the twenty said that they were the initiators of action to resolve the problem.

In all, 18 respondents said that they had actually attended one or more mediation sessions by the time of the interview. Six respondents had attended one mediation session; three had attended two sessions; four had attended three sessions; and five respondents had attended four or more sessions.

In most cases some kind of agreement was reached at the end of the mediation or conciliation (11 out of 18), but in nine of the cases where there had been some kind of agreement respondents reported that the case had gone on to be the subject of a court or tribunal decision (mostly divorce or separation cases). In the seven cases where no agreement had been reached at the final mediation or conciliation session, two cases had later ended in an agreement between the parties, three had gone on to be adjudicated in court or in a tribunal, and two cases remained unresolved.

Advice and Representation

Of those respondents who had some involvement with mediation or conciliation services, all but two had received some kind of advice about their problem and most of those had received legal advice from a solicitor (14 of the 18 who were advised). All but four had taken legal advice at some time in the past about other matters.

All respondents were asked whether or not they had been accompanied at their mediation or conciliation and whether there had been anyone to speak on their behalf. Those respondents who had attended more than one session were asked about the final session only. Most attended without any kind of representation although in seven cases respondents brought partners, friends and relatives with to support them. In one case a solicitor provided representation and in two cases a trade union or staff association representative provided representation. Those who were represented did not think that they would have been better off without representation and all three evaluated their representative as having done well or very well at the mediation or conciliation session.

Those who had attended their session without representation were asked why they did not have a representative with them. Of the 16 who attended without a representative, twelve said that they did so because they did not think that they needed anyone to represent them; one respondent said that he could not afford a representative; and one said that he had been advised to represent himself. Of these 16 respondents who attended their mediation or conciliation without representation, three said that they had felt at a disadvantage because they had not been represented at the session, but the remainder said that they felt at *no* disadvantage without representation. In three of the 16 cases when respondents attended unrepresented the other side was represented at the mediation/conciliation by a solicitor and in one case by a barrister. In three cases another person represented the other side.

ASSESSMENT OF MEDIATION AND CONCILIATION

Most mediation or conciliation sessions were fairly brief. In five cases respondents said that the final session had lasted for less than 30 minutes and eight respondents said that the session had lasted for between half an hour and two hours. In one case the session lasted for a whole day.

Most respondents felt that during the mediation/conciliation session they had had the opportunity to say all (9 respondents) or most (4 respondents) of what they wanted to say. Three respondents reported that they had said "some" of what they wanted to say, but no respondents thought that they had said very little or none of what they wanted to say. Three respondents thought that there were important facts about their problem that they felt did not get discussed at the session.

Most of those respondents who attended a mediation or conciliation session thought that the mediator/conciliator understood their case very well (11 out of 15 answering). All but three respondents thought that the mediator/conciliator was entirely neutral and the three who perceived bias thought that the mediator/conciliator favoured the other party.

Of the 18 respondents who attended mediation/conciliation sessions, seven said that they would definitely go to mediation/conciliation again if in the same position (39%), five said that they would probably do so again (28%), three thought that they might repeat the experience and one respondent said that they would probably not do it again if in the same position. No one said that they would definitely not repeat the experience.

Of those who attended mediation/conciliation sessions, 11 reported that an agreement had been reached at the end of the final session and of these, seven thought that the agreement reached was fair, but four thought that the agreement reached had not been fair (i.e. one-third of those reaching agreement). Despite the small number involved, the level of perception that agreements were unfair is notable. However, the generally positive assessments of mediation made by the few respondents who experienced this form of alternative dispute resolution process are consistent with other recent research on experiences of mediation in this country[1].

COURT AND TRIBUNAL HEARINGS

"The judge was fine, brilliant. **In what way fine, brilliant?** *Well he gave me what I wanted . . ."*

Among respondents to the main questionnaire about 14% reported that there had been a court, tribunal or arbitration hearing in connection with their dispute. Of those who said that there had been no hearing, about 4% said that papers had been sent to a court or tribunal for a decision without a hearing.

Among those who stated that there had been a court or tribunal hearing about their dispute, just over one-half (53%) said that they had started the action and just fewer than one-half (47%) said that the legal action had been started against them.

[1] See for example Genn 1998, op. cit.; Mulcahy et al, *Mediating Medical Negligence Claims—An Option for the Future?* HMSO, 1999.

It was reported in Chapter 4 that among those whose case went to a court or tribunal hearing, over one-third (38%) went to the county courts; one-quarter (24%) went to a magistrates court; and just under one in ten (9%) went to a small claims hearing in the county court, although the identification of courts is somewhat unreliable. A further 12 respondents said that their case had come before an Ombudsman.

A little over half of those respondents who reported that there had been a court or tribunal hearing in connection with their problem said that they attended the final hearing of the matter (56%).

Advice and representation

Most of those who actually attended court or tribunal hearings had received advice about resolving their dispute (92%) and of those who were advised, over three-quarters had received advice from a solicitor about the problem (78%). The small minority who said that they *had not* received any advice were those attending hearings in a tribunal, magistrates court or county court.

Of those attending hearings in a court or tribunal, about a quarter (26%) said that they attended without anyone accompanying them. About 40% were accompanied by a solicitor and/or barrister; five percent said that they were accompanied by an advice worker; three percent were accompanied by a representative from a Law Centre; and three percent were accompanied by a Trade Union or Staff Association representative. Over one-half were accompanied by a partner, friend or relative (with or without a specialist advocate)[2].

Although it would be illuminating fully to analyse representation according to the type of court or tribunal attended, the number of respondents attending most types of courts was so small that the analysis has had to be limited, and based on unweighted numbers rather than percentages. The results are therefore presented as indicative only.

Of the 24 respondents who said that they attended a hearing at the county court, four said that they attended without representation, twelve said that a solicitor represented them and five said that a barrister represented them. Some six people said that they had attended a small claims arbitration and of these three said that they attended without representation and three said that a friend or relative accompanied

---

[2] The numbers add up to more than 100% because respondents mentioned all of those who accompanied them.

them. Among the 18 respondents who said that they attended a hearing at a magistrates court, four said that they went without representation, ten said that they were represented by a solicitor, one had a representative from a Law Centre and one from an advice agency. Of the seven ✓ respondents who attended an industrial tribunal hearing, all had representation either from a solicitor, barrister, Law Centre, or Trade Union. Only two respondents said that they had attended a hearing at the High Court. One said that they attended without representation and the other said that they had a barrister to represent them.

Those who attended hearings without representation were asked why they had attended unrepresented. The most common reason given was that the respondent did not think that they needed anyone to represent them. The next most common reason given was that the respondent could not afford to have a representative. A few unrepresented respondents said that they had been advised to represent themselves at the hearing. In response to the question of whether they had felt at a disadvantage without an advocate at the hearing, a quarter of unrepresented respondents reported that they *did* feel at a disadvantage, but three out of four said that they felt at *no* disadvantage[3].

Of all the hearings attended, with, or without representation, the respondent was facing a represented opponent in a little under two-thirds of cases. Where the opponent was represented this was most often by a solicitor (63%) and also quite often by a barrister (15%). In a tiny minority of cases the opponent was represented by a trade union or staff association representative (1%) and in a similar proportion by the partner, friend, or relative of the opponent (1%).

Assessments of representatives' performance at hearings were generally very favourable. A little over two-thirds of respondents (69%) thought that they had been represented very well and a further one-quarter (23%) thought that they had been represented fairly well. About seven percent thought that they had not been well represented, all of whom were respondents who had *lost* their case at their hearing.

In about one-half of cases respondents said that they had won their case (51%). One-third (34%) said that they had lost the case, and the remainder (14%) gave another response.

The overwhelming majority (93%) of represented respondents thought that they would *not* have been better off at the hearing with-

---

[3] Similar reasons for lack of representation at court hearings have been found elsewhere. Cf, Genn and Genn, 1989, op. cit. However that study found that applicants at tribunal hearings often felt at a distinct disadvantage without representation.

out a representative, although three percent thought that they w
have been better off alone and four percent thought that they m
have been better off alone.

ASSESSMENTS OF COURT AND TRIBUNAL HEARINGS

In most cases the final hearing attended by respondents lasted for less
than 30 minutes (55%), with a further one-third lasting for up to two
hours. A very small minority (4%) lasted for two days or more.

Most respondents had little difficulty understanding what was going
on at the hearing, although about one in ten (11%) said that they had
not understood the procedures; about 12% said that they had not
understood why particular questions had been asked; and a similar
proportion said that they had not been sure who were the various
people at the hearing.

Levels of satisfaction also seemed to be quite high in relation to the
ability to get points across during the hearing. Almost two-thirds of
respondents (65%) said that they had the opportunity to say everything
they wanted to say and a further ten percent reported that they had said
most of what they wanted to say. However, a quarter of respondents
reported that they had said only some, very little or none of what they
wanted to say at the hearing.

About half of those who had experienced difficulty in getting points
across during the hearing said that there had been important facts about
their problem which they felt did not get discussed at the hearing.

On the question of the judge's or tribunal's understanding of their
case, about half of those who attended hearings thought that the decision-maker had understood the case very well (50%) and another one-
quarter (29%) thought the decision-maker had understood the case
fairly well. The remaining respondents were divided between those
who thought that the decision-maker had not understood the case very
well (13%) or not at all well (7%).

Interestingly, assessments of impartiality were considerably less positive. Less than half of respondents attending hearings felt that the
judge/tribunal "favoured" neither side (47%), while a fifth (20%)
thought the judge/tribunal favoured the respondent and a third (33%)
thought that the judge/tribunal favoured the opposing side[4].

---

[4] It is of course possible that some respondents interpreted this question in terms of
whether the judge/tribunal thought that one side or the other had the stronger case rather
than that the judge/tribunal was in some way biased against or in favour of the respondent.

Most respondents said that the judge or tribunal had explained the reasons for the decision very clearly (63%) or fairly clearly (27%), although about one in ten thought that that decision had not been explained clearly (10%).

Another indication that the court or tribunal experience had been largely positive was the proportion of respondents reporting that they would be prepared to go to a court or tribunal again if faced with similarly circumstances. Some 85% of respondents who attended hearings said that they would definitely (59%) or probably (26%) go to court again if they found themselves in the same position again. Some six percent said that they would definitely not go again and another eight percent said that they would probably not go to a court or tribunal again if in the same position. Those who said that they would probably or definitely not repeat the experience if they were in the same position in the future had principally been to hearings in the magistrates court, social security appeals tribunal, or before an education appeals committee.

The generally positive responses to questioning about experiences in court are not entirely consistent with other recent research on litigants' experiences of court. Baldwin's comparison of litigants' experiences of small claims hearings and open court procedures in the county court suggests that those litigants whose cases were dealt with through normal open court procedure often found the experience to be intimidating and frightening. He comments, "the views expressed about formal court adjudication presented a depressing picture . . . over 40 percent of this sample could be described as disgruntled people."[5] On the other hand, he found that those litigants who had experienced small claims hearings were much more positive about the experience and had felt able to take the hearing in their stride.

Although many of the court hearings reported by respondents in the present survey were identified simply as county court proceedings and only a small proportion of respondents said that the had been to a small claims hearing, it is possible that a far higher percentage of cases were actually dealt with in small claims hearings than was reported by respondents during the survey and this might account for the positive assessment of court experiences. Moreover, the largely favourable findings that emerge from respondents' answers to the survey questions about their experience of court proceedings are somewhat at odds with

---

[5] Baldwin 1997, Lord Chancellor's Department, op. cit., pp 24–25.

findings relating to the negative effects of dealing with justiciable problems through the legal system reported in the previous chapter, and with some of the accounts given by respondents during open questioning in qualitative interviews. Although many respondents suggested that their court or tribunal experience had not been particularly upsetting, there were also several vivid accounts of traumatic court experiences. For example:

"I was absolutely petrified. The day we actually did go to court I was a nervous wreck. **What was it that petrified you?** I just felt like a criminal, even though I hadn't done anything. I just felt awful. Didn't like it at all. And there was a lot of people there. It was quite busy when we first went. . . . and to speak publicly as well and it's the authority of it all. I just didn't like the idea of it . . . I'd seen the law courts in Croydon so I knew them from the outside, but I didn't know what the inside was like. I mean it was pretty comfortable in there, it wasn't all hard benches. It was quite a nice place. But just going through where they check your handbags and the security men. I thought 'I wonder what they think I'm here for? Have I been really naughty?' And really I'm just here to protect my children. It was embarrassment as well. And I was angry with my husband for taking me to court, after all we'd been through with him. It should have been me taking him to court . . . And to drag the kids through. But I did it, I had to do it. That was it."

"It was all absolutely new. I have never been to a court in my life in any offence, I never wanted to see the courts. I'm just scared of courts basically. I'm just scared of law. And I don't like to get my hands dirty into the law and I was worrying about legal fees and it was scaring me up that I literally couldn't fight the case against [the large company] and me a small Asian person trying to take them to the court. I didn't have that sort of guts in me. Though my case was genuine . . . I was very nervous. I was a nervous wreck. **What was making you nervous?** Oh just somebody asking lots of questions, just making me scared. And then the solicitor says 'You can't say this word, you can't say that word, you have to say these words' . . . When I went to the court and there's only two of us, me and the solicitor from the Law Centre and there was five of them from the company, they had two barristers. And that was just the first hearing. And when the judge saw those five people sitting round with big massive briefcases and folders and he said, 'For a start the application was delayed for 24 hours and secondly you haven't submitted a new case. You haven't filled out the proper forms.' And he just chucked the case out. 'Sorry, no case.' **Did you understand what was going on?** It was a bit of a mystery to me. I mean it was just like going into sort of a puzzle and coming out. My first thought was that they might have bloody bribed the judge. That the company might have bribed him. That was my first initial thought. Sitting in front of five people and there's me, made redundant and the other person is a Law Centre person, not even a barrister. We just looked like chickens in front of them. It was really frightening. Very frightening. You know you could see those people and they already had that big folder prepared in front of them and I was there with two A4 papers. And my solicitor had a filofax and two A4 papers in his hand."

In addition to the unfamiliarity of the physical surroundings there were also complaints about the mysterious procedures involved in court behaviour. Many practices, which are central to preparation for appearance in court and to the settlement of proceedings, appear alien and sometimes inappropriate to those who have had no relevant experience. For example, the fact that opposing representatives meeting at court are known to each other and interact in a courteous and perhaps even friendly manner can strike those unfamiliar with professional behaviour and protocol as sinister. Those involved in litigation employ a partisan representative to fight their corner in adversarial procedures. They are not repeat-players and are unlikely to have had previous experience of court proceedings. They may be very emotional about their case and expect their representative to be equally involved. In this context, friendly conversations between representatives seem out of place. Moreover, although some litigants who arrive at the court door might be relieved that a settlement can be achieved without being subjected to a hearing, others want their opportunity to be heard and expect matters to be decided by the judge, rather than compromised in the corridor as a result of discussions between representatives. For example:

> "I also found that system very unfair. I found that my solicitor and his solicitor were talking about the case before they even went in and deciding what was going to happen before you even went into the court. And I found that totally against anything that I believe in. It was the first time I'd ever been to court for anything, and I imagined that your solicitor would be on your side, and his solicitor would be on the other side and you would go in and you would fight it out in court and that would be it. And no, I couldn't believe that these two solicitors were like this in the corner, you know, and coming back to me and saying, 'This is what's going to happen and we're going for this and going for that.' And I thought, 'Well you've just decided before we've even gone into the court. So what is the whole point of it?' "
> (*Divorce/separation problem*)

There were however, respondents who described court experiences in more positive terms, who had been well prepared for what was to happen, or who received more consideration and sensitivity than had been expected. For example:

"The procedure in the court itself, did that have any worries for you or not? Not really 'cause my solicitor actually told me that it'd only be obviously the judge or whoever like has to be in that courtroom and just me and [ex-husband], no one else. So I knew I'd be fine once I got in that courtroom. There was a barrister. Had you met the barrister previously? Yeah. Was that someone you felt confident about? Yeah I did, yeah. 'Cause I mean she deals with those kinds of situations. I knew exactly what was going to happen and virtually what was going to be said because as I said my solicitor informed me about everything. How helpful was that to you do you think? Very. 'Cause obviously I didn't really know what to expect in the actual court-room but like she explained it to me. And I thought yeah everything is going to be dealt with, you know, it's fine . . ."

"I actually turned up at the court for the Decree Absolute. Even the judge did-n't understand why I turned up because he asked me 'Do you want to with-draw the application?' So I said 'No', but I couldn't tell anybody why I'd turned up. I had been told I didn't have to, but that I could if I wanted to. The Judge was very nice. He took me into his private chambers and he said 'Are you sure this is what you want?' And he laughed and said, 'You're just here to make sure I do a proper job, aren't you?' I laughed and he signed it, stamped it, and gave me the papers and said, 'You're a free woman.' I felt dreadful. When I came out I felt absolutely sick." [*Female divorcing husband*]

What emerged from qualitative interviews were graphic descriptions of how individuals felt on entering the alien world of the court: anxiety, difficulty of coping with vocabulary, uncertainty about procedure and a pervasive sense that courts are about wrongdoing. However, these accounts are not necessarily inconsistent with the answers provided to the main survey which suggested that in the end respondents were able to overcome their anxieties and get most of their points across. The sig-nificance of respondents' expectations and how those expectations of courts and the judiciary are formed are discussed further below.

EXPLORING ATTITUDES TO THE LEGAL SYSTEM

In order to explore general attitudes to the legal system five statements were read out to all respondents to the main survey, whether or not they had taken any action to try and resolve their problem, and respon-dents were asked to say how much they agreed or disagreed with each statement. The statements were largely drawn from comments made by members of the public during focus group discussions at the developmental stage of the research. The introduction to the attitude statements deliberately set the context, which was worded as follows: *"I would now like to ask you a few general questions about your feelings about the justice system in Britain. I am going to read out a few statements—please tell me for each one how much you agree or disagree with it."* Three of the statements were posed in positive terms and two in negative terms and the statements were always read to respondents in the following order:

(a) "If I went to court with a problem, I am confident that I would get a fair hearing.

(b) "Most judges are out of touch with ordinary people's lives."

(c) "Lawyers' charges are reasonable for the work they do."

(d) "Courts are an important way for ordinary people to enforce their rights."

(e) "The legal system works better for rich people than for poor people."

These attitude statements about the justice system in Britain produced, on the whole, rather negative responses, which were consistent with the views and attitudes that had been expressed by members of the public who joined focus group discussions during the developmental stage of the project. Analysis of attitudes in relation to respondents' demographic characteristics and experience of the legal system displayed few *consistent* differences of view between groups, although there was some interesting variation in response to individual questions depending on social group and past experience of using legal advice. These are discussed in relation to each question.

The generally negative responses to attitude statements posed on the main survey questionnaire were also reflected in many of the qualitative interviews conducted after the main survey and during which respondents were asked completely open questions about their attitudes to the courts, the judiciary and the legal system as a whole. Some typical responses to this open questioning are presented in relation to each of the attitude statements in the main survey in order to flesh out some of the perceptions that the public hold of the courts and procedures for enforcing rights and claims.

THE IMPORTANCE OF COURTS FOR ENFORCING RIGHTS

It seems clear that the *idea* of courts as a place in which ordinary citizens can enforce rights is important in the national consciousness. The symbolic value of the courts, irrespective of any immediate concerns of the public about access and cost, is clearly demonstrated by the three-quarters of respondents who agreed or strongly agreed with the statement *"Courts are an important way for ordinary people to enforce their rights"* (Figure 7.1). It is also important to note that this particular question produced the lowest number of non-committal responses, suggesting that most people have a view on this subject, and that in the vast majority of cases that view is positive. The question, however, is estimating the extent to which the public subscribes to the ideal of the courts and commitment to the rule of law. To that extent the question is rather different from some of the other attitude questions which were tapping experience, expectations and beliefs.

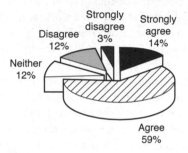

Figure 7.1. "Courts are an important way for ordinary people to enforce their rights". (Base = All respondents 1134 weighted)

There were some significant differences in response to this question among respondents depending on demographic characteristics and experience of the legal system. For example, the oldest (over 65) and youngest (under 25) age groups were the most likely of all age groups to agree that courts are important for enforcing individual rights. As far as education is concerned, respondents with degree level educational qualifications were the *most* likely to *disagree* with the statement, while those with no qualifications or up to CSE level were the *least* likely to disagree with the statement.

Respondents experiencing accidental injury or work-related ill health, money problems and employment problems were the most likely of all problem types to *disagree* with the statement. While respondents' experience of using advisers to deal with their most recent problem did not appear to be related to their attitude to the importance of courts, those respondents who had taken no action at all to deal with their problem were significantly *more* likely than those who took action to *disagree* with the statement. This may suggest that alienation from the legal system plays a role in decisions not to try and obtain redress when faced with a justiciable problem, or that both factors are a manifestation of a more general sense of alienation. Respondents who lost their case in a court or tribunal were significantly more likely to *disagree* with the statement than those who had won their case, suggesting that those who lost had not been able to accept the decision and that this negative experience of legal proceedings has an impact on expressed support for the legal system.

Interestingly, respondents who had sought legal advice in the past for some matter, whether or not they had done so for the most recent problem, were significantly more likely to *disagree* with the view that the courts are important for enforcing legal rights, when compared with those who had never taken legal advice in the past. This may reflect a cynicism borne of previous unhappy experiences.

It seems then that although there is a high level of agreement with the idea of the significance of the courts as a place for enforcing individual rights, those expressing least confidence were those who had recently lost a case in court, and middle-aged, well-educated people with previous experience of legal advice. This may reflect scepticism rather than alienation on the part of some people concerned to offer a sophisticated response to a rather blunt statement.

FAIRNESS OF THE COURTS

A second attitude statement aimed at tapping broad confidence in the legal system concerned perceptions of the fairness of courts (*"If I went to court with a problem I am confident that I would get a fair hearing"*). Questions such as this have been used in numerous studies in the United States to measure the degree of "diffuse support" for the courts. Diffuse support recognises the legitimacy of an institution, even in the face of decisions viewed as wrong or inimical to the individual's own interests[6]. Diffuse support is regarded as more generalised and more persistent than the kind of specific support measured by questions

---

[6] Olsun and Huth (1998) "Explaining Public Attitudes Towards Local Courts", *The Justice System Journal*, vol 20/1 p 42.

aimed at evaluating the extent to which institutions have achieved specific objectives. It is therefore a reasonable indication of underlying confidence in the courts.

The results of the analysis of questionnaire responses to the proposition that the respondent would receive a fair hearing in court show that a bare majority of respondents agreed with the statement (53%), and only one in twenty respondents was prepared to say that they strongly agreed with the statement. What is also somewhat disconcerting about the responses to this question in the context of public confidence in the judicial system, is that one in five respondents could not, or would not, commit themselves to a view on the question of the fairness of proceedings. While one in five saying, in effect, that they did not know whether or not they would receive a fair hearing if they went to court cannot be interpreted as a negative finding, it is clearly not a positive finding to a statement probing confidence in the courts.

There were relatively few statistically significant differences in the responses to this particular attitude statement either in relation to demographic characteristics or in experience of the legal system. However, respondents with degree level qualifications were less likely to disagree with the statement and more likely to express no opinion than other groups. Indeed, one in four of those with degree level qualifications expressed no opinion, about 17% disagreed, and 58% agreed or strongly agreed. By contrast, respondents with no educational qualifications were more likely to express an opinion. One in four in this group disagreed with the statement, but six out of ten agreed or strongly agreed with the statement.

There was also a significant difference between men and women on this question, with men expressing greater confidence than women (62% agreeing or strongly agreeing with the statement as compared with 52% of women). Women's relatively lower confidence may be a reflection of the domination of the courts by males. Women were also more likely than men to offer no view, with one in four women saying that they neither agreed nor disagreed with the statement.

There was no significant difference in the response to the attitude statement on perceptions of the fairness of courts between age groups or income groups on this subject.

One factor, however, that did seem to be associated with different responses to confidence in the fairness of court proceedings was experience of obtaining legal advice. Those respondents who said that they had at some time in the past obtained legal advice about any matter

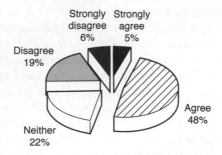

Figure 7.2. "If I went to court with a problem, I am confident that I would get a fair hearing". (Base = All respondents 1134 weighted)

were *less* likely than others to agree that they had confidence that they would get a fair hearing in court (49% as compared with 60% of those who had never sought legal advice) and more likely to say that they had no view (24% as compared with 17% of those who had never sought legal advice). On the other hand, there was no difference in view between those who had obtained legal or other advice for the problem about which they were currently being interviewed and those who handled the problem alone. Moreover, responses to this question did not vary according to the outcome of the problem or whether respondents had been involved in any legal proceedings in the course of trying to resolve the problem about which they were being interviewed. This suggests that immediate experience of being involved in legal proceedings has little impact on persistent expressions of confidence in the courts, although the immediate experience of losing at a court or tribunal hearing clearly does. Those respondents whose problem ended in a court or tribunal hearing and who lost their case were significantly *more* likely to *disagree* with the statement than those who won (38% of those who lost their hearing disagreeing with the statement as compared with 19% of those who won).

PERCEPTIONS OF COURTS

"Courts are for people to sort their problems out aren't they. They are also there to punish people who've done bad things. So that's why I think there should be two different types."

In order to probe perceptions and experiences of courts more deeply, open questions were asked about respondents' views on courts during qualitative interviews. These questions produced interesting responses. Although questioning about courts in interviews was always related to the civil courts, the instinctive response of most respondents was to make reference to features of the criminal courts. Many people found it hard to understand questions like *"What are the courts for?"* since their only understanding of courts was in a criminal context. Members of the public do not hold a distinction in their minds between civil and criminal courts. The public image of "court" is a place where criminals are taken to be tried. This means that initiating or considering initiating court proceedings (let alone being the subject of civil court proceedings) involves an automatic sense of being involved in wrongdoing and a fear that one might somehow be punished. *"I have never had to go to court because I have never done anything wrong, thank goodness"* was a common sentiment. For example:

> "Do you think you would get a fair hearing if you went to court? I don't know. I haven't been involved in anything like that really. I've never been in trouble with the police for anything."

> "Do you have confidence in the court system? Not really, no. Because I think people that should be prosecuted get away with absolute murder."

In some cases this view of courts as being essentially criminal leads to a reluctance to use the courts or even go to court to defend one's position. An example of this effect was provided by a respondent who had been threatened with possession proceedings and who refused to attend court:

> "We were very naive and we knew absolutely nothing about court, only what we'd ever seen on television. I didn't know anybody that had been to court, so I had no idea. I expected a Crown Court. I expected to go to the Old Bailey, because we had absolutely no idea. Looking back with hindsight, maybe I could have gone to court but . . . **Could you just explain in more detail why you think you didn't go to court?** Well like I said a lot of the time somebody steals money from a bank or something, not armed robbery, embezzlement things, they tend to get life for it and I just found that I felt that the courts were biased towards money. Money was more important than peoples' lives. We didn't realise that in this situation the court was the other way round. We had a fairly negative view of the court . . . the news, on a documentary or a programme . . . So we had no idea of what would happen and basically it's fear I think. I didn't want to go to prison. I thought, 'I'll end up in bloody prison!' So we just wanted to get rid of it as quickly as

we could . . . We pleaded guilty by letter. They said we owed them the money."

Moreover, the fact that respondents automatically interpreted "courts" as being "criminal courts" meant that their expressed lack of confidence in courts was often a reflection of dissatisfaction with the state of the criminal law and decisionmaking in criminal cases. Most respondents interviewed in qualitative interviews had no personal experience of courts and their opinions, beliefs and stereotypes had been formed and modified by televised representations of courts, newspaper atrocity stories and, less frequently, by reported experiences of family and friends. In discussing attitudes to courts, respondents commented about juries, about criminal defendants and most often about the problem of lack of consistency in judicial sentencing of criminals and the failure of the law to address certain forms of behaviour seen as anti-social and worthy of punishment. Several references were made to the fact that causing death by dangerous driving is not treated with sufficient severity and a recent case that had involved a driver who killed a child as a result of drunken driving was used to illustrate the fact that the law does not reflect public opinion, leading to lack of confidence in the courts. Other examples fresh in the public consciousness were expensive fraud trials in which juries had acquitted the defendants.

> "There are areas where courts get things wrong, but they often get things wrong because they are reflecting what society wants of them. What society wants done or what society wants punished. Fashions change. Things become less acceptable to the public and some things become more acceptable. I find it sad that fairly major frauds involving what I would regard as theft of vast amounts of money are punished in a minor way whereas relatively small thefts by people who haven't got very much are sometimes punished by imprisonment. The public aren't so worried about fraud. They are worried about their possessions being stolen but if somebody actually defrauds a bank of some money or lose an awful lot of money I don't think the public would worry so much about that. But they do worry about someone breaking in and stealing their television."

> "I think watching court cases, dramas on telly and things like that, you get a picture in your head about how law works and it doesn't seem to work right, and that's probably where it's come from. **Doesn't seem to work right, what do you mean by that?** It doesn't seem fair. No, not from what I watch on telly and read in the newspapers. Sometimes people don't win the money they should and then some people win thousands of pounds because some-

one called them a pig or something. It seems unjust, the results seem unjust. But then again I'm just catching on the radio, on the telly and I'm making assumptions maybe. I don't have first hand experience. I don't know anyone who's got in trouble or who's owed money or who's challenged someone. I don't know how the court works."

Even those with experience of courts expressed rather negative views:

"I think there's a big class thing around in the legal profession and in courts. I've seen it in my work, when I worked in a children's home and had to accompany some adolescents to court and families and things. They would go to a solicitor, or get legal advice and that person would be their advisor and offering them a service and you would think that they were offering them the best service. Then you would get to court and it was a bit like an old boys' network and obviously all these solicitors knew everyone and then they started to do deals outside of court and bargaining. And I just felt it was more about solicitors', lawyers', barristers', and judges' interests, rather than actually other people."

Not all respondents however held such negative views. There were examples of considerable confidence and recognition of the important role of courts in underpinning legal rights. For example:

"I think the civil courts are very important. I suppose it is always right for people to try to come to an amicable arrangement by themselves without involving lots of expense and time and worry, but when you can't achieve an agreement between two parties then you have to use a court. It's essential. There is no other way of doing that . . . I think I do have confidence in the court system."

"I think I would get a fair hearing. Yeah, I think if I was passionate and I went to court about an issue I'd feel I would get a fair hearing, I think I've got faith in it. If you're telling the truth and what you say is right and you're not making it all to be something that it wasn't, if you're honest I think I would get a fair hearing."

DIFFERENTIAL RESOURCES AND THE LEGAL SYSTEM

"There is a legal system and I feel that it is just not available to me. If I were poor enough it would be available to me and if I were rich enough it would be available to me and we are one of the 94% of the British population who fall somewhere between the two."

The scepticism conveyed in the responses to the question about fairness of hearings may, in part, be a reflection of the very strong feelings aroused by a related attitude statement suggesting that the wealthy have an advantage in the legal system. Almost three-quarters of respondents agreed or strongly agreed with the proposition that the legal system works better for the rich than the poor. Only eleven per-cent of all respondents disagreed with the statement and only two per-cent strongly disagreed, although about 15% of respondents did not offer a view.

There were, on the whole, rather few differences between groups of respondents associated with the view of the legal system working best for those with resources. However, respondents with a degree level qualification appeared to be somewhat *less likely* than groups with lower educational qualifications to agree that the legal system works better for the rich than the poor. On the other hand, over half of those with incomes over £41,000 *strongly agreed* with the statement, perhaps suggesting that they were aware of the advantage that they might have in legal proceedings with a higher income. Other differences worth not-ing were that women were more likely to *disagree* with the statement than men, and respondents who were unemployed or defined as long-term sick and disabled at the time of the interview were significantly more likely to *strongly agree* with the statement than other groups.

Although responses to this particular attitude question did not appear to vary significantly depending on involvement in legal pro-ceedings for the most recent problem, or whether respondents had obtained advice about the most recent problem, those who had lost their case at court or tribunal hearings were more likely to agree and

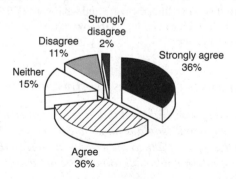

Figure 7.3. "The legal system works better for rich people than for poor people". (Base = All respondents 1134 weighted)

less likely to disagree with the statement than those who had won their case.

Interviews with respondents and discussions during focus groups at the developmental stage of the research revealed a number of strands to the argument. Trying to unravel some of threads it seems clear that most people feel that using the legal system requires expertise. The courts and paraphernalia of the legal system are reserved for the most important cases, and legal proceedings are not something that the ordinary person should plunge into without advice. Free advice is in short supply or of dubious quality. Even purchased advice is of variable quality and the better the advice the more it costs. What many respondents seem to believe is needed to succeed with legal proceedings is good quality legal advice, which may be expensive. Thus, those who can afford to pay for good quality legal advice will inevitably have an advantage over those who cannot afford to pay for anything at all, and those who can afford to pay *more* will have a further advantage. For example:

"We've got to fight for ourselves because money talks. If we had thousands of pounds in the bank and we could go to a top solicitor we could say 'This is my problem. You sort it out.' Because you wouldn't be worried that your bill's mounting up with the solicitor. The money would be there to pay. Whereas we have to go through all the different agencies. You just go from one to the other and you get nowhere because we can't really afford to do anything else about it because we're on limited money even if we work."

"This is what it's all about—time and money—whatever problem you are talking about. Solicitors and what have you—it's all to do with money."

"If you could get George Carman QC to argue your case you'd be housed tomorrow. It would cost £100,000 to get a report. He's never lost a case that man, so you can't tell me that you can't buy justice. You can buy it, but you can't always get it at our level."

These basic principles, however, become somewhat muddled by the rules relating to legal aid, perceptions of legal aid being gradually withdrawn, and concerns about the way in which legal aid seems to be easily available for wealthy high-profile defendants in criminal cases i.e. that those with resources can work the system both legitimately and illegitimately. Recent media reports had clearly had an effect, for example:

"The Maxwell brothers have had Legal Aid for £3million. So how can the system say to us, who can't get no justice, there is justice out there for you?

He ain't living in a block of flats. If it was true and he hadn't nicked that money, he wouldn't be living in a lovely detached house in those conditions. He'd be over at the Council saying 'Can you find me a flat for my wife and the kids?' "

"The Maxwell brothers they got theirs [legal aid] for nothing and it cost millions and the case was slung out. And I have to pay £59.50 a month (for a personal injury claim)."

There were, however, concerns that the system worked best for those who could afford to use it and those who were financially eligible for legal aid—leaving those in the middle either without the means of obtaining redress or the prospect of unaffordable legal bills. These views came sometimes through direct experience, but also through hearing about the experiences of others.

"[*My sister is going through a divorce*] But she can't afford justice. That's the thing, she can't afford twenty five thousand pounds. She hasn't got it. Her husband has refused to pay any of the bills for the divorce because she's taking the divorce. He went off with another woman and it's been pretty awful anyway. You can't afford that money. I'd have to sell the house. And I have known people who have pushed this through and they're left with nothing. They've had to sell the house, the car to pay off the solicitor's fees. And it's just amazing . . . Justice is for the poor. It's for the poor on the dole who get Legal aid. And the wealthy of course. They can afford it . . . So us lot, we haven't got a chance . . . It would be the last thing any of us would ever want to do, we'd want to stay as far out of it as possible . . . And it's mainly because of the money."

THE COST OF LEGAL ADVICE

These concerns about the extent to which the legal system requires resources are directly reflected in or perhaps a reflection of, a pervasive belief that the cost of legal advice is unaffordable for most ordinary people. About three out of four respondents disagreed or strongly disagreed with the suggestion that lawyers' charges are reasonable for the work that they do (72%).

Despite the widespread disagreement with the statement, there were some differences between groups in their response to the question. For example, respondents with no educational qualifications were the most likely of all respondents to *agree* with the statement (21% agreeing and one percent strongly agreeing) while those respondents with degree level

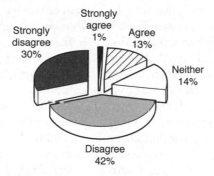

Figure 7.4. "Lawyers' charges are reasonable for the work they do". (Base = All respondents 1134 weighted)

qualifications or higher were the least likely to agree with the statement (ten percent agreeing and less than one percent strongly agreeing).

Respondents with an annual income of less than £10,000 and those with an annual income of £41,000 or more were the two groups most likely to agree with the statement that lawyers' charges are reasonable for the work that they do. Among respondents with an income of less than £10,000 some 22% agreed or strongly agreed with the statement. Among respondents with incomes of over £41,000, about 19% agreed with the statement although none strongly agreed. These figures can be compared with the responses from respondents with incomes between £32,000 and £40,000 among whom not a single respondent agreed with the statement. These findings lend some support to the contention that only the well-off and the poor (through legal aid) can afford legal ser- vices, as does the finding that as far as employment status was con- cerned, those most likely to agree that lawyers' charges are reasonable were those who were unemployed at the time of the interview.

There was little difference in response according to the type of prob- lem that respondents had experienced although those who had been dealing with divorce and separation problems were among the most likely to agree with the statement that lawyers' charges are reasonable (20% agreeing and 3% strongly agreeing) as were those who had prob- lems with their landlord (23% agreeing and none strongly agreeing).

There were also some differences in views depending on whether or not respondents had obtained advice to deal with their most recent problem. Among those who had obtained advice from a solicitor, about 18% agreed or strongly agreed that lawyers' charges are reasonable for the work that they do as compared with only eleven percent of those who had obtained non-legal advice about their problem and 14% of those who had handled their problem without advice.

Qualitative interviews and focus group discussions indicated that concerns about legal costs emanated both from personal experience and from reports in the press about high legal costs accruing in cases. It is also important to note that the fieldwork was taking place during a period of upheaval in the civil justice system and unusual amounts of press coverage of matters to do with proposed changes to legal aid. In the propaganda war under way between policy-makers and the professions the messages being received by the public are relatively crude. Press reports about fees paid to 'fat cat lawyers' serve to create or reinforce concerns about the unaffordability of legal advice for the average citizen:

"Sometimes they go to astronomical levels. You see all these things with solicitors and how much solicitors' bills are and you see this thing like with the two Princes. £400,000 for solicitors! And you think, 'God how much would they charge me?' But if you knew that you could go to a solicitor and all it would cost you for some decent advice was say £30 or something like that, or to a body of people who was set up. I mean I'd willingly pay for advice, but it's going through my mind all the time, 'Oh what happens if it's this amount of money', and you think to yourself 'Oh can I pay for it?' "

"Solicitors charge a fortune. When we were going through with the mortgage for where we lived when we first got married it was £10 for this and £15 for that. You can't get legal aid can you? You have to be on Income Support. But there are genuine people like us that don't get income support but haven't got any money anyway."

"At work we recently had a bill from a solicitor who read our lease and he charged £550. He read the lease—that's all he did. If it cost £550 to read a lease God help you if you wanted them to fight your case. If that's a sign of how much solicitors charge! And the sting in the tail was a letter came with the bill saying 'I've tried to reduce my costs as much as I can bearing in mind your situation at the moment and I've reduced the bill to £550'. And all he did was read through four sheets of paper!"

"There is no possibility that I would ever go to a solicitor for anything medium range because I am not going to get it paid for. It's just not worth it. It's going to have to be so big an issue that basically I'm going to go bust either way before it's going to be worth going to a solicitor. It just costs too much."

"We are involved with solicitors over a will. Its been going on for years. And if we do get any money the solicitor is going to make more money than we are."

"You said another reason for not pursuing it through legal channels, through a solicitor would be the cost. How much do you think something like that would cost? Thousands . . . Thousands and thousands because it would go on for months and months and months. Oh yes you're looking at a very hefty, very hefty sum. I know what legal fees are. We are talking probably £20,000 at least. Oh yes it would be costly. And we're just not prepared to spend that sort of money. There would be such a fight and a wrangle it would go on for months and months. Especially with an outside solicitor because they'd have to start from scratch. It would be horrendous."

THE JUDICIARY

"Well it's that whole 'glasses-on-the-end-of-the-nose' sort of thing."

A final attitude question posed to all respondents that provoked rather negative responses concerned the judiciary. Respondents were asked whether or not they agreed with the statement that most judges were out of touch with ordinary peoples' lives. The wording of the attitude statement was borrowed from expressions that occurred frequently during open-ended focus group discussions with members of the public during developmental work prior to the main survey. The strength and consistency of feeling expressed during those group discussions were confirmed in the survey responses and then further elaborated during open questioning in qualitative interviews.

Among respondents to the main survey questionnaire, about two-thirds (66%) agreed or strongly agreed with the statement, 13% disagreed or strongly disagreed with the statement, and a relatively sizeable proportion (21%) felt unable to agree or disagree with the statement.

There were virtually no significant differences in the response to this question depending on age, education, employment status, problem type, previous experience of legal advice, or involvement in legal proceedings. This is important because many of those most likely to have had experience of judicial behaviour expressed the same negative attitudes as those who had not.

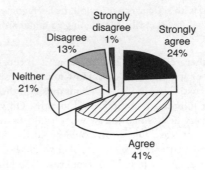

Figure 7.5. "Most judges are out of touch with ordinary people's lives". (Base = All respondents 1134 weighted)

There were some differences in view on this question according to income, but even these were inconsistent. Although respondents with incomes in excess of £41,000 were the most likely of all income groups to *disagree* with the statement (26% disagreeing as compared with 10% of those with incomes under £10,000), they were also the group most likely to *strongly agree* with the statement (45% strongly agreeing as compared with 24% of those with incomes under £10,000).

It seems, therefore, that the view that judges are out of touch, or at least the sentiment conveyed by the statement, is one that holds across social boundaries and irrespective of experience of the legal system. It was also an issue about which respondents in qualitative interviews appeared to hold relatively strong views. In each qualitative interview respondents were asked completely open questions about their views of judges. The questioning overwhelmingly stimulated negative responses relating to perceptions of remoteness based on social distance, inconsistency in sentencing, and examples of insensitive judicial comments reported in the media. Indeed several respondents exhumed ancient examples of cases that had made a deep impression[7]. There also appeared to be some disapproval of court robes and wigs which were seen as being anachronistic and which possibly contributed to the impression of judges being outdated.

---

[7] A notorious case repeated more than once during interviews and focus group discussion was one in which a young woman who had been raped was accused by the judge of contributing to the rape by having worn a mini-skirt. The case was reported more than five years ago.

It is notable that although only a very few respondents to qualitative interviews had ever met or appeared before a judge, most of those interviewed in depth were nonetheless generally opinionated and fluent on this subject. This is because judges, and caricatures of judges, through media communication, regularly enter the homes of the public, and because the behaviour of judges has a high public salience. Members of the public have views about judges, because of the importance attached to the office of judge in the public imagination. The occasionally strong disapproval of the judiciary expressed by respondents related to the imagined typical incumbent rather than to the office. It also reflects a degree of apprehension, which may be a necessary part of social order, but is not wholly functional in the context of a modern civil justice system.

The opinions expressed about the judiciary during qualitative interviews could fill a book on their own. The comments tended to cluster around several themes: age, values and bias, inconsistency, and dress. The extracts from interview transcripts speak for themselves.

Antiquity

"**I wondered what you felt about the judges in this country?** Not a lot from what I hear. They sound like a bunch of pompous old weirdoes. They're just old men. That's the impression I've got. They need to be a bit more with it. They all seem to be so out of touch. That's just my view, my impression of what I see. Out of touch, older people. **Where do you get these impressions from?** I don't know. Media. Newspapers. TV."

"The people who are up there who are making decisions are some fuddy old judge. He might have lived in the real world 40 years ago but now he is living in a mansion in the middle of Berkshire and when was the last time he went down Soho late at night and got mugged because he didn't have anyone with him? They are not in touch with reality."

"It just seems a very old system. The people at the top are just very old and I don't think they can understand technical problems. Generally they may not understand your situation. Like a District Judge or something. You know they are going to be much older, and they are not going to be the same age as a younger disputant, and you think this person is going to have completely different ideas to where this dispute is coming from because he comes from a different generation."

"There is a perceived risk about it coming to court because you don't know what doddery old guy you are going to get on the day."

"I would say they're too old. My stereotype comes from the telly and they are always portrayed as 70+, wrinkly, upper class fellows. I think it's bad for the system because it's having an effect on me, and I should know better."

Values and Bias

"I don't know what the mix of judges is but most of them seem to be, you know, white middle aged men . . . I think you'll find a woman judge has far more listening power because she has far more experience . . . It depends on what the case is about, but I think women on the whole tend to be more open minded. . . . They can think how other people think. They're not biased, they're not sort of narrow-minded, I think's the word, like you get some of the old judges, the old men."

"Most judges come from a very good background. A lot of people say we haven't a class system . . . There will always be a class system in this country; it's embedded in us. People say 'I'm not working class or middle class'. But we are. The way we think, the way we do things. And in that respect judges will have a less than objective view on cases brought before them. I'm not saying it's deliberate, but it's just in the way we're brought up and the way we are. It's like with a bigot . . . that's the way he's been brought up. It's just the way it's embedded, it's so embedded that you really don't have a choice anymore. It's all the brainwashing."

"Some of them come out with very strange statements sometimes and strange rulings. But generally they seem to work. . . . I'm not sure that the way they're appointed is particularly good, it's all a bit political . . . I'd like them to be elected, democratically like every person in high position should be. **What difference would that make?** Well it's a bit like jobs for the boys isn't it? It depends who you know; it depends what school you went to. It would increase maybe numbers of female judges. And judges of other races as well. And people with maybe a more broader outlook on life rather . . . they would seem to be from one area of society really, and some of them I think don't really even know how the rest of us live. I don't think they actually know what life is like for the rest of us . . . They're obviously very bright, very intelligent people who know a lot about the law, . . . but they're not seeing things the way maybe that they need to see it, the way the rest of us see it. And they should reflect society. They should reflect opinions of society, not just their own sort of opinions."

"I found the magistrates that were involved are not everyday people anyway. You know, they had no worries. They're not living in the real world a lot of them. I mean that was my experience anyway. The way they spoke to me, the way they made their decisions. I thought 'You are not real people. You've obviously never been through problems with people'. And I feel a lot of people making these decisions don't have any idea of reality, you know. **What about the judge?** I think judges are not in touch with reality either to be honest. I mean they were upstanding people, perhaps not all of them, a lot of them are, a lot of them aren't. But there again, most of them have come from a privileged background, been to private school what have you, not that I've got anything against or for private schools, But they've not had the life that the people that they are dealing with have had . . . And they are making judgements on people. They have no idea how these people have been brought up, how they've lived, how they're living."

Although the survey could not deal adequately with minorities, survey questionnaires and qualitative interviews occasionally revealed some telling comments about expectations of majority justice. For example:

"Tell you the truth, I think if I was to go to court now, if there was a white person against me, I know that it won't be fair anyway . . . Because there would be some prejudice. Because obviously the judge, the lawyers and everything they're all going to be white and do you know what I mean? From my point of view I know I would lose. **Why do you think that would be? Because they have a prejudice against you?** Yeah, that's what I think. Yeah judges would be in a way. It's the judges. **What makes you think that?** I've heard about so many cases. You do hear a lot of things about any ethnic person. Anyone who's got a case I mean they've always lost. Just going by Stephen Lawrence's case . . . And whoever stabbed him got away . . . 'Cause they were white . . . **So do you think the judicial system favours white people?** Yeah. **Do you feel that about organisations that give advice like Citizens Advice Bureau?** No, not really no. **So who is it exactly that you think has this prejudice?** Many courts. The judges. The police."

Consistency

A constant theme in discussions and interviews was the inconsistency of courts in relation to the sentencing of convicted offenders. The public holds strong views about appropriate punishment and the need for what are seen as 'proportionate' penalties.

"The top judges are not living in the real world with the kind of comments and kind of sentences they give out . . . The thing with the judges you get the same case come up and one will get a suspended sentence and someone else will go to a different court with another judge and they will get 10 years. They are not consistent."

"**Do you have confidence in the judges?** No because of some of the things they come out with. And the decisions. Do you know? They just seem totally ridiculous. In the newspapers when you read it and you think, how did he come to that? And on the news when you see these judges—a girl gets raped and one of them tells them that he should take her out for a meal or she gets a thousand pounds."

Physical characteristics and dress

Although respondents were never asked questions about judicial dress, respondents often raised the subject when they were explaining their views of the judiciary. There was generally very little support expressed for wigs and gowns. Rather it was felt that they merely accentuated age, distance, and a degree of menace.

"Well why's someone got to dress up like that? Everybody in court is exactly the same. You are putting a judge up there like the king. He's there to decide, but why has he got to wear long wigs? I just think it's silly. Do they think they get more respect by looking like that? They are only human beings. I think they get more respect from being seen to be a human being than being someone up there judging you, really as if they are God. It's just what you see on the television. They can wear nice pin stripe suits, which they do before they go into court, so why have they got to put a gown and wig on to go into court? A magistrate to me would come across as more of a human being that understood your problem. They are not above the people they are dealing with."

"I think it would scare me, if I was up in front of a judge. It would terrify me. **Why would you be so frightened of them?** I don't know, I just would be. I think probably more than a jury. **But you've never seen a judge in real life?** No, no I haven't. **So where does your picture of these judges come from?** Probably off the telly! And you do hear things in the news about judges and things that they've done. I can't think of any examples, but I know I've built up a picture. I'm sure there's plenty of nice judges. **What is it about them that makes them so fearsome?** Well I don't think they need them wigs. I think that's really outdated and I just don't think we need that and all the robes. Make them more like normal human beings I think. **Why would that be better?** I just don't like it. I just don't like that feeling, that they are so grand and you're just this small little person, I think that's what it is."

POSITIVE VIEWS OF THE JUDICIARY

Not all views expressed about the judiciary were negative. A minority of respondents in the survey questionnaire and in qualitative interviews expressed general approval of the judiciary and an appreciation of the demands of the job. One or two even approved of wigs and gowns.

"I do like judges wearing wigs and I do like the cloaks. I like all that . . . Because it's history. It's from way, way back. They must have worn a wig for a reason and I think possibly the reason was to make people frightened of them and it would still do it. If you're a bad person and you'd been naughty and there's somebody having a go at you with a great big wig and what have you, you're going to feel a bit daunted aren't you? It's a bad thing as far as I'm concerned. But if you're talking about a murderer or somebody I think it's a good thing."

"We read newspapers and we hear stories about quirky judges and judges that are past their prime and I think that tends to influence one a little. I've met a few judges and I've been quite impressed by the ones I have met. Most of them seem to be quite sensible people. So I don't have a thing about judges."

"Judges are human. I think it must be a difficult job at times because they've got to remain impassive, they can't be seen to be taking sides, they've got to be objective. I think they do a good job with the facilities that are available to them."

"I think that most people are terrified of courts or they get a perverted view of the courts. Some judge high up, passing judgment on everybody before him. Everyone thinks of all the judges as frustrated old men that don't live in the real world, which it is in some cases, but only a small portion. Only a small minority. Most judges have to know what they are doing to be in their position."

"I think they sometimes come out with things where you just don't know what planet they're on. I think because they are so far removed from everyday life, but then part of their role, or maybe you could almost say their mystique is that they have to be removed from everyday life."

CONCLUSION

The survey data on attitudes to the legal system, together with information from focus group discussions and qualitative interviews offer some rather contradictory and disconcerting evidence. The experiences of those respondents who had been involved in court and tribunal hearings seem to be broadly positive on key measures of participation and fairness. However, those with first-hand experience of court hearings, even within a sample of members of the public selected because of their experience of justiciable problems, comprise a very small minority. Expectations of courts, judges, and lawyers are not shaped by personal experience, but by televised representations and tabloid atrocity stories. Most people's experience of courts is as a spectator—watching and reading about what goes on in high-profile and generally criminal cases.

The responses to questioning in this study suggest that although the public regard the courts as important, there is some lack of confidence in the fairness of hearings, a belief that the courts serve the interests of the wealthy, and that the judiciary are remote and out of touch. There is also a strong view that lawyers' charges are unreasonably high.

Some of these findings are broadly consistent with recent surveys of public perceptions of the courts in the United States. A recent review of the findings of 23 statewide surveys suggests that the public is generally poorly informed about the role of the courts and court procedures, and unaware of court reforms[8]. The review of the surveys also concludes that the public "holds certain strong negative images of the state courts: that trial courts are difficult to access, slow to reach decisions, costly to use, difficult to understand . . ."[9]. Other negative views of the courts in the US include a perception of unfairness resulting from racial bias in the courts. However, the strongest and most widespread perception apparently relates to the belief that "the rich are far more likely than others to prevail in legal proceedings."[10]

The most recent study to be published in the United States on "Public Trust and Confidence in the Justice System" involved a survey of 1,826 Americans in early 1999. Respondents were asked to express their opinions regarding the "courts in their community".[11] The results of the study revealed a number of areas of public dissatisfaction with the courts. For example, over two-thirds of respondents did not agree that it was affordable to bring cases to court; 87% felt that having a lawyer

[8] David B Rottman, *Public Trust and Confidence in the State Courts: A Primer*, National Center for State Courts, Working Paper, March 1999.

[9] Ibid p 4.

[10] Ibid p 5.

[11] *How the Public Views The State Courts: A 1999 National Survey*, National Center for State Courts, May 1999.

contributed a lot to the cost of going to court; only 10% of respondents felt that courts in their communities handled cases in an excellent manner; and 70% of African-Americans felt that as a group they were treated somewhat worse or far worse than other groups by courts. Some 44% of respondents felt that judges were out of touch with what was going on in their community. The findings of the present study seem to be remarkably consistent with some of the results of North American studies of public perceptions of courts.

The evidence of qualitative interviews in the present study revealed a depth of ignorance about the legal system and a widespread inability to distinguish between criminal and civil courts. As a result of this confusion about the work of the courts, attitudes towards the judicial system are strongly influenced by media stories about criminal cases and televised representations of criminal trials. The assumption that "court" means a criminal court contributes to a reluctance voluntarily to become involved in court proceedings in order to enforce or defend civil claims. Respondents' views of the legal system often conveyed a sense of alienation from the institutions and processes of the law, despite the fact that the courts are regarded as important and that they would be used if something terrible occurred. There is a lack of sympathy with the jargon of the law, the mystifying procedures of the courts, the closed world of the profession, and what is seen as a worrying camaraderie between opposing advocates. Fears about the cost of embarking on legal proceedings and a belief that resources are crucially important to the outcome of litigation lead many people to feel that the courts are largely irrelevant to their lives and to the resolution of their problems. The view of judges as inconsistent, old and remote is simply a part of this picture.

These are important matters. The courts have a crucial role in maintaining social order, in providing for the peaceful resolution of disputes and in protecting citizens from arbitrary power. Public confidence in the judicial system is also fundamental to the legitimacy that enables the courts to rely on voluntary compliance with promulgated decisions.

8

Paths to Justice: Which Way Now?

"There aren't enough courts, there's not enough lawyers to deal with everybody's problems. And basically, at the end of the day, 85% of the problems in this country are forgotten because people just get frustrated and they just don't think it's worth it. **Does it matter?** Of course it matters—because everybody's problem is important."

"I'm not sure if it's a good idea or not to keep suing people all the time. I think it all comes back to us in the end by higher prices, higher premiums and insurance, so is it a good idea?"

UBIQUITOUS PROBLEMS

Justiciable problems that are more than trivial are a feature of life. Many involve substantial threats to the security and comfort of individuals. Others involve financial loss or the danger of loss. Still others involve merely muddle and inconvenience. The results of this study have shown that the most common problems encountered by the public involve problems to do with faulty goods and services; money problems; injuries and work-related health problems; problems with neighbours; employment problems; and problems flowing from divorce and separation. About forty percent of the population experienced at least one of these problems on one occasion during the five year period covered in the survey; many experienced the same problem more than once, *and* more than one particular type of problem. In fact, as might be expected, problems have a tendency to appear in clusters. Some fourteen percent of the population reported having experienced two or more non-trivial problems during the previous five years. Divorce is often accompanied by problems over children; employment problems and money problems unsurprisingly often appear together. People who suffer accidental injury are often likely to have money problems and employment problems. Consumer problems seem to crop up everywhere—and so it goes on.

Responding to problems

The most common strategy adopted by members of the public when faced with a justiciable problem is to try and sort out the problem or to take some direct personal action that might lead to a resolution of the problem. Only a tiny minority of people faced with a justiciable problem does nothing at all. When this occurs, it is generally a matter of deliberate choice rather than apathy. The kinds of problems about which people do absolutely nothing are those where some harm might flow from taking action (such as damaging a relationship or risking violent retaliation), where respondents believe they are powerless, or where they believe that the process of gaining recompense will be too traumatic. The types of problems most likely to be "lumped" by respondents were those to do with employment, injury, family matters, clinical negligence, and unfair treatment by the police. The types of problems about which respondents were most likely to take action were those to do with divorce and separation, children, neighbours, and faulty goods and services.

When people decide to taken action the most common course is first to make direct contact with the opposing side, in person or writing, to try and achieve their objective or some kind of satisfactory response. Going directly to seek outside advice or assistance to resolve the problem, without first having tried to resolve the problem directly, occurs in only a small minority of specific kinds of cases; for example, some matters to do with divorce, separation and family violence; accidental injury or work-related ill-health; some employment matters; and occasionally when there are problems with neighbours. Failure to attempt a direct approach in those situations may be the result of fear, a total breakdown in relations and communication, or a perception that the only appropriate route to a remedy is via legal proceedings.

Achieving a result

When members of the public handle the resolution of their problems alone they meet with varying degrees of success. About half of those members of the public interviewed in the survey who dealt with their problem without advice or assistance eventually abandoned the matter. This is a relatively high figure that demonstrates the difficulty of

achieving a resolution for many types of problem and the need for
advice and assistance in enforcing rights and defending claims. It also
indicates that the impact of justiciable problems in a high proportion
of cases is apparently simply absorbed by the public, although it takes
a toll. About half of those who had failed to resolve their problem after
taking some action to reach a resolution reported that they had found
the whole business stressful, and one in five reported that their health
had suffered.

The evidence of the study demonstrates clearly, however, that success in resolving problems using self-help strategies depends on the type
of problem being dealt with. Self-helpers who took on the other side in
consumer matters were comparatively successful in achieving a resolution of the problem by comparison with, say, those who tried to deal
with employment problems alone. Success in handling the problem
alone depends on the type of problem, the competence of the person
dealing with the problem and the intransigence of the opposition. Self-
helpers faced with intransigence either gave up or sought help. This
means that the problems taken to advisers are, by definition, the more
serious and intractable.

The problems most frequently taken to advisers are those concerning divorce and separation, neighbours, ownership of property,
employment, and accidental injury. Those least likely to find their way
to advisers are consumer problems, money problems, and landlord and
tenant problems. The problems that are most often taken *directly* to
solicitors, or that eventually end up with solicitors, are divorce and separation problems, accidental injury or work related ill-health, and
matters to do with owning residential property. This reflects the seriousness of these matters to individuals, the extent to which the legal
system is perceived as being relevant to the resolution of the problem
or to securing a remedy, and to some extent the availability of legal aid
or other means of subsidising legal costs.

Once problems have been taken to advisers there are still varying
degrees of success in reaching a resolution of the problem. In cases where
advice had been obtained from a solicitor in private practice, about one
in three were resolved by agreement, just under one in three ended with
a court or tribunal decision or order and a little over one in three
remained unresolved. When advice was obtained from advice agencies
or other non-legal sources, agreement was reached in a third of cases,
around one in ten ended in a court or tribunal hearing, but in just over
half of the cases no agreement or other resolution was achieved.

Some problems appear to have a generally low rate of resolution, for example employment problems, neighbour problems and problems with landlords. On the other hand, if legal advice is obtained or agencies or other advisers provide positive assistance, the likelihood that a resolution will be achieved is increased. For example, an employment problem or personal injury with the benefit of advice from a solicitor or active assistance from another adviser will have an above average rate of resolution. However, the same types of problems without advice from solicitors or active assistance from other advisers have a lower than average rate of resolution.

The problems with the highest rate of resolution are divorce and separation problems, money problems and consumer problems, although in the case of divorce and money problems the resolution was often that the respondent was ordered to pay out money as a result of a court hearing. Cases in which relatively small sums of money are being contested, cases where individuals are being propelled into court by an institution, and cases in which individuals are bringing matters before a tribunal have relatively high resolution rates, although that is often in the form of a formal hearing.

What emerges clearly from the approach of the public to the resolution of justiciable disputes is the very limited use made of formal legal proceedings. About eight in ten justiciable problems are dealt with either successfully or unsuccessfully apparently without any legal proceedings being commenced, without an ombudsman being contacted or any other ADR processes being used. This is despite the fact that about three in five members of the public took some advice about trying to resolve their problem, and that of those, about half received advice from a solicitor at some point about their problem.

Making Choices

This simplified account of the outcome of justiciable problems obscures the complexity of the factors that influence choices about whether to take action, what kind of action to take, how much to persevere and when to give up. At each stage in the process that follows the recognition that something bad has happened or is about to happen, the decision about what to do will be determined by a vast range of factors: Do people have any inkling of what their rights and remedies might be? Do they have the knowledge or confidence to pursue those rights and remedies? Do they feel able to handle the matter alone? If not do they know where to go for help? If they know where to go for help can they access that help, when accessibility depends on the willingness or ability to pay (or be paid for), or on the willingness or ability to join long queues at advice agencies during normal working hours.

All of these matters have to be evaluated against the nature of the threat to be averted or the value to be gained, the uncertainty of the outcome in the light of the obduracy of the opponent, and within the context of beliefs about the expense and trauma involved in bringing the law to bear in the enforcement or defence of rights. The study reveals clearly the error in thinking about legal or other advice needs in relation to what certain kinds of "people" do, rather than focusing on what people do *in relation to particular problems*. The most self-reliant and confident people will, for certain kinds of problems almost automatically obtain legal advice, because the matter is important and because it is immediately characterised as a problem for which legal assistance is required.

> "I didn't turn to anyone for advice [about the consumer problem]. I just did it myself. I don't discuss my business with other people. I don't want to involve others . . . I have always had to do these things myself. I have always been very self-reliant . . . But I have got someone doing my hand—it's in the hands of solicitors. . . . That is very very important. I am suing. I tripped over a raised wire in a motor caravan showroom and I am suing the company. The hand is ruined for ever . . . I wrote to them and I got a letter back from this man saying we don't think it's our fault at all. More or less implying that I wasn't looking. He said very sorry about it but that's it. So of course that got my goat up. So then I went for a solicitor. They advertise in the newspaper, no win no charge. I got legal aid for the first bit." (*Woman interviewed about consumer problem that she resolved without obtaining advice who had previously suffered injury*)

The importance of problem-type as well as person-type in influencing the approach taken to the resolution of justiciable problems means that policy aimed at providing more effective access to successful dispute resolution must have regard not only to the *number* of justiciable problems confronted by the public, but to the *types* of problems experienced, and the ease or difficulty with which those problems can be resolved.

What do people want?

When faced with a justiciable event most people simply want to solve the problem or to obtain compensation for harm and loss. The impulse for punishment, revenge, apologies, or altruistic solutions is far less important than the desire to be rid of the problem, free of the threat, or compensated for the loss. In finding pathways to solutions, members of the public want routes that are quick, cheap, and relatively stress-free. That is true for all social groups. People want to get on with their lives as quickly as possible and few relish the thought of having to pay to obtain what they believe is their right or what is due to them. Individuals take action or defend their position largely (although not exclusively) because they believe that they have a moral claim to the outcome that they seek, however that belief has been formed and irrespective of the accuracy of the belief in strictly legal terms.

In seeking these solutions there is little evidence from this study of any "rush" to law. On the contrary, for most type of problems (excluding divorce and separation, accidental injury and tribunal matters) involvement in legal proceedings is a rare exception. However, the avoidance of legal proceedings requires some interpretation. Members of the public do not necessarily avoid law because they have an instinctive reluctance to press what they believe to be their legal rights. Most people *do* try to press their claims or defend their position, presumably by some reference to rights that have moral or legal force. Many express a strong sense of injustice and unfairness about the problem with which they have been faced. It is not the law that is remote from attempts to resolve justiciable problems, but rather it is formal legal proceedings that are largely remote from the resolution of many day to day justiciable problems. This remoteness derives from the real and imagined cost and discomfort of becoming involved in the procedures that currently exist for the resolution of civil disputes and claims. There is a widespread perception that legal proceedings involve uncertainty, expense and potential long-term disturbance and that only the most serious matters could justify enduring those conditions. Were there to be a revolution in public dispute resolution processes—and this means more than tinkering with procedures and small claims limits—public enthusiasm for mobilising the courts might increase. While it might not be regarded as a social good for the public to be engaged in perpetual litigation, the inability to secure redress for what are seen

as morally justifiable claims and a sense of exclusion from the appara-
tus provided by the state for dispute resolution can lead to frustration,
cynicism, apathy and lack of confidence in institutions.

What do people need?

A clear message that emerges from the study is the profound need for
knowledge and advice about obligations, rights, remedies, and procedures for resolving justiciable problems. This is a need that exists to
varying degrees across all social, educational, and cultural boundaries
and for all types of justiciable problem. It is a trite observation that citizenship requires knowledge, but the pervasive lack of the most rudi-
mentary knowledge about legal rights and procedures for enforcing or
defending rights can lead to an unnecessary level of helplessness even
among the more competent and resourceful.

> "I think if they made information more readily available that would help. I
> believe it is available, something called the Government White Papers.
> Where you get them from I don't know. I have no idea. You could go and
> read it up, but where do you go? That's the thing. The information, if it's
> there, it's not easily accessible. You just need somebody to say if you go to
> this place and talk to them, or you can get the information printed out or
> whatever. Most businessmen have the information there because they deal
> with solicitors all the time, but the ordinary man and woman who get these
> problems find themselves in the middle of nowhere because they don't know
> . . . and they panic and they feel very stupid."

It is unclear what the effect would be of providing effective and accessible procedures for dispute resolution, together with more widespread
knowledge about rights, and procedures for enforcing those rights or
defending claims. There are at least three possibilities. First that it
might lead to greater use of the courts because the public had more
knowledge and the courts would be more accessible. Second it might
result in less resort to the courts because the public would have the
knowledge and confidence to resolve their own disputes directly. Third
it might help to avoid problems and disputes from occurring, and the
need for litigation. At the moment the emphasis in advice provision
tends to be geared towards disaster management. There are few pro-
grammes of public education about rights, obligations and remedies
that might equip the public to take steps to avoid disputes from arising
or to deal confidently and appropriately with difficulties before they

have escalated into something more intractable. As the experiences of respondents to the survey have graphically illustrated, accessing advice when a disaster is looming is as difficult as when the disaster has occurred. In some respects it may be more difficult since the most obvious sources of free advice such as CABx are reported by respondents to suffer from restricted opening hours requiring those in work to take time off in order to obtain advice. They also reportedly suffer from overcrowded offices, unanswered telephones, and difficulties in arranging appointments.

Although in theory information technology offers possibilities for easy access to information, there is still a considerable way to go before the average *adult* member of the public will possess the skill to access such information. Aside from levels of computer literacy there is also the matter of ordinary literacy to be addressed. According to a 1998 survey of 8,000 members of the public aged 16 to 60 for whom English was their first language, around sixteen percent of the adult population is functionally illiterate and in some areas of the country one in four adults are unable to read a parcel label. The study estimated that about eight million people are so bad at reading and writing that they cannot cope with the demands of modern life.[1]

Moreover, the present study has shown that in any case information alone is not helpful for all types of people or for all types of problems. Members of the public with low levels of competence in terms of education, income, confidence, verbal skill, literacy skill, and emotional fortitude are likely to need some help in resolving justiciable problems no matter what the importance of the problem and no matter how intransigent or accommodating the opposition, although this need is likely to be greater where the problem is serious and the opponent is particularly intransigent.

IMPLICATIONS IN THE CONTEXT OF CURRENT REFORMS

The study has demonstrated how common are non-trivial justiciable problems. It has also established that although in most cases action is taken to resolve the problem or to achieve a remedy, about eight in ten problems do not involve any kind of formal court or tribunal proceeding, nor are they taken to ombudsmen, mediation or other alternative

[1] *Adults' Basic Skills*, Basic Skills Agency Survey, 1998.

dispute resolution processes. In about half of all cases no resolution to the problem appears to have been achieved by means of agreement, judicial decision, or court order. These statistics suggest a large "dark figure" of hidden potential demand for the civil justice system. What are the likely implications of these and other key findings of the study for the operation of the civil justice system and for the interests of the public in the context of the current reform agenda?

The study has shown that strategies for dealing with justiciable problems are influenced principally by the nature of the problem, but also by a complicated mix of factors such as: the knowledge and competence of the individual; the resources of the individual or the resources available to them; the accessibility of advice and assistance; the nature of formal legal procedures for resolving problems; and the capacity of the substantive law to offer an effective remedy.

Whether individual members of the public will find it more easy or more difficult to resolve their problems in the future, and whether litigation is likely to increase or decrease, will be influenced by a number of developments affecting individual competence, procedural change to the civil justice system, changes to public subsidisation of legal services and changes in substantive law.

Competence

As far as individual competence is concerned, it is likely that average levels of competence will rise rather than fall in the future. For example, an increasing proportion of the population is receiving higher education; greater emphasis is being placed in schools on improving standards of literacy and numeracy; computer literacy is taught at an early age. These developments should equip the public to make good use of information and advice about rights and obligations, about the legal system and about alternative dispute resolution processes, if that information were to be made more readily available. At the moment there is no place in the national curriculum for information about the most basic rudiments of legal rights and obligations or the nature of the legal system. It is perhaps bizarre that although members of the public will have been taught to distinguish between, say different varieties of trees, they are unable as adults to distinguish between the criminal and civil courts. As the study has shown, "education" about rights and obligations and about the activity of courts is received through the haphazard and selective reports of journalists, whose primary interest is in selling newspapers, and via televised representations of legal proceedings in which the principal objective is entertainment. These "information" sources cannot satisfy the expressed need for greater understanding of rights, obligations and procedures for redress, nor is it desirable that they should be filling the knowledge gap. The evident influence of the media on the public imagination of the legal system is a direct result of the absence of any competing accurate and regular information flow.

There are challenges here for the Community Legal Service, for the courts, for schools, and, indeed, for the judiciary in considering how a co-ordinated programme of public education could be mounted to provide a better understanding of matters that are fundamental to citizenship.

Procedural changes

Given the large number of justiciable problems that are *not* currently being taken to the courts, it is worth considering the likely effect of Lord Woolf's procedural changes on the future behaviour of the public, particularly since a primary aim of those changes was to improve the accessibility of the courts and reduce the cost of obtaining legal redress.

The study has shown that only about twenty percent of non-trivial justiciable problems experienced by private individuals lead to any kind of legal proceedings. However, the extent to which legal proceedings are involved in the resolution of justiciable problems varies substantially depending upon the type of problem being experienced. Those experiencing problems flowing from divorce and separation most frequently commence legal proceedings (about two in every three cases). Legal proceedings are also relatively common in the resolution of problems surrounding the ownership of residential property, where about one in three cases involves legal proceedings. Problems relating to benefits and the schooling of children are also quite likely to involve legal procedures, with about two in five of those matters leading to tribunal proceedings. However, other types of problems are much less likely to involve the commencement of legal proceedings. Only about one in five of those with an employment problem become involved in legal proceedings; about one in ten of those experiencing problems with landlords commences legal proceedings; one in twenty of those with consumer problems issues legal proceedings; and one in fifty of those experiencing a problem with a neighbour tries to use the legal system to resolve the problem.

The procedural changes introduced by Lord Woolf will not have any direct impact on most matters relating to divorce and separation problems since the court procedures for dealing with such cases are different from ordinary civil disputes, nor will they have any direct impact on the way in which tribunal proceedings are conducted for matters to do with social security benefits, employment, education etc, since each individual tribunal is responsible for devising and modifying its own procedures. On the other hand, it is possible that any developing change in judicial culture flowing from the Woolf "revolution" might spill over so that the new emphasis on proportionality and speed and intolerance of delaying tactics may affect the handling of cases in other judicial forums.

For the most common categories of civil dispute, such as consumer problems, money problems, accidental injury, neighbour problems and landlord and tenant problems, Lord Woolf's changes to court procedures are likely to have a mixed effect. The new multi-track procedure for cases with a value in excess of £15,000 has little relevance for the majority of justiciable problems experienced by members of the public as private individuals. The study has shown that disputes over money and legal compensation most commonly involve relatively small sums. Only a handful of cases reported in the study had values in excess of £15,000 and they were mostly divorce and separation problems. Only one or two cases of money problems, accidental injury and employment problems had a value of more than £15,000. There were also remarkably few cases involving sums of between £5,000 and £15,000, which is the scope of the new "fast track" procedure for most civil cases other than personal injury and some housing cases. These last two categories of case will most often be dealt with under the fast track procedure, but the future use of the courts to obtain a remedy for personal injury and housing matters is likely to be more greatly influenced by changes to legal aid provision than by changes in court procedure, as discussed below.

It seems then that the principal impact of the Woolf reforms on the use of the courts by those experiencing justiciable problems will result from the changes to the scope of the small claims jurisdiction. The study shows that in about nine out of ten justiciable problems experienced by private individuals with a money value, the amount in dispute did not exceed £5,000, which is the new limit for the small claims jurisdiction. How will this affect the interest of the public in using the courts? The evidence of this study suggests that those members of the public who had experience of small claims hearings found the experience broadly satisfactory and said that they would be prepared to repeat the experience if it was necessary in the future. This is consistent with other research on the experience of litigants involved in small claims hearings.[2] However, the question of whether those respondents who were unable to secure a satisfactory resolution of their problem by direct means and who expressed reluctance to become involved in legal proceedings might become more enthusiastic now that most cases will be dealt with under this simplified procedure is unclear. Knowledge of the small claims procedure does not appear to be particularly widespread and the information and advice that might arm the public with the necessarily knowledge and skill to handle a small claim hearing on their own is difficult to obtain without some cost, unless people have access to friends and relatives who can offer advice[3]. In this context it is worth noting that among respondents to the survey who reported that their case had reached a small claims hearing, almost all were defendants. Indeed the likelihood of going to any kind of court was far higher for defendants than for plaintiffs. Less than one in ten plaintiffs was involved in a court hearing. This demonstrates the reluctance voluntarily to become involved in legal proceedings that respondents graphically explained during interviews.

The evidence of the survey and qualitative interviews suggests that the average person does not have the necessary knowledge or confidence to launch into even small claims proceedings without guidance and information about their legal position. The problems for those with poor levels of education and literacy are all the more extreme. Herein lies another challenge for the Community Legal Service.

There is also the problem of recent exponential increases in court costs. The attraction of the wider availability of the simplified procedures of the small claims jurisdiction may be reduced by the relatively substantial fees that are now required for the issue of legal proceedings and the new additional charges made for court allocation of cases to the new court "tracks".

---

[2] John Baldwin, *Small Claims in the County Courts in England and Wales*, Oxford, Clarendon Press, 1997; John Baldwin, *Monitoring the Rise of the Small Claims Limit: Litigants' Experiences of Different Forms of Adjudication*, Lord Chancellor's Department, Research Series No 1/97, 1997.

[3] Baldwin has argued on the basis of his research that it is desirable for those attending small claims hearings to obtain prior legal advice: "Lawyers have a very important part to play in the offering of preliminary legal advice to litigants in person, particularly about the merits of their case and about how they should prepare for the hearing." Ibid. p 76.

In any case, even the relatively simple small claims procedure cannot offer much help for those involved in intractable problems such as those involving neighbours, where there appears to be scope perhaps for changes in the law and for the development of alternative methods of dispute resolution.

Alternative Dispute Resolution

The results of the study have demonstrated very clearly how little impact the development of mediation, conciliation and other ADR techniques has had on the way that members of the public seek to resolve their justiciable problems, or on the suggested strategies offered by those providing advice. Quite simply, current ADR activity in the context of civil and family disputes appears to be negligible. The reasons for this are lack of knowledge about ADR services among the general public and to some extent among advisers and the legal profession; suspicion about what is a relatively new development in this country; and also principled objections to the compromise of legal rights and entitlements[4]. However, knowledge about ADR is beginning to increase partly as a result of its vigorous promotion by ADR providers, but more importantly as a result of Lord Woolf's procedural changes. The new power of the courts to direct parties to attempt to settle their difference by means of ADR and to stay proceedings for these attempts to take place, could have a profound influence on the development of ADR. Knowledge of ADR is likely to spread more rapidly if solicitors and other advisers are required by the courts to try it. Moreover, solicitors may begin to experiment with ADR in anticipation of such directions.

The Lord Chancellor's Department is developing its policy on ADR. If future policy leads to a situation in which having attempted ADR becomes a condition of access to trial facilities, this could have a substantial impact on the character of litigation.

Public funding of legal services through the Community Legal Service

Although information about legal costs is notoriously difficult to obtain from members of the public, the results of the study suggest that just over one in four of those respondents who appear to have incurred

---

[4] See Genn, 1998 op. cit., Mulcahy 1999 op. cit., for a discussion of recent experiments in mediating civil disputes.

legal costs in the process of trying to resolve their justiciable problem received legal aid and about two percent had entered into a conditional fee arrangement with a solicitor to deal with their problem. Of those who received legal aid almost six in ten commenced or became involved in legal proceedings. Of the small number who had a conditional fee arrangement, only a tiny minority became involved in legal proceedings. The statistical analysis of advice seeking has shown that those on the lowest incomes were as likely to obtain advice about their problems as those on higher incomes and that the rate at which those on the lowest incomes consulted solicitors was at least as high as for those on higher incomes.

Evidence from qualitative interviews with respondents has demonstrated the relative ease with which those eligible for legal aid can currently access the legal system if that is what they wish and if they have sufficient understanding to seek advice about their problem in the first place. However, of all those who apparently incurred legal costs, less than one in three had received legal aid. By far the greatest use of legal aid was among those experiencing divorce and separation problems, where a little over half of those incurring legal costs received legal aid. Those experiencing other kinds of justiciable problem who incurred legal costs were far less likely to have received legal aid. For example, among those who incurred legal costs in the course of dealing with a dispute with their landlord, about one in three had obtained legal aid; a little under one in five of those with employment problems incurring legal costs obtained legal aid; and about one in ten of those bringing personal injury claims who incurred legal costs had received legal aid. There were also small proportions of neighbour problems, consumer problems, and money problems where legal costs had been incurred and legal aid had been obtained.

It is not clear how changes to legal aid eligibility under the new Community Legal Service Fund will affect this pattern, although it is certain, for example, that members of the public suffering personal injury and other money claims who are currently receiving legal aid will in future have to seek any legal remedy on the basis of a conditional fee arrangement.

The objectives of the new Community Legal Service are to provide general information about the law and legal system and the availability of legal services, as well as providing advice and assistance in the resolution of disputes. The evidence of this study is that there is a great unmet demand for such information, advice and assistance and that this demand runs across a wide income spectrum. The way in which priorities for the provision of services under the Community Legal Service are set will inevitably determine the types of existing need that will be met. This study has demonstrated that in setting those priorities attention should be paid to the volume of problems experienced by the public, the way in which problems of certain kinds tend to cluster[5], the seriousness and intractability of certain types of problems and differential need for *assistance* rather than *advice*, which will depend at least in part on severity of the problem and the competence of the individual[6].

Substantive Law

The problem of how rights and remedies are pursued does not stand still. The establishment of new rights inevitably carries with it the potential for a growth in demand for judicial determination and in this context the implementation of the provisions of the Human Rights Act 1998 has considerable implications for the work of the civil courts. The constant expansion of rights through new legislation carries with it a concomitant expansion of expectations that there ought to be forums in which the rights of private individuals can be made effective.

The access to justice dilemma

The central dilemma in the access to justice argument is whether the objective of legal policy should be to enhance access to legal forums for the resolution of disputes, or whether it should be aimed at preventing problems and disputes from arising, equipping as many members of the public as possible to solve problems when they do arise without recourse to legal action, and diverting cases away from the courts into private dispute resolution forums. It is not an answer to say that they should be twin objectives of policy, because they logically conflict. The more that is done to enhance access to the courts, the less the public will be interested in wasting time in possibly fruitless self-help remedies or alternative dispute resolution processes.

In democracies governed by the rule of law the peaceful resolution of disputes and the protection of the citizen from the exercise of arbitrary

---

[5] See the discussion in Chapter 2.
[6] See the discussion in Chapters 4 and 5.

power are among the primary functions of law. Courts backed by the coercive power of the State are fundamental to these objectives, and the responsibility of the State in the provision of *effective* access to the courts has an impact that goes much wider than the interests of litigants who find their way to court. The contribution of courts to the resolution of disputes is not limited to those cases that are fully adjudicated[7]. It has been persuasively argued that as well as dealing with cases brought to court, disputes can be prevented by what courts do, for example by enabling the public to behave in a way that will avoid disputes from arising[8]. The decisions of courts define the norms that influence private dispute settlement; they approve private settlements and provide guarantees of compliance, without which parties might be unwilling to agree a private settlement. Courts also provide devices for learning about the other side's case, which increases the likelihood of settlement by reducing uncertainty.[9] Thus an effective system for dispute resolution that could be easily mobilised by the public and that was backed by coercive power might eventually lead to *less* rather than more litigation.

The evidence of this study has shown that despite efforts by members of the public to resolve their problems by means of self-help strategies and even after having enlisted the help of advisers, a high proportion of problems are abandoned without any resolution. Greater understanding about the law and greater certainty about the enforcement of legal rights and obligations in the civil context might have an impact on the behaviour of those who evade their responsibilities and obligations when the opportunity exists and when the likelihood of sanction seems remote.

[handwritten:) This is a fact which the gov must take into consideration.]

[7] Marc Galanter, "The Radiating Effects of Courts" in K Boyum and L Mather (eds), *Empirical Theories About Courts*, New York, Longman, 1983, pp 117–38.

[8] Ibid.

[9] Richard O Lempert, "More Tales of Two Courts: Exploring Changes in the 'Dispute Settlement Function' of Trial Courts,' " *Law and Society Review*, 1978, 13:91.

Appendix A
Technical Report

As explained in the introduction to the main report, the study comprised three distinct stages:

1. A face-to-face screening survey of the general population of adults (aged over 18), designed to estimate the incidence of events for which a legal remedy exists ("justiciable problems") in the previous five years. This involved a random sample of 4,125 individuals ("the screening survey").
2. Follow-up face-to-face interviews with 1,134 individuals identified as having experienced a non-trivial justiciable problem ("the main survey").
3. In-depth qualitative interviews with 40 respondents who had experienced a justiciable problem ("the qualitative interviews").

SAMPLE DESIGN

The objective of the sample design was to achieve main interviews with 1,000 people who had experienced problems with a potential legal remedy. As it was not known what proportion of the population would be eligible for a main interview, as having experienced a problem with a potential legal remedy, it was necessary to draw the sample in two stages. The first stage was designed to allow the strike rate to be assessed so that an appropriate number of addresses could be issued at the second stage in order to achieve the target number of interviews.

The screening sample was drawn from the Postcode Address (Small Users) File (PAF). The sample was drawn in the following stages:

1. Postcode sectors with fewer than 550 delivery points were grouped together with an adjacent sector.
2. The list of sectors, including the grouped sectors, was stratified by region, population density and Census data for household tenure.
3. Sectors were selected systematically with probability proportional

to the number of delivery points using a random start and fixed interval method.

4. A fixed number of delivery points were selected per selected sector.

THE ADVANCE LETTER

An advance letter was mailed to sampled households shortly before fieldwork was due to begin, printed on University College London letterhead and signed by author. The letter introduced the subject matter of the study in general terms as "a study to investigate the extent to which people have problems in their daily lives which are difficult to sort out". The letter avoided mention of the legal system, the courts or access to justice and interviewers were briefed to avoid using these terms when introducing the survey. This approach was adopted in order to minimise the risk of respondents focusing on the sorts of problems which involve solicitors and courts to the exclusion of the wider types of problem of concern to the study. Another consideration was that mention of legal processes might discourage respondents who had not had contact with the legal system from co-operating with the study. A copy of the letter appears at Appendix C.

THE SCREENING SURVEY

A random sample of 4,125 individuals aged 18 or over were screened for whether or not they had experienced problems of various sorts over the past five or so years. The majority of these individuals were interviewed in person although in the case of partners a single interview was allowed to cover two individuals, with the respondent providing proxy information for their partner. In order to facilitate collection of screening details for a partner, the screening questionnaire has separate columns for answers for respondents and partners to be recorded.

The screening questionnaire collected information about the following types of problems:

• Employment
• Owning residential property
• Renting out rooms or property
• Living in rented accommodation
• Faulty goods and services

- Money
- Divorce
- Family
- Children
- Accident or injury
- Discrimination.

For each type of problem respondents were presented with a show card listing common examples of these problems and asked the following questions:

- *"Since January 1992, have you (or your husband/wife/partner) had any problems or disputes that were difficult to solve to do with (PROBLEM TYPE)?"*
- The number of such problems they had experienced in this period
- For up to three most recent problems of that type, whether they had done anything to resolve the problem
- If they had done nothing to resolve the problem, the reason why not.
- The date when the problem or dispute began.

The following rules were adopted in classifying problems experienced by respondents:

- Where both the respondent and his/her partner were involved in a problem the problem was recorded for both individuals
- Problems which started before January 1992 were included if they were on-going after that date
- Problems which started before the respondent turned 18 years of age were excluded
- Problems experienced by a respondent in their role as a business person were excluded
- Situations in which the respondent was helping someone else out with their problem were not counted as a problem, except where the respondent was acting on behalf of a child (under the age of 16)
- Criminal problems where a respondent had been legitimately questioned or arrested by the police were not counted. However, perceived unfair treatment by the police was counted
- Problems which occurred abroad were excluded.

EVENT SELECTION FOR THE MAIN SURVEY

An event selection form was completed for each individual who had experienced an eligible problem and had either taken action over it or not taken action for a reason other than the triviality of the problem. "Trivial" problems were defined as those where respondents stated that they felt the problem was not important or they had no dispute with anyone regarding it or they thought the other person in the dispute was right.

The event selection form was designed to identify a single problem to be asked about in the main interview and, in the case of shared problems, to identify the best person in the household to ask about this problem in the main interview. Where respondents had been involved in more than one problem within the reference period, the event selection form identified the *second most recent* problem as the one to be covered in the main interview.

THE MAIN QUESTIONNAIRE

The main questionnaire focused on the single problem identified using the event selection form and covered the following issues in sequence:

1. The nature of the dispute.
2. Advice—sources of advice, the nature of advice received and the respondent's satisfaction with it.
3. Where no advice was sought, the reason why.
4. Objectives—the main reasons for taking action and the extent to which these were achieved.
5. Experiences of court and dispute resolution processes, including mediation, tribunals and dealings with imbudsmen.
6. Settlements reached, with or without help from advisers.
7. Amounts recovered.
8. Amounts paid out.
9. Dispute resolution: whether the dispute was ended by agreement or adjudication.
10. Costs—legal costs, financial support and other financial costs of the dispute.
11. General assessments of the experience of dealing with the problem:

regrets, the impact of the problem and respondents' attitudes to the legal system.

A copy of the main interview questionnaire appears at Appendix C.

QUESTIONNAIRE DEVELOPMENT

The questionnaires and other fieldwork instruments were developed by the author and researchers at the *National Centre for Social Research*. The key elements of the design were discussed and agreed with members of the project advisory panel convened by the Nuffield Foundation.

Several stages of questionnaire development were carried out in the Spring and Summer of 1997 including focus group discussions with advice agencies, members of the public and solicitors and pilots of the questionnaire and other survey instruments.

FIELDWORK PROCEDURES AND RESPONSE RATES

Interviewers called at each issued address in order to check that it was a private address and to ascertain how many adults aged 18 or over lived there. Eleven per cent of issued addresses were found to be ineligible because they were untraceable, were empty, demolished or not yet built, because they contained a business, institution or holiday home. (Table 1). At the remainder of addresses, which were private households, interviewers sought to establish how many adults aged 18 years or over lived there. This information was recorded for 79% of private households (Table 1).

Where the interviewers found more than one dwelling unit at the address they were required to list them all and then randomly select one dwelling unit to be contacted for the study, using instructions provided with the sample details.

A total of 4,608 adults aged 18 or over were identified within the 2,595 addresses where information was obtained, an average of 1.6 adults per address. Screening interviews were completed with 4,125 of these adults, representing a response rate of 89% (Table 2).

A total of 1,419 respondents to the screening survey (34% of the sample) were classified as eligible for the main interview as having experienced one or more problems for which a legal remedy exists and having

Table 1. Incidence of private households and success rate for establishing the number of residents in them.

	Number	%	%
Addresses issued for screening	3,702	100	
Of which:			
Contain no private households	416	11	
—not traced	36	1	
—empty, demolished, not yet built	226	6	
—business or institution only	71	2	
—weekend or holiday home	53	1	
—other	30	1	
Contain private households	3,286	89	100
Of which:			
No information obtained about residents	691	21	
—no contact made	174	5	
—information refused on doorstep	456	14	
—refusal to head office	60	2	
Information obtained about residents	2,595		79

Table 2. Success rate for screening individuals.

	Number	%
Number of adults identified at addresses where information obtained	4,608	100
Of which:		
Number of adults not screened	483	11
Number of adults screened	4,125	89

taken action or not taken action for a reason other than the triviality or the problem (Table 3). Where two or more adults in the same household had a shared problem only one was selected for the main interview, by a random method. Thus, of the 1,419 people who were eligible, 1,248 (88%) were issued for the main stage of fieldwork.

Table 3. Eligibility rate of screened adults.

	Number	%	%
Number of adults screened	4,125	100	
Of which:			
Not eligible for main interview	2,706	66	
Eligible for main interview	1,419	34	100
Of which:			
Not issued for main interview as shared problem covered by another interview in the household	171		12
Issued for main interview	1,248		88

At the main stage of fieldwork interviews were completed with 1,134 people, representing a response rate of 91% of the issued sample (Table 4).

Table 4. Response rate for main interview.

	Number	%
Issued for main interview	1,248	100
No interview achieved	114	9
Interview completed	1,134	91

Taking the information in Tables 1 to 4 together a cumulative response rate can be calculated by multiplying together the proportion of private addresses at which information was obtained (79%), the proportion of identified adults who were screened (89%) and the proportion of selected adults for whom a main interview was completed (91%). This calculation produces a cumulative response rate of 64%.

FIELDWORK

The survey was carried out in Autumn 1997 and Spring 1998 by interviewers of the *National Centre for Social Research*. Interviewers were personally briefed by the author and project researchers in briefing conferences in regional centres. Fieldwork was managed by staff at the *National Centre*'s offices in Brentwood and by a network of local field managers. Following the *National Centre*'s usual quality control procedures a proportion of interviews were supervised during the survey or had their work back-checked by the office by re-contacting respondents.

DATA PROCESSING AND ANALYSIS

Interviews were edited and coded at the *National Centre*'s data processing department in Brentwood. Data were entered by keying. Initial analysis and weighting was carried out at the *National Centre* using Quantum. Subsequent analyses were carried out by the author and the *National Centre* using SPSS analysis software.

WEIGHTING

The dataset of problems for which a main interview was completed was designed to be representative of all problems for which a legal remedy exists which were experienced by adults in England and Wales in the reference period of the past five years. The following weighting corrections were applied:

- A screening weight was applied to correct the composition of the screening sample to match that of the population as a whole
- A correction for the number of eligible problems experienced by respondents to correct for the tendency for problems experienced by respondents who had multiple problems to be under-represented in the unweighted sample
- A correction for the incidence of shared problems to correct for the tendency of shared problems to be over-represented in the unweighted sample.

A single weighting factor was calculated for each interview to make the above three corrections and ensure that the total weighted sample was scaled back to the unweighted number of interviews, that is 1,134.

QUALITATIVE INTERVIEWS

The sample for the qualitative interviews was purposely selected in order to include a range of common problem types including personal injury problems, neighbour disputes, consumer disputes, employment disputes and family disputes. The sample was organised in five groups according to the type of action the respondent took in response to the problem.

A Those who took no action to resolve problem
   (No to QA17(a), and no to Q18(a), and no to QA32, and no to QA33).
B Those who took action to resolve problem and did so without using an adviser of any kind
   (No to QA17(a) and Yes to QA32).
C Those who sought non-legal advice and dealt with the problem themselves
   (Yes to QA17 *but not* code 02, or 10, or 11, or 12, or 15).
D Those who sought legal advice and resolved problem without court hearing
   (Yes to QA17 code 02, or 10, or 11, or 12, or 15; AND No to QD1(a); AND Yes to D14(a)).
E Those who sought legal advice and resolved problems via court hearing
   (Yes to QA17 code 02, or 10, 0r 11, or 12, or 15 and YES to AD1(a)).

A total of 40 qualitative interviews were carried out by interviewers from the *National Centre*'s qualitative research department in the autumn of 1998. The interviewers were briefed and debriefed by the author. The topic guide is reproduced in Table 5.

Table 5. Topic guide for qualitative follow-up interviews.

---

1. *Initial motivations for taking or not taking action*
   - What effect was the problem having—impact on life/work/health?
   - Why did something have to be done?
   - Or why was nothing done despite effect of problem—was it lack of knowledge? Lack of money? Not wanting more trouble? Just too much bother? Too upset?
   - If no action taken, was there anything that could have been provided that would have assisted them to resolve the problem? Advice? Information? Support?

2. *Reasoning leading to approach taken*:
   - How did they formulate the problem?
   - What did they think could be done? Why did they think nothing could be done?
   - Feelings of blame, anger, injustice? Or not?

3. *Objectives in taking action*
   - What were they seeking?
   - What did they *really* want? [this needs careful probing]
   - Did anyone else have a part in framing those objectives or expectations?

4. *Why did they seek advice or not seek advice*:
   - What made them think advice was necessary?
   - What were they hoping for?
   - How did they come to go to that/those advisers?
   - What did they get from the adviser(s)?
   - Assessment of quality of adviser—knowledge, approach, how could they have been better?

5. *Resolving the dispute*:
   - What steps were taken with or without help to resolve the dispute?
   - How did it end (if at all)?
   - Why did it end in that way?
   - Responses to court based resolution processes
   - Responses to non-court based resolution processes

6. *Assessments*:
   Did they achieve their objectives? If not, why not?
   Was the outcome worth the effort expended?
   Whether took action or not: how would they act differently if they were faced with a similar situation in the future?
   How could the process have been made easier/better?
   How should a problem like theirs be dealt with in a well-ordered society?

Positive aspects of dealing with the problem?
Negative aspects of dealing with the problem?

7. *General attitudes to the civil justice system:*
    • What are the courts for?
    • Should ordinary people be able to use the courts effectively?
    • What agencies, organisations, institutions should be made available to help people resolve problems such as theirs?

Appendix B

Logistic regression analysis

The objective of the analysis was to identify and explain the factors and respondent characteristics that are important in influencing:

- whether the respondent sought advice for the problem
- whether the dispute was resolved
- whether the main objective was achieved
- perceived fairness of the outcome

The statistical method utilised was mainly multiple logistic regression. Regression analysis is a versatile data analysis technique that can be used to study relations among variables. Logistic regression is a multivariate statistical technique that is used to predict a binary dependent variable from a set of independent variables, i.e. the probability that an event will occur. There are many ways of identifying the significant independent variables, but the most well known way is by means of the 'forward stepwise selection'.

Using this method, initially the model contains only the constant and no independent variables. At each step, the value with the smallest significance level for the score statistic is entered into the model, provided that is less than the chosen significance level (e.g. 0.05). All variables in the forward stepwise block that have been entered are then examined to see if they meet removal criteria. If the significance level for the log likelihood for the model, or the significance level for the Wald statistic for a variable exceeds the chosen cut-off point for removal (usually 0.1), the variable is removed from the model. If no variables meet removal criteria, the next eligible variable is entered into the model. The process continues until no variables meet entry or removal criteria.

The analysis used the following 4 (binary) dependent variables (variable names are given in brackets using capital letters):

- whether any advice was sought about the problem(DEPEND1)
- whether the dispute was resolved i.e. agreement reached or court/tribunal/ombudsman's decision or order given (DEPEND2)

- whether main objective was achieved (either completely or partly) (DEPEND3)
- whether the outcome achieved was fair (only for those who reached agreement or where there was a court/tribunal/ombudsman's decision or order) (DEPEND4).

The independent variables used in the analysis were:

- AGE2 – Age group
- DADTYP – Type of advice sought
- DADTYP1 – Type of advice and whether positive assistance given by CABx and other advisers
- DADSETT2 – Type of advice and problem resolved
- DAMOUNT3 – Type of remedy sought (revised to include two levels of lump sum)
- DINCOME2 – Income group
- DLAWATT – Attitude to courts (whether confident of a fair hearing)
- DNEGEFF – Whether any negative effects while sorting out problem
- DPLAINT2 – Whether a plaintiff or defendant
- DPROB – Problem type
- MJ3B2 – Employment status
- MJ3D2 – Social class
- MJ8B2 – Highest educational qualification
- SEX – Sex

Their use in the four models is summarised below:

	Depend1: whether any advice sought	Depend2: whether dispute resolved completely or partly	Depend3: whether main objective achieved	Depend4... whether outcome was fair
AGE2	X	X	X	X
DADTYP			X	
DADTYP1		X		
DADSETT2				X
DAMOUNT3	X	X	X	X
DINCOME2	X	X	X	X
DLAWATT	X			X
DNEGEFF			X	X
DPLAINT2	X	X	X	X

	Depend1: whether any advice sought	Depend2: whether dispute resolved completely or partly	Depend3: whether main objective achieved	Depend4... whether outcome was fair
DPROB	X	X	X	X
MJ3B2	X	X	X	X
MJ3D2	X		X	X
MJ8B2	X	X	X	
SEX	X	X	X	X

The following tables provide the regression coefficients (log odds), odds ratios, p-values and the absolute value of the R-statistic (the partial correlation between the dependent and each of the independent variables, indicating the contribution of each independent variable in the logistic regression model) for the four logistic regression models discussed in Chapters 4, 5 and 6. The models were fitted using SPSS (Statistical Package for the Social Sciences). The tables present the variables that are significant after a forward conditional stepwise logistic regression model for identifying the factors associated with advice seeking, resolving disputes, achievement of objectives and fairness of outcome. Unless stated, all coefficients are compared with the theoretical average, i.e. there is no reference category.

Table B1 Obtaining advice

Variable	Coef. (log odds)	Odds ratio	p-value	R
Respondent's age [age2]			0.000	0.10
18–24	–0.49	0.61	0.000	
25–34	–0.25	0.78	0.005	
35–44	–0.03	0.98	0.786	
45–54	0.63	1.87	0.000	
55–64	0.27	1.31	0.052	
65+	–0.07	0.93	0.645	
Missing	–0.07	0.94	0.749	
Remedy sought [DAMOUNT3]			0.000	0.06
Smaller lump sum: £500 or less	–0.04	0.96	0.802	
Larger lump sum: £501 or more	0.74	2.10	0.000	
Money amount: regular payments	–0.14	0.87	0.319	

Table B1 cont.

Variable	Coef. (log odds)	Odds ratio	p-value	R
No money amount	−0.26	0.77	0.002	
Not applicable/not answered	−0.31	0.74	0.001	
Income [DINCOME2]			0.024	0.03
Under £8,000	−0.06	0.94	0.504	
£8,000–£14,999	0.04	1.04	0.665	
£15,000–£28,999	0.10	1.11	0.206	
£29,000 and over	0.24	1.27	0.010	
Missing	−0.32	0.73	0.006	
Attitude to courts [DLAWATT]			0.004	0.04
Positive (confident)	0.17	1.19	0.026	
Neither positive not negative / can't say	0.29	1.34	0.002	
Negative (not confident)	0.08	1.09	0.338	
Not answered	−0.55	0.58	0.001	
Whether defendant [DPLAINT2]			0.015	0.03
Assumed to be defendant	−0.16	0.85	0.015	
Others / can't say	0.16	1.18	0.015	
Problem type [DPROB]			0.000	0.29
Employment	0.47	1.60	0.004	
Neighbour problems	0.66	1.93	0.000	
Divorce/separation	1.77	5.89	0.000	
Accident or injury	0.13	1.14	0.398	
Money (excluding benefits)	−1.22	0.30	0.000	
Landlord and tenant	−0.41	0.67	0.001	
Consumer problems	−1.58	0.21	0.000	
Owning property	0.91	2.48	0.000	
DSS/Education	−0.24	0.78	0.147	
Other problem types	−0.48	0.62	0.000	
Education [MJ8B2]			0.000	0.11
no qualifications	−0.45	0.64	0.000	
degree etc.	0.04	1.05	0.573	
A levels etc.	0.64	1.89	0.000	
O-levels/CGEs/ungraded/other	−0.24	0.79	0.001	
Sex			0.022	0.03
Male	−0.10	0.91	0.022	
Female	0.10	1.10	0.022	
Constant	0.73		0.000	

Table B2 Problem resolution (agreement/court/trib/omb decision)

Variable	Coef. (log odds)	Odds ratio	p-value	R
Age [AGE2]			0.000	0.069
18–24	−0.12	0.89	0.325	
25–34	0.28	1.32	0.001	
35–44	−0.06	0.95	0.536	
45–54	−0.24	0.79	0.022	
55–64	0.12	1.13	0.356	
65+	−0.46	0.63	0.005	
Missing	0.48	1.61	0.012	
Remedy sought [DAMOUNT3]			0.000	0.117
Smaller lump sum: £500 or less	−0.11	0.90	0.454	
Larger lump sum: £501 or more	0.85	2.33	0.000	
Money amount: regular payments	0.15	1.16	0.283	
No money amount	−0.20	0.82	0.011	
Not applicable/not answered	−0.68	0.51	0.000	
Income [DINCOME2]			0.000	0.056
Under £8,000	−0.29	0.75	0.002	
£8,000–£14,999	0.02	1.02	0.785	
£15,000–£28,999	−0.01	0.99	0.845	
£29,000 and over	0.36	1.44	0.000	
Missing	−0.08	0.92	0.467	
Problem type [DPROB]			0.000	0.138
Employment	−0.36	0.69	0.012	
Neighbour problems	−0.67	0.51	0.000	
Divorce/separation	0.52	1.68	0.000	
Accident or injury	−0.07	0.93	0.623	
Money (excluding benefits)	0.50	1.65	0.000	
Landlord and tenant	−0.46	0.63	0.001	
Consumer problems	0.61	1.84	0.000	
Owning property	−0.16	0.85	0.382	
DSS/Education	0.16	1.17	0.340	
Other problem types	−0.06	0.94	0.572	
Employment status [MJ3B2]			0.039	0.023
Self–employed	−0.16	0.86	0.160	
Managers	−0.23	0.79	0.035	
Foremen	0.12	1.13	0.296	
Other and NA	−0.05	0.95	0.467	
Missing	0.32	1.38	0.013	
Education [MJ8B2]			0.004	0.043
no qualifications	−0.21	0.81	0.019	

Table B2 cont.

Variable	Coef.	Odds ratio (log odds)	p-value	R
degree etc.	−0.12	0.89	0.119	
A levels etc.	0.21	1.23	0.011	
O–levels/CGEs/ungraded/other	0.12	1.13	0.084	
Type of advice [DADTYP1]			0.000	**0.080**
Legal advice *(reference)*	0.00	1.00		
Other advice (not legal) with action	−0.13	0.88	0.342	
Other advice (not legal) with no action	−0.35	0.70	0.009	
No advice	−0.60	0.55	0.000	
Whether plaintiff [DPLAIN2]			0.000	**0.098**
Defendant	0.45	1.57	0.000	
Other	−0.45	0.64	0.000	
Constant	0.63		0.000	

Table B3 **Achieving objectives**

Variable	Coef.	Odds ratio (log odds)	p-value	R
Age [AGE2]			0.000	0.13
18–24	−0.13	0.88	0.301	
25–34	0.50	1.65	0.000	
35–44	0.17	1.19	0.065	
45–54	0.38	1.47	0.000	
55–64	−0.99	0.37	0.000	
65+	−0.11	0.90	0.484	
Missing	0.18	1.20	0.412	
Remedy sought [DAMOUNT3]			0.006	0.04
Smaller lump sum: £500 or less	−0.20	0.82	0.189	
Larger lump sum: £501 or more	0.50	1.65	0.003	
Money amount: regular payments	0.04	1.04	0.735	
No money amount	−0.06	0.94	0.458	
Not applicable/not answered	−0.28	0.75	0.004	
Income [DINCOME2]			0.000	0.06
Under £8,000	0.04	1.04	0.679	
£8,000–£14,999	0.24	1.28	0.007	
£15,000–£28,999	0.15	1.16	0.053	
£29,000 and over	−0.35	0.70	0.000	
Missing	−0.08	0.92	0.483	

Variable	Coef.	Odds ratio (log odds)	p-value	R
Problem type [DPROB]			0.000	0.16
Employment	−0.27	0.76	0.061	
Neighbour problems	−0.34	0.71	0.013	
Divorce/separation	−0.19	0.83	0.164	
Accident or injury	0.64	1.90	0.000	
Money (excluding benefits)	−0.11	0.89	0.364	
Landlord and tenant	−1.14	0.32	0.000	
Consumer problems	0.44	1.55	0.000	
Owning property	0.20	1.22	0.272	
DSS/Education	0.54	1.72	0.001	
Other problem types	0.23	1.26	0.036	
Employment status [MJ3B2]			0.000	0.08
Self–employed	0.00	1.00	0.985	
Managers	−0.91	0.40	0.000	
Foremen	−0.34	0.71	0.044	
other and NA	−0.30	0.74	0.026	
Missing	1.56	0.49	0.002	
Education [MJ8B2]			0.003	0.05
no qualifications	−0.02	0.98	0.811	
degree etc.	0.10	1.11	0.226	
A levels etc.	−0.26	0.77	0.002	
O–levels/CGEs/ungraded/other	0.18	1.20	0.011	
Sex			0.021	0.03
Male	0.11	1.11	0.021	
Female	−0.11	0.90	0.021	
Type of advice [DADTYP]			0.043	0.02
Legal advice	−0.08	0.92	0.240	
Other advice (not legal)	0.16	1.17	0.012	
No advice	−0.08	0.92	0.219	
Class [MJ3D2]			0.000	0.08
Professional	0.05	1.05	0.810	
Intermediate	0.57	1.77	0.000	
skilled (non–man.)	0.47	1.60	0.000	
skilled (manual)	−0.05	0.96	0.749	
partly skilled	−0.05	0.95	0.739	
Unskilled	0.50	1.64	0.010	
Other	−1.50	0.22	0.003	
Whether plaintiff [DPLAINT2]			0.000	0.06
Assumed to be defendant	0.28	1.32	0.000	
Others/can't say	−0.28	0.76	0.000	

Table B3 (Cont.):

Variable	Coef.	Odds ratio (log odds)	p-value	R
Negative effects [DNEGEFF]			0.000	0.10
Yes	−0.31	0.73	0.000	
No/not answered	0.31	1.36	0.000	
Constant	0.44		0.000	

Table B4: **Perceived fairness of outcome**

Variable	Coef.	Odds ratio (log odds)	p-value	R
Remedy sought [DAMOUNT3]			0.000	0.153
Smaller lump sum: £500 or less	0.00	1.00	0.995	
Larger lump sum: £501 or more	−0.46	0.63	0.055	
Money amount: regular payments	−0.63	0.53	0.001	
No money amount	0.71	2.02	0.000	
Not applicable/not answered	0.38	1.47	0.015	
Income [DINCOME2]			0.000	0.107
Under £8,000	0.20	1.22	0.264	
£8,000–£14,999	−0.22	0.80	0.157	
£15,000–£28,999	0.04	1.04	0.801	
£29,000 and over	−0.72	0.49	0.000	
Missing	0.71	2.04	0.008	
Problem type [DPROB]			0.000	0.143
Employment	−1.44	0.24	0.042	
Neighbour problems	5.56	259.36	0.353	
Divorce/separation	−1.10	0.33	0.116	
Accident or injury	−0.14	0.87	0.852	
Money (excluding benefits)	−0.14	0.87	0.846	
Landlord and tenant	−1.29	0.28	0.071	
Consumer problems	−1.18	0.31	0.090	
Owning property	0.52	1.68	0.508	
DSS/Education	−0.68	0.51	0.346	
Other problem types	−0.17	0.89	0.866	
Employment status [MJ3B2]			0.000	0.099
self–employed	1.07	2.93	0.000	
Managers	−0.03	0.97	0.892	
Foremen	−0.33	0.72	0.063	
Other and NA	−0.31	0.73	0.018	
Missing	−0.41	0.67	0.084	

Variable	Coef.	Odds ratio (log odds)	p-value	R
Sex			0.006	0.060
Male	–0.21	0.81	0.006	
Female	0.21	1.24	0.006	
Whether plaintiff [DPLAINT2]			0.000	0.084
Assumed to be defendant	–0.35	0.71	0.003	
Others / can't say	0.35	1.42	0.003	
Negative effects [DNEGEFF]			0.000	0.124
Yes	–0.47	0.62	0.000	
No/not answered	0.48	1.61	0.000	
Advice/outcome [DADSETT2]			0.000	0.109
Legal advice and problem resolved	0.44	1.56	0.000	
No legal advice but problem resolved	–0.44	0.64	0.000	
Attitude to courts [DLAWATT]			0.000	0.167
Positive (confident)	0.63	1.87	0.000	
Neither positive nor negative/ can't say	0.33	1.39	0.067	
Negative (not confident)	–0.59	0.56	0.001	
Not answered	–0.37	0.69	0.323	
Constant	1.80		0.009	

CHAID ANALYSIS

Logistic regression analysis identified a number of factors that appear to discriminate between people in terms of the various outcome measures. It is not, however, clear how these factors interact in order to produce a number of different and defined population subgroups with a specific size. To address this an analysis has been undertaken using the CHAID (CHi–squared Automatic Interaction Detector) module within SPSS, in order to divide the population into groups who differ in terms of advice seeking and settling disputes.

CHAID is a multivariate statistical technique, which operates broadly as follows: first, a dependent variable that divides the population into two or more groups is defined (for example, those who seek advice and those who do not). Second, a set of independent variables (possible discriminators) is identified for inclusion in the analysis. Third, the CHAID algorithm searches these independent variables and selects the variable that discriminates best in terms of the dependent variable (for example having or not having had advice) and divides the population into groups based on this variable. Fourth, within each of these groups, CHAID searches through the remaining variables for the next best discriminator and further sub–divides the population within the group into sub–groups based on this variable. Finally, this sub–division process stops when no further split can be found that satisfies the chi–squared criterion for statistical significance.

The following tables provide the seeking advice and resolving dispute rates for the population subgroups identified by CHAID and discussed in Chapters Four and Five. The tables are presented in ascending order of percentage obtaining advice and resolving the dispute respectively.

Table B5 **Obtaining Advice**

GROUP	% of total	% seeking advice
Money or consumer problems, earning up to £29K, no money amount sought	7.2%	20%
Money or consumer problems, earning up to £29K, money amount sought, no qualifications or O-levels etc.	8.9%	28%
Landlord and tenant, DSS education or other problem, no qualifications or O-levels, negative attitude to law	5.5%	31%
Money or consumer problems, earning more than £29K	7.6%	51%
Landlord and tenant, DSS education or other problem, no qualifications or O-levels, positive or neutral attitude to law	11.6%	54%
Money or consumer problems, earning up to £29K, money amount sought, degree or A-levels	5.3%	59%
Landlord and tenant, DSS education or other problem, degree or A-levels	16.2%	68%
Accident or injury problems	7.1%	69%
Employment, neighbour or owning property problem, earning more than 29K a year	7.2%	72%
Employment, neighbour or owning property problem, earning less than 15K a year	7.3%	78%
Employment, neighbour or owning property problem, earning more than £15K and less than £29K a year	6.4%	90%
Divorce / separation problems	9.8%	92%
Total	100.0%	

Table B6 Resolving Problems

GROUP	% of total	% sresolving
Neighbour or landlord and tenant problems, with no qualifications	5.4%	17%
Divorce/separation, money, consumer, owning property, DSS/education or other type of problem, above 65 years old	3.9%	23%
Employment, accident or injury problem, other type of advice without action taken, or no advice	6.1%	23%
Divorce/separation, money, consumer, owning property, DSS/education or other type of problem, up to 64 years old, money value not applicable, with other type of employment status	8.3%	28%
Neighbour or landlord and tenant problems, with degree, A-level or O-level etc.	13.7%	33%
Employment, accident or injury problem, with legal advice or other type of advice with action taken	8.9%	47%
Divorce/separation, money, consumer, owning property, DSS/education or other type of problem, up to 64 years old, money value not applicable, self–employed, managers or foremen	6.2%	55%
Divorce/separation, money, consumer, owning property, DSS/education or other type of problem, up to 64 years old, seeking either no money or less than £500	37%	56%
Divorce/separation, money, consumer, owning property, DSS/education or other type of problem, up to 64 years old, seeking regular payments or more than £500	10.5%	66%
Total	100.0%	

Appendix C

Faculty of Laws

UNIVERSITY COLLEGE LONDON
BENTHAM HOUSE ENDSLEIGH GARDENS LONDON WC1H 0EG
Tel 0171 391 1440

Dear Sir or Madam,

I am writing to ask for your help with a study to investigate the extent to which people have problems in their daily lives which are difficult to sort out. We are interested in experiences in many aspects of life - working life, family life, money matters, renting or owning property and many more. This is the first national study of its kind which will seek to explore how people deal with their problems - some may seek advice or help from other people or organisations, some may try to sort out the problem on their own, others may do nothing. This study will enable us to identify successful and unsuccessful ways of dealing with problems, and we hope will lead to improvements in the advice and help available to people.

The study is being carried out by researchers at University College London and Social and Community Planning Research (an independent non-profit making research institute). The research is funded by the Nuffield Foundation.

So that we can get the national picture we have selected addresses at random from a list kept by the Post Office of all addresses in England and Wales. An SCPR interviewer will be calling at your address in the near future to ask your household to help with the study. The interviewer will carry an identification card with a photograph.

Even if you think you have not had any problems in the last few years we would still like to speak to you - without your help we will not be able to estimate the numbers of people in the population who have not experienced problems in recent years. The usefulness of the survey depends very much on the cooperation of all those selected and I do hope you will agree to take part.

The information you provide will be treated in the strictest confidence and the report of the study will be produced in such a way that no individuals will be identifiable.

If you have any queries about the survey, please contact one of the researchers at SCPR (Sarah Beinart or Patten Smith) on 0171 250 1866.

Many thanks in anticipation of your help.

Yours sincerely,

Professor Hazel Genn

Head Office: 35 NORTHAMPTON SQUARE
LONDON EC1V 0AX
Tel: 0171 250 1866 Fax 0171 250 1524

Field and DP Office: 100 KINGS ROAD
BRENTWOOD, ESSEX CM14 4LX
Tel: 01277 200 600 Fax: 01277 214 117

P1606   **SCREENING QUESTIONNAIRE**   **1997**

SERIAL NO : ☐☐☐☐☐☐   PERSON NO. (Respondent): ☐☐

DATE: ☐☐☐☐☐☐

START TIME: ☐☐☐☐
(24 hour clock)

PERSON NO. (Partner): ☐☐
(if 'Yes' at Q1a)

1a Can I just check, do you have a (husband/wife) or partner
living in this household?

Yes	1	ASK b)	222
No	2	GO TO d)	

IF SPOUSE / PARTNER IN HOUSEHOLD
b **REFER TO ARF, AND TRANSFER PERSON NUMBER OF PARTNER AT TOP OF PAGE**

c **READ OUT:**
I would like to ask you about different sorts of problems you or your
(husband / wife / partner) might have had.

Please only include problems you have had <u>yourselves</u>, not situations
where you helped somebody else with *their* problem.

We are interested in those problems you or your (husband / wife / partner)
have experienced as <u>individuals</u>, not those experienced by your employer
or any business you might run.

We are also only interested in problems you or your (husband / wife / partner) had
since the age of 18.

ASK Q2 - Q15 FOR RESPONDENT <u>AND</u> PARTNER | **GO TO Q2** |

IF <u>NO</u> SPOUSE / PARTNER IN HOUSEHOLD
d **READ OUT:**
I would like to ask you about different sorts of problems you might have had.

Please only include problems you have had <u>yourself</u>, not situations where
you helped somebody else with *their* problem.

We are interested in those problems you have experienced as an <u>individual</u>,
not those experienced by your employer or any business you might run.

We are also only interested in problems you had since the age of 18.

ASK Q2 - Q15 FOR RESPONDENT <u>ONLY</u>

2

SHOW SCREEN CARD A
2a Since January 1992, have you (or your husband/wife/partner)
had any problems or disputes that were difficult to solve
to do with employment?
CODE ALL THAT APPLY

| INCLUDE ALL PROBLEMS |
| SINCE JAN '92 EVEN IF |
| **STARTED** BEFORE THEN. |

| EXCLUDE PROBLEMS |
| BEFORE AGE OF 18. |
| INCLUDE IF BECAME 18 |
| DURING DISPUTE. |

	Respondent	Partner	
... losing a job	1	1	223-29
... getting pay or a pension	2	2	
... other rights at work (eg maternity leave, sickness pay, holiday entitlement, working hours)	3	3	
... changes to your terms and conditions of employment	4 → b)	4 → b)	
... unsatisfactory or dangerous working conditions	5	5	
... harassment at work	6	6	
... unfair disciplinary procedures	7	7	
NO, NONE OF ABOVE	0 → Q3	0 → Q3	

IF PROBLEM
SHOW SCREEN CARD A
b How many problems of this sort have you (has your
husband / wife / partner) had since January 1992?

ENTER NUMBER: ☐☐ ☐☐   230-31

c **COMPLETE GRID ON NEXT PAGE FOR RESPONDENT
(AND PARTNER) FOR UP TO 3 PROBLEMS SINCE
JANUARY 1992, STARTING WITH THE MOST RECENT.**

WORK <u>DOWN</u> THE GRID FOR EACH PROBLEM

**IF FOUR OR MORE PROBLEMS, TAKE THE THREE MOST
RECENT.**

3

SHOW SCREEN CARD X (coloured)

2d Thinking of the (most recent / 2nd most recent / 3rd most recent) problem, did you (your husband/wife/partner) do any of the things on this card to try to resolve it?
CODE ALL THAT APPLY IN APPROPRIATE COLUMN

Cd 2

	Respondent			Partner			
	Most recent	2nd most recent	3rd most recent	Most recent	2nd most recent	3rd most recent	
Talked or wrote to the other side about solving the problem	1 *	1 *	1 *	1 *	1 *	1 *	1st 32-38
Sought advice about trying to solve the problem	2 *	2 *	2 *	2 *	2 *	2 *	2nd 39-45
Threatened other side with legal action	3 *	3 *	3 *	3 *	3 *	3 *	3rd 46-52
Went to court, tribunal or arbitration / Started a court or tribunal case or an arbitration	4 * →f	4 * →f	4 * →f	4 * →f	4 * →f	4 * →f	
Went to mediation or conciliation	5 *	5 *	5 *	5 *	5 *	5 *	
Took the problem to an ombudsman	6 *	6 *	6 *	6 *	6 *	6 *	
Took some other kind of action to try to solve the problem	7 *	7 *	7 *	7 *	7 *	7 *	
(DID NOTHING)	8 → e	8 → e	8 → e	8 → e	8 → e	8 → e	

IF DID NOTHING
SHOW SCREEN CARD Y (coloured)

e Why did you (your husband/wife/partner) do nothing?
CODE ALL THAT APPLY

Other side was already taking action	0 *	0 *	0 *	0 *	0 *	0 *	1st 53-61
Thought it would cost too much	1 *	1 *	1 *	1 *	1 *	1 *	2nd 62-70
Thought it would take too much time	2 *	2 *	2 *	2 *	2 *	2 *	3rd 71-79
Did not think there was anything that could be done	3 *	3 *	3 *	3 *	3 *	3 *	
Did not think it was very important	4	4	4	4	4	4	
No dispute with anybody / Thought the other person/side was right	5	5	5	5	5	5	
Was scared to do anything	6 *	6 *	6 *	6 *	6 *	6 *	
Thought it would damage relationship with other side	7 *	7 *	7 *	7 *	7 *	7 *	
Other reason (**SPECIFY**)	8 *	8 *	8 *	8 *	8 *	8 *	

Cd 3

f When did this problem or dispute begin?
ENTER DATE DISPUTE BEGAN.

MONTH

YEAR

IF DON'T KNOW MONTH, ENTER 98

1st 10-13
2nd 14-17
3rd 18-21

4

SHOW SCREEN CARD B

3a Since January 1992, have you (or has your husband/wife/partner) had any problems or disputes which were difficult to solve to do with owning residential property? **CODE ALL THAT APPLY**

> INCLUDE ALL PROBLEMS
> SINCE JAN '92 EVEN IF
> STARTED BEFORE THEN.

> EXCLUDE PROBLEMS
> BEFORE AGE OF 18.
> INCLUDE IF BECAME 18
> DURING DISPUTE.

	Resp.	Partner	
.. alterations to property, or planning permission	1	1	22-26
... selling or buying property *(eg misleading property survey, problems with terms of lease or title to property)*	2	2	
.. communal repairs or maintenance	3 → b)	3 → b)	
... neighbours *(eg disputes about noise, boundaries, access)*	4	4	
... dealing with squatters	5	5	
repossession of the home	6	6	
NO, NONE OF ABOVE	0 → **Q4**	0 → **Q4**	

IF PROBLEM
SHOW SCREEN CARD B

b How many problems of this sort have you (has your husband / wife / partner) had since January 1992?

ENTER NUMBER: ☐☐ ☐☐ 27-28

c **COMPLETE GRID ON NEXT PAGE FOR RESPONDENT (AND PARTNER) FOR UP TO 3 PROBLEMS SINCE JANUARY 1992, STARTING WITH THE MOST RECENT.**

WORK DOWN THE GRID FOR EACH PROBLEM

IF FOUR OR MORE PROBLEMS, TAKE THE THREE MOST RECENT.

5

SHOW SCREEN CARD X (coloured)

3d Thinking of the (most recent / 2nd most recent / 3rd most recent) problem, did you (your husband/wife/partner) do any of the things on this card to try to resolve it?
CODE ALL THAT APPLY IN APPROPRIATE COLUMN

Cd 3

	Respondent			Partner		
	Most recent	2nd most recent	3rd most recent	Most recent	2nd most recent	3rd most recent	
Talked or wrote to the other side about solving the problem	1 *	1 *	1 *	1 *	1 *	1 *	1st 29-35
Sought advice about trying to solve the problem	2 *	2 *	2 *	2 *	2 *	2 *	2nd 36-42
Threatened other side with legal action	3 *	3 *	3 *	3 *	3 *	3 *	3rd 43-49
Went to court, tribunal or arbitration / Started a court or tribunal case or an arbitration	4 * →f	4 * →f	4 * →f	4 * →f	4 * →f	4 * →f	
Went to mediation or conciliation	5 *	5 *	5 *	5 *	5 *	5 *	
Took the problem to an ombudsman	6 *	6 *	6 *	6 *	6 *	6 *	
Took some other kind of action to try to solve the problem	7 *	7 *	7 *	7 *	7 *	7 *	
(DID NOTHING)	8 → e	8 → e	8 → e	8 → e	8 → e	8 → e	

IF DID NOTHING
SHOW SCREEN CARD Y (coloured)

e Why did you (your husband/wife/partner) do nothing?
CODE ALL THAT APPLY

Other side was already taking action	0 *	0 *	0 *	0 *	0 *	0 *	1st 50-58
Thought it would cost too much	1 *	1 *	1 *	1 *	1 *	1 *	2nd 59-67
Thought it would take too much time	2 *	2 *	2 *	2 *	2 *	2 *	3rd 68-76
Did not think there was anything that could be done	3 *	3 *	3 *	3 *	3 *	3 *	
Did not think it was very important	4	4	4	4	4	4	
No dispute with anybody / Thought the other person/side was right	5	5	5	5	5	5	
Was scared to do anything	6 *	6 *	6 *	6 *	6 *	6 *	
Thought it would damage relationship with other side	7 *	7 *	7 *	7 *	7 *	7 *	
Other reason (**SPECIFY**)	8 *	8 *	8 *	8 *	8 *	8 *	

Card 4

f When did this problem or dispute begin?
ENTER DATE DISPUTE BEGAN.

| **IF DON'T KNOW MONTH, ENTER 98** | MONTH | | | | | | |
| | YEAR | | | | | | |

1st 10-13
2nd 14-17
3rd 18-21

6

SHOW SCREEN CARD C

4a Since January 1992, have you (or your husband/wife/partner had any problems or disputes that were difficult to solve to do with renting out rooms or property to a lodger or tenant? **CODE ALL THAT APPLY**

> EXCLUDE PROBLEMS/DISPUTES TO DO
> WITH RESPONDENT'S BUSINESS

> INCLUDE ALL PROBLEMS
> SINCE JAN '92 EVEN IF
> <u>STARTED</u> BEFORE THEN.

> EXCLUDE PROBLEMS
> BEFORE AGE OF 18.
> INCLUDE IF BECAME 18
> DURING DISPUTE.

	Resp.	Partner	
... repeated non-payment of rent (rent arrears)	1	1	22-29
... repairs, return of deposits or early abandonment of tenancy	2	2	
...agreeing on council tax or housing benefit payments or other terms of the lease or tenancy agreement	3	3	
... evicting a lodger or tenant	4 → b)	4 → b)	
... tenant sub-letting the property	5	5	
... problems with managing agents or letting agents	6	6	
... complying with safety regulations	7	7	
... anti-social tenants	8	8	
NO, NONE OF ABOVE	0 → Q5	0 → Q5	

IF PROBLEM
SHOW SCREEN CARD C

b How many problems of this sort have you (has your husband / wife / partner) had since January 1992?

ENTER NUMBER:

30-31

c **COMPLETE GRID ON NEXT PAGE FOR RESPONDENT (AND PARTNER) FOR UP TO 3 PROBLEMS SINCE JANUARY 1992, STARTING WITH THE MOST RECENT.**

WORK <u>DOWN</u> THE GRID FOR EACH PROBLEM

IF FOUR OR MORE PROBLEMS, TAKE THE THREE MOST RECENT.

SHOW SCREEN CARD X (coloured)

4d Thinking of the (most recent / 2nd most recent / 3rd most recent) problem, did you (your husband/wife/partner) do any of the things on this card to try to resolve it?

CODE ALL THAT APPLY IN APPROPRIATE COLUMN

	Respondent			Partner			Cd 4
	Most recent	2nd most recent	3rd most recent	Most recent	2nd most recent	3rd most recent	
Talked or wrote to the other side about solving the problem	1 *	1 *	1 *	1 *	1 *	1 *	1st 32-38
Sought advice about trying to solve the problem	2 *	2 *	2 *	2 *	2 *	2 *	2nd 39-45
Threatened other side with legal action	3 *	3 *	3 *	3 *	3 *	3 *	3rd 46-52
Went to court, tribunal or arbitration / Started a court or tribunal case or an arbitration	4 * →f	4 * →f	4 * →f	4 * →f	4 * →f	4 * →f	
Went to mediation or conciliation	5 *	5 *	5 *	5 *	5 *	5 *	
Took the problem to an ombudsman	6 *	6 *	6 *	6 *	6 *	6 *	
Took some other kind of action to try to solve the problem	7 *	7 *	7 *	7 *	7 *	7 *	
(DID NOTHING)	8 → e	8 → e	8 → e	8 → e	8 → e	8 → e	

IF DID NOTHING
SHOW SCREEN CARD Y (coloured)

e Why did you (your husband/wife/partner) do nothing?
CODE ALL THAT APPLY

Other side was already taking action	0 *	0 *	0 *	0 *	0 *	0 *	1st 53-61
Thought it would cost too much	1 *	1 *	1 *	1 *	1 *	1 *	2nd 62-70
Thought it would take too much time	2 *	2 *	2 *	2 *	2 *	2 *	3rd 71-79
Did not think there was anything that could be done	3 *	3 *	3 *	3 *	3 *	3 *	
Did not think it was very important	4	4	4	4	4	4	
No dispute with anybody / Thought the other person/side was right	5	5	5	5	5	5	
Was scared to do anything	6 *	6 *	6 *	6 *	6 *	6 *	
Thought it would damage relationship with other side	7 *	7 *	7 *	7 *	7 *	7 *	
Other reason (**SPECIFY**)	8 *	8 *	8 *	8 *	8 *	8 *	

f When did this problem or dispute begin?
ENTER DATE DISPUTE BEGAN.

| IF DON'T KNOW MONTH, ENTER 98 |

MONTH

YEAR

Card 5
1st 10-13
2nd 14-17
3rd 18-21

8

SHOW SCREEN CARD D

5a Since January 1992, have you (or your husband/wife/ partner) had any problems or disputes that were difficult to solve ... to do with living in rented accommodation? **CODE ALL THAT APPLY**

> INCLUDE ALL PROBLEMS
> SINCE JAN '92 EVEN IF
> STARTED BEFORE THEN.

> EXCLUDE PROBLEMS
> BEFORE AGE OF 18.
> INCLUDE IF BECAME 18
> DURING DISPUTE.

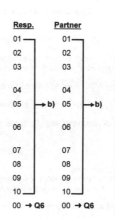

	Resp.	Partner	
... poor or unsafe living conditions	01	01	22-41
... getting a deposit back from the landlord or council	02	02	
.. renting out rooms to lodgers or sub-letting	03	03	
... getting other people in the accommodation to pay their share of the bills	04	04	
... getting the landlord or council to do repairs *(eg dampness)*	05 →b)	05 →b)	
... agreeing on rent, council tax or housing benefit payments or other terms of the lease or tenancy agreement	06	06	
...getting the landlord to provide a written lease, or tenancy agreement	07	07	
... neighbours *(eg disputes about noise, boundaries, access etc)*	08	08	
... harassment by the landlord	09	09	
... being evicted, or threatened with eviction	10	10	
NO, NONE OF ABOVE	00 → **Q6**	00 → **Q6**	

IF PROBLEM
SHOW SCREEN CARD D

b How many problems of this sort have you (has your husband / wife / partner) had since January 1992?

ENTER NUMBER: 42-43

c **COMPLETE GRID ON NEXT PAGE FOR RESPONDENT (AND PARTNER) FOR UP TO 3 PROBLEMS SINCE JANUARY 1992, STARTING WITH THE MOST RECENT.**

WORK <u>DOWN</u> THE GRID FOR EACH PROBLEM

IF FOUR OR MORE PROBLEMS, TAKE THE THREE MOST RECENT.

SHOW SCREEN CARD X (coloured)

5d Thinking of the (most recent / 2ⁿᵈ most recent / 3ʳᵈ most recent) problem, did you (your husband/wife/partner) do any of the things on this card to try to resolve it?
CODE ALL THAT APPLY IN APPROPRIATE COLUMN

Cd 5

	Respondent			Partner			
	Most recent	2ⁿᵈ most recent	3ʳᵈ most recent	Most recent	2ⁿᵈ most recent	3ʳᵈ most recent	
Talked or wrote to the other side about solving the problem	1 *	1 *	1 *	1 *	1 *	1 *	1ˢᵗ 44-50
Sought advice about trying to solve the problem	2 *	2 *	2 *	2 *	2 *	2 *	2ⁿᵈ 51-57
Threatened other side with legal action	3 *	3 *	3 *	3 *	3 *	3 *	3ʳᵈ 58-64
Went to court, tribunal or arbitration / Started a court or tribunal case or an arbitration	4 * →f	4 * →f	4 * →f	4 * →f	4 * →f	4 * →f	
Went to mediation or conciliation	5 *	5 *	5 *	5 *	5 *	5 *	
Took the problem to an ombudsman	6 *	6 *	6 *	6 *	6 *	6 *	
Took some other kind of action to try to solve the problem	7 *	7 *	7 *	7 *	7 *	7 *	
(DID NOTHING)	8 → e	8 → e	8 → e	8 → e	8 → e	8 → e	

IF DID NOTHING
SHOW SCREEN CARD Y (coloured)

e Why did you (your husband/wife/partner) do nothing?
CODE ALL THAT APPLY

Cd 6

	Most recent	2ⁿᵈ most recent	3ʳᵈ most recent	Most recent	2ⁿᵈ most recent	3ʳᵈ most recent	
Other side was already taking action	0 *	0 *	0 *	0 *	0 *	0 *	1ˢᵗ 10-18
Thought it would cost too much	1 *	1 *	1 *	1 *	1 *	1 *	2ⁿᵈ 19-27
Thought it would take too much time	2 *	2 *	2 *	2 *	2 *	2 *	3ʳᵈ 28-36
Did not think there was anything that could be done	3 *	3 *	3 *	3 *	3 *	3 *	
Did not think it was very important	4	4	4	4	4	4	
No dispute with anybody / Thought the other person/side was right	5	5	5	5	5	5	
Was scared to do anything	6 *	6 *	6 *	6 *	6 *	6 *	
Thought it would damage relationship with other side	7 *	7 *	7 *	7 *	7 *	7 *	
Other reason (**SPECIFY**)	8 *	8 *	8 *	8 *	8 *	8 *	

f When did this problem or dispute begin?
ENTER DATE DISPUTE BEGAN.

MONTH

IF DON'T KNOW
MONTH, ENTER 98

YEAR

1ˢᵗ 37-40
2ⁿᵈ 41-44
3ʳᵈ 45-48

SHOW SCREEN CARD E

6a Since January 1992, have you (or your husband/wife/partner) had any problems or disputes that were difficult to solve to do with receiving faulty goods or services - some examples are shown on this card?

Card 6

CODE ALL THAT APPLY

> INCLUDE ALL PROBLEMS SINCE JAN '92 EVEN IF STARTED BEFORE THEN.

> EXCLUDE PROBLEMS BEFORE AGE OF 18. INCLUDE IF BECAME 18 DURING DISPUTE.

		Resp.	**Partner**	
Yes		1 ⟩ **b)**	1 ⟩ **b)**	49
No		2 → **Q7**	2 → **Q7**	

IF PROBLEM

SHOW SCREEN CARD E

b How many problems of this sort have you (has your husband / wife / partner) had since January 1992?

ENTER NUMBER: ☐☐ ☐☐   50-51

c COMPLETE GRID ON NEXT PAGE FOR RESPONDENT (AND PARTNER) FOR UP TO 3 PROBLEMS SINCE JANUARY 1992, STARTING WITH THE MOST RECENT.

WORK <u>DOWN</u> THE GRID FOR EACH PROBLEM

IF FOUR OR MORE PROBLEMS, TAKE THE THREE MOST RECENT.

SHOW SCREEN CARD X (coloured)

6d Thinking of the (most recent / 2nd most recent / 3rd most recent) problem, did you (your husband/wife/partner) do any of the things on this card to try to resolve it?
CODE ALL THAT APPLY IN APPROPRIATE COLUMN

Cd 6

	Respondent			Partner			
	Most recent	2nd most recent	3rd most recent	Most recent	2nd most recent	3rd most recent	
Talked or wrote to the other side about solving the problem	1 *	1 *	1 *	1 *	1 *	1 *	1st 52-58
Sought advice about trying to solve the problem	2 *	2 *	2 *	2 *	2 *	2 *	2nd 59-65
Threatened other side with legal action	3 *	3 *	3 *	3 *	3 *	3 *	3rd 66-72
Went to court, tribunal or arbitration / Started a court or tribunal case or an arbitration	4 * →f	4 * →f	4 * →f	4 * →f	4 * →f	4 * →f	
Went to mediation or conciliation	5 *	5 *	5 *	5 *	5 *	5 *	
Took the problem to an ombudsman	6 *	6 *	6 *	6 *	6 *	6 *	
Took some other kind of action to try to solve the problem	7 *	7 *	7 *	7 *	7 *	7 *	
(DID NOTHING)	8 → e	8 → e	8 → e	8 → e	8 → e	8 → e	

IF DID NOTHING
SHOW SCREEN CARD Y (coloured)
e Why did you (your husband/wife/partner) do nothing?
CODE ALL THAT APPLY

Cd 7

Other side was already taking action	0 *	0 *	0 *	0 *	0 *	0 *	1st 10-18
Thought it would cost too much	1 *	1 *	1 *	1 *	1 *	1 *	2nd 19-27
Thought it would take too much time	2 *	2 *	2 *	2 *	2 *	2 *	3rd 28-36
Did not think there was anything that could be done	3 *	3 *	3 *	3 *	3 *	3 *	
Did not think it was very important	4	4	4	4	4	4	
No dispute with anybody / Thought the other person/side was right	5	5	5	5	5	5	
Was scared to do anything	6 *	6 *	6 *	6 *	6 *	6 *	
Thought it would damage relationship with other side	7 *	7 *	7 *	7 *	7 *	7 *	
Other reason (**SPECIFY**)	8 *	8 *	8 *	8 *	8 *	8 *	

f When did this problem or dispute begin?
ENTER DATE DISPUTE BEGAN.

MONTH

| IF DON'T KNOW |
| MONTH, ENTER 98 |

YEAR

1st 37-40
2nd 41-44
3rd 45-48

12

SHOW SCREEN CARD F

7a Since January 1992, have you (or your husband/wife/ partner) had any problems or disputes that were difficult to solve ... to do with money?

Card 7

CODE ALL THAT APPLY

> EXCLUDE PROBLEMS/DISPUTES TO DO
> WITH RESPONDENT'S BUSINESS OR
> EMPLOYER

> INCLUDE ALL PROBLEMS
> SINCE JAN '92 EVEN IF
> STARTED BEFORE THEN.

> EXCLUDE PROBLEMS
> BEFORE AGE OF 18.
> INCLUDE IF BECAME 18
> DURING DISPUTE.

	Resp.	Partner	
... getting someone to pay money that they owe	01	01	49-66
... insurance companies unfairly rejecting claims	02	02	
... incorrect or disputed bills	03	03	
... incorrect or unfair tax demands (including Council Tax)	04	04	
... the DSS not giving benefits, pensions, grants or loans that you (or your husband/wife/partner) are legally entitled to	05 → b)	05 → b)	
... being given incorrect information or advice about insurance, pensions or other financial products	06	06	
... mismanagement of a pension fund to which you (or your husband/wife/partner) contribute	07	07	
... unfair refusal of credit as a result of incorrect information about you (or your husband/wife/partner)	08	08	
... unreasonable harassment from creditors	09	09	
NO, NONE OF ABOVE	00 → Q8	00 → Q8	

IF PROBLEM
SHOW SCREEN CARD F

b How many problems of this sort have you (has your husband / wife / partner) had since January 1992?

ENTER NUMBER: ☐☐ ☐☐ 67-68

c **COMPLETE GRID ON NEXT PAGE FOR RESPONDENT (AND PARTNER) FOR UP TO 3 PROBLEMS SINCE JANUARY 1992, STARTING WITH THE MOST RECENT.**

WORK DOWN THE GRID FOR EACH PROBLEM

IF FOUR OR MORE PROBLEMS, TAKE THE THREE MOST RECENT.

	Respondent			Partner			
7d SHOW SCREEN CARD X (coloured) Thinking of the (most recent / 2nd most recent / 3rd most recent) problem, did you (your husband/wife/partner) do any of the things on this card to try to resolve it? **CODE ALL THAT APPLY IN APPROPRIATE COLUMN**	Most recent	2nd most recent	3rd most recent	Most recent	2nd most recent	3rd most recent	Cd 7
Talked or wrote to the other side about solving the problem	1 *	1 *	1 *	1 *	1 *	1 *	1st 69-75 Cd 8
Sought advice about trying to solve the problem	2 *	2 *	2 *	2 *	2 *	2 *	2nd 10-16
Threatened other side with legal action	3 *	3 *	3 *	3 *	3 *	3 *	3rd 17-23
Went to court, tribunal or arbitration / Started a court or tribunal case or an arbitration	4 * →f	4 * →f	4 * →f	4 * →f	4 * →f	4 * →f	
Went to mediation or conciliation	5 *	5 *	5 *	5 *	5 *	5 *	
Took the problem to an ombudsman	6 *	6 *	6 *	6 *	6 *	6 *	
Took some other kind of action to try to solve the problem	7 *	7 *	7 *	7 *	7 *	7 *	
(DID NOTHING)	8 → e	8 → e	8 → e	8 → e	8 → e	8 → e	
IF DID NOTHING **SHOW SCREEN CARD Y (coloured)** e Why did you (your husband/wife/partner) do nothing? **CODE ALL THAT APPLY**							
Other side was already taking action	0 *	0 *	0 *	0 *	0 *	0 *	1st 24-32
Thought it would cost too much	1 *	1 *	1 *	1 *	1 *	1 *	2nd 33-41
Thought it would take too much time	2 *	2 *	2 *	2 *	2 *	2 *	3rd 42-50
Did not think there was anything that could be done	3 *	3 *	3 *	3 *	3 *	3 *	
Did not think it was very important	4	4	4	4	4	4	
No dispute with anybody / Thought the other person/side was right	5	5	5	5	5	5	
Was scared to do anything	6 *	6 *	6 *	6 *	6 *	6 *	
Thought it would damage relationship with other side	7 *	7 *	7 *	7 *	7 *	7 *	
Other reason (**SPECIFY**)	8 *	8 *	8 *	8 *	8 *	8 *	
f When did this problem or dispute begin? **ENTER DATE DISPUTE BEGAN.** MONTH IF DON'T KNOW MONTH, ENTER 98 YEAR							1st 51-54 2nd 55-59 3rd 60-63

14

| 8a | Can I just check, have you (or has your husband/wife partner) been involved in divorce proceedings, even if no divorce was obtained, since January 1992? **INCLUDE PROCEEDINGS AGAINST CURRENT OR PREVIOUS SPOUSE** | | | | Card 8 |

INCLUDE EVEN IF PROCEEDINGS <u>STARTED</u> BEFORE JAN'92.	EXCLUDE PROCEEDINGS BEFORE AGE OF 18. INCLUDE IF BECAME 18 DURING PROCEEDINGS.

	Resp.	Partner	
Yes	1 * → b)	1 * → b)	64
No	2 → Q9	2 → Q9	

IF YES

b| When did these divorce proceedings begin?
ENTER DATE DIVORCE PROCEEDINGS STARTED.

65-68

IF DON'T KNOW MONTH, ENTER 98

Month

Year

SHOW SCREEN CARD G

9a| Since January 1992, have you (or your husband/wife/partner) had any experience of any of the things on this card to do with relationships and other family matters?
CODE ALL THAT APPLY

INCLUDE ALL PROBLEMS SINCE JAN '92 EVEN IF <u>STARTED</u> BEFORE THEN.	EXCLUDE PROBLEMS BEFORE AGE OF 18. INCLUDE IF BECAME 18 DURING DISPUTE.

...division of money, pensions or property in connection with divorce or separation	1	1	69-74
... getting or paying maintenance or child support payments	2	2	
... fostering or adopting children or becoming a legal guardian	3 →b)	3 →b)	
... violent or abusive relationships with a partner, ex-partner or other family member	4	4	
... problems after the death of a family member or partner *(eg disputed wills, division of property, funeral arrangements, succession of tenancy)*	5	5	
NO, NONE OF ABOVE	0 → Q10	0 → Q10	

IF PROBLEM
SHOW SCREEN CARD G

b| How many problems of this sort have you (has your husband / wife / partner) had since January 1992?

ENTER NUMBER:

75-76

c| **COMPLETE GRID ON NEXT PAGE FOR RESPONDENT (AND PARTNER) FOR UP TO 3 PROBLEMS SINCE JANUARY 1992, STARTING WITH THE MOST RECENT.**

WORK <u>DOWN</u> THE GRID FOR EACH PROBLEM

IF FOUR OR MORE PROBLEMS, TAKE THE THREE MOST RECENT.

15

9d SHOW SCREEN CARD X (coloured)

Thinking of the (most recent / 2nd most recent / 3rd most recent) problem, did you (your husband/wife/partner) do any of the things on this card to try to resolve it?

CODE ALL THAT APPLY IN APPROPRIATE COLUMN

Cd 9

	Respondent			Partner			
	Most recent	2nd most recent	3rd most recent	Most recent	2nd most recent	3rd most recent	
Talked or wrote to the other side about solving the problem	1 *	1 *	1 *	1 *	1 *	1 *	1st 10-16
Sought advice about trying to solve the problem	2 *	2 *	2 *	2 *	2 *	2 *	2nd 17-23
Threatened other side with legal action	3 *	3 *	3 *	3 *	3 *	3 *	3rd 24-30
Went to court, tribunal or arbitration / Started a court or tribunal case or an arbitration	4 * →f	4 * →f	4 * →f	4 * →f	4 * →f	4 * →f	
Went to mediation or conciliation	5 *	5 *	5 *	5 *	5 *	5 *	
Took the problem to an ombudsman	6 *	6 *	6 *	6 *	6 *	6 *	
Took some other kind of action to try to solve the problem	7 *	7 *	7 *	7 *	7 *	7 *	
(DID NOTHING)	8 → e	8 → e	8 → e	8 → e	8 → e	8 → e	

IF DID NOTHING
SHOW SCREEN CARD Y (coloured)

e Why did you (your husband/wife/partner) do nothing?

CODE ALL THAT APPLY

Other side was already taking action	0 *	0 *	0 *	0 *	0 *	0 *	1st 31-39
Thought it would cost too much	1 *	1 *	1 *	1 *	1 *	1 *	2nd 40-48
Thought it would take too much time	2 *	2 *	2 *	2 *	2 *	2 *	3rd 49-57
Did not think there was anything that could be done	3 *	3 *	3 *	3 *	3 *	3 *	
Did not think it was very important	4	4	4	4	4	4	
No dispute with anybody / Thought the other person/side was right	5	5	5	5	5	5	
Was scared to do anything	6 *	6 *	6 *	6 *	6 *	6 *	
Thought it would damage relationship with other side	7 *	7 *	7 *	7 *	7 *	7 *	
Other reason (**SPECIFY**)	8 *	8 *	8 *	8 *	8 *	8 *	

f When did this problem or dispute begin?

ENTER DATE DISPUTE BEGAN.

IF DON'T KNOW
MONTH, ENTER 98

MONTH

YEAR

1st 58-61
2nd 62-65
3rd 66-69

16

10a Can I just check, do you (or your husband/wife/partner) have any children aged 23 or younger?

	Resp.	Partner
Yes, children aged 23 or younger	1 → b)	1 → b)	70
No	2 → Q11	2 → Q11
Can't say	8 → Q11	8 → Q11

**IF HAS CHILDREN AGED 23 OR YOUNGER
SHOW SCREEN CARD H**
b Since January 1992, have you (or your husband/wife/partner) had any problems or disputes that were difficult to solve ... to do with children who were under 18 at the time?
CODE ALL THAT APPLY

> INCLUDE ALL PROBLEMS
> SINCE JAN '92 EVEN IF
> STARTED BEFORE THEN.

... residence and contact (custody and access) arrangements for children — 1 — 1 — 71-75
...children being taken into care, or being on the Child Protection register — 2 — 2
... abduction (or threatened abduction) of the children — 3 → c) — 3 → c)
...children going to the school you (or your husband/wife/partner) want, or receiving the type of education they need (eg special needs) — 4 — 4
... children being unfairly excluded or suspended from school — 5 — 5

NO, NONE OF ABOVE — 0 → Q11 — 0 → Q11

**IF PROBLEM
SHOW SCREEN CARD H**
c How many problems of this sort have you (has your husband / wife / partner) had since January 1992?

ENTER NUMBER: ☐☐ ☐☐ 76-77

d **COMPLETE GRID ON NEXT PAGE FOR RESPONDENT (AND PARTNER) FOR UP TO 3 PROBLEMS SINCE JANUARY 1992, STARTING WITH THE MOST RECENT.**

WORK DOWN THE GRID FOR EACH PROBLEM

IF FOUR OR MORE PROBLEMS, TAKE THE THREE MOST RECENT.

SHOW SCREEN CARD X (coloured)

10e Thinking of the (most recent / 2nd most recent / 3rd most recent) problem, did you (your husband/wife/partner) do any of the things on this card to try to resolve it?
CODE ALL THAT APPLY IN APPROPRIATE COLUMN

Cd 10

	Respondent			Partner		
	Most recent	2nd most recent	3rd most recent	Most recent	2nd most recent	3rd most recent	
Talked or wrote to the other side about solving the problem	1 *	1 *	1 *	1 *	1 *	1 *	1st 10-16
Sought advice about trying to solve the problem	2 *	2 *	2 *	2 *	2 *	2 *	2nd 17-23
Threatened other side with legal action	3 *	3 *	3 *	3 *	3 *	3 *	3rd 24-30
Went to court, tribunal or arbitration / Started a court or tribunal case or an arbitration	4 * →g	4 * →g	4 * →g	4 * →g	4 * →g	4 * →g	
Went to mediation or conciliation	5 *	5 *	5 *	5 *	5 *	5 *	
Took the problem to an ombudsman	6 *	6 *	6 *	6 *	6 *	6 *	
Took some other kind of action to try to solve the problem	7 *	7 *	7 *	7 *	7 *	7 *	
(DID NOTHING)	8 → f	8 → f	8 → f	8 → f	8 → f	8 → f	

IF DID NOTHING
SHOW SCREEN CARD Y (coloured)

f Why did you (your husband/wife/partner) do nothing?
CODE ALL THAT APPLY

Other side was already taking action	0 *	0 *	0 *	0 *	0 *	0 *	1st 31-39
Thought it would cost too much	1 *	1 *	1 *	1 *	1 *	1 *	2nd 40-48
Thought it would take too much time	2 *	2 *	2 *	2 *	2 *	2 *	3rd 49-57
Did not think there was anything that could be done	3 *	3 *	3 *	3 *	3 *	3 *	
Did not think it was very important	4	4	4	4	4	4	
No dispute with anybody / Thought the other person/side was right	5	5	5	5	5	5	
Was scared to do anything	6 *	6 *	6 *	6 *	6 *	6 *	
Thought it would damage relationship with other side	7 *	7 *	7 *	7 *	7 *	7 *	
Other reason (SPECIFY)	8 *	8 *	8 *	8 *	8 *	8 *	

g When did this problem or dispute begin?
ENTER DATE DISPUTE BEGAN.

MONTH

IF DON'T KNOW
MONTH, ENTER 98

YEAR

1st 58-61
2nd 62-65
3rd 66-69

18

SHOW SCREEN CARD I
11a Since January 1992, have you (or your husband/wife/partner)
suffered any injury or health problem because of an accident or
because of poor working conditions?
Some examples are shown on this card.
IF YES: Did you (he/she) have to see a doctor or dentist or go to a
hospital as a result of this?

Card 10

> INCLUDE ALL PROBLEMS
> SINCE JAN '92 EVEN IF
> STARTED BEFORE THEN.

> EXCLUDE PROBLEMS
> BEFORE AGE OF 18.
> INCLUDE IF BECAME 18
> DURING DISPUTE.

	Resp.	Partner	
Yes - suffered injury or health problem; went to doctor/dentist/hospital	1 → b)	1 → b)	70
Yes - suffered injury or health problem; did <u>not</u> go to doctor/hospital	2 → Q12	2 → Q12	
No	3 → Q12	3 → Q12	

IF CODE 1 AT a)
SHOW SCREEN CARD I
b How many problems of this sort have you (has your
husband / wife / partner) had since January 1992
- please only include those where you had to see
a doctor or dentist or go to hospital?

ENTER NUMBER: ☐☐ ☐☐ 71-72

c **COMPLETE GRID ON NEXT PAGE FOR RESPONDENT
(AND PARTNER) FOR UP TO 3 PROBLEMS SINCE
JANUARY 1992, STARTING WITH THE MOST RECENT.**

WORK <u>DOWN</u> THE GRID FOR EACH PROBLEM

**IF FOUR OR MORE PROBLEMS, TAKE THE THREE MOST
RECENT.**

SHOW SCREEN CARD X (coloured)
11d Thinking of the (most recent / 2nd most recent / 3rd most recent) problem, did you (your husband/wife/partner) do any of the things on this card to try to resolve it?
CODE ALL THAT APPLY IN APPROPRIATE COLUMN

	Respondent			Partner			
	Most recent	2nd most recent	3rd most recent	Most recent	2nd most recent	3rd most recent	Cd 10
Talked or wrote to the other side about solving the problem	1 *	1 *	1 *	1 *	1 *	1 *	1st 73-79 Cd 11
Sought advice about trying to solve the problem	2 *	2 *	2 *	2 *	2 *	2 *	2nd 10-16
Threatened other side with legal action	3 *	3 *	3 *	3 *	3 *	3 *	3rd 17-23
Went to court, tribunal or arbitration / Started a court or tribunal case or an arbitration	4 * →f	4 * →f	4 * →f	4 * →f	4 * →f	4 * →f	
Went to mediation or conciliation	5 *	5 *	5 *	5 *	5 *	5 *	
Took the problem to an ombudsman	6 *	6 *	6 *	6 *	6 *	6 *	
Took some other kind of action to try to solve the problem	7 *	7 *	7 *	7 *	7 *	7 *	
(DID NOTHING)	8 → e	8 → e	8 → e	8 → e	8 → e	8 → e	

IF DID NOTHING
SHOW SCREEN CARD Y (coloured)
e Why did you (your husband/wife/partner) do nothing?
CODE ALL THAT APPLY

Other side was already taking action	0 *	0 *	0 *	0 *	0 *	0 *	1st 24-32
Thought it would cost too much	1 *	1 *	1 *	1 *	1 *	1 *	2nd 33-41
Thought it would take too much time	2 *	2 *	2 *	2 *	2 *	2 *	3rd 42-50
Did not think there was anything that could be done	3 *	3 *	3 *	3 *	3 *	3 *	
Did not think it was very important	4	4	4	4	4	4	
No dispute with anybody / Thought the other person/side was right	5	5	5	5	5	5	
Was scared to do anything	6 *	6 *	6 *	6 *	6 *	6 *	
Thought it would damage relationship with other side	7 *	7 *	7 *	7 *	7 *	7 *	
Other reason (**SPECIFY**)	8 *	8 *	8 *	8 *	8 *	8 *	

f When did this problem or dispute begin?
ENTER DATE DISPUTE BEGAN.

IF DON'T KNOW MONTH, ENTER 98

MONTH ☐☐ ☐☐ ☐☐ ☐☐ ☐☐ ☐☐

YEAR ☐☐ ☐☐ ☐☐ ☐☐ ☐☐ ☐☐

1st 51-54
2nd 55-58
3rd 59-62

20

SHOW SCREEN CARD J
12a Since January 1992, have you (or your husband/wife/partner) had any problems or disputes that were difficult to solve ... to do with any of these issues?
CODE ALL THAT APPLY

Card 11

EXCLUDE CASES OF POLICE NOT DOING JOB PROPERLY

INCLUDE ALL PROBLEMS SINCE JAN '92 EVEN IF STARTED BEFORE THEN.

EXCLUDE PROBLEMS BEFORE AGE OF 18. INCLUDE IF BECAME 18 DURING DISPUTE.

	Resp.	Partner	
... being discriminated against because of race, sex or disability	1	1	63-67
... unfair treatment by the police *(eg assault by the police, or being unreasonably arrested)*	2 ▶ b)	2 ▶ b)	
... immigration or nationality issues	3	3	
... being given medical or dental treatment that was negligent or wrong	4	4	
NO, NONE OF THESE	0 ➔ **Q13**	0 ➔ **Q13**	

IF PROBLEM
SHOW SCREEN CARD J
b How many problems of this sort have you (has your husband / wife / partner) had since January 1992?

ENTER NUMBER: ☐☐ · ☐☐   68-69

c **COMPLETE GRID ON NEXT PAGE FOR RESPONDENT (AND PARTNER) FOR UP TO 3 PROBLEMS SINCE JANUARY 1992, STARTING WITH THE MOST RECENT.**

WORK DOWN THE GRID FOR EACH PROBLEM

IF FOUR OR MORE PROBLEMS, TAKE THE THREE MOST RECENT.

12d SHOW SCREEN CARD X (coloured)
Thinking of the (most recent / 2nd most recent / 3rd most recent) problem, did you (your husband/wife/partner) do any of the things on this card to try to resolve it?
CODE ALL THAT APPLY IN APPROPRIATE COLUMN

Cd 11

	Respondent			Partner			
	Most recent	2nd most recent	3rd most recent	Most recent	2nd most recent	3rd most recent	
Talked or wrote to the other side about solving the problem	1 *	1 *	1 *	1 *	1 *	1 *	1st 70-76 Cd 12
Sought advice about trying to solve the problem	2 *	2 *	2 *	2 *	2 *	2 *	2nd 10-16
Threatened other side with legal action	3 *	3 *	3 *	3 *	3 *	3 *	3rd 17-23
Went to court, tribunal or arbitration / Started a court or tribunal case or an arbitration	4 * →f	4 * →f	4 * →f	4 * →f	4 * →f	4 * →f	
Went to mediation or conciliation	5 *	5 *	5 *	5 *	5 *	5 *	
Took the problem to an ombudsman	6 *	6 *	6 *	6 *	6 *	6 *	
Took some other kind of action to try to solve the problem	7 *	7 *	7 *	7 *	7 *	7 *	
(DID NOTHING)	8 → e	8 → e	8 → e	8 → e	8 → e	8 → e	

IF DID NOTHING
SHOW SCREEN CARD Y (coloured)
e Why did you (your husband/wife/partner) do nothing?
CODE ALL THAT APPLY

	Most recent	2nd most recent	3rd most recent	Most recent	2nd most recent	3rd most recent	
Other side was already taking action	0 *	0 *	0 *	0 *	0 *	0 *	1st 24-32
Thought it would cost too much	1 *	1 *	1 *	1 *	1 *	1 *	2nd 33-41
Thought it would take too much time	2 *	2 *	2 *	2 *	2 *	2 *	3rd 42-50
Did not think there was anything that could be done	3 *	3 *	3 *	3 *	3 *	3 *	
Did not think it was very important	4	4	4	4	4	4	
No dispute with anybody / Thought the other person/side was right	5	5	5	5	5	5	
Was scared to do anything	6 *	6 *	6 *	6 *	6 *	6 *	
Thought it would damage relationship with other side	7 *	7 *	7 *	7 *	7 *	7 *	
Other reason (SPECIFY)	8 *	8 *	8 *	8 *	8 *	8 *	

f When did this problem or dispute begin?
ENTER DATE DISPUTE BEGAN.

■ IF DON'T KNOW
MONTH, ENTER 98

MONTH □□ □□ □□   □□ □□ □□

YEAR □□ □□ □□   □□ □□ □□

1st 51-54
2nd 55-58
3rd 59-62

22

13a Apart from anything you have already told me about in this
interview - since January 1992, has any legal action been taken against you
(or your husband/wife/partner), for example have you been sent a
solicitor's letter or had court proceedings started against you?

Card 12

		Resp.	Partner	
EXCLUDE ACTION BY POLICE ABOUT ALLEGED CRIME				
INCLUDE ALL ACTION SINCE JAN '92 EVEN IF STARTED BEFORE THEN.	Yes	1 * → h)	1 * → l)	63
	No	2 → Q14	2 → Q14	
EXCLUDE ACTION BEFORE AGE OF 18. INCLUDE IF BECAME 18 DURING DISPUTE.				

IF YES
b How many legal actions have been taken against you (your
husband/wife/partner) since January 1992?
**EXCLUDE CASES COVERED EARLIER
IN INTERVIEW**

EXCLUDE CRIMINAL
PROSECUTIONS

WRITE IN NUMBER: ☐☐   ☐☐   64-65

c **FOR EACH LEGAL ACTION, STARTING
WITH THE MOST RECENT:**
When did the dispute which led to this legal
action begin?

IF 4 OR MORE LEGAL
ACTIONS, ASK ABOUT 3
MOST RECENT

IF DON'T KNOW
MONTH, ENTER 98

	Respondent			Partner		
	Most recent	2nd most recent	3rd most recent	Most recent	2nd most recent	3rd most recent
MONTH	☐☐	☐☐	☐☐	☐☐	☐☐	☐☐
YEAR	☐☐	☐☐	☐☐	☐☐	☐☐	☐☐

1st
66-69
2nd
70-73
3rd
74-77

23

ALL

14a Apart from this, since January 1992 have you (has
your husband/wife/partner) been <u>threatened</u> with
legal action by anyone?

		Resp.	Partner	
EXCLUDE CRIMINAL PROSECUTIONS	Yes	1 → b)	1 → b)	10
	No	2 → Q15	2 → Q15	

INCLUDE ALL SUCH
PROBLEMS SINCE JAN '92
EVEN IF STARTED
BEFORETHEN.

EXCLUDE PROBLEMS
BEFORE AGE OF 18.
INCLUDE IF BECAME 18
DURING DISPUTE.

IF YES

b Did you (your husband/wife/partner) disagree with what
the other party was demanding (on any of these occasions)?

	Resp.	Partner	
Yes, disagreed	1 * → c)	1 * → c)	11
No	2 → Q15	2 → Q15	

IF DISAGREED

c Now I would like you to think of the occasions on which
you were (your husband/wife/partner was) threatened with
legal action and did not agree with what was being demanded.
On how many occasions has this happened since January 1992?
**EXCLUDE ACTUAL LEGAL ACTIONS AND
THREATENED CRIMINAL PROSECUTIONS**

WRITE IN NUMBER: [ ][ ]   [ ][ ]   12-13

d **FOR EACH THREATENED LEGAL ACTION,
STARTING WITH THE MOST RECENT:**
When did the dispute that led to this threat
being made begin?

IF 4 OR MORE THREATS,
ASK ABOUT 3 MOST
RECENT

IF DON'T KNOW
MONTH, ENTER 98

	Respondent			Partner		
	Most recent	2nd most recent	3rd most recent	Most recent	2nd most recent	3rd most recent
MONTH	[ ]	[ ]	[ ]	[ ]	[ ]	[ ]
YEAR	[ ]	[ ]	[ ]	[ ]	[ ]	[ ]

1st
14-17
2nd
18-21
3rd
22-25

ALL

15a **SHOW SCREEN CARD K**
(Apart from anything you have already told me about
in this interview), have you (has your husband/wife/partner)
had any other problems since January 1992 for which you
have done or thought about doing any of the things
on this card?

Card 13

	Resp.	Partner	
Yes	1 * → b)	1 * → b)	26
No	2 → Q16	2 → Q16	

INCLUDE ALL SUCH
PROBLEMS SINCE JAN '92
EVEN IF STARTED
BEFORE THEN,

EXCLUDE PROBLEMS
BEFORE AGE OF 18.
INCLUDE IF BECAME 18
DURING DISPUTE.

IF YES

b On how many occasions have you (has your
husband/wife/partner) done this?
**EXCLUDE CASES COVERED EARLIER IN
INTERVIEW.**

WRITE IN NUMBER: 27-28

c **FOR EACH PROBLEM/DISPUTE FOR
WHICH RESPONDENT STARTED OR
CONSIDERED STARTING COURT
PROCEEDINGS, STARTING WITH THE
MOST RECENT:**
When did the dispute that led to you (thinking
about) starting court proceedings begin?

IF 4 OR MORE SUCH
PROBLEMS OR DISPUTES,
ASK ABOUT 3 MOST RECENT

IF DON'T KNOW
MONTH, ENTER 98

	Respondent			Partner		
	Most recent	2nd most recent	3rd most recent	Most recent	2nd most recent	3rd most recent
MONTH						
YEAR						

1st
29-32
2nd
33-36
3rd
37-40

16a Can I check, how old were you (was your husband/wife/partner)
on your (his/her) last birthday?

	Resp.	Partner	
ENTER AGE:			41-42

b **CODE SEX:**

Male	1	1	43
Female	2	2	

25

17a **INTERVIEWER CHECK Q2-15 RESPONDENT COLUMN**
Are any starred (*) codes ringed in respondent column?
(All starred codes are shaded in grey)

| | Yes | 1 | GO TO b) | 44 |
| | No | 2 | GO TO Q18 | |

IF YES
b Respondent is eligible for main interview.

BEFORE PROCEEDING WITH AN EVENT SELECTION FORM WITH THE
RESPONDENT, PLEASE CHECK THAT (S)HE WAS 18 OR OVER AT THE
OF THE PROBLEM(S) CODED.

> INCLUDE IF BECAME 18
> DURING DISPUTE

IF (S)HE WAS UNDER 18 AT THE TIME OF A PROBLEM, IT SHOULD NOT
HAVE BEEN CODED - GO BACK AND AMEND APPROPRIATE QUESTION
AND SUBSEQUENT ROUTING. YOU MAY ALSO NEED TO AMEND THE
CODE GIVEN AT A17a).

18a **INTERVIEWER CHECK Q1a, page 1**

| Spouse / partner in household (code 1 at Q1a) | 1 | GO TO b) | 45 |
| No spouse / partner in household (code 2) | 2 | END. | |

IF SPOUSE / PARTNER IN HOUSEHOLD
b **INTERVIEWER CHECK Q2-15 PARTNER COLUMN**
Are any starred (*) codes ringed?
(All starred codes are shaded in grey)

| | Yes | 1 | GO TO c) | 46 |
| | No | 2 | END. | |

IF YES
c Partner is eligible for main interview.

BEFORE PROCEEDING WITH AN EVENT SELECTION FORM WITH THE
PARTNER, PLEASE CHECK THAT (S)HE WAS 18 OR OVER AT THE
OF THE PROBLEM(S) CODED.

> INCLUDE IF BECAME 18
> DURING DISPUTE

IF (S)HE WAS UNDER 18 AT THE TIME OF A PROBLEM, IT SHOULD NOT
HAVE BEEN CODED - GO BACK AND AMEND APPROPRIATE QUESTION
AND SUBSEQUENT ROUTING. YOU MAY ALSO NEED TO AMEND THE
CODE GIVEN AT A18a).

INTERVIEWER TO COMPLETE:

END TIME: ☐☐☐   47-50

INTERVIEWER NAME: _____

INTERVIEWER NUMBER: ☐☐☐☐☐   51-54

26

INTERVIEWER:
IF RESPONDENT REPORTS A PROBLEM, AND YOU ARE NOT SURE WHETHER IT IS WITHIN SCOPE FOR THE SURVEY, PLEASE TAKE THE DETAILS DOWN HERE, AND CONTACT THE OFFICE BEFORE PROCEEDING WITH A MAIN INTERVIEW.

Head Office: 35 NORTHAMPTON SQUARE
LONDON EC1V 0AX
Tel: 0171 250 1866 Fax 0171 250 1524

SOCIAL & COMMUNITY
SCPR
PLANNING RESEARCH

Field and DP Office: 100 KINGS ROAD
BRENTWOOD, ESSEX CM14 4LX
Tel: 01277 200 600 Fax: 01277 214 117

P1606

MAIN QUESTIONNAIRE

1997

Card 15

SERIAL NUMBER: ⬚⬚⬚⬚⬚ ⬚   **PERSON NUMBER:** ⬚⬚

RECORD TIME NOW: ⬚⬚⬚⬚

01-05
06-07
Cd:08-09
10-13

A1. CHECK EVENT SELECTION FORM (Q2b/Q2c):

Screen question number **Q2** (employment)	01	**GO TO A2, page 2**
Screen question number **Q3** (owning residential property)	02	**GO TO A3, page 2**
Screen question number **Q4** (renting out rooms or property)	03	**GO TO A4, page 2**
Screen question number **Q5** (living in rented accommodation)	04	**GO TO A5, page 2**
Screen question number **Q6** (faulty goods or services)	05	**GO TO A6, page 3**
Screen question number **Q7** (money)	06	**GO TO A7, page 3**
Screen question number **Q8** (divorce proceedings)	07	**GO TO A8, page 3**
Screen question number **Q9** (family matters)	08	**GO TO A9, page 3**
Screen question number **Q10** (children)	09	**GO TO A10, page 4**
Screen question number **Q11** (accident or injury)	10	**GO TO A11, page 4**
Screen question number **Q12** (discrimination / police / immigration / medical treatment)	11	**GO TO A12, page 4**
Screen question number **Q13** (legal action taken against respondent)	12	
Screen question number **Q14** (threatened with legal action)	13	**GO TO A13, page 4**
Screen question number **Q15** (started / thought about starting case in court / tribunal / arbitration / going to mediation / ombudsman)	14	

14-15

2

IF SCREEN Q2 (*employment*)
A2. (Can I just check), who (were / are) you in dispute or disagreement with -
was it your employer, a work colleague or some other person
or organisation?
CODE ALL THAT APPLY

Employer	1		1516-18
Work colleague(s)	2	**GO TO A14, page 5**	
Other person / organisation	3		

(SPECIFY) _____

IF SCREEN Q3 (*owning residential property*)
A3. **SHOW CARD A.**
(Can I just check), who (were / are) you in dispute or disagreement with?
CODE ALL THAT APPLY

Freeholder	01		1519-28
Neighbour	02		
Bank / Building society / Mortgage company	03	**GO TO A14, page 5**	
Insurance company	04		
Estate agent	05		
Surveyor	06		
Council / Local Authority	07		
Squatters	08		
Other person / organisation	09		

(SPECIFY) _____

IF SCREEN Q4 (*renting out rooms or property*)
A4. **SHOW CARD B.**
(Can I just check), who (were / are) you in dispute or disagreement with?
CODE ALL THAT APPLY

Tenant / Lodger	1		1529-32
Managing or letting agent	2	**GO TO A14, page 5**	
Council / Local Authority	3		
Other person / organisation	4		

(SPECIFY) _____

IF SCREEN Q5 (*living in rented accommodation*)
A5. **SHOW CARD C.**
(Can I just check), who (were / are) you in dispute or disagreement with?
CODE ALL THAT APPLY

Landlord / Council / Housing association	1		1533-37
Neighbour(s)	2		
Co-tenant(s) / Flat mate(s)	3	**GO TO A14, page 5**	
Lodger / Sub-tenant	4		
Other person / organisation	5		

(SPECIFY) _____

3

IF SCREEN Q6 (*faulty goods / services*)
A6. **SHOW CARD D.**
(Can I just check), who (were / are) you in dispute or disagreement with?
CODE ALL THAT APPLY

Shop / Mail order company / Travel agent	1		1538-41
Tradesman (eg plumber, electrician, double glazing installation, car mechanic)	2		
Professional (eg lawyer, accountant, surveyor)	3	**GO TO A14, page 5**	
Other person / organisation	4		

(SPECIFY) _____

IF SCREEN Q7 (*money*)
A7. **SHOW CARD E.**
(Can I just check), who (were / are) you in dispute or disagreement with?
CODE ALL THAT APPLY

Bank / building society / mortgage company / credit card company	01		1542-51
Utility company (eg gas, electricity, water)	02		
Insurance company	03		
Pension company	04	**GO TO A14, page 5**	
Inland Revenue	05		
Other business	06		
Employer	07		
Council / Local authority	08		
DSS	09		
Accountant / financial adviser	10		
(Ex) husband / wife / partner	11		
Other family member	12		
Other person / organisation	13		

(SPECIFY) _____

IF SCREEN Q8 (*divorce proceedings*)
A8. **IN SUBSEQUENT QUESTIONS,**
"…OTHER SIDE…" = (EX) HUSBAND / WIFE

GO TO A14, page 5

IF SCREEN Q9 (*family matters*)
A9. **SHOW CARD F.**
(Can I just check), who (were / are) you in dispute or disagreement with?
CODE ALL THAT APPLY

(Ex) Husband / wife / partner	1		1552-57
Other family member	2		
Local authority / Social Services	3		
Fostering or adoption agency	4	**GO TO A14, page 5**	
Child Support Agency (CSA)	5		
Other person / organisation	6		

(SPECIFY) _____

4

A10.
IF SCREEN Q10 (*children*)
SHOW CARD G.
(Can I just check), who (were / are) you in dispute or disagreement with?
CODE ALL THAT APPLY

(Ex) Husband / wife / partner	1	1558-62
Other family member	2	
Local authority / Social Services	3	**GO TO A14, page 5**
School / Teacher / Local Education Authority (LEA)	4	
Other person / organisation	5	
(SPECIFY) _____		

A11.
IF SCREEN Q11 (*accident / injury*)
SHOW CARD H.
(Can I just check), who (were / are) you in dispute or disagreement with?
CODE ALL THAT APPLY

Employer	1	1563-67
Council / Local authority	2	
Shop	3	
Restaurant / café / bar	4	**GO TO A14, page 5**
Driver of car, van, bicycle, motorcycle or other vehicle	5	
Other person / organisation	6	
(SPECIFY) _____		

A12.
IF SCREEN Q12 (*discrimination etc*)
SHOW CARD I.
(Can I just check), who (were / are) you in dispute or disagreement with?
CODE ALL THAT APPLY

Police	1	1568-71
Immigration authorities	2	
Hospital / Doctor / dentist / other medical practitioner	3	**GO TO A14, page 5**
Other person / organisation	4	
(SPECIFY) _____		

A13.
IF SCREEN Q13-15 (*legal action taken/threatened/started*)
(Can I just check), who (were / are) you in dispute or disagreement with?
WRITE IN:

_____

1572-79

5

ALL

A14. PLEASE ESTABLISH AN APPROPRIATE WORD OR PHRASE TO DESCRIBE
THE PERSON / ORGANISATION THAT RESPONDENT WAS IN DISPUTE OR
DISAGREEMENT WITH.

_____

THROUGHOUT THE QUESTIONNAIRE, WHERE QUESTIONS REFER TO
"...OTHER SIDE...". YOU SHOULD INSERT THE APPROPRIATE WORD
OR PHRASE

A15a) Can you tell me in more detail exactly what the problem or dispute (was / is) about?
IF NECESSARY:
PROBE: What (was / is) the key thing that you and ... OTHER SIDE ... (were / are)
in dispute about?

PROBE FOR THE KEY ARGUMENTS OF <u>BOTH SIDES</u>

GUIDANCE ABOUT LEVEL OF DETAIL REQUIRED:

e.g. IF DISPUTE ABOUT LOSS OF JOB
Threatened or actual loss of job (dismissal / early retirement / redundancy)?
Disputed grounds for loss of job or dispute about package on leaving (eg pension,
redundancy package) or something else?

IF NEIGHBOUR DISPUTE:
Dispute about boundaries, noise levels, communal maintenance or other problem?
Respondent complaining about other side, or other side complaining about respondent?

IF DISPUTE WITH LANDLORD ABOUT EVICTION:
Actual or threatened eviction? On what grounds? Did respondent dispute these grounds?

IF DISPUTE ABOUT CHILD SUPPORT PAYMENTS:
Payments by respondent or other party?
If previous agreement not being met - in what way? Why?

IF DISPUTE ABOUT FAULTY SERVICE:
In what way was the service faulty?
Was respondent withholding payment, or was the other side refusing to complete job, or what?

1610-29

b) PLEASE ESTABLISH AN APPROPRIATE WORD OR PHRASE TO DESCRIBE
THE PROBLEM / DISPUTE / SITUATION.

_____

THROUGHOUT THE QUESTIONNAIRE, WHERE QUESTIONS REFER TO "...PROBLEM ..." YOU
SHOULD EITHER INSERT THE APPROPRIATE WORD OR PHRASE OR REFER TO "THIS PROBLEM/
DISPUTE".

c) INTERVIEWER: SUBSEQUENT QUESTIONS OFFER DIFFERENT TENSES.
USE AS APPROPRIATE FOR EACH RESPONDENT.

6

ALL

A16a) **SHOW CARD J**
Before I ask you some more detailed questions about ...PROBLEM,
can you look at this card and tell me whether you have *ever* contacted
any of the people or organisations on this card about any matter?

Yes	1	**ASK b)**	1630
No	2	**GO TO A17**	

IF YES
b) **SHOW CARD J**
Which ones?
CODE ALL THAT APPLY

Citizens Advice Bureaux (OAB)	01	1631-74
Law Centre	02	
Welfare Rights Officer (WRO)	03	
Consumer advice centre /Trading Standards Officer	04	
Other advice agency / worker	05	
Employer	06	
Trade Union or Staff Association	07	
Professional body *(eg BMA, Law Society)*	08	
Trade association *(eg ABTA, Which, AA)*	09	
Solicitor	10	
Barrister	11	
Claims agency *(eg Direct Legal)*	12	
Court staff	13	
Ombudsman	14	
Other legal consultant *(eg employment law / immigration law consultant)*	15	
Member of Parliament (MP) or Local councillor	16	
Local council department	17	
Housing association	18	
Social worker / Social Services	19	
Police	20	
Religious organisation *(eg church, mosque, synagogue)*	21	
Insurance company	22	

7

A17a) **SHOW ADVISER CARD**
Now please think about ...PROBLEM. (Did you have / Have you had) any contact at any stage
with any of the people or organisations on this card about ... PROBLEM...?
(IF NECESSARY: - please do not include contact with ...OTHER SIDE)
MAKE SURE RESPONDENT READS FULL LIST.

Yes, contact with adviser(s)	1 **ASK b)**	1710
No	2 **GO TO A18**	

IF YES
b) **SHOW ADVISER CARD**
Who did you contact first about ... PROBLEM?
RING ONE CODE IN 1ST COLUMN BELOW

	1st	2nd	3rd	4th	5th	6th/7th etc	
Citizens Advice Bureaux (CAB)	01	01	01	01	01	01	1st
Law Centre	02	02	02	02	02	02	1711-2
Welfare Rights Officer (WRO)	03	03	03	03	03	03	2nd
Consumer advice centre / Trading Standards Officer	04	04	04	04	04	04	1713-4
Other advice agency / worker	05	05	05	05	05	05	3rd
Employer	06	06	06	06	06	06	1715-6
Trade Union or Staff Association	07	07	07	07	07	07	4th
Professional body (eg BMA, Law Society)	08	08	08	08	08	08	1717-8
Trade associations (eg ABTA, Which, AA)	09	09	09	09	09	09	5th
Solicitor	10	10	10	10	10	10	1719-20
Barrister	11	11	11	11	11	11	6th
Claims agency (eg Direct Legal)	12	12	12	12	12	12	1721-30
Court staff	13	13	13	13	13	13	
Ombudsman	14	14	14	14	14	14	
Other legal consultant (eg employment law / immigration law consultant)	15	15	15	15	15	15	
Member of Parliament (MP) or Local councillor	16	16	16	16	16	16	
Local council department	17	17	17	17	17	17	
Housing association	18	18	18	18	18	18	
Social Worker / Social Services	19	19	19	19	19	19	
Police	20	20	20	20	20	20	
Religious organisation (eg church, mosque, synagogue)	21	21	21	21	21	21	
Insurance Company	22	22	22	22	22	22	
Other person / organisation	23	23	23	23	23	23	
(SPECIFY) _____							
No further advice sought	00	00	00	00	00	00	

c) Who did you contact next?
RING ONE CODE IN 2ND COLUMN ABOVE

ONLY INCLUDE PARTNER / FRIENDS /
RELATIVES IF THEY ARE ONE OF THE TYPES OF
ADVISERS ON THE CARD.

d) Who did you contact next?
RING ONE CODE IN 3RD COLUMN ABOVE

e) Who did you contact next?
RING ONE CODE IN 4TH COLUMN ABOVE

IF CONTACTED MORE THAN ONE OF THE SAME
TYPE OF ADVISER, EG MORE THAN ONE SOLICITOR
CONSULTED, RING CODE FOR SOLICITOR IN AS
MANY COLUMNS AS IS APPROPRIATE.

f) Who did you contact next?
RING CODE IN 5TH COLUMN ABOVE

g) Who did you contact next?
RING CODE IN 6TH COLUMN ABOVE
IF CONTACTED MORE THAN 6 SOURCES, CODE ALL THAT APPLY IN '6th/7th' COLUMN ABOVE.

8

ALL
A18a) SHOW ADVISER CARD
(Did / Have) you (try / tried) unsuccessfully to contact any of the (other) people
or organisations on this card for help or advice about...PROBLEM?

| | Yes | 1 | ASK b) | 1731 |
| | No | 2 | GO TO c) | |

IF YES
b) SHOW ADVISER CARD
Who?
CODE ALL THAT APPLY

Citizens Advice Bureaux (CAB)	01	1732-41
Law Centre	02	
Welfare Rights Officer (WRO)	03	
Consumer advice centre /Trading Standards Officer	04	
Other advice agency / worker	05	
Employer	06	
Trade Union or Staff Association	07	
Professional body *(eg BMA, Law Society)*	08	
Trade association *(eg ABTA, Which, AA)*	09	
Solicitor	10	
Barrister	11	
Claims agency *(eg Direct Legal)*	12	
Court staff	13	
Ombudsman	14	
Other legal consultant *(eg employment law / immigration law consultant)*	15	
Member of Parliament (MP) or Local councillor	16	
Local council department	17	
Housing association	18	
Social worker / Social Services	19	
Police	20	
Religious organisation *(eg church, mosque, synagogue)*	21	
Insurance company	22	
Other person / organisation (SPECIFY)	23	

c) SHOW ADVISER CARD
(Did /Have) you consider(ed) contacting any of the (other) people or
organisations on this card for help or advice about...PROBLEM?

| | Yes | 1 | ASK d) | 1742 |
| | No | 2 | GO TO A19 | |

9

d) IF YES
SHOW ADVISER CARD
Who?
CODE ALL THAT APPLY

Citizens Advice Bureaux (CAB)	01
Law Centre	02
Welfare Rights Officer (WRO)	03
Consumer advice centre /Trading Standards Officer	04
Other advice agency / worker	05
Employer	06
Trade Union or Staff Association	07
Professional body *(eg BMA, Law Society)*	08
Trade association *(eg ABTA, Which, AA)*	09
Solicitor	10
Barrister	11
Claims agency *(eg Direct Legal)*	12
Court staff	13
Ombudsman	14
Other legal consultant *(eg employment law / immigration law consultant)*	15
Member of Parliament (MP) or Local councillor	16
Local council department	17
Housing association	18
Social worker / Social Services	19
Police	20
Religious organisation *(eg church, mosque, synagogue)*	21
Insurance company	22
Other person / organisation (SPECIFY)	23

1743-56

e) Why did you decide not to contact .. ADVISERS MENTIONED AT d)?
PROBE FULLY. RECORD VERBATIM.

OR CODE: (Intend to / May) contact in future   01

1757-66

A19a) INTERVIEWER CHECK A17a), page 7

Contact with adviser(s) about problem (code 1 at A17a)	1	**GO TO b)**
No contact with adviser (code 2 at A17a)	2	**GO TO A31, page 16**

1767

10

IF ADVISER CONTACTED
b) **INTERVIEWER CHECK page 7 - A17b) GRID, COLUMN 1**
   FOR 1ST ADVISER CONTACTED

c) Before you consulted .. 1ST ADVISER ..., had there
   been any contact between you and ...OTHER SIDE... to try
   to sort out ...PROBLEM?

Yes	1	**GO TO f)**	1768
No	2	**ASK d)**	

IF NO
d) Before you consulted ...1ST ADVISER..., had you
   tried to contact ...OTHER SIDE .. to sort out ...PROBLEM?

Yes	1	1769
No	2	

e) And before you consulted ...1ST ADVISER..., had
   ...OTHER SIDE... tried to contact you to sort out ...PROBLEM?

Yes	1		1770
No	2	**GO TO A20**	
(Can't say)	8		

IF CONTACT BETWEEN TWO PARTIES
f) Did you manage to come to any sort of agreement with .. OTHER SIDE...
   before you consulted .. 1ST ADVISER?

Yes	1	**ASK g)**	1771
No	2	**GO TO A20**	
(Can't say)	8		

IF YES
g) What sort of agreement?
   PROBE FULLY. RECORD VERBATIM.

1772-81

A20a) What made you think of contacting ...1st ADVISER...?   1810-13
   CODE ALL THAT APPLY

It was advised or suggested by a friend / relative / work colleague	1
Saw (or heard) advertisement for ...ADVISER	2
Previous experience of similar situation	3
Other (*specify*)	4

_____

_____

(Can't say)	8

11

b) When did you contact ...1ST ADVISER?
ENTER MONTH AND YEAR.
ESTIMATE ACCEPTABLE.

1814-17

MONTH: ☐☐

YEAR: ☐☐

c) About how long after .. PROBLEM.. started was this?

CODE ONE ONLY

As soon as problem started	01
1- 2 weeks	02
3 - 4 weeks	03
5 - 6 weeks	04
2 months	05
3 months	06
4 months	07
5 months	08
6 months	09
More than 6 months	10
(Can't say)	98

1818-19

d) **INTERVIEWER CHECK GRID AT A17b), page 7**

One adviser contacted	1	**GO TO e)**
Two or three advisers contacted	2	**GO TO f)**
Four or more advisers contacted	3	**GO TO g)**

1820

IF ONE ADVISER CONTACTED
e) NOW PLEASE COMPLETE GRID ON NEXT PAGE FOR THE ADVISER CONTACTED
(RECORDED AT A17b)

WORK DOWN THE FIRST COLUMN UNTIL YOU REACH THE BOTTOM OF PAGE 15.

IF TWO OR THREE ADVISERS CONTACTED
f) NOW PLEASE COMPLETE GRID ON NEXT PAGE FOR EACH ADVISER CONTACTED,
STARTING IN FIRST COLUMN WITH THE FIRST ADVISER CONTACTED (RECORDED AT A17b)

WORK DOWN THE 1ST COLUMN UNTIL YOU REACH THE BOTTOM OF PAGE 15, THEN RETURN
TO PAGE 12 AND COMPLETE THE 2ND COLUMN FOR THE 2ND ADVISER CONTACTED.

IF FOUR OR MORE ADVISERS CONTACTED
g) NOW PLEASE COMPLETE GRID ON NEXT PAGE FOR THE **FIRST TWO** ADVISERS CONTACTED,
STARTING IN FIRST COLUMN WITH THE FIRST ADVISER CONTACTED (RECORDED AT A17b)

OUT OF THE REMAINING 3RD / 4TH, 5TH etc ADVISERS RECORDED AT 17b),
ESTABLISH **WHICH ADVISER DID THE MOST FOR THE RESPONDENT**.
THEN COMPLETE THE THIRD COLUMN FOR THIS ADVISER.

WORK DOWN EACH COLUMN UNTIL YOU REACH THE BOTTOM OF PAGE 15, THEN RETURN TO
PAGE 12 AND COMPLETE FURTHER COLUMNS AS APPROPRIATE FOR SUBSEQUENT ADVISERS.

		1st ADVISER	2nd ADVISER	3rd ADVISER
A21	**INTERVIEWER CHECK A17b)** WRITE IN TYPE OF 1st ADVISER IN COLUMN 1, TYPE OF 2nd ADVISER IN COLUMN 2 ETC *(eg CAB, Solicitor)*	1821-2	1926-7	2026-7
A22	(Sometimes people seek advice from friends or relatives who work in particular jobs such as advice agencies or the legal profession). Can I just check, was ...ADVISER... that you contacted a friend or relative of yours?	1823	1928	2028
	Yes	1	1	1
	No	2	2	2
A23	**SHOW CARD K** When you contacted .. ADVISER ... about .. PROBLEM, what sort of advice or help were you looking for? **CODE ALL THAT APPLY**	1824-30	1929-35	2029-35
	Advice about my legal rights	1	1	1
	Advice about procedures / what to do next *(eg how to deal with summons, court procedures)*	2	2	2
	Advice about ways to solve the problem	3 → A24	3 → A24	3 → A24
	Advice about financial position	4	4	4
	Someone to represent me in court / tribunal	5	5	5
	Other advice or help (SPECIFY IN ROW BELOW)	6 ↓ ROW 1	6 ↓ ROW 2	6 ↓ ROW 3

ROW 1 (1st ADVISER)   1831-40

                                                                                GO TO A24

ROW 2 (2nd ADVISER)   1936-45

                                                                                GO TO A24

ROW 3 (3rd ADVISER)   2036-45

                                                                                GO TO A24

		1st ADVISER	2nd ADVISER	3rd ADVISER
A24	Did .. ADVISER.. think that there was something that could be done about .. PROBLEM... - either by you, or with the help of someone else?	1841	1946	2046
	Yes	1	1	1
	No	2	2	2
A25.	**SHOW CARD L** Did ...ADVISER... give you advice about any of the things on this card at any time? **CODE ALL THAT APPLY**	1842-44	1947-49	2047-49
	Your legal rights	1	1	1
	Procedures / what to do next *(eg how to deal with summons, court procedures)*	2	2	2
	The financial position	3	3	3
	None of these types of advice	4	4	4

13

		1st ADVISER	2nd ADVISER	3rd ADVISER
A26a)	**SHOW CARD M** Did ...ADVISER... suggest that you do any of the things on this card? **CODE ALL THAT APPLY**	1845-49	1950-54	2050-54
	Contact other side to try to resolve the problem	1	1	1
	Seek advice or help from another person / organisation	2	2	2
	Threaten other side with legal action	3 → b	3 → b	3 → b
	Go to court, tribunal or arbitration / start a court, tribunal or arb. case against other side	4	4	4
	Go to mediation / conciliation	5	5	5
	Take the problem to an ombudsman	6	6	6
	None of these	0 → A27	0 → A27	0 → A27
b)	**INTERVIEWER CHECK a)**	1850	1955	2055
	Advised to seek advice from other person/organisation (code 2 at a)	1 → c	1 → c	1 → c
	Others	2 → A27	2 → A27	2 → A27
c)	**IF ADVISED TO SEEK ADVICE FROM OTHER** Who did (s)he suggest that you contact for advice or help? **CODE ALL THAT APPLY**	1851-60	1956-65	2056-65
	Citizens Advice Bureaux (CAB) 01	01	01	01
	Law Centre 02	02	02	02
	Welfare Rights Officer (WRO) 03	03	03	03
	Consumer advice centre / Trading Standards Officer 04	04	04	04
	Other advice agency / worker 05	05	05	05
	Employer 06	06	06	06
	Trade Union or Staff Association 07	07	07	07
	Professional body 08	08	08	08
	Trade associations 09	09	09	09
	Solicitor 10	10	10	10
	Barrister 11	11	11	11
	Claims agency 12	12	12	12
	Court staff 13	13	13	13
	Ombudsman 14	14	14	14
	Other legal consultant 15	15	15	15
	Member of Parliament (MP) or Local councillor 16	16	16	16
	Local council department 17	17	17	17
	Housing association 18	18	18	18
	Social Worker / Social Services 19	19	19	19
	Police 20	20	20	20
	Religious organisation 21	21	21	21
	Insurance Company 22	22	22	22
	Other person / organisation 23 (SPECIFY)	23 _____	23 _____	23 _____
	(Can't say) 98	98	98	98

14

		1st ADVISER 1861-66	2nd ADVISER 1966-71	3rd ADVISER 2066-71
A27	**SHOW CARD N** Did ...ADVISER... give you any of the types of help on this card? **CODE ALL THAT APPLY**			
	None of these types of help	0	0	0
	Contacted other side on my behalf	1	1	1
	Negotiated with other side on my behalf	2	2	2
	Contacted another person/organisation on my behalf	3	3	3
	Helpéd me to contact another person/organisation (e.g. by making an appointment, giving me a list of people to approach)	4 → A28	4 → A28	4 → A28
	Accompanied me to court/ tribunal/ arbitration/ mediation	5	5	5
	Spoke on my behalf in court/ tribunal/ arbitration/ mediation	6	6	6
	Gave me other advice or help (specify in row below)	7 ↓ ROW 1	7 ↓ ROW 2	7 ↓ ROW 3

ROW 1 (1st ADVISER) 1867-76

GO TO A28
ROW 2 (2nd ADVISER) 1972-81

GO TO A28
ROW 3 (3rd ADVISER) 2072-81

					GO TO A28
A28a)	Did you actually meet .. ADVISER . face-to-face?		1910	2010	2110
	Yes	1 → b	1 → b	1 → b 0	
	No	2 → c	2 → c	2 → c	
b)	**IF MET ADVISER FACE-TO-FACE** How far did you have to travel to see ...ADVISER? **IF ADVISER = EMPLOYER** **CODE "NO TRAVEL"**		1911	2011	2111
	(No travel / Adviser travelled to respondent)	0	0	0	
	Less than 5 miles	1	1	1	
	6 - 14 miles	2	2	2	
	15 - 29 miles	3	3	3	
	30 - 49 miles	4	4	4	
	50 miles or more	5	5	5	
	(Can't say)	8	8	8	

15

			1st ADVISER	2nd ADVISER	3rd ADVISER
A28c)	About how many times did you speak to .. ADVISER.., either in person or on the phone?		1912	2012	2112
		Never	1	1	1
		Once or twice	2	2	2
		3 - 5 times	3	3	3
		6 - 10 times	4	4	4
		11 - 15 times	5	5	5
		16 - 20 times	6	6	6
		More than 20 times	7	7	7
		(Can't say)	8	8	8
A29	Overall, how helpful did you find the advice or help you received from .. ADVISER...**READ OUT**...		1913	2013	2113
		..very helpful,	1	1	1
		fairly helpful,	2	2	2
		not very helpful	3	3	3
		or not at all helpful?	4	4	4
		(Can't say)	8	8	8
A30a)	Would you recommend other people in your situation to consult ...TYPE OF ADVISER ..? PROBE: Definitely or probably (not)?		1914	2014	2114
		Yes - definitely	1→ c	1→ c	1→ c
		Yes - probably	2→ c	2→ c	2→ c
		Probably not	3→ b	3→ b	3→ b
		Definitely not	4→ b	4→ b	4→ b
		(Can't say)	8→ c	8→ c	8→ c
b)	**IF WOULD NOT RECOMMEND** Why is that?		RECORD IN ROW I BELOW	RECORD IN ROW II BELOW	RECORD IN ROW III BELOW
	ROW 1 (1st ADVISER)				1915-24
					GO TO c
	ROW 2 (2nd ADVISER)				2015-24
					GO TO c
	ROW 3 (3rd ADVISER)				2115-24
					GO TO c
c)	**INTERVIEWER CHECK A17b, page 7**		1925	2025	2125
		Further adviser coded at A17b)	1→A21, next col. page 12	1→A21, next col. page 12	1→A21, next col. page 12
		Others	2→ B1, page 22	2→ B1, page 22	2→ B1, page 22

16

IF NO ADVISER CONTACTED

A31. Can I just check, as far as you know (did / does) ...OTHER SIDE... have
a solicitor or other adviser to help them deal with .. PROBLEM?
IF YES: Who?
CODE ALL THAT APPLY

Citizens Advice Bureaux (CAB)	01
Law Centre	02
Welfare Rights Officer (WRO)	03
Consumer advice centre /Trading Standards Officer	04
Other advice agency / worker	05
Employer	06
Trade Union or Staff Association	07
Professional body *(eg BMA, Law Society)*	08
Trade association *(eg ABTA, Which, AA)*	09
Solicitor	10
Barrister	11
Claims agency *(eg Direct Legal)*	12
Court staff	13
Ombudsman	14
Other legal consultant *(eg employment law / immigration law consultant)*	15
Member of Parliament (MP) or Local councillor	16
Local council department	17
Housing association	18
Social worker / Social Services	19
Police	20
Religious organisation *(eg church, mosque, synagogue)*	21
Insurance company	22
Other person / organisation (SPECIFY)	23
No advice or help	00
Can't say	98

A32a) (Was there / Has there been) any contact between you and ...OTHER SIDE...
to try to sort out ...PROBLEM?

Yes, contact with other side	1	**GO TO A33**
No	2	**ASK b)**
(No other side in this problem/dispute)	3	**GO TO A33**

IF NO

b) (Did you try / Have you tried) to contact ...OTHER SIDE...
to sort out ...PROBLEM?

Yes, tried to contact other side	1
No	2

17

c) (Did / Has) ...OTHER SIDE... (try / tried) to contact you   2138
   to sort out ...PROBLEM?

                                                        Yes   1

                                                        No   2

                                                  (Can't say)   8

IF NO ADVISER CONTACTED
A33 (Apart from this), (did you do / have you done) anything else   2139-48
   about ... PROBLEM ?
   CODE ALL THAT APPLY

                    Threatened other side with legal action   01

                         Went to court, tribunal or arbitration
   / started court, tribunal or arbitration case against other side   02

                         Went to mediation or conciliation   03

                      Took the problem to an ombudsman   04

   Sought advice or help from other person / organisation (*specify*)   05

   _____

                         Paid other side some money   06

                              Other action (*specify*)   07

   _____

   _____

                              No - done nothing   00

                                  (Can't say)   98

A34a) **INTERVIEWER CHECK A32a)**

Yes, contact with other side	1	**GO TO B1, page 22**	2149
No	2	**GO TO b)**	
(No other side in this problem/dispute)	3	**GO TO c)**	

   IF NO CONTACT
b) **INTERVIEWER CHECK A32b)**

Respondent tried to contact other side	1	**GO TO B1, page 22**	2150
No attempted contact	2	**GO TO c)**	

   IF NO ATTEMPTED CONTACT / NO OTHER SIDE
c) **INTERVIEWER CHECK A33**

Respondent did something else (code 01-06)	1	**GO TO B1, page 22**	2151
Others (code 00 or 98)	2	**ASK A35**	

18

IF NO ACTION TAKEN
A35a) Do you intend to do anything about .. PROBLEM ?
IF YES: Definitely or probably?
IF NO: Probably not or definitely not?

Yes, definitely	1		2152
Yes, probably	2	GO TO A36	
Maybe	3		
Probably not	4	ASK b)	
Definitely not	5		

IF DOES NOT INTEND TO DO ANYTHING
b) Why don't you intend to do anything about ... PROBLEM?   2153-62
PROBE FULLY. RECORD VERBATIM

GO TO A41, page 21

IF (MAYBE) INTENDS TO DO SOMETHING
A36. What do you intend to do?   2163-72
CODE ALL THAT APPLY

Contact the other side	01
Threaten other side with legal action	02
Go to court, tribunal or arbitration / start court, tribunal or arbitration case against other side	03
Go to mediation or conciliation	04
Take the problem to an ombudsman	05
Seek advice or help from other person / organisation (*specify*)	06
Pay other side some money	07
Other (planned) action (*specify*)	08
(Can't say)	98

19

A37a) I would now like to ask you about what you want to achieve by doing something about ...PROBLEM.
What is the <u>main</u> thing you want to achieve in trying to sort out ...PROBLEM?
PROBE FULLY.   RECORD VERBATIM.

2210-19

b) What other things (if any) do you want to achieve?
PROBE FULLY.   RECORD VERBATIM.

2220-29

OR CODE: No other things   00

A38a) All in all, how likely do you think it is that you will achieve what you want ...**READ OUT**...

2230

...very likely,	1	**GO TO A39**
fairly likely,	2	
not very likely,	3	**ASK b)**
or not at all likely?	4	
(Can't say)	8	**GO TO A39**

IF NOT LIKELY
b) Why do you say that?
PROBE FULLY.   RECORD VERBATIM.

2231-40

IF INTENDS TO DO SOMETHING ABOUT PROBLEM
A39a) **INTERVIEWER CHECK ANSWERS GIVEN AT A37a) AND b),**
AND CODE:

Respondent wanted to get **money** from other side	1	**GO TO d)**
Respondent wanted other side to **reduce** amount of money he/she/they were asking for *(eg bill / child support etc)*	2	**GO TO c)**
Others	3	**GO TO b)**

2341

IF OTHERS
b) Can I just check, are you trying to get ...OTHER SIDE... to pay you some money?

2342

Yes	1	**GO TO d)**
No	2	**GO TO A41, page 21**

IF WANTED REDUCTION IN BILL / EXPECTED PAYMENTS etc
c) I would now like to ask you some questions about when you decided that you wanted ...OTHER SIDE... to reduce the amount of money (he/she/they) was/were asking you for.

Can I just check, were you trying to get a reduction in a *bill* that you were being asked to pay, or a reduction in *regular payments* that you were being asked to make?

2343

Bill	1	**GO TO A40**
Reduced payments	2	**GO TO A41**
Both	3	**GO TO A40**
Can't say	8	**GO TO A41**

IF WANTS OTHER SIDE TO PAY MONEY
d) Can I just check, are you trying to get a lump sum of money or regular payments from ...OTHER SIDE...?

2244

Lump sum of money from other side	1	**ASK A40**
Regular payments from other side (eg maintenance, benefits etc).	2	**GO TO A41**
Both	3	**ASK A40**
Can't say	8	

IF WANTS LUMP SUM / REDUCED BILL / CAN'T SAY
A40a) How much money are you trying to get ...OTHER SIDE... to (pay / reduce the bill or payment by)?
PROMPT WITH CODES IF NECESSARY
ESTIMATE ACCEPTABLE

INCLUDE MONEY OWED AND
COMPENSATION

£50 or less	01	2245-46
£51 - £100	02	
£101 - £200	03	
£201 - £500	04	
£501 - £750	05	
£751 - £1,000	06	
£1,001 - £1,500	07	
£1,501 - £3,000	08	**ASK b)**
£3,001 - £5,000	09	
£5,001 - £10,000	10	
£10,001 - £15,000	11	
£15,001 - £25,000	12	
£25,001 - £50,000	13	
£50,001 - £75,000	14	
£75,001 - £100,000	15	
More than £100,000	16	
(Can't say)	98	**GO TO A41**

21

IF VALUE GIVEN AT a)

b) Where did you get the idea from that you could expect to get this amount of money?

CODE ALL THAT APPLY

2247-55

Suggested or advised by *friend / relative / work colleague*　01

Suggested or advised by *other person / organisation* (*specify*)　02

_____

Reports in the *media* about these kinds of cases　03

Previous experience of similar kind of situation　04

Other (*specify fully*)　05

_____

_____

(Can't say)　98

IF NO ACTION (YET) TAKEN

A41. Can I just check, (has / did) ...OTHER SIDE...threaten(ed) you with legal action at any stage, or taken you to court to sort out ...PROBLEM?

2256

Yes	1	**GO TO C1, page 26**
No	2	**GO TO H4, page 62**

SECTION B: OBJECTIVES	22

IF ANY ACTION TAKEN

B1a) Thinking back to when you first decided to do something about
...PROBLEM..., what was the <u>main</u> thing you wanted to achieve?
RECORD VERBATIM IN COLUMN 1 OF TABLE AGAINST "MAIN AIM"

b) (Did / Have) you achieve(d) this aim?
IF YES: Completely or partly?
RING CODE IN COLUMN 2

c) At that stage, were there any <u>other</u> things you hoped to achieve?
RECORD VERBATIM AGAINST "2ⁿᵈ AIM", "3ʳᵈ AIM" etc

        OR CODE: No other things | 00 **GO TO B2** | (2257-58)

FOR EACH AIM RECORDED, ASK:

d) (Did / Have) you achieve(d) this aim?
IF YES: Completely or partly?
RING CODE IN COLUMN 2

Column 1		Column 2	
Things respondent hoped to achieve		Whether achieved or not	
Main aim:	2257-63	Achieved completely 1	2264
		Achieved partly 2	
		Not achieved 3	
		Too early to say 4	
2ⁿᵈ aim:	2265-71	Achieved completely 1	2272
		Achieved partly 2	
		Not achieved 3	
		Too early to say 4	
3ʳᵈ aim:	2273-79	Achieved completely 1	2280
		Achieved partly 2	
		Not achieved 3	
		Too early to say 4	
4ᵗʰ aim:	2310-16	Achieved completely 1	2317
		Achieved partly 2	
		Not achieved 3	
		Too early to say 4	

B2a) You've now told me about what you wanted to achieve *initially*.
During the course of trying to sort out ...PROBLEM..., (have / did)
you change(d) your mind at any time about what you want(ed) to
achieve?

        Yes | 1 **ASK b)** | 2318
        No | 2 **GO TO B3**
        Can't say | 8

23

IF YES
b) What <u>other</u> things did you decide that you wanted to achieve?
RECORD EACH NEW AIM IN COLUMN 1 OF TABLE AGAINST
"NEW AIM 1", "NEW AIM 2" etc

OR CODE: No other things | 00   **GO TO B3** | (2319-20)

c) **FOR EACH 'NEW' AIM RECORDED, ASK:**
(Did / Have) you achieve(d) this aim? **IF YES:** Completely or partly?
RING CODE IN COLUMN 2

Column 1	Column 2	
Other things respondent hoped to achieve	Whether achieved or not	
New aim 1: 2319-25	Achieved completely 1	2326
	Achieved partly 2	
	Not achieved 3	
	Too early to say 4	
New aim 2: 2327-33	Achieved completely 1	2334
	Achieved partly 2	
	Not achieved 3	
	Too early to say 4	
New aim 3: 2335-41	Achieved completely 1	2342
	Achieved partly 2	
	Not achieved 3	
	Too early to say 4	
New aim 4: 2343-49	Achieved completely 1	2350
	Achieved partly 2	
	Not achieved 3	
	Too early to say 4	

B3a) All in all, when you first decided to do something about ...PROBLEM...,
how likely did you think it was that you would achieve what you
wanted ...**READ OUT**...

...very likely,	1 **GO TO B4**	2351
fairly likely,	2	
not very likely,	3	
or not at all likely?	4 **ASK b)**	
(can't say)	8	

IF NOT LIKELY
b) Why did you think that?
PROBE FULLY.   RECORD VERBATIM.   2352-61

24

B4a) INTERVIEWER CHECK ANSWERS GIVEN IN
GRIDS AT B1 AND B2

Respondent wanted to get **money** from other side	1	**GO TO d)**	2362
Respondent wanted other side to **reduce** amount of money he/she/they was/were asking for *(eg bill, child support etc)*	2	**GO TO c)**	
Others	3	**GO TO b)**	

IF OTHERS
b) Can I just check, were you trying to get ...OTHER SIDE... to pay you some money?

Yes	1	**GO TO d)**	2363
No	2	**GO TO C1, page 26**	

IF WANTED REDUCTION IN BILL / EXPECTED PAYMENTS etc
c) I would now like to ask you some questions about when you decided that you wanted ...OTHER SIDE... to reduce the amount of money (he/she/they) was asking you for.
Can I just check, were you trying to get a reduction in a *bill* that you were being asked to pay, or a reduction in *regular payments* that you were being asked to make?

2364

Bill	1	**GO TO B5**
Reduced payments	2	**GO TO C1, page 26**
Both	3	**GO TO B5**
Can't say	8	**GO TO C1, page 26**

IF WANTED TO GET MONEY
d) I would now like to ask you some questions about when you decided that you wanted some money from ...OTHER SIDE.
Can I just check, at that stage were you trying to get a lump sum of money or regular payments from ...OTHER SIDE...?

Lump sum of money from other side	1	**ASK B5**	2365
Regular payments from other side (eg maintenance, benefits etc).	2	**GO TO C1, page 26**	
Both	3	**ASK B5**	
(Can't say)	8		

25

IF WANTED LUMP SUM / CAN'T SAY / REDUCED BILL
B5a) How much money were you trying to get ...OTHER SIDE... to
(pay / reduce the bill or payment by)?
PROMPT WITH CODES IF NECESSARY
ESTIMATE ACCEPTABLE

INCLUDE MONEY OWED AND COMPENSATION	£50 or less	01	2366-67
	£51 - £100	02	
	£101 - £200	03	
IF AMOUNT OF MONEY SOUGHT CHANGED OVER TIME, ASK ABOUT LATEST AMOUNT	£201 - £500	04	
	£501 - £750	05	
	£751 - £1,000	06	
	£1,001 - £1,500	07	
	£1,501 - £3,000	08 **ASK b)**	
	£3,001 - £5,000	09	
	£5,001 - £10,000	10	
	£10,001 - £15,000	11	
	£15,001 - £25,000	12	
	£25,001 - £50,000	13	
	£50,001 - £75,000	14	
	£75,001 - £100,000	15	
	More than £100,000	16	
	(Can't say)	98 **GO TO C1, page 26**	

IF VALUE GIVEN AT a)
b) Where did you get the idea from that you could expect to get
this amount of money?
CODE ALL THAT APPLY

Suggested or advised by *friend / relative / work colleague*   01   2368-77

Suggested or advised by *other person / organisation* (*specify*)   02

_____

Reports in the *media* about these kinds of cases   03

Previous experience of similar kind of situation   04

Other (*specify fully*)   05

_____

(Can't say)   98

26

SECTION C: MEDIATION

C1a) **SHOW CARD O**
On this card are some examples of organisations that offer mediation
or conciliation to people to help resolve disputes.
Did you attend any mediation or conciliation sessions with any of
these types of organisations to try to resolve ... PROBLEM ... ?

Yes - help received	1	**ASK b)**	2410
No	2		
(Mediation / conciliation session planned for future)	3	**GO TO D1, page 31**	
(Can't say)	8		

IF YES
b) **SHOW CARD O**
What was the name of the organisation?
CODE ONE ONLY

Advisory, Conciliation and Arbitration Service (ACAS)	01	2411-12
Alternative Dispute Resolution (ADR)	02	
Centre for Dispute Resolution (CEDR)	03	
Mediation UK	04	
Academy of Experts	05	
Chartered Institute of Arbitrators	06	
National Family Mediation (NFM)	07	
Family Mediators Association (FMA)	08	
BALM	09	
SFLA	10	
Other mediation/conciliation organisation (SPECIFY)	11	
_____		
(Can't say)	98	

c) How many (mediation / conciliation) sessions were there?   2413

One	1
Two	2
Three	3
Four or more	4

d) (I would now like to ask you a few questions about the <u>final</u>
(mediation / conciliation) session).

What was the date of the (final) mediation / conciliation session?   2414-17

WRITE IN MONTH AND YEAR: ☐☐ **19** ☐☐
ESTIMATE ACCEPTABLE.

27

C2a)   **SHOW CARD P**
At the (final) mediation / conciliation session, were you accompanied by
any of the people on this card?

Barrister	1		2418-22
Solicitor	2		
Law Centre adviser	3		
Advice worker (CAB / WRO)	4		
Trade Union or Staff association representative	5	**ASK b)**	
Partner / friend / relative	6		
Other (SPECIFY)	7		
Not accompanied	0	**GO TO C4**	

IF ACCOMPANIED
b)   **SHOW CARD P**
Was there anyone at the mediation / conciliation session(s) to speak
on your behalf?
IF YES: Who spoke on your behalf?

Barrister	1		2423-27
Solicitor	2		
Law Centre adviser	3		
Advice worker (CAB / WRO)	4	**ASK C3**	
Trade Union or Staff Association representative	5		
Partner / friend / relative	6		
Other (SPECIFY)	7		
No-one to speak on respondent's behalf	0	**GO TO C4**	
(Can't say)	8		

IF REPRESENTED AT MEDIATION SESSION
C3a)   How well do you feel that your (barrister / solicitor / adviser)
represented you at the (mediation / conciliation) session
... READ OUT ...

...very well,	1	2428
fairly well,	2	
not very well,	3	
or not at all well?	4	
(Can't say)	8	

c)   Do you think you would have been better off without
a (barrister / solicitor / adviser) to represent you?

Yes	1		2429
No	2	**GO TO C5**	
Maybe	3		
(Can't say)	8		

28

IF NO-ONE TO SPEAK ON RESP'S BEHALF

C4a) Why did you not have anyone representing you at the
(mediation / conciliation) session?
CODE ALL THAT APPLY
PROBE: Any other reason?

Could not afford it	1
Was advised that I should represent myself	2
Didn't think I needed anyone to represent me	3
Other (*specify fully*)	4

2430-34

_____

_____

(Can't say)	8

b) Did you feel that you were at a disadvantage because you
did not have anybody to speak on your behalf?

Yes	1	2435
No	2	
(Can't say)	8	

IF MEDIATION/CONCILIATION

C5a) **SHOW CARD P**
Did ...OTHER SIDE... have anyone to speak on (his / her / their)
behalf at the (mediation / conciliation) session?
IF YES: Who spoke on ...OTHER SIDE's... behalf?
CODE ALL THAT APPLY

Barrister	1	2436-40
Solicitor	2	
Law Centre adviser	3	
Advice worker (CAB / WRO)	4	**ASK b)**
Trade Union or Staff Association representative	5	
Partner / friend / relative	6	
Other (SPECIFY)	7	

No-one to speak on other side's behalf	0	**GO TO C6**
(Can't say)	8	

b) How well do you feel that ...OTHER SIDE...'s (barrister / solicitor / adviser)
represented (him / her / them) ... READ OUT ...

...very well,	1	2441
fairly well,	2	
not very well,	3	
or not at all well?	4	
(Can't say)	8	

29

C6a) How long did the (mediation / conciliation)
session last?
CODE ONE ONLY

Less than 30 minutes	01	2442-3
30 minutes, under 2 hours	02	
2 hours, under 4 hours	03	
4 hours, under a day	04	
Whole day	05	
Two days	06	
Three days or more	07	
Can't say	98	

b) **SHOW CARD Q**
Did you feel that you had an opportunity to say what you wanted
to say during the (mediation / conciliation) session - please choose
your answer from this card?

2444

I had an opportunity to say ... everything I wanted to say	1	**GO TO C7**
...most of what I wanted to say	2	
...some of what I wanted to say	3	
...very little of what I wanted to say	4	**ASK c)**
... none of what I wanted to say	5	
(Can't say)	8	

IF DID NOT SAY EVERYTHING (S)HE WANTED
c) Were there any important facts about ... PROBLEM... which
you feel did not get discussed at the (mediation / conciliation) session?

Yes	1	2445
No	2	
(Can't say)	8	

C7a) How well do you think that the (mediator / conciliator)
understood your case ... READ OUT ....

...very well,	1	2446
fairly well,	2	
not very well,	3	
or not at all well?	4	
(Can't say)	8	

b) Did you feel that the (mediator / conciliator) tended to favour
one of the parties?

Yes - favoured respondent	1	2447
Yes - favoured other party	2	
No	3	
Can't say	8	

30

c) If you were in the same position again, would you be prepared
to go to (mediation / conciliation) again?
IF YES: Probably or definitely?
IF NO: Probably not or definitely not?

Yes, probably	1	2448
Yes, definitely	2	
Probably not	3	
Definitely not	4	
Maybe	5	
(Can't say)	8	

C8a) Can I just check, did you come to an agreement at the end of the
(mediation / conciliation) session?

Yes, agreement reached	1	**ASK b)**	2449
No	2	**GO TO D1, page 31**	

IF AGREEMENT REACHED
b) Do you think the agreement reached was fair?

Yes	1	**GO TO D1, page 31**	2450
No	2	**ASK c)**	
(Can't say)	8	**GO TO D1, page 31**	

IF NO
c) Why do you say that?
PROBE FULLY.   RECORD VERBATIM.

2451-60

31

SECTION D: COURT / TRIBUNAL / ARBITRATION / OMBUDSMAN

D1a) (Was there / Has there been) a court, tribunal or arbitration hearing about
... PROBLEM... - even if <u>you</u> didn't attend it?

IF NO COURT HEARING YET, CODE "NO"	EXCLUDE ANY ASSOCIATED CRIMINAL PROCEEDINGS STARTED BY THE POLICE.

Yes - court / tribunal / arbitration hearing	1	GO TO D3	2461
No	2	ASK b)	

IF NO

b) Sometimes papers are sent to a court, tribunal or arbitration and
a decision is made without a hearing. Can I just check, (have / were)
papers about ...PROBLEM... (been) sent to a court, tribunal or arbitration
for such a decision?

Yes, papers sent to court/ tribunal/ arbitration for decision without a hearing	1	GO TO D2	2462
No	2	ASK c)	

IF NO

c) Has ...PROBLEM...come before an Ombudsman?

Yes - came before ombudsman	1	GO TO D10, page 36	2463
No	2	GO TO D12, page 37	

IF PAPERS SENT TO COURT etc FOR DECISION WITHOUT HEARING
D2a) **SHOW CARD R**
What kind of court or tribunal was it?
CODE ONE ONLY

Small claims court or arbitration (*county court*)	01	2464-65
County court	02	
High Court	03	
Magistrates court	04	
Industrial Tribunal	05	
Social Security Appeal Tribunal (SSAT)	06	
Other tribunal (SPECIFY)	07	
_____		
Other court (SPECIFY)	08	
_____		
Other arbitration (SPECIFY)	09	
_____		
Can't say	98	

b) Can I check, did you start the action or was the action
started against you?
CODE ONE ONLY

Respondent started action	1		2466
Action started against respondent	2	GO TO D10, page 36	
(Can't say)	8		

32

IF HEARING IN COURT / TRIBUNAL / ARBITRATION

D3a) **SHOW CARD R**

What kind of court or tribunal was it?

CODE ONE ONLY

Small claims court or arbitration (*county court*)	01
County court	02
High Court	03
Magistrates court	04
Industrial Tribunal	05
Social Security Appeal Tribunal (SSAT)	06
Other tribunal (SPECIFY)	07
Other court (SPECIFY)	08
Other arbitration (SPECIFY)	09
Can't say	98

2467-68

b) Can I check, did you start the action or was the action started against you?

CODE ONE ONLY

Respondent started action	1
Action started against respondent	2
(Can't say)	8

2469

c) How many hearings or arbitrations have there been - please include all hearings, whether or not you attended them?

One	1
Two	2
Three	3
Four or more	4
(Can't say)	8

2470

d) (I would like to ask you a few questions about the final hearing or arbitration).

What was the date of (your / that) hearing or arbitration?

WRITE IN MONTH AND YEAR

ESTIMATE ACCEPTABLE.

☐☐ **19** ☐☐

2471-74

IF PROCEEDINGS ON-GOING, GIVE DATE OF MOST RECENT HEARING / ARBITRATION

OR CODE: (Can't say)   9998

D4a) Did you attend the (hearing / arbitration) yourself?

Yes, attended hearing / arbitration	1	**ASK b)**
No	2	**GO TO c)**

2475

33

IF YES
b) **SHOW CARD P**
Were you accompanied by any of the people on this card?
CODE ALL THAT APPLY

Barrister	1		2510-14
Solicitor	2		
Law Centre adviser	3		
Advice worker (CAB / WRO)	4	**ASK c)**	
Trade Union or Staff Association representative	5		
Partner / friend / relative	6		
Other (SPECIFY)	7		

Not accompanied	0	**GO TO D6**
(Can't say)	8	

IF ACCOMPANIED / DID NOT ATTEND HEARING
c) **SHOW CARD P**
Was there anyone at the (hearing / arbitration) to speak on your behalf
- please do not include witnesses who gave evidence for you?
IF YES: Who spoke on your behalf?
CODE ALL THAT APPLY

Barrister	1		2515-19
Solicitor	2		
Law Centre adviser	3		
Advice worker (CAB / WRO)	4	**ASK D5**	
Trade Union or Staff Association representative	5		
Partner / friend / relative	6		
Other (SPECIFY)	7		

No-one to speak on respondent's behalf	0	**GO TO D6**
(Can't say)	8	

IF REPRESENTED AT HEARING / ARBITRATION
D5a) How well do you feel that your (barrister / solicitor / adviser)
represented you at the (hearing / arbitration) ... READ OUT ...

...very well,	1	2520
fairly well,	2	
not very well,	3	
or not at all well?	4	
(Can't say)	8	

b) Do you think you would have been better off without
a (barrister / solicitor / adviser) to represent you?

Yes	1	2521
No	2	**GO TO D7**
Maybe	3	
(Can't say)	8	

34

IF NO-ONE TO SPEAK ON RESP'S BEHALF

D6a) Why did you not have anyone representing you at the
(hearing / arbitration)?
CODE ALL THAT APPLY
PROBE: Any other reason?

2522-26

Could not afford it	1
Was advised that I should represent myself	2
Didn't think I needed anyone to represent me	3
Other (*specify fully*)	4

_____

_____

_____

(Can't say)	8

b) Did you feel that you were at a disadvantage because you
did not have anybody to speak on your behalf?

2527

Yes	1
No	2
(Can't say)	8

IF HEARING / ARBITRATION

D7a) **SHOW CARD P**
Did ...OTHER SIDE... have anyone to speak on (his / her / their)
behalf at the (hearing / arbitration) - please do not include witnesses
who gave evidence for (him/her/them)?
IF YES: Who spoke on (his / her / their) behalf?
CODE ALL THAT APPLY

2528-32

Barrister	1	
Solicitor	2	
Law Centre adviser	3	
Advice worker (CAB / WRO)	4	**ASK b)**
Trade Union or Staff Association representative	5	
Partner / friend / relative	6	
Other (SPECIFY)	7	
_____		
No-one to speak on respondent's behalf	0	**GO TO D8**
(Can't say)	8	

c) How well do you feel that ...OTHER SIDE...'s (barrister / solicitor / adviser)
represented (him / her / them) at the (hearing / arbitration)... READ OUT ...
CODE ONE ONLY

2533

...very well,	1
fairly well,	2
not very well,	3
or not at all well?	4
(Can't say)	8

35

D8a) How long did the (hearing / arbitration) last?
PROMPT IF NECESSARY
CODE ONE ONLY

Less than 30 minutes	1	2534
30 minutes - 2 hours	2	
2 - 4 hours	3	
Whole day	5	
Two days	6	
Three days or more	7	
Can't say	8	

b) **INTERVIEWER CHECK D4a), page 32**

2535

Respondent attended hearing / arbitration	1	**ASK c)**
Others	2	**GO TO D10, page 36**

IF ATTENDED HEARING / ARBITRATION
c) Did you have any difficulties understanding what was going
on at the (hearing / arbitration) - for example....
... READ OUT AND CODE YES OR NO FOR EACH....

	Yes	No	(Can't say)	
..the (court / tribunal / arbitration) procedures?	1	2	8	2536
... why particular questions were being asked?	1	2	8	2537
... who the various people at the (hearing / arbitration) were?	1	2	8	2538

d) **SHOW CARD Q**
Did you feel that you had an opportunity to say what you wanted
to say at the (hearing / arbitration) - please choose your answer
from this card?

2539

At the hearing, I had an opportunity to say ... everything I wanted to say	1	**GO TO D9**
...most of what I wanted to say	2	
...some of what I wanted to say	3	
...very little of what I wanted to say	4	**ASK e)**
... none of what I wanted to say	5	
(Can't say)	8	

IF DID NOT SAY EVERYTHING (S)HE WANTED
e) Were there any important facts about ... PROBLEM... which
you feel did not get discussed at the (hearing / arbitration)?

2540

Yes	1
No	2
(Can't say)	8

D9a) How well do you think that the (judge / tribunal / magistrate / arbitrator)
understood your case ... READ OUT ....

...very well,	1	2541
fairly well,	2	
not very well,	3	
or not at all well?	4	
(Can't say)	8	

b) Did you feel that the (judge / tribunal / magistrate / arbitrator) favoured one of the parties?

Yes - favoured respondent	1	2542
Yes - favoured other party	2	
No	3	
Can't say	8	

c) If you were in the same position again, would you be prepared to go to (court / tribunal / arbitration) again?
IF YES: Probably or definitely?
IF NO: Probably not or definitely not?

Yes, probably	1	2543
Yes, definitely	2	
Probably not	3	
Definitely not	4	
Maybe	5	
(Can't say)	8	

IF PROBLEM PUT BEFORE COURT / TRIBUNAL / ARBITRATION / OMBUDSMAN
D10a) Can I just check, was a decision given by the (judge / tribunal / magistrate / arbitrator / ombudsman)?
CODE 'YES' IF CASE 'THROWN OUT OF COURT'

CODE 'NO' IF SETTLED OUT OF COURT	Yes, decision given	1	**ASK b)**	2544
	No	2	**GO TO D12, page 37**	
	(Case ongoing / Still awaiting decision)	3	**GO TO F1, page 50**	

IF DECISION GIVEN
b) Did you win or lose the case?

Respondent won	1	2545
Respondent lost	2	

Other *(specify)* _____

(Can't say)	8	

c) Do you think the (judge's / tribunal's / magistrate's / arbitrator's / ombudsman's) decision was fair?

2546

Yes	1	**GO TO e)**	
No	2	**ASK d)**	
(Can't say)	8	**GO TO e)**	

IF NO
d) Why do you say that?
PROBE FULLY. RECORD VERBATIM.

2547-56

e) **INTERVIEWER CHECK D4a), page 32**

Respondent attended hearing / arbitration	1	**GO TO g)**	2557
Others	2	**GO TO f)**	

37

IF OTHERS
f) **INTERVIEWER CHECK D1c, page 31**

Case came before Ombudsman	1	**ASK g)**	25?
Others	2	**GO TO D11**	

IF ATTENDED HEARING / CASE CAME BEFORE OMBUDSMAN
g) How clearly did the (judge / tribunal / magistrate / arbitrator / ombudsman) explain the reasons for (the / his / her) decision - READ OUT...

...very clearly,	1	25?
fairly clearly,	2	
not very clearly,	3	
or not at all clearly?	4	
(Can't say)	8	

D11. What would you say was the main reason that you did not come to an agreement or settlement with ...OTHER SIDE...before (the hearing / the arbitration / sending the case to the Ombudsman)? **PROBE FULLY. RECORD VERBATIM.**

2560-?

GO TO E1, page 41

IF PROBLEM NOT COME BEFORE COURT / TRIBUNAL / ARBITRATION / OMBUDSMAN (YET)
D12a) Can I just check, was a court, tribunal or arbitration case ever <u>started</u> - for a <u>court</u> case, this would mean that a writ or summons was issued?

Yes, court / tribunal / arbitration case started	1	**ASK b)**	257?
No	2	**GO TO D14**	
Can't say	8		

IF YES
b) **SHOW CARD R**
What kind of court or tribunal was it?
CODE ONE ONLY

Small claims court or arbitration (*county court*)	01
County court	02
High Court	03
Magistrates court	04
Industrial Tribunal	05
Social Security Appeal Tribunal (SSAT)	06
Other tribunal (SPECIFY)	07
Other court (SPECIFY)	08
Other arbitration (SPECIFY)	09
Can't say	98

2571-7

38

c) Can I check, did you start the action or was the action
started against you?
CODE ONE ONLY

Respondent started action	1	2573
Action started against respondent	2	
(Can't say)	8	

D13. Can I just check, was a date ever set for ... PROBLEM ... to come before
a court, tribunal or arbitrator?

Yes, date set for hearing	1	2574
No	2	
(Can't say)	8	

**IF NO DECISION GIVEN
/ NOT (YET) COME BEFORE COURT/TRIBUNAL/ARBITRATION**
D14a) (Can I just check) did you at any stage reach an agreement or settlement
with ...OTHER SIDE...to end the dispute?

Yes, agreement / settlement reached	1	**ASK b)**	2575
No	2	**GO TO F1, page 50**	
(Problem resolved itself without agreement)	3		

IF AGREEMENT / SETTLEMENT REACHED
b) **SHOW ADVISER CARD**
Did you reach this agreement with the help of any of the people
on this card? **IF YES:** Who?

CODE ALL THAT APPLY　Citizens Advice Bureaux (CAB)	01	2610-19
Law Centre	02	
Welfare Rights Officer (WRO)	03	
Consumer advice centre /Trading Standards Officer	04	
Other advice agency / worker	05	
Employer	06	
Trade Union or Staff Association	07	
Professional body (eg BMA, Law Society)	08	
Trade association (eg ABTA, Which, AA)	09	
Solicitor	10	
Barrister	11	
Claims agency (eg Direct Legal)	12	
Court staff	13	
Ombudsman	14	
Other legal consultant (eg employment law / immigration law consultant)	15	
Member of Parliament (MP) or Local councillor	16	
Local council department	17	
Housing association	18	
Social worker / Social Services	19	
Police	20	
Religious organisation (eg church, mosque, synagogue)	21	
Insurance company	22	
Other person / organisation (SPECIFY)	23	

No help from anyone on this card	00

39

c) **SHOW ADVISER CARD**
Did ...OTHER SIDE... have a solicitor or other adviser to help
with coming to this agreement? **IF YES:** Who?
CODE ALL THAT APPLY

Citizens Advice Bureaux (CAB)	01	2620-29
Law Centre	02	
Welfare Rights Officer (WRO)	03	
Consumer advice centre /Trading Standards Officer	04	
Other advice agency / worker	05	
Employer	06	
Trade Union or Staff Association	07	
Professional body (eg BMA, Law Society)	08	
Trade association (eg ABTA, Which, AA)	09	
Solicitor	10	
Barrister	11	
Claims agency (eg Direct Legal)	12	
Court staff	13	
Ombudsman	14	
Other legal consultant (eg employment law / immigration law consultant)	15	
Member of Parliament (MP) or Local councillor	16	
Local council department	17	
Housing association	18	
Social worker / Social Services	19	
Police	20	
Religious organisation (eg church, mosque, synagogue)	21	
Insurance company	22	
Other person / organisation (SPECIFY)	23	

No advice or help	00
(Can't say)	98

d) Who made the first move to settle the dispute - was it
you, (your solicitor/adviser) or ...OTHER SIDE?
CODE ONE ONLY

Respondent	1	2630
Respondent's solicitor / adviser	2	
Other side	3	
Other side's solicitor / adviser	4	
Both sides	5	
Other (SPECIFY) _____	6	
(Can't say)	8	

e) When was this agreement reached?
WRITE IN MONTH AND YEAR
ESTIMATE ACCEPTABLE.

☐☐ **19** ☐☐   2631-34

OR CODE: (Can't say)   9998

40

D15a) **INTERVIEWER CHECK D13, page 38**

Date set for hearing	1 **ASK b)**	2635
Others	2 **GO TO D16**	

IF PROCEEDINGS STARTED AND DATE SET FOR HEARING
b) How soon before the hearing date did you come to the agreement / settlement?
CODE ONE ONLY

Day of hearing	1	2636
Less than one week	2	
One week, less than one month	3	
One month, less than 3 months	4	
3 months, less than 6 months	5	
6 months or more	6	
(Can't say)	8	

c) Why was it settled at that stage, rather than at a (court / tribunal / arbitration) hearing?   2637-46
PROBE FULLY. RECORD VERBATIM.

GO TO E1, page 41

IF CODE 2 AT D15a)
D16a) **INTERVIEWER CHECK D1a), D1b) AND D1c) - page 31**

Problem came before court / tribunal / arbitration / ombudsman *(i.e. code 1 at D1a, D1b or D1c)*	1 **ASK b)**	2647
Others	2 **GO TO E1, page 41**	

IF COURT / TRIBUNAL / ARBITRATION / OMBUDSMAN
b) Why was the case settled at that stage, rather than waiting for a   2648-57
decision from the (court / tribunal / arbitration / ombudsman)?
PROBE FULLY. RECORD VERBATIM.

41

SECTION E: IF AGREEMENT REACHED / DECISION GIVEN

E1a) I would now like to ask you about what was agreed or decided.
If there has been more than one agreement, settlement or decision
about ...PROBLEM, I would like to ask you in detail about the most recent one.

Can I first check, has there been more than one agreement or decision
reached about ...PROBLEM?
IF YES: How many?

No, one only	1	2658
Yes, more than one agreement - two	2	
- three	3	
- four or more	4	

b) **SHOW CARD S**
Can I just check, during the course of trying to sort out
...PROBLEM..., have any of the circumstances on this card
applied to you?

> - LEGAL ADVICE OR REPRESENTATION FROM A
>   SOLICITOR, BARRISTER OR OTHER LEGAL CONSULTANT
> - PROBLEM CAME BEFORE COURT / TRIBUNAL /
>   ARBITRATION
> - COURT / TRIBUNAL / ARBITRATION CASE STARTED
> - PROBLEM WENT TO MEDIATION OR CONCILIATION
> - PROBLEM WENT TO OMBUDSMAN

Yes, card applied	1	**ASK c)**	2659
No	2	**GO TO d)**	

IF YES
c) **SHOW CARD S**
The circumstances on the card almost always lead to legal costs.
Sometimes, it is agreed that the other side will pay your legal costs
- these costs might not necessarily be paid directly to you; they may
be paid directly to your solicitor or other legal adviser.

Can I just check, (in the most recent agreement or decision) was
it decided that ...OTHER SIDE... should pay any of your legal costs?

Yes	1	2660
No	2	
(No legal costs)	3	
(Can't say)	8	

d) (Apart from legal costs) was it decided that ...OTHER SIDE...
should pay you any money for anything else?

REDUCTION IN BILL = YES

Yes	1	**ASK e)**	2661
No	2	**GO TO f)**	

42

IF YES
e) **SHOW CARD T**
Did this money include compensation for anything - that is money to
make up for any pain, distress or inconvenience you have suffered,
or any money that you have lost?
IF YES: What was this compensation for?
CODE ALL THAT APPLY

Yes, compensation to make up for :	
- pain	1
- distress	2
- inconvenience	3
- money lost	4
- extra expenses incurred as a result of the problem	5
- something else (SPECIFY)	6

2662-66

No compensation   7

(Can't say)   8

f) **INTERVIEWER CHECK E1c) AND E1d), page 41**

Other side to pay money *(code 1 at E1c) and/or code 1 at E1d)*	1	**ASK g)**
Others	2	**GO TO E4**

2667

IF OTHER SIDE TO PAY MONEY TO RESPONDENT
g) (Including any compensation and legal costs), how much
money was it decided that ...OTHER SIDE... should pay?
WRITE IN AMOUNT OF MONEY AS APPROPRIATE BELOW:
EITHER AS A TOTAL AMOUNT *(Option 1)* OR AS REGULAR PAYMENTS *(Option 2)*

IF 2+ SOURCES OF PAYMENT ENTER TOTAL

IF A BILL WAS REDUCED, ENTER AMOUNT REDUCED BY

2668-73

Option 1: **TOTAL AMOUNT OF MONEY:**   Total: £ ☐☐☐☐☐☐

OR

Option 2: **REGULAR PAYMENTS:**   Regular payments: £ ☐☐☐☐

2674-77

RING APPROPRIATE CODE TO INDICATE
HOW OFTEN PAYMENTS TO BE MADE:

Weekly	1
Fortnightly	2
Monthly	3
Quarterly	4
Six monthly	5
Yearly	6
Other (SPECIFY)	7

2678

(Can't say)   8)

43

E2a) Was this more, less or about the same amount of money
as you had hoped for?
IF MORE: Much more or a bit more than you hoped for?
IF LESS: Much less or a bit less than you hoped for?

2710

Much more than hoped for	1	**GO TO E3**
A bit more than hoped for	2	
A bit less than hoped for	3	**ASK b)**
Much less than hoped for	4	
About the same	5	**GO TO E3**
(Can't say)	8	

IF LESS
b) **INTERVIEWER CHECK D10a), page 36**

Decision given by judge / tribunal / magistrate / arbitrator / ombudsman	1	**GO TO E3**
Others	2	**ASK c)**
(including D10a not asked)		

2711

IF NO DECISION GIVEN
c) Why did you accept this amount of money, rather than trying to
get more?
PROBE FULLY.   RECORD VERBATIM.

2712-21

IF OTHER SIDE TO PAY MONEY
E3a) Since the (agreement was reached / decision was given), have you
had any difficulties actually obtaining this money from ...OTHER SIDE...?

2722

Yes	1	**ASK b)**
No	2	**GO TO E8, page 47**

IF YES
b) Since the (agreement was reached / decision was given),
(have you done / did you do) anything to try to get ...OTHER SIDE... to
pay the money?
CODE ALL THAT APPLY

Yes - wrote to the other side	1	
- spoke to (or tried to speak to) the other side	2	
- threatened other side with legal action	3	
- started court or tribunal proceedings against other side	4	
- other (*specify*)	4	**GO TO E8, page 47**
No - did not do anything	0	

2723-27

44

IF NO ARRANGEMENT FOR OTHER SIDE TO PAY MONEY
E4a) **SHOW CARD S**
Please look at this card again about the sorts of things which lead to legal costs.
Can I just check, (in the most recent agreement or decision) was it decided that you should pay any of ...OTHER SIDE's... legal costs?

- LEGAL ADVICE OR REPRESENTATION FROM A SOLICITOR, BARRISTER OR OTHER LEGAL CONSULTANT	Yes	1	**ASK b)**	2728
- PROBLEM CAME BEFORE COURT / TRIBUNAL / ARBITRATION	No	2		
- COURT / TRIBUNAL / ARBITRATION CASE STARTED	(No legal costs)	3	**GO TO c)**	
- PROBLEM WENT TO MEDIATION OR CONCILIATION	(Can't say)	8		
- PROBLEM WENT TO OMBUDSMAN				

IF YES
b) How much was it agreed that you should pay to cover these legal costs?

2729-34

WRITE IN: Other side's legal costs: £ ☐☐☐☐☐☐

    OR CODE: (Can't say)   999998

c) And (apart from legal costs) was it decided that you should pay ...OTHER SIDE... any money for anything else?

	Yes	1	**ASK d)**	2735
	No	2	**GO TO e)**	

IF YES
d) **SHOW CARD T**
Did this money include compensation for anything - that is money to make up for any pain, distress or inconvenience that ...OTHER SIDE... suffered, or any money that (he / she / they) lost?
IF YES: What was this compensation for?
CODE ALL THAT APPLY

Yes, compensation to make up for :		
- pain	1	2736-41
- distress	2	
- inconvenience	3	
- money lost	4	
- extra expenses incurred as a result of the problem	5	
- something else (SPECIFY)	6	
_____		
No compensation	7	
(Can't say)	8	

e) **INTERVIEWER CHECK E4a) AND c)**

Respondent to pay money (code 1 at E4a) and/or code 1 at E4c)	1	**ASK E5**	2742
Others	2	**GO TO E8, page 47**	

45

IF RESPONDENT TO PAY MONEY TO OTHER SIDE

E5a) (Apart from ...OTHER SIDE's... legal costs), how much money was it
decided that you should pay ...OTHER SIDE?
INCLUDE COMPENSATION
WRITE IN AMOUNT OF MONEY AS APPROPRIATE BELOW:
EITHER AS A TOTAL AMOUNT *(Option 1)* **OR AS REGULAR PAYMENTS** *(Option 2)*

2743-48

Option 1: **TOTAL AMOUNT OF MONEY:**   Total: **£**

OR

2749-52

Option 2: **REGULAR PAYMENTS:**   Regular payments: **£**

RING APPROPRIATE CODE TO INDICATE
HOW OFTEN PAYMENTS TO BE MADE:

Weekly	1
Fortnightly	2
Monthly	3
Quarterly	4
Six monthly	5
Yearly	6
Other (SPECIFY)	
_____	7
(Can't say)	8

2753

b) Was this more, less or about the same amount as the other
party had originally asked for?

More than other party had asked for	1
Less than asked for	2
About the same	3
(Can't say)	8

2754

E6a) Was it more, less or about the same amount of money
as you had expected to pay?
IF MORE: Much more or a bit more than you expected?
IF LESS: Much less or a bit less than you expected?

2755

Much more than expected	1	**ASK b)**
A bit more than expected	2	
A bit less than expected	3	
Much less than expected	4	
About the same	5	**GO TO E7**
(Can't say)	8	

IF MORE THAN EXPECTED
b) **INTERVIEWER CHECK D10a), page 36**

Decision given by judge / tribunal / magistrate / arbitrator / ombudsman	1	**GO TO E7**
Others	2	**ASK c)**
(including D10a not asked)		

2756

46

IF NO DECISION GIVEN

c) Why did you agree to pay this amount of money, rather than negotiating a lower figure?
PROBE FULLY. RECORD VERBATIM.

2757-66

E7a) Since the (agreement was reached / decision was given), have you paid any of the money?

Yes	1	**GO TO E8**
No	2	**ASK b)**

2767

IF NOT ANY OF THE MONEY

b) How likely do you think it is that you will pay the money ... READ OUT ....

... very likely,	1
fairly likely,	2
not very likely,	3
or not at all likely?	4
(Can't say)	8

2768

c) Since the (agreement was reached / decision was given), has ...OTHER SIDE... done anything to try to get you to pay the money?
CODE ALL THAT APPLY

Yes - wrote to me	1
- spoke to (or tried to speak to) me	2
- threatened me with legal action	3
- started court or tribunal proceedings against me *(i.e. sent me a writ or summons)*	4
- other (*specify*)	5
No - has not done anything	0
(Can't say)	8

2769-73

d) Why have you not (yet) paid the money?
PROBE FULLY. RECORD VERBATIM.

2810-19

47

IF AGREEMENT MADE / DECISION GIVEN

E8a) (Apart from the money payment), were any other arrangements agreed
or decided, for example that you or ...OTHER SIDE... would do something,
or stop doing something?

Yes	1	**ASK b)**	2820
No	2	**GO TO E11**	

IF YES

b) What was agreed / decided?
PROBE FULLY. RECORD VERBATIM.   2821-30

c) **INTERVIEWER CODE FROM ANSWER GIVEN AT b)**

Certain action / behaviour required of respondent only	1	**ASK E9**	2831
Action / behaviour required of other side only	2	**GO TO E10**	
Action / behaviour required of both sides	3	**ASK E9**	

IF ACTION REQUIRED OF RESPONDENT

E9a) Have you kept to (your part of) these agreed arrangements?

Yes	1	**GO TO c)**	2832
No	2	**ASK b)**	

IF NO

b) Why is that?
PROBE FULLY. RECORD VERBATIM.

2833-42

c) **INTERVIEWER CHECK E8c)**   2843

Certain action / behaviour required of respondent only	1	**GO TO E11**	
Action / behaviour required of both sides	3	**ASK E10**	

IF ACTION REQUIRED OF OTHER SIDE

E10a) Has ...OTHER SIDE... kept to (his / her / their) part of these
agreed arrangements?   2844

Yes	1	**GO TO E11**	
No	2	**ASK b)**	

48

IF NO
b) Have you done anything to try and make ...OTHER SIDE... keep
to the agreed arrangements?
CODE ALL THAT APPLY

Yes - wrote to the other side	1	2845-49
- spoke to (or tried to speak to) the other side	2	
- threatened other side with legal action	3	**GO TO E11**
- started court or tribunal proceedings against other side	4	
- other (*specify*)	5	

_____

_____

No - did not do anything	0	**ASK c)**

IF DONE NOTHING TO ENFORCE AGREEMENT
c) Why is that?   2850-59
PROBE FULLY.   RECORD VERBATIM.

IF AGREEMENT REACHED / DECISION GIVEN
E11a) Before this (agreement was reached / decision was given), had you rejected   2860
any offers... from ...OTHER SIDE... - by this I mean formal offers from
(him/her/them) to pay you money or to do something else to resolve the
dispute?

Yes   1

No   2

b) And before this (agreement was reached / decision was given), did <u>you</u> make
any offers that were rejected by...OTHER SIDE...?
IF NECESSARY: By this I mean formal offers to pay ...OTHER SIDE...
money or to do something else to resolve the dispute?

Yes   1   2861

No   2

IF AGREEMENT REACHED / DECISION GIVEN
E12a) **INTERVIEWER CHECK D10a), page 36**

Decision given by judge / tribunal / magistrate / arbitrator / ombudsman	1	**GO TO E13**	2862
Others	2	**ASK b)**

IF OTHERS
b) Taking everything into consideration, do you think that the
agreement was fair?

Yes	1	**GO TO E13**	2863
No	2	**ASK c)**

49

IF NO
c) In what ways do you think it was unfair?
PROBE FULLY.   RECORD VERBATIM.

2864-73

d) Why did you agree to settle the case if you did not
think that it was fair?
PROBE FULLY.   RECORD VERBATIM.

2910-19

IF AGREEMENT / DECISION
E13a) Did the (agreement / decision) actually end the dispute between
you and ...OTHER SIDE...?
IF YES: Completely or only partly?

2920

Yes, completely	1	**GO TO G1, page 53**
Yes, partly	2	**ASK b)**
No	3	

IF PARTLY / NO
b) Is the problem still on-going?

2921

Yes, problem still on-going	1	**GO TO F4, page 51**
No, problem resolved	2	**ASK c)**

IF PROBLEM RESOLVED
c) How did the problem resolve itself?
PROBE FULLY.   RECORD VERBATIM.

2922-31

GO TO G1, page 53

50

SECTION F: IF NO AGREEMENT REACHED / NO DECISION GIVEN

F1a) Can I just check, is the problem still on-going?

Yes, problem still on-going	1	**GO TO F2**	2932
No, problem resolved	2	**ASK b)**	

IF PROBLEM RESOLVED
b) How did the problem resolve itself?   2933-42
PROBE FULLY. RECORD VERBATIM.

IF NO AGREEMENT / DECISION
F2a) **SHOW ADVISER CARD**
(Did / Does)...OTHER SIDE... have a solicitor or other adviser at any stage
to help sort out .. PROBLEM?
IF YES: Who?
CODE ALL THAT APPLY

Citizens Advice Bureaux (CAB)	01	2943-52
Law Centre	02	
Welfare Rights Officer (WRO)	03	
Consumer advice centre /Trading Standards Officer	04	
Other advice agency / worker	05	
Employer	06	
Trade Union or Staff Association	07	
Professional body (eg BMA, Law Society)	08	
Trade association (eg ABTA, Which, AA)	09	
Solicitor	10	
Barrister	11	
Claims agency (eg Direct Legal)	12	
Court staff	13	
Ombudsman	14	
Other legal consultant (eg employment law / immigration law consultant)	15	
Member of Parliament (MP) or Local councillor	16	
Local council department	17	
Housing association	18	
Social worker / Social Services	19	
Police	20	
Religious organisation (eg church, mosque, synagogue)	21	
Insurance company	22	
Other person / organisation (SPECIFY)	23	

No advice or help	00
(Can't say)	98

51

b) (Before the problem was resolved,) did you at any stage reject any offers from ...OTHER SIDE... - by this I mean formal offers from (him/her/them) to pay you money or to do something else to resolve the dispute?

Yes	1	2953
No	2	

c) And did you make any offers to ...OTHER SIDE... that were rejected?
IF NECESSARY: By this I mean formal offers to pay ...OTHER SIDE.... money or to do something else to resolve the dispute?

Yes	1	2954
No	2	

F3. **INTERVIEWER CHECK F1a)**

Problem still on-going	1	**ASK F4**	2955
Problem resolved	2	**GO TO F6**	

IF PROBLEM STILL ON-GOING
F4a) Apart from what you have already told me about, are you doing anything else to sort out this problem?

			2956
Yes	1	**GO TO c)**	
No	2	**ASK b)**	

IF NO
b) Do you intend to do anything about .. PROBLEM ?
IF YES: Definitely or probably?
IF NO: Probably not or definitely not?

Yes, definitely	1		2957
Yes, probably	2	**ASK c)**	
Maybe	3		
Probably not	3		
Definitely not	4	**GO TO F5**	
Maybe	5		
(Can't say)	8		

IF DOING / LIKELY TO DO SOMETHING
c) What are you doing or planning to do?
CODE ALL THAT APPLY

Contact the other side	01	2958-67
Threaten other side with legal action	02	
Go to court, tribunal or arbitration / start court, tribunal or arbitration case against other side	03	
Go to mediation or conciliation	04	
Take the problem to an ombudsman	05	
Seek advice or help from other person / organisation (*specify*)	06	

_____

Pay other side some money	07
Other (planned) action (*specify*)	08

_____

_____

_____

(Can't say)	98

52

d) Do you think that you will be able to sort out ... PROBLEM?
IF YES: Definitely or probably?
IF NO: Probably not or definitely not?   2968

Yes - definitely	1	
Yes - probably	2	
Probably not	3	**GO TO G1, page 53**
Definitely not	4	
(Can't say)	8	

IF NOT PLANNING TO DO ANYTHING ABOUT PROBLEM
F5 Why don't you intend to do anything about ... PROBLEM?   2969-78
PROBE FULLY. RECORD VERBATIM.

IF NOT PLANNING TO DO ANYTHING /
PROBLEM RESOLVED ITSELF WITHOUT AGREEMENT
F6 What would you say was the main reason that you (did / have)   3010-19
not manage(d) to come to an agreement or settlement with
..OTHER SIDE?
PROBE FULLY. RECORD VERBATIM.

53

SECTION G: COSTS

ALL
G1a) **INTERVIEWER CHECK E1b), page 41**

Yes, card applied *(i.e. legal costs probably incurred)*	1	GO TO c)
No	2	ASK b)

3020

IF NO
b) **SHOW CARD S**
Can I just check, during the course of trying to sort out
...PROBLEM..., (did / have) any of the circumstances on this card
(apply / applied) to you?

> - LEGAL ADVICE OR REPRESENTATION FROM A
>   SOLICITOR, BARRISTER OR OTHER LEGAL CONSULTANT
> - PROBLEM CAME BEFORE COURT / TRIBUNAL /
>   ARBITRATION
> - COURT / TRIBUNAL / ARBITRATION CASE STARTED
> - PROBLEM WENT TO MEDIATION OR CONCILIATION
> - PROBLEM WENT TO OMBUDSMAN

Yes, card applied *(i.e. legal costs probably incurred)*	1	ASK c)
No	2	GO TO G9

3021

IF CARD APPLIED
c) Can I just check, during the course of trying to sort out ...PROBLEM...,
(were you / have you been) offered any financial support from any of
the following sources...
...**READ OUT AND CODE YES OR NO FOR EACH**...

	Yes	No	Can't say	
...Legal Aid?	1	2	8	3022
...Legal Expenses Insurance?	1	2	8	3023
...Trade Union or Staff Association?	1	2	8	3024
Employer?	1	2	8	3025

d) **INTERVIEWER CHECK c)**

Respondent offered at least one type of support (at least one code 1 at c)	1	ASK G2
Others	2	GO TO G6

3026

IF OFFERED FINANCIAL SUPPORT
G2a) **INTERVIEWER CHECK G1c)**

Respondent offered Legal Aid	1	ASK b)
Others	2	GO TO G3

3027

IF OFFERED LEGAL AID
b) You said you were offered Legal Aid. Did you accept it?

Yes	1	GO TO d)
No	2	ASK c)

3028

54

IF NO
c) Why was that?
PROBE FULLY. RECORD VERBATIM.

3029-38

GO TO G3

IF LEGAL AID ACCEPTED
d) Was this Legal Aid backing withdrawn at
at any stage?

Yes	1	3039
No	2	
(Can't say)	8	

G3a) **INTERVIEWER CHECK G1c), page 53**

Respondent offered Legal Expenses Insurance	1	**ASK b)**	3040
Others	2	**GO TO G4**	

b) You said that you were offered Legal Expenses Insurance.
Was this Legal Expenses Insurance backing withdrawn at
at any stage?

Yes	1	3041
No	2	
(Can't say)	8	

c) **SHOW CARD S**
(This card shows examples of the sorts of things which
lead to legal costs).
(Did / Has) Legal Expenses Insurance actually (pay / paid)
any money to cover your legal costs?

3042

```
- LEGAL ADVICE OR REPRESENTATION FROM A
  SOLICITOR, BARRISTER OR OTHER LEGAL CONSULTANT
- PROBLEM CAME BEFORE COURT / TRIBUNAL /
  ARBITRATION
- COURT / TRIBUNAL / ARBITRATION CASE STARTED
- PROBLEM WENT TO MEDIATION OR CONCILIATION
- PROBLEM WENT TO OMBUDSMAN
```

Yes	1	**ASK d)**
No	2	
Not yet but expected to	3	**GO TO G4**
(Can't say)	8	

IF YES
d) How much did the Legal Expenses Insurance pay to cover these
legal costs?
ESTIMATE ACCEPTABLE

£ ☐☐☐☐☐☐   3043-48

(Can't say)   999998

55

G4a) **INTERVIEWER CHECK G1c), page 53**

Respondent offered financial support from Trade Union/ Staff Assocn.	1	**ASK b)**	3049
Others	2	**GO TO G5**	

IF OFFERED TRADE UNION SUPPORT
b) You said you were offered financial support from your
Trade Union or Staff Association. Did they withdraw their backing at
at any stage?

Yes	1	3050
No	2	
(Can't say)	8	

G5a) **INTERVIEWER CHECK G1c), page 53**

Respondent offered financial support from employer	1	**ASK b)**	3051
Others	2	**GO TO G6**	

IF OFFERED EMPLOYER SUPPORT
b) You said that you were offered financial support by your
employer. Did your employer withdraw this backing at
any stage?

Yes	1	3052
No	2	
(Can't say)	8	

c) **SHOW CARD S**
(This card shows examples of the sorts of things which
lead to legal costs).
(Did / Has) your employer actually (pay / paid) any money to
cover your legal costs?

> - LEGAL ADVICE OR REPRESENTATION FROM A
>   SOLICITOR, BARRISTER OR OTHER LEGAL CONSULTANT
> - PROBLEM CAME BEFORE COURT / TRIBUNAL /
>   ARBITRATION
> - COURT / TRIBUNAL / ARBITRATION CASE STARTED
> - PROBLEM WENT TO MEDIATION OR CONCILIATION
> - PROBLEM WENT TO OMBUDSMAN

Yes	1	**ASK d)**	3053
No	2		
Not yet but expected to	3	**GO TO G6**	
(Can't say)	8		

IF YES
d) How much did your employer pay to cover these
legal costs?
ESTIMATE ACCEPTABLE

£ ☐☐☐☐☐☐

3054-59

(Can't say)   999998

56

G6a) **SHOW CARD S**
(This card shows examples of the sorts of things which lead to legal costs).
Can I just check, did any person or organisation offer to cover
your legal costs on a "no win, no fee" basis?
IF NECESSARY:
- by this, I mean did they offer to cover your legal costs if you
lost the case? This arrangement is sometimes referred to as
conditional or speculative fees.

```
- LEGAL ADVICE OR REPRESENTATION FROM A
  SOLICITOR, BARRISTER OR OTHER LEGAL CONSULTANT
- PROBLEM CAME BEFORE COURT / TRIBUNAL /
  ARBITRATION
- COURT / TRIBUNAL / ARBITRATION CASE STARTED
- PROBLEM WENT TO MEDIATION OR CONCILIATION
- PROBLEM WENT TO OMBUDSMAN
```

Yes, offered on a "no win, no fee" basis	1	**ASK b)**	3060
No	2	**GO TO G7**	
(Can't say)	8		

IF YES
b) Who was this?
CODE ALL THAT APPLY

Solicitor	1	3061-65
Barrister	2	
Claims agency (eg Direct Legal)	3	
Other legal consultant (eg employment law / immigration law consultant)	4	
Partner / friend / relative	5	
Other (SPECIFY)	6	

_____

c) Did you have a written agreement about this "no win, no fee"
arrangement?

Yes	1	3066
No	2	
(Can't say)	8	

d) Was this "no win, no fee" offer withdrawn at any stage?

Yes	1	3067
No	2	
(Can't say)	8	

G7a) **SHOW CARD S**
(Apart from this) can I just check, (were you / have you been) offered any financial
support by any <u>other</u> person or organisation - this may have been an offer to pay some
of your legal costs, or to provide legal advice or services free of charge?

```
- LEGAL ADVICE OR REPRESENTATION FROM A
  SOLICITOR, BARRISTER OR OTHER LEGAL CONSULTANT
- PROBLEM CAME BEFORE COURT / TRIBUNAL /
  ARBITRATION
- COURT / TRIBUNAL / ARBITRATION CASE STARTED
- PROBLEM WENT TO MEDIATION OR CONCILIATION
- PROBLEM WENT TO OMBUDSMAN
```

Yes	1	**ASK b)**	3068
No	2	**GO TO G8**	

57

IF YES
b) Who offered you this support?
   CODE ALL THAT APPLY

Solicitor	1	3069-74
Barrister	2	
Claims agency (eg Direct Legal)	3	
Other legal consultant (eg employment law / immigration law consultant)	4	
Partner / friend / relative	5	
Other (SPECIFY)	6	

_____

c) Was this offer of financial support withdrawn at any stage?

Yes	1	3110
No	2	
(Can't say)	8	

d) And did (this person or organisation / any of these people or organisations) actually pay any money to cover your legal costs?

Yes	1	**ASK e)**	3111
No	2		
Not yet, but expected to	3	**GO TO G8**	
(Can't say)	8		

IF YES
e) How much did (he/she/they) pay to cover these legal costs?
   ESTIMATE ACCEPTABLE

£ [| | | | | |]   3112-17

(Can't say)   999998

G8a) **SHOW CARD S**
And did <u>you</u> personally have to pay any of your legal costs?

- LEGAL ADVICE OR REPRESENTATION FROM A SOLICITOR, BARRISTER OR OTHER LEGAL CONSULTANT - PROBLEM CAME BEFORE COURT / TRIBUNAL / ARBITRATION - COURT / TRIBUNAL / ARBITRATION CASE STARTED - PROBLEM WENT TO MEDIATION OR CONCILIATION - PROBLEM WENT TO OMBUDSMAN			
Yes	1	**ASK b)**	3118
No	2		
Not yet, but expect to	3	**GO TO G9**	
(Can't say)	8		

IF YES
b) How much did you pay?
   ESTIMATE ACCEPTABLE   3119-24

£ [| | | | | |]

(Can't say)   999998

58

c) How much had you expected to pay?
ESTIMATE ACCEPTABLE

£ ⬚⬚⬚⬚⬚⬚

3125-30

ASK d)

OR CODE: (Nothing) 000000

(Can't say) 999998 **GO TO G9**

IF EXPECTED AMOUNT GIVEN
d) Where did you get the idea from that you might have to pay (that amount / nothing)?
CODE ALL THAT APPLY

Suggested or advised by *friend / relative / work colleague*	01
Suggested or advised by *other person / organisation* (specify)	02

3131-40

_____

Previous experience of similar kind of situation	03
Other (*specify fully*)	04

_____

_____

(Can't say) 98

G9a) As far as you know, during the course of trying to sort out ...PROBLEM...,
(was ....OTHER SIDE... / has ....OTHER SIDE... been) offered any financial
support from any of the following sources...
...READ OUT AND CODE YES OR NO FOR EACH...

	Yes	No	Can't say	
...Legal Aid?	1	2	8	3141
...Legal Expenses Insurance?	1	2	8	3142
...Trade Union?	1	2	8	3143
Employer?	1	2	8	3144

b) And as far as you know, did any person or organisation offer to cover
...OTHER SIDE's.... legal costs on a "no win, no fee" basis?
IF NECESSARY:
- by this, I mean did they offer to cover (his/her/their) legal costs if
(he/she/they) lost the case?

Yes, offered on a "no win, no fee" basis	1
No	2
(Can't say)	8

3145

59

G10. (Were you / Have you been) worried at any stage about having to pay any
legal costs - either your own costs or ...OTHER SIDE's...costs?
IF YES: Your costs or ...OTHER SIDE's?
CODE ONE ONLY

Yes - worried about paying own legal costs	1	3146
Yes - worried about paying other side's legal costs	2	
Yes - worried about both	3	
No	4	
(Can't say)	8	

ALL
G11a) **SHOW CARD U**
(Were there / Have there been) any (other) financial costs
related to sorting out ....PROBLEM - some examples are
shown on this card?
IF YES: What were these costs for?
CODE ALL THAT APPLY

Loss of earnings	1	3147-51
Cost of travelling *(eg to visit lawyers / advice agencies / court etc)*	2	
Cost of telephone calls	3	
Other costs *(specify)*	4	
_____		
No other financial costs (yet)	0	
(Can't say)	8	

b) **SHOW CARD V**
About how much in total were these costs?
ESTIMATE ACCEPTABLE

£10 or less	01	
£11 - £50	02	3152-53
£51 - £100	03	
£101 - £200	04	
£201 - £500	05	
£501 - £750	06	
£751 - £1,000	07	
£1,001 - £1,500	08	
£1,501 - £3,000	09	
£3,001 - £5,000	10	
£5,001 - £10,000	11	
More than £10,000	12	
(Can't say)	98	

c) (Did you have / Have you had) to take any time off work, or use
any of your annual leave to sort out ...PROBLEM?

Yes	1	3154
No / Not yet	2	

60

SECTION H: OVERALL ASSESSMENT AND ATTITUDES

IF ACTION TAKEN

H1a) Thinking back to when you first decided to do something
about ...PROBLEM..., how long had you thought that it
would take to solve the problem?

CODE ONE ONLY

PROBE FOR ESTIMATE

Less than a week	01	3155-56
1 week less than 2 weeks	02	
2 weeks, less than a month	03	
1 - 2 months	04	
3 - 4 months	05	
5 - 6 months	06	
7 - 9 months	07	
10 - 12 months	08	
More than a year	09	
(Can't say)	98	

b) **INTERVIEWER CHECK E13b) page 49 OR F1a) page 50**

Yes, problem still on-going	1	**GO TO H2**	3157
No, problem resolved	2	**ASK c)**	

IF PROBLEM RESOLVED

c) Did (Has) solving this problem take(n) a shorter time than
you expected, about as long as you expected, or a longer
time than you expected?
IF SHORTER: Much shorter or a bit shorter?
IF LONGER: Much longer, or a bit longer?

Much shorter than expected	1	3158
A bit shorter than expected	2	
About as long as you expected	3	
A bit longer than expected	4	
Much longer than expected	5	
(Can't say)	8	

IF ACTION TAKEN

H2a) Looking back over the experience of trying to sort out.. PROBLEM (so far),
is there anything about the way in which you handled the situation
that you regret?

Yes	1	**ASK b)**	3159
No	2	**GO TO H3**	

IF YES

b) What is that?
PROBE FULLY. RECORD VERBATIM.

3160-69

61

IF ACTION TAKEN

H3a) Can I just check, (were you / have you been) in paid work at any time
during the course of sorting out .. PROBLEM?

Yes	1	**ASK b)**	3170
No	2	**GO TO c)**	

IF YES

b) **SHOW CARD W**
As a result of trying to sort out this problem, (did / have)
you experience(d) any of the things on this card?
CODE ALL THAT APPLY

Had to take time off work due to stress	1	3171-75
Chances of promotion were badly affected	2	
Relationships with colleagues suffered	3	
Had to move to another job	4	
Other effect on working life (SPECIFY)	5	

_____

None of these effects	0

c) **SHOW CARD X**
As a result of trying to sort out this problem, (did / have)
you experience(d) any of the things or feelings on this card?
CODE ALL THAT APPLY

The experience has made me feel that I have some control over my situation	01	3210-29
I have found the experience of trying to sort out ...PROBLEM ...stressful	02	
I have had difficulty sleeping	03	
My health has suffered	04	
I am glad to (be enforcing / have enforced) my rights	05	
My relationships with family and friends have suffered	06	
I am glad to (be clearing / have cleared) my name	07	
I have had to move to another house / flat	08	
I have had to move to another area	09	
Other effect on life (SPECIFY)	10	

_____

None of these effects	00

62

H4a) **ALL**
I would now like to ask you a few general questions about your
feelings about the justice system in Britain.

SHOW CARD Y
I am going to read out a few statements - please tell me for each
one how much you agree or disagree with it.
READ OUT EACH STATEMENT BELOW AND RING ONE CODE FOR EACH

		Strongly Agree	Agree	Neither agree nor disagree	Disagree	Strongly Disagree	(Can't say)	
a)	If I went to court with a problem, I am confident that I would get a fair hearing	1	2	3	4	5	8	3230
b)	Most judges are out of touch with ordinary people's lives	1	2	3	4	5	8	3231
c)	Lawyers' charges are reasonable for the work they do	1	2	3	4	5	8	3232
d)	Courts are an important way for ordinary people to enforce their rights	1	2	3	4	5	8	3233
e)	The legal system works better for rich people than for poor people	1	2	3	4	5	8	3234

63

SECTION J: CLASSIFICATION

ALL

J1a) And now a few questions about yourself to help us to analyse
the findings of the survey.
ASK OR CODE:
Can I just check, are you .. READ OUT ...

... married and living with your (husband/wife),	1	**GO TO J2**

3235

married and separated from your (husband / wife),	2	
... widowed,	3	**ASK b)**
.. divorced,	4	
...or single and never married?	5	

IF SEPARATED / WIDOWED / DIVORCED / SINGLE

b) Can I just check, are you living with someone as a couple ?

Yes	1
No	2

3236

J2a) **SHOW CARD Z**
Which of the phrases on this card best describes what you were doing last
week, that is the seven days ending last Sunday?
CODE ONE ONLY

In paid work as employee / self-employed - <u>full-time</u> (30 or more hours per week) - *or temporarily away from full-time job*	01

3237-38

In paid work as employee / self-employed - <u>part-time</u> (less than 30 hours per week) - *or temporarily away from part-time job*	**GO TO J3** 02

In full-time education - *or on vacation from full-time education*	03	**ASK b)**
In part-time education - *or on vacation from full-time education*	04	
On government training scheme	05	
Waiting to take up paid work	06	
Unemployed	07	
Long-term sick or disabled	08	
Wholly retired from work	09	
Looking after the home / family	10	
Doing something else (SPECIFY) _____	11	

64

IF NOT IN PAID WORK LAST WEEK

b) Can I just check, apart from government schemes, have you been in paid work at any time in the last ten years - please do NOT include part-time or vacation work you may have done while you were a full-time student?

Yes - in paid work in the last 10 years	1	**ASK J3**	3239
No - not in paid work in the last 10 years	2	**GO TO J6**	

IF IN PAID WORK IN LAST 10 YEARS

J3a) Now I'd like to ask you about your current (most recent) job.
What is (was) the name or title of the job?
IF 2+ JOBS AT ONCE, TAKE MAIN JOB
(IF QUERIED, MOST REMUNERATIVE)

b) What kind of work do (did) you do most of the time?
PROBE FULLY.

SOC ☐☐☐ 3240-42

ES ☐☐ 3243-44

c) What materials or machinery do (did) you use?
PROBE FULLY.

SEG ☐☐ 3245-46

SC ☐ 3247

d) What skills or qualifications are (were) needed for the job?
PROBE FULLY.

J4a) Are (were) you ... READ OUT....

.. an employee	1	**ASK b)**	3248
or self-employed?	2	**GO TO J5**	

IF EMPLOYEE

b) Do (did) you supervise, or are (were) you responsible for other people's work?

Yes	1	**ASK c)**	3249
No	2	**GO TO d)**	

65

IF YES
c) How many people?

1 - 4	1	
5 - 24	2	
25 - 99	3	
100 - 499	4	
500 or more	5	
(Can't say)	8	

3250

d) Including yourself, about how many people are (were) employed at the place where you work(ed)?

1 - 4	1	
5 - 24	2	
25 - 99	3	**GO TO J6**
100 - 499	4	
500 or more	5	
(Can't say)	8	

3251

IF SELF-EMPLOYED
J5a) Do (Did) you have any employees?

Yes	1	**ASK b)**
No	2	**GO TO J6**

3252

IF YES
b) How many?

1 - 4	1	
5 - 24	2	
25 - 99	3	
100 - 499	4	
500 or more	5	
(Can't say)	8	

3253

J6 **SHOW CARD AA**
Which of the letters on this card best represents the total income of your household at the moment - please think about your household income from all sources, before tax and other deductions?
ESTIMATE ACCEPTABLE

B	06
C	13
D	11
F	09
G	14
H	12
J	10
K	04
L	05
M	08
N	16
O	03
P	15
Q	01
T	02
Z	07
(Can't say)	98
(Refused)	97

3254-55

66

J7 Are you a member of a Trade Union, Staff Association or Professional association?

	Yes	1
	No	2

3256

J8a) Now a couple of questions about your education.
At what age did you finish your continuous full-time education?
IGNORE GAPS OF ONE YEAR OR LESS

WRITE IN AGE: ☐☐

3257-58

OR CODE: (Never went to school) 96
(Still in full-time education) 97

b) **SHOW CARD BB**
Please look at this card and tell me whether you have any of the qualifications listed. Please start at the top of the list and tell me the first one you come to that you have obtained.
CODE FIRST TO APPLY

No qualifications 00

3259-60

Degree / Higher degree (or degree level qualification)
Teaching qualification
HNC/HND 01
BEC/TEC Higher, BTEC Higher
City and Guilds Full Technological Certificate
Nursing qualification (SRN, SCM, RGN, RM RHV, Midwife)
GNVQ - Levels 4 & 5
NVQ - Levels 4 & 5

"A" levels / "AS" levels / SCE Higher
ONC/OND
BEC / TEC / BTEC not Higher 02
SCOTBEC / TEC or SCOTVEC not Higher
Higher School Certificate
City and Guilds Advanced / Final
GNVQ - Level 3 / Advanced / Intermediate
NVQ - Levels 2 & 3

"O" level passes (Grades A-C if after 1975)
GCSE (Grades A-C)
CSE (Grade 1)
SCE Ordinary (Bands A-C)
Standard Grade (Levels 1-3) 03
SLC Lower
SUPE Lower or Ordinary
School Certificate or Matric
City and Guilds Craft / Ordinary level
GNVQ - Levels 1 & 2 / Foundation
NVQ - Level 1

CSE Grades 2-5
GCE "O" level Grades D & E (if after 1975)
GCSE (Grades D, E, F, G)
SCE Ordinary (Bands D & E) 04
Standard grade (Level 4,5)
Clerical or commercial qualifications
Apprenticeship
City and Guilds Foundation

CSE Ungraded 05

Other qualifications (specify) _____ 06

(Can't say) 98

67

J9a) SHOW CARD CC
In which of these ways do you occupy this accommodation?

Own it outright	1	3261
Buying it with the help of mortgage or loan	2	**GO TO J10**
Pay part rent and part mortgage (shared ownership)	3	
Rent it	4	**ASK b)**
Live here rent-free (including rent-free in relative's / friend's property; excluding squatting)	5	
(Squatting)	6	**GO TO J10**

IF RENT / RENT-FREE
b) Do you rent from the council, a housing association, from an employer or from a private individual?

Council / Local Authority / New Town Devt / Scottish Homes	1
Housing associations / Charitable or co-operative trusts	2
Employer	3
Privately	4
(Bed and breakfast)	5
Other (SPECIFY) _____	6

3262

J10. SHOW CARD DD
Finally, to which of these groups do you consider you belong?
CODE ONE ONLY

White	01
Black - Caribbean	02
Black - African	03
Black - neither Caribbean nor African	04
Indian	05
Pakistani	06
Bangladeshi	07
Chinese	08
None of these	09
Can't say	98
Refused	97

3263-64

J11 RECORD TIME NOW: 3265-68

J12 RECORD INTERVIEW LENGTH: *(minutes)* 3269-71

J13 INTERVIEWER NAME: _____

J14 INTERVIEWER NUMBER: 3272-75